SEARCH NO MORE

SEARCH NO MORE

THE KEYS TO TRUTH AND HAPPINESS

Steven R. Hemler

TAN Books
Charlotte, North Carolina

Cover design by Caroline K. Green

Library of Congress Control Number: 2018961067
ISBN: 978-1-5051-1274-0

Published in the United States by
TAN Books
Charlotte, NC 28241
www.TANBooks.com
Printed in the United States of America

CONTENTS

Part 4: The Community of the Church

ACKNOWLEDGMENTS

I gratefully acknowledge the many contributions of family and friends in the development of this book. I am very thankful for the review comments and excellent suggestions provided by Fr. James Glass, Fr. Peter Reynierse, Deacon Dr. Frank Fischer, Dr. Joanne Depue, Ben Keast, Brian Shrader, Matt Nelson, Karlo Broussard, Rhonda Kerr, David Carradini, Kaila Brosey, Kelly Key, Travis Salisbury, Marc Garcia, Jill Devine, Bill Re, Susan and Mark Hope, and several others. I especially appreciate the work of Matt Neuman who initially developed the presentations on Jesus and the Mass that were used as a basis for several chapters in this book. I am also very appreciative of Sr. Mary Margaret Ann Schlather and Catholic Distance University for implementing new apologetics seminars on Jesus, salvation, and the Church, since it was these online seminars that prompted me to adapt several of our multimedia presentations into the text-based lecture format that was the basis of this book. I am most grateful for the love and support of my wife, Linda, and our children Jonathan, Christopher, and Allison. I have been truly blessed with a wonderful wife and fantastic children. May God bless everyone involved in this labor of love and all who read this book.

PUBLISHER'S NOTE

It is our hope and the author's that many "seekers" will read this book who are likely unfamiliar with standard biblical citations and abbreviations. So we have included an appendix with those abbreviations at the back of the book. Biblical citations include the abbreviation for the book of the Bible cited, as well as the chapter and verse or verses. For example, the famous John 3:16 signs that were seen at football stadiums throughout the 70s and 80s referred to the Gospel of John, chapter 3, verse 16. *For God so loved the world that he gave his only begotten son, that whoever believes in him should not perish but have eternal life.* In this book, you would see that verse cited like this: (Jn 3:16). If more verses were cited, it would be something like this (Jn 3:16–17). So, if you are such a seeker, welcome. It is our sincere hope that this book will help you find what you are looking for, what you were made for.

Jesus said, "And so I say to you,
you are Peter, and upon this rock I will
build my church, and the gates of the
netherworld shall not prevail against it.
I will give you the keys to the kingdom of
heaven. Whatever you bind on earth
shall be bound in heaven; and whatever you
loose on earth shall be loosed in heaven."

—MATTHEW 16:18-19—

Part 1

THE KEYS TO TRUE HAPPINESS

Chapter 1

WHY AREN'T WE HAPPIER?

We all hunger for happiness. This is why we do what we do—we believe it will bring us happiness. We typically seek happiness in money and the things it will buy, in academic achievement or a successful career, in how we look or dress, in sports or hobbies, in being entertained, in parties and socializing, in recreational activities and family relationships.

How often do we try to feel good by satisfying the need for material possessions, the hunger for approval, or our desire for fun? We all feel a temptation to focus our lives on these things. This temptation is based on the belief that "the good life" is found in satisfying our physical and emotional desires. As shared by my young friend Ben Keast:

> Many people of my generation have been lured into the "more, more, more!" mentality, since now we are surrounded with so much advertising. There are so many people in the world that really believe that the good life is living in a mansion, or having

a fancy car, or whatever (there are even reality TV shows about people with all this), and so few people are just happy with what they already have. Moreover, so many people tie their happiness to their self-image, whether it be how much they own to impress others or how they look (especially when it comes to social media).

How often do we tell ourselves that we're not happy because we do not have all the things that we should have or that we want to have? So we strive and work to get more nice things—cars, homes, electronic devices, clothes—and then we find that these do not satisfy us for long. Thus we strive and strive, and for many people, life becomes a constant quest to acquire more, to attain more, to achieve more.

If we get a good grade, we want a better grade next time. If we get a good job, we want a better job. If we get a promotion, we want the next promotion. When we earn money, we want more money. When we buy something nice, we want to buy something even better. After we get together with friends and family, we can't wait to be with them again. After having fun at one party, we want to have even more fun at the next party. When we reach a goal, the "bar is raised" and we never feel like we have fully achieved our desire. We keep looking for happiness in what comes next.

I first came to this realization after attending an endless stream of parties and other social events one weekend after another in college. After each weekend, I felt an inner drive to make sure I had parties or other social activities to attend with friends the next weekend—because being alone with nothing to do on a weekend in college was a dreadful prospect! But I eventually came to realize that seeking happiness in this way just never ends, because after one party must come another, then another, and so on. All this "fun" was not bringing me true happiness. Once the present party was over, the next was needed in order to have more fun. It just never ends.

Our desires for fun, fame, the esteem of others, material possessions, and our own enjoyment are insistent, constantly clamoring for attention. While they may be worthwhile, seeking to be happy by getting more of these things is not fully satisfying because we can never have enough of them. We always want more pleasure, prestige, popularity, power, possessions, and prosperity.

Of course, there is nothing wrong with having enough possessions to live comfortably or with enjoying good times with friends and family. What we are talking about is when pursuit of these things becomes a major driving force and central purpose in our life. As many people have discovered, the endless pursuit of self-indulgent activities in the hope of finding happiness is not a fulfilling lifestyle. We eventually find that something is missing. As affirmed by author Ravi Zacharias: "The real problem is that even pleasure ultimately leaves us empty and unfulfilled. When the pleasure button is pressed incessantly, we are left feeling bewilderingly empty and betrayed. . . . Pleasure without boundaries produces life without purpose."[1]

Our culture confuses pleasure with true happiness. *The simple truth is that the pleasures of this world cannot be sustained beyond the activity producing them.* The fun of a party lasts only until the end of the party. True happiness, on the other hand, can be sustained beyond the activity producing it. At most, the pleasures of this world bring only a fleeting happiness, not true happiness and lasting joy—the kind of joy that is serene and untouchable, self-contained, and independent of the changing circumstances in life.[2]

The Happiness Hole in Our Hearts

Many people eventually discover that wholehearted and single-minded pursuit of worldly pleasures leads, in the end, not to lasting happiness but to pain, sorrow, and guilt.[3] If we talk with anyone who is addicted to food, alcohol, drugs, or sex, we realize what happens when worldly pleasures are made too central in our lives. How many rich and famous people, who seem to have all this world offers, end up in rehab?

Drinking and drugs will not fill the happiness hole in our heart, nor will being busy with more wholesome pursuits like recreational activities, socializing, travel, sports, or entertainment. Do we, for instance, sometimes find ourselves watching too much television? If so, could we be using television as an escape from the nagging feeling that there must be more to life?

Our lives will never expand to greater depth and meaning as long as we are dominated by selfish pursuits. Life means so much more. Love, relationships, family, moral excellence, and serving God and others are much more important. As Rick Warren writes, "Don't settle for just achieving 'the good life,' because the good life is not good enough. Ultimately it doesn't satisfy. You can have a lot to live *on* and still have nothing to live *for*. Aim instead for *'the better life'*—serving God in a way that expresses your heart. Figure out what you love to do—what God gave you a heart to do—and then do it for his glory."[4]

Our "heart" is the core of our self, the deepest center of who we are, that place from which our thoughts and actions arise. *Only God can fill the happiness hole we feel in our heart.* Philosopher Peter Kreeft reinforced this point when he wrote, "Trying to fill the God-sized hole in our hearts with things other than God is like trying to fill the Grand Canyon with marbles."[5] When we hook our inherent desire for God onto something less than God— such as pleasure, power, money, success, prestige—we eventually feel unhappiness and disharmony inside.

This is not a new realization. Saint Augustine of Hippo, a famous Catholic bishop who lived about sixteen hundred years ago, astutely captured this reality when, after living his youth in wayward pursuit of worldly pleasures before emerging into the light of Christianity, he wrote, "*God, you have made us for Yourself, and our hearts are restless till they find their rest in You.*"[6]

St. Augustine realized that we all have an innate desire for God ("God, you have made us for Yourself") and nothing in this world will ever be able to fully satisfy us as God can ("our hearts are restless until they rest in You"). We are designed to seek after and look for God. But have we spent too much of our lives looking for

happiness in all the wrong places, beguiled by the pleasures and enticements of this world?

Former atheist and famous Oxford professor C. S.
Lewis summed up things well when he stated, "All that
we call human history—money, poverty, ambition, war,
prostitution, classes, empires, slavery—is the long terrible story of man trying to find something other than God
which will make him happy."[7] He also stated, "We are
half-hearted creatures, fooling about with drink and sex
and ambition when infinite joy is offered us, like an ignorant child who wants to go on making mud pies in a slum
because he cannot imagine what is meant by the offer of
a holiday at the sea. We are far too easily pleased."[8]

As St. Augustine also wrote, "But my mistake was this,
that I looked for pleasure, beauty, and truth not in God
but in myself and His other creatures, and the search led
me instead to pain, confusion, and error."[9] We all share
an ache for joy in our heart that longs to be filled by a
Person who is not just loving but is Love itself. Diocese
of Arlington Bishop Emeritus Paul S. Loverde addressed
this when he stated, "Young adults so often are searching
for what will really satisfy the inner longing of the heart.
Some among us—many perhaps, have come to realize, as
did centuries ago Saint Augustine—that what our society
tells us and models before us does not fulfill our longing.
Yes, at the moment, it seems to fulfill and satisfy, but later
on, we feel empty once again. 'Is this all there is,' we ago-
nizingly ask? Yes, there is more—a Person whose name is
Jesus Christ."[10]

Even when we ignore or reject God, God continues
to draw us to himself so that we may find the fullness

of truth and happiness we desire. The *Catechism of the Catholic Church* (27) emphasizes this: "The desire for God is written in the human heart, because man is created by God and for God; and God never ceases to draw man to himself. Only in God will he find the truth and happiness he never stops searching for."

As we grow older, we typically discover that we are most fully alive when we live in accord with our God-given conscience and moral values. We find that when we follow the moral law written in our heart and the teachings of the Church, we are not burdened by feelings of guilt and shame and we can become more than a slave to our human passions and desires.[11]

For example, in today's hook-up culture, many people come to feel guilty and unhappy about their sexual behavior. They "hook up," usually feel awful afterwards, and have no idea why.[12] But they know something has gone terribly wrong. This is especially true after being repeatedly hurt and realizing that too often "guys play at love to get sex, while girls play at sex to get love."

In other words, sex can become a means of self-gratification at the expense of another person. How many young women, in particular, feel they have been "played" and consequently develop a jaded view of romantic relationships? These effects of the "sexual revolution" have resulted in many people today yearning for real emotional intimacy and a committed relationship.[13] The number of young adults, primarily young women, suffering from eating disorders, addiction, anxiety, and depression is at an all-time high.[14] It is no coincidence that the top two prescribed drugs at most college health care centers are anti-depressants and the birth-control pill.[15]

Many people have found that poor decisions and destructive behavior result from failing to follow God's guidance for our lives as found in the Bible and the teachings of the Church. As wisely observed by Cardinal George Pell, "The validity of Christian teaching on sexuality and marriage is demonstrated in the wounds of those who do not practice it. Infidelity and irresponsibility do not bring freedom; they bring slavery, imprisonment to bad habits, and even addiction."[16]

Fr. Dwight Longenecker also observed:

> The damaged lives we see when love goes wrong remind us why the church has such stringent standards when it comes to sexual sin. Catholic rules about sexuality are not random. The rules about sex are not a long list cooked up by old men in red robes in Rome who thought they should be party-poopers and stop everyone from having fun. Catholic rules about love and marriage are not arbitrary prohibitions. They are disciplines that protect marriage, protect children and protect men and women from being casualties in the risky battlefield called love.[17]

Mastering Our Passions

Christians, moreover, understand that sex is about self-giving, not self-gratification. Christians realize that God's gift of human sexuality has two distinct and equally important purposes: life-making and love-making. Our sexuality is naturally about making new life and deepening a couple's bond of love through their mutual self-giving and enduring commitment within marriage.[18]

The indwelling power and presence of God's Holy Spirit enables Christians to overcome and not be controlled by our selfish and ultimately self-destructive desires, including unbridled sexual and romantic desires that often leave us feeling hurt and emotionally empty. Faith gives us the ability to become more than our pleasure-seeking human nature would have us be. As St. Dominic said in the thirteenth century, "A man who governs his passions is master of the world. We must either rule them, or be ruled by them. It is better to be the hammer than the anvil."[19]

Some things about human nature never seem to change. God, however, wants to free us from all that would keep us captive to selfishness and sin. To sin literally means "to miss the mark" or "to be off target." We all sin. We all do things we know are wrong. The problem with sin is that it moves us away from God and from our real purpose in life, which is to know, love, and serve God—the source of all goodness, joy, and truth—and to be united with God in the everlasting joy of heaven.

However, there is a great misconception about the Christian life. Many people—including many Christians—believe that Christian living is essentially about delayed gratification. In other words, if I put off fun and happiness in this life, God will give me a hundredfold in the next. But that is not (and never has been) Christian

teaching. This is explained well in the following statement from the Archdiocese of Melbourne:

> A willingness to do God's will is built on two con-
> victions. We have to believe that God loves us more
> than we love ourselves and that God wants our
> happiness more than we want it. In other words,
> we have to believe that God knows more than we
> do about what will make us truly happy. If God had
> given us everything we ever asked for we would be
> seriously unhappy. The basis of our desire to find
> and to do the will of God should be the belief that
> God's will for us is our only chance to be truly and
> lastingly happy.[20]

We do not have to worry about Jesus taking away
our fun and happiness. Rather, we will find the true joy
and deep happiness we are searching for in life through
a prayerful and personal relationship with the Lord Jesus
Christ together in community with other Christians in
the Church. If we turn to Jesus in a spirit of repentance
and humility, he will free us free from slavery to our sinful and hurtful desires and bring us true happiness and
joy. For as Jesus said, "I have told you this so that my
joy may be in you and your joy may be complete" (Jn
15:11).[21] How we can find true happiness and fulfillment
in Jesus and his Church is what we will explore next.

Chapter 2

HOW DOES BEING A CHRISTIAN BRING TRUE HAPPINESS?

Like St. Augustine and C. S. Lewis, many people find that when we open our hearts and our lives to God, the inner hunger for meaning and happiness goes away. God satisfies the deepest desires of those who believe in and have a prayerful relationship with God. Life with God ceases to be mere existence and becomes a thing of both joy and peace. Only in God does the human heart find the happiness it is searching for. Pope St. John Paul II expressed this realization beautifully when he addressed the millions of young people gathered for World Youth Day 2000:

> It is Jesus in fact that you seek when you dream of happiness; he is waiting for you when nothing else you find satisfies you; he is the beauty to which you are so attracted; it is he who provokes you with that thirst for fullness that will not let you settle for compromise; it is he who urges you to shed the masks of a false life; it is he who reads in your hearts your most genuine choices, the choices that others try

13

to stifle. It is Jesus who stirs in you the desire to do something great with your lives, the will to follow an ideal, the refusal to allow yourselves to be grounded down by mediocrity, the courage to commit yourselves humbly and patiently to improving yourselves and society, making the world more human and more fraternal.[22]

A number of modern scientific studies have confirmed that religious people are generally happier than non-religious people. For example, the Pew Research Center found that "Americans who are highly religious are more likely than those who are less religious to report being very happy in their lives (40% vs. 29%)."[23] And as the *Washington Post* reported on a study of nine thousand adults, "A new study suggests that joining a religious group could do more for someone's 'sustained happiness' than other forms of social participation, such as volunteering, playing sports or taking a class. A study in the *American Journal of Epidemiology* by researchers at the London School of Economics and Erasmus University Medical Center in the Netherlands found that the secret to sustained happiness lies in participation in religion."[24]

Educational psychology professor, international speaker, and veteran teacher Dr. Kathy Koch has identified five core needs that we all have in life.[25] A prime need is *identity—who am I?* Another important need we have is for *security—who can I trust?* A third need is *belonging—who wants me?* Our fourth need is *purpose—why am I alive?* And fifth, *competence—what do I do well?*

Meeting these five core needs is key to finding the

happiness and wholeness that we all seek. As Dr. Koch writes about meeting these five needs, "Trying to meet our needs in anyone or anything other than Jesus Christ can result in a temporary or shallow sense of wholeness, but not a long-lasting or authentic, real, actual, legitimate, true genuine wholeness."[26] Being an active and committed Christian is the best way to meet our five core needs that have been created by God and to find true happiness, as explained below.

Identity—Who Am I?

Our identity—how we define and describe ourselves—determines our behavior and is important to our happiness.[27] Many people define their identity in terms of their physical appearance, abilities, career, or material possessions, and this identity strongly influences what they do or say. But our behavior can easily become self-centered, and our identity can become rooted in pride when it is grounded in how we see ourselves or how others see us rather than in how God sees us.[28]

Christian identity is grounded in the realization that each of us is a gifted child of a loving and merciful God (see 1 Jn 3:1). God's love for us does not depend on what we do or don't do. God loves us unconditionally, and no sin, no failing, no weakness can keep God from loving each of us like there is only one of us to love.[29]

God's deep and permanent love for each of us is even greater than the love of a mother for her child and the love of a lover who gives all for his beloved. *The deepest need in the human heart is to know we are loved, and Christians recognize that we are deeply loved by the God of the universe.* Catholic author Don Schwager addresses this in a daily Scripture meditation:

> Jesus on many occasions spoke to his disciples about the nature of God's unquenchable love. *God is love* (1 John 4:16) because he is the creator and source of all that is true love. His love is unconditional, unmerited, and unlimited. We can't buy it, earn it, demand it. It is a pure gift, freely given, and freely received. God's love doesn't change or waver. It endures because it is eternal and timeless. It's the beginning and the end—the purpose for which God created us and why he wants us to be united with him in a bond of unbreakable love. And it's the essence of what it means to be a son or daughter of God the eternal Father.[30]

The realization of how deeply God loves us enables Christians to overcome burdens of inferiority, inadequacy, or low self-esteem by helping us realize that our worth and value does not come from how we look, how talented we are, or what people say about us. Rather, we are valuable because of who made us. We are each God's creation and are made in the image and likeness of God (see Gn 1:26–27). Our value, therefore, comes directly from God, and our worth goes well beyond our looks, abilities, or achievements. As shared by Ashley Oliver, a contributor to *The Upper Room*:

> When I was a freshman in high school, I was

diagnosed with an eating disorder. For over two years, I despised my body. In this state it was impossible for me to believe that I had been created in God's image or that God loved me the way I was. When I finally began my journey to recovery, I slowly began to understand that everyone has been created in God's perfect image. Through the years, I have learned that every single thing that God created is beautiful and wonderful, including each of us. Regardless of the flaws we see in ourselves, God doesn't make mistakes. The way we are is the way God intended us to be. So as we go through life, we try to remember that God loves us exactly as we are. God's works are wonderful; and God loves and accepts us, flaws and all. With God's help, we can love ourselves and others as God loves us.[31]

While devout Christians constantly strive with God's help to become better persons, we are able to accept the self-worth and dignity that come from being a beloved child of an all-loving and all-knowing God. As children of God, we can abandon the need to compare ourselves with others and we can hold onto the truth that each of us has been blessed with the individual talents and unique gifts that God has chosen to give us. This awareness helps Christians accept and love who we are, especially when we also realize that *God doesn't make junk.*[32]

God loves us wholly, completely, and perfectly. God is love, and everything God does flows from his love for each of us.[33] There is no limit, no holding back, no compromising on God's love. God loves each of us even in our weakness and sinful condition. God's love is why the Father sent his eternally begotten Son, the Lord Jesus Christ, to redeem us from sin and slavery to our disordered passions, desires, and addictions, as well as to dwell within us (see 1 Jn 4:9–10 and chapters 7–8 herein).[34]

Since the beginning, Christians have believed Jesus revealed that the one, true God is a mysterious trinity of three divine persons—Father, Son, and Holy Spirit—united in a community of love.[35] As such, Jesus teaches us to address God as "our Father" (Mt 6:9) because our heavenly Father loves each of us as beloved sons and daughters (Jn 1:12). Jesus also calls us his brothers and sisters (Mk 3:34–35) as well as his friends (Jn 15:15).

And if being a child of God and a brother/sister/friend of Jesus Christ is not enough, we are also temples of the Holy Spirit. "Do you not know," St. Paul asks, "that your body is a temple of the Holy Spirit within you, whom you have from God, and that you are not your own?" (1 Cor 6:19). Christians know that being a child of God the Father, a brother/sister/friend of Jesus Christ, and a temple of the Holy Spirit makes us extremely significant and important.

Furthermore, through the Holy Spirit within us, we have direct access to God (Eph 2:18), who accepts us completely and totally. Isn't it quite amazing that the triune God, in the persons of the Father, Son, and Holy Spirit, loves us and wants a personal relationship with each of us through prayer? We can confidently ask God for whatever we need because God delights in giving his children good things (Mt 7:11).

Christians find strength and hope in being able to

pray to the Father, through the Son, in the Holy Spirit, and we know that God actually hears and answers our individual prayers according to what is best for us—but not always what we want. The power of prayer is the confidence that we are being guided and cared for, even when that guidance and care are not immediately apparent.

Even though God knows what we need before we ask, prayer strengthens our faith and our dependence upon God. We do not pray to change God's mind or tell God something he doesn't already know. God is not like a big city boss whom we have to persuade. The entire point of prayer is to make us humble before God. Prayer is a trusting surrender and confidence that God will act in his own time and way for our ultimate good. This is expounded upon in a daily Scripture reflection in *The Word Among Us*:

> To a large extent, the way we petition God depends on our concept of who he is. Advocates of "prosperity gospel" approach God like a benevolent benefactor—the Great Provider in the sky. They ask for wealth, position, success and all the other things they think will ensure a happy life. At the other end of the spectrum are those who feel too sinful or unworthy of God's favor. If they ask for anything at all, it is for forgiveness—usually over and over again.
>
> Both approaches miss the mark. God doesn't want us to be selfish in our petitions, nor does he want us to avoid asking because we feel undeserving. He does, however, want us to ask. His answer

may surprise us, and it may not always be what we
expect, but we can be sure that he will give us the
best possible response to our requests.

So aim high. Believe that if you keep on knocking on heaven's door, your prayers will be answered
with the wisdom and generosity that come from a
loving, gracious God.[36]

Christians are heartened and empowered by frequent
communication in prayer with the personal and loving
God and Creator of the universe. We can pray to God
anytime, anywhere, and about anything. Prayer is a great
power and privilege that any Christian possesses, with the
highest form of prayer being the Mass (see chapter 10).

Prayer is an expression of great faith, and nothing
pleases God more than faith. In this way, prayer helps us
build a trusting relationship with God, which is the only
foundation of true happiness and lasting joy. As Jesus
said, "Ask and you will receive, so that your joy may be
complete" (Jn 16:24).

Christians also know that we can be free of and not
burdened by guilt and shame for our wrongdoings—no
matter what we may have done in the past. Our loving
Father in heaven has unlimited mercy and constant hope
for all of his children, no matter how far from God we
may be at the moment. God longs for us to return from
our mistaken wandering and is delighted to bestow abundant love and forgiveness when we turn toward him. Don
Schwager also writes:

There are no limits to the mercy of God, but we can
reject his mercy by refusing to ask God's pardon

for our wrongdoing and by refusing to accept the help he gives us to turn away from sin and from whatever would keep us from doing his will. God gives sufficient grace (his favor and mercy towards us) and he gives sufficient help (his wisdom and strength) to all who humbly call upon him. Giving up on God and refusing to turn away from sin and disbelief results from our own sinful pride, stubborn will, and the loss of hope in God's promises. God never turns a deaf ear to those who seek his help and listen to his voice—his word of hope, pardon, and freedom from sin and oppression.[37]

Christians repeatedly testify to experiencing the help and healing of God's grace and the indwelling Holy Spirit. There is no addiction, no hurt, no regret that is too big to be redeemed by the love and mercy of God. God's grace and healing empower us to forgive those who have hurt us and help us let go of any seething resentment or nagging bitterness we may feel toward anyone who has harmed us.

The good news of Christianity is that God offers to every person a more abundant life of merciful love, forgiveness, healing, peace, joy, and eternal salvation. Christians know that if we are truly sorry for what we have done in the past, we will experience God's infinite mercy and tender forgiveness. God will liberate us from the burden of guilt and from the oppression of sinful habits and hurtful desires. Only God can lift the burden of excessive worry or guilt about what came before, since God is much more interested in our future than in our past.

As Oscar Wilde astutely observed, "Every saint has a past and every sinner has a future."[38] This quote reflects the reality that most of those who have been declared a saint by the Church did, at one time, have a less-than-saintly past. God's bountiful mercy, forgiveness, and grace mean that each of us has a hopeful future, no matter how dubious our past.

God knows our failings and weaknesses better than we do. God pardons and heals those who ask for his mercy and forgiveness. Only God's love and forgiveness can clear our conscience and bring us healing, pardon, and peace. This is most vividly experienced when Catholics confidentially confess our sins to an ordained priest in what the Catholic Church calls the sacrament of Reconciliation (also called confession). The reality of God's mercy and forgiveness is powerfully and personally felt when hearing the words of absolution spoken by the priest in the sacrament of Reconciliation.

Catholics appreciate experiencing God's grace, strength, and healing found in the sacraments of the Church (i.e., Baptism, Eucharist, Reconciliation, Confirmation, etc.). God's help and power received in the sacraments, especially Reconciliation and the Eucharist, help us overcome our weaknesses and grow personally and spiritually into a better, happier person. This is discussed more fully in part 4 of this book.

Security—Who Can I Trust?

Establishing and maintaining a sense of security is vital for the happiness we seek. We feel anxious and afraid without a sense of security in life. Young children first place their security in their parents and rightfully trust that parents will provide for their physical and emotional needs. As we grow older, we often try to base our sense of security on *things* like popularity, grades, money, knowledge, talent, or "being cool."[39] However, none of these things provide lasting security, because they fade away, break down, or lose their glamour. Disappointment then follows and despair may not be far behind. The most meaningful question, therefore, is not *what* can I trust, but *who* can I trust?

Christians routinely find that our deepest need for security is best met through a personal and prayerful relationship with God, our Creator.[40] Christians find we can truly depend upon God and our Christian friends as we face our daily cares and concerns. We can trust God because God is in control, even during the difficult times of our lives, and things will work out according to God's will.

We can easily fall into worry during difficult times, even though worrying does not really do any good. While stressful and difficult times occur for all of us, Christians know that excessive worry separates us from God by focusing our energy on the problem instead of on God. Christians can confidently rest assured and trust that we are held in God's loving hands and that everything will truly be all right. Christians are fortified by their faith.

Trusting in God allows us to experience peace and joy, instead of falling into worry and despair. As St. Paul states in the Bible, "We know that all things work for good for those who love God, who are called according to his purpose" (Rom 8:28). This knowledge frees Christians from being consumed by paralyzing worry and fear.

When we love God above all other things, we are rooted in a power that transcends space and time, a power that governs the universe in its entirety, a power that is greater than life and death. Moreover, this power is a loving, personal God who knows me intimately and guides me according to his divine purposes.

As Jesus stated, "Are not two sparrows sold for a small coin? Yet not one of them falls to the ground without your Father's knowledge. Even all the hairs of your head are counted. So do not be afraid; you are worth more than many sparrows" (Mt 10:29–31). Because of this worth, we have nothing to fear from anything or anybody in this world.

Being a follower of Christ, however, does not mean we will be safe from suffering, from disease, or from hardship. Jesus did not come to guarantee his followers health, wealth, or prosperity. As Jesus stated to his disciples, "In the world you will have trouble, but take courage, I have conquered the world" (Jn 16:33).

The radical difference is that Christians know we are not alone when hardships befall us. As Jesus promised, "I am with you always" (Mt 28:20). Jesus is still with us today to help us, comfort us, and encourage us, especially in the midst of our suffering. We can either face the trials and difficulties of this life alone, or we can face them together with Jesus Christ.

Though he was God, Jesus became fully human and experienced life as we do. He was tempted as we are. He dealt with grief, sadness, pain, and rejection. Whenever we think that nobody understands or cares, Christians remember that Jesus knows what we are going through because he has been through it himself.

When we are troubled and in distress, we can turn to Jesus in confidence that he will be with us. If we trust in the Lord Jesus, he will strengthen and comfort us during times of hardship and suffering. Jesus gives strength and courage to those who humbly acknowledge their dependence upon him.

Jesus will support and guide us in whatever situation we find ourselves. He will see us through any calamity or trial that comes our way. The risen Jesus is here with us today to share in our pain and suffering, and he invites us to rest safely in his loving care.

Jesus assures us that we do not have to give in to fear or discouragement if we place our trust and hope in him and remember his great love for us. The Lord Jesus Christ offers his followers a supernatural joy that enables us to bear any sorrow or pain. If we truly trust in him, Jesus will help us bear our burdens with a deep peace and real joy (see Phil 4:6–7).

Christians know that God's unconditional love is supporting us, and we can feel at peace about ourselves and the world even during troubling times. Living a life of faith and trust in God brings a calming sense of hope and joy.

This inner strength and hope can be a potent witness to the power of the Christian faith. Seeing God's power in action in this way, for example, led bestselling author Malcolm Gladwell to rediscover his Christian faith.[41] While Gladwell was writing his book *David and Goliath*, he went to visit Cliff and Wilma Derksen in Winnipeg, Canada. Thirty years earlier, the Derksens had experienced every parent's worst nightmare: their daughter Candace had been abducted and murdered. Gladwell was amazed by what Candace's parents said at the time.

At a news conference after Candace's funeral, her father, Cliff, said, "We would like to know who the person or persons are [who murdered Candace] so we could share, hopefully, a love that seems to be missing in these peoples' lives." Her mother, Wilma, added, "I can't say at this point I forgive this person," but the stress was clearly on the phrase "at this point." She continued, "We have all done something dreadful in our lives, or have felt the urge to." As Gladwell wrote, "I wanted to know where the Derksens found the strength to say those things. A sexual predator had kidnapped and murdered their daughter, and Cliff Derksen could talk about sharing his love with the killer and Wilma could stand up and say, 'We have all done something dreadful in our lives, or have felt the urge to.' Where do two people find the power to forgive in a moment like that?"[42]

Gladwell realized the Derksens' Christian faith was the source of this unusual and mysterious power that came from within, and this led him to rediscover his faith in Christ. The truth of the Christian faith is important, but faith also brings a higher purpose and meaning to our problems.

We all have problems and challenges. Devout Christians, however, see challenges in life as opportunities for personal and spiritual growth, as opportunities to become more like Jesus Christ. Christians know that every problem is a character-building opportunity, and the more difficult the problem, the greater is its character-building potential.

God gives committed Christians the grace needed to go through life faithfully and to enter heaven joyfully when our life on earth is done. This realization gives Christians patience, hope, comfort, and peace, even during the inevitable hard times in life.

Belonging—Who Wants Me?

Practicing Christians not only believe in but also belong to God, each other, and to the Church. The essence of being a Christian is about more than doctrine, rules, and commandments. It is first and foremost about relationship, our personal relationship with God and with others. God offers each of us the greatest of all relationships: union of heart, mind, and spirit with the one, true God who is the very source of life and love (1 Jn 4:8, 16). God wants us not because of what we do but because God loves each of us.

The local Church community also wants us. Christians have close friends and companions among our fellow brothers and sisters in Christ. Christians share relationships of trust, affection, commitment, loyalty, faithfulness, kindness, thoughtfulness, compassion, mercy, helpfulness, encouragement, support, strength, and so many other qualities that bring people together in mutual love and unity.[43] We are bound together by our faith and supported in our common calling and mission. Our shared faith makes us coworkers in the "vineyard of the Lord."

While Christians are still sinners, we understand that "the Church is a hospital for sinners, not a museum for saints."[44] We truly value the support and friendship of other Christians in our journey through life. Christians take comfort in the great gift of the Church because we do not have to navigate challenging times alone. Rather, as members of the Church community, we can rely on our brothers and sisters in Christ for strength, inspiration, and encouragement.

In our fellowship and friendship with other Christians, we typically experience a sense of belonging, acceptance, love, and support. Feelings of loneliness are significantly diminished or even vanish. This is especially true during the hard times. Christians are there for each other in the good times as well as the bad. The Christian community supports us when we experience pain, loss, sadness, sickness, or need. Surveys show that practicing Catholic young adults report having the social support they need to cope with the difficult times in life.[45]

I first experienced the beauty of Christian community when in high school. While in the eleventh grade, I was encouraged by my parish religious education teacher to attend a powerful Christian Awakening weekend retreat for high school juniors and seniors. Afterward, my teacher and her husband hosted weekly "Prayer and Share" meetings in their home for the youth from our church who went on this retreat. Others eventually joined us. I attended those weekly prayer meetings for three years and cannot convey how much my faith grew during that time. Belonging to this close Christian community, where I felt valued, loved, and accepted, was a truly wonderful and life-changing experience.

This led me to become actively involved in high school youth ministry and religious education for many years. I have belonged to several other church-based faith sharing and Bible study groups over the years, including attending a weekly men's prayer breakfast during the thirteen years that we lived in the Middle East.

Catholics are part of a two-thousand-year heritage that gives "roots" and meaning to our existence. One's heritage is one's inheritance. Christians are heartened to realize that we stand on the shoulders of those who have gone before us marked with the sign of faith, including many in our own family lineage. Christians are part of a very long legacy of faith. Many people vividly experience this when they go on a pilgrimage to the Holy Land, Rome, or other sacred sites.

Christians recognize that our true destiny is to belong to God and live in God's joy, both here and in the hereafter. We realize that our life on earth is preparation for eternity. We know we are forgiven and look forward to spending eternity with God and the faithfully departed saints in heaven. Christians believe we are saved for eternal life by God's grace and not by our own efforts alone.

We don't have to try to work our way into heaven by being "good enough" or "nice enough." We merely need to accept in gratitude the redemption that Jesus won for us on the cross, commit our lives to being an active follower of Jesus, and then live accordingly while being helped by the power and presence of the indwelling Holy Spirit that is available in the sacraments of the Church.

Purpose—Why Am I Alive?

When we fluctuate from one activity, college major, career, or relationship to the next, it is often because we are unsure of our reason for living.[46] We may be searching for what to do or who to be. It is all part of trying to address our need for purpose, to know why we exist, to know why we are alive. Many of us, however, still feel empty inside and sense that we are just going through the motions.

We often find that our purpose cannot be fully met in the typical *p*'s—pleasure, prestige, popularity, power, possessions, prosperity, or pursuits.[47] It can only be met in a Person, God. Christians find true meaning and purpose from a personal and prayerful relationship with God and active involvement in a committed Christian community.

Devout Christians throughout the centuries testify that faith brings a deeper meaning and purpose to life by leading us to more fully serve God and help others. Most people feel that we are destined not to just exist but to make a positive difference in the world. As famously stated by poet Ralph Waldo Emerson, "The purpose of life is not to be happy. It is to be useful, to be honorable, to be compassionate, to have it make some difference that you have lived and lived well."[48]

When we focus our lives on lovingly serving God and others, we experience the truth of the saying, "It is more blessed to give than to receive." Civil rights leader Martin Luther King, Jr., captured this well when he stated, "Those who are not looking for happiness are the most likely to find it, because those who are searching forget that the surest way to be happy is to seek happiness for others."[49] True happiness is found in the satisfaction we receive from fulfilling our God-given purpose in life.

Many Christians have discovered real meaning in life by using their talents and gifts to lovingly serve God and others, including through the many service opportunities available in their local church community (see chapter 11). Christians know that God enables us to be all we can be by empowering us to give all we can give. We are comforted and empowered when we let God's love and grace touch our lives. Accepting that we are truly loved and cherished by God enables us to better love others in return. For as Jesus said, "As I have loved you, so you also should love one another" (Jn 13:34). Don Schwager writes:

> God loved us first (1 John 4:19) and our love for him is a response to his exceeding goodness and kindness towards us. The love of God comes first and the love of neighbor is firmly grounded in the love of God. The more we know of God's love,

truth, and goodness, the more we love what he
loves and reject whatever is hateful and contrary to
his will. God commands us to love him first above
all else—his love orients and directs our thoughts,
intentions, and actions to what is wholly good and
pleasing to him. He wants us to love him personally, wholeheartedly, and without any reservation
or compromise.

What is the nature of love? Love is the gift of
giving oneself for the good of others—it is wholly
other oriented and directed to the welfare and
benefit of others. Love which is rooted in pleasing
myself is self-centered and possessive—it is a selfish love that takes from others rather than gives to
others. It is a stunted and disordered love which
leads to many hurtful and sinful desires—such as
jealousy, greed, envy, and lust. The root of all sin is
disordered love and pride which is fundamentally
putting myself above God and my neighbor—it is
loving and serving self rather than God and neighbor. True love, which is wholly directed and oriented to what is good rather than evil, is rooted in
God's truth and righteousness (moral goodness).[50]

Pride can keep us from the love and knowledge of
God and close our minds to God's wisdom and will for
our lives. Just as pride is the root of sin and evil, so humility is the soil in which the love and grace of God can take
root.[51] The virtue of humility enables us to put our trust in
God and not just in ourselves. God gives help and strength
to those who humbly place their hope and trust in him.

True humility is not feeling bad about yourself, or having a low opinion of yourself, or thinking of yourself as inferior to others.[52] True humility allows us to honestly assess our personal strengths and weaknesses, which helps us avoid both despair and pride. A humble person is free to be his or her true self and does not feel the need to wear a mask or put on a façade in order to look good to others. Humility frees us from preoccupation with ourselves, whereas a low self-esteem tends to focus our attention on ourselves. Rick Warren writes, "Humility is not thinking less of yourself; it is thinking of yourself less."[53]

We feel best about ourselves when we don't put ourselves at the center of the universe. That's because our lives are ultimately not about ourselves. Humility leads to true self-knowledge and dedication to give ourselves to something greater than ourselves.[54] Humility frees us to love and serve others selflessly for their sake rather than for our own. To be a servant, therefore, requires an attitude of humility. We feel most right about what we are doing when we are giving our lives away in loving service to God and others.

We experience true happiness and joy in life when we give of ourselves out of love for one another. New parents frequently discover this after their first baby is born. Our family life and career often provide excellent opportunities to serve God and others. Christians understand that any occupation, any job, is a vocation—a legitimate vehicle for finding God and serving others.

Competence—What Do I Do Well?

Competence is having the necessary skills and qualifica-
tions for our given work or situation.[55] When we're competent, we are well qualified and capable. We do not need
to be perfect in what we do. We just need to be competent.

Christians rely on God as the source of our competence. We know that each of us is a good and valuable
person because we are each created in God's own image
and likeness. We also know our Creator has given each of
us special gifts and talents that we can use effectively in
serving God and others.

As St. Paul wrote, "We have gifts that differ according to the grace given to us" (Rom 12:6). He also stated,
"For we are his handiwork, created in Christ Jesus for
the good works that God has prepared in advance, that
we should live in them" (Eph 2:10). Since we are each
God's handiwork, we have just the personal strengths and
weaknesses that God desires us to have.

Even though we may feel inadequate, we can trust
that God does not expect us to accomplish a task without
giving us the ability to accomplish it. Christians find that
God empowers us to do things better than we can do just
by ourselves. That's because God gives sufficient means
(grace and wisdom) for using our gifts and talents far
beyond what we could do on our own. For as God told
St. Paul, "My grace is sufficient for you, for power is made
perfect in weakness" (2 Cor 12:9).

However, it is not necessary to first try to figure out
our talents before beginning to serve God and others. We
often discover our gifts and talents just by trying. God is

pleased when we are willing to use what we have to serve God and others regardless of how inadequate we think we are. Throughout history, God has used people who were less than perfect. *God cares more about our availability than our ability.*

God understands our limitations and shortcomings and can use us if we just make ourselves available. Christians discover that we are capable of serving in ways we could not have imagined because God empowers us. God equips ordinary people, like you and me, and uses the ordinary circumstances of our daily lives and work situations as opportunities to serve God and others.

Despite our flaws and weaknesses, we can have confidence in our ability to competently serve God and others because we know that God empowers us to do what God calls us to do. *Christians can do well whatever God asks us to do because God doesn't just call the equipped, but God always equips the called.*

God's strength, power, love, and wisdom are working in Christians through the indwelling power and presence of the Holy Spirit. It is God working within us that enables us to be competent.[56] God's grace and help is enough and is all that we need to be competent.

God's only request is that we appreciate what we have been given and humbly use our gifts and talents fully and wisely. We should pray for wisdom to recognize our gifts and seek opportunities to lovingly use them in God's service. God honors and helps those who use their gifts and talents for doing good. There is nothing better we can do with our lives than to use them in service of the God of the universe.

Finding True Happiness

Following Jesus in the Church community is the key to meeting all five of our core needs and experiencing authentic wholeness and true happiness. Devout Christians find that Jesus was indeed right when he said he came so we "might have life and have it more abundantly" (Jn 10:10). Although this joyful and abundant life cannot be experienced perfectly until we get to heaven, we can begin to experience it in this life, here and now. As Christians, we experience a new vitality and a superabundance of life when we walk with Jesus. When we live with and for God, life becomes truly worth living and we begin to live in the fullest sense of the word.

Since we are made for God, we must place God at the forefront and center of our lives in order to truly flourish. When our life is centered on God, all our energies and aspirations fall into a fulfilling and satisfying pattern. Jesus expressed this when he said, "seek first the kingdom [of God] and his righteousness, and all these things will be given you besides" (Mt 6:33). The kingdom of God that Jesus frequently spoke about is found in the community of those who sincerely seek to follow Jesus and allow God to reign in our lives and in our world. As the National Study of Youth and Religion found, "Emerging adult Catholics who were more involved in their faith— as measured by Mass attendance, prayer, and self-rated importance of faith—are doing what most people would consider to be better in life on many outcomes. . . . Positive life-course experiences and outcomes seem more likely to be associated among Catholic emerging adults who are more seriously practicing and committing to religious faith."[57]

Faith is not just one of the many components of our life—like work, school, sports, socializing, recreation, entertainment, etc. *Religious faith is the foundation from which all other aspects of life flow and is vital to the happiness we were made for and that we all seek.*

Having a personal relationship with God enhances and amplifies many other aspects of life, including our personal relationships and goals. For instance, we are likely to have a more rewarding career because our faith and the grace of God give us a more positive and productive attitude. Christians also understand that our career can be a good way to serve God and others.

We are what we love. When we consciously make God the center and ground of our life, the result is wholeness and joy. Practicing Christians do not live life on the rim of the circle but rather at the center—at that reliable, unchanging point where God resides. When Jesus Christ is the center of our life, our mind, our will, our emotions, our private life, our public life—all of it—finds its harmonious place around that center.

As expanded upon throughout this book, Catholics know that *the keys to true happiness are Jesus and his Church.* For as Jesus said when he instituted his Church, "And so I say to you, you are Peter, and upon this rock I will build my church, and . . . I will give you the keys to the kingdom of heaven" (Mt 16:18–19). Jesus knows what is best for us and that the keys to true joy and lasting happiness are found in following him in his Church.

We are all wired for God. There is a hunger in us that

nothing in this world can possibly satisfy. God will continue to knock on the door of our restless hearts until we finally make the choice to open it and let God in (see Mt 7:7; Lk 11:9; Rv 3:20). As we will look at next, it is never too late to respond to God's loving invitation and accept God's promise of a new life and a rewarding personal relationship with God himself, the source of true joy and lasting happiness.

Chapter 3

WHY TURN TO GOD?

Every decision in life shapes the kind of person we become. Our character determines to a large extent the kind of future we will have both in this life and in the next. It is possible to gain everything that we desire, only to ultimately discover that we have missed out on the most important things of all. Of what value are pleasure, money, success, and prestige if they do not bring true happiness and help us gain what is really important? Nothing in this world lasts. Nothing in this world should, therefore, be the object of our deepest longings or our strongest commitments.

Feelings of restlessness, boredom, and a sense that something is missing in life begin to have answers once we start actively practicing the Christian faith by following Jesus in the Church. Only God can save us from dejection, hopelessness, and emptiness in life. To live our life as if God and Christ's community of followers (the Church) do not exist is like being the heir to a great fortune, but instead choosing to live as a homeless person.

Gale Richards, a contributor to *The Upper Room*, shares the following personal experience:

> We are God's creation, yet God has given us the freedom to choose to turn away. For years, out of fear or busyness, I made the choice to turn away. But turning away left a separation between God and me. Something was missing, and life felt incomplete. I finally realized that I could draw close to God by responding to the inner nudges and calls of the Spirit. The first few times were scary. But I followed God's leading and now give thanks for the blessings this has brought me. Relationship with God brings a whole new dimension of fullness to life.[58]

Talking with God, even if we don't fully believe in God, helps us to sort out the clutter inside our head and enables us to deal with those things that are nagging at us. We need to take it in steps. God talks to us all the time wherever we are. We just need to sit quietly and listen to God speaking to us.

Then life starts to make more sense and becomes much more than a monotonous grind. We stop feeling as if we are just reacting to events. Instead, we feel like we have some safe distance from things, so we are able to reflect before we respond. Life begins to have a natural rhythm and takes on a deeper meaning and purpose.

More and more, we discover that being a practicing Christian does not lead to feelings of subjugation from having to follow "the rules" but rather to positive feelings of belonging, love, joy, peace, hope, and true happiness. These are the fruit of the Holy Spirit in the lives of those who actively practice the Christian faith (see Gal 5:22). As C. S. Lewis stated:

> People often think of Christian morality as a kind of bargain in which God says, "If you keep a lot of rules I'll reward you, and if you don't I'll do the other thing." I do not think that is the best way of looking at it. I would much rather say that every time you make a choice you are turning the central part of you, the part of you that chooses, into something a little different from what it was before. And taking your life as a whole, with all your innumerable choices, all your life long you are slowly turning this central thing either into a heavenly creature or into a hellish creature: either into a creature that is in harmony with God, and with other creatures, and with itself, or else into one that is in a state of war and hatred with God, and with its fellow-creatures, and with itself. To be the one kind of creature is heaven: that is, it is joy and peace and knowledge and power. To be the other means madness, horror, idiocy, rage, impotence, and eternal loneliness. Each of us at this moment is progressing to the one state or the other.[59]

While we do have a choice in how we will live our lives, Christianity is not about following some arbitrary rules by our own strength alone. Rather, God became man so that we could become more like God. Christians become "divinized" through a prayerful relationship with God and through the grace of the sacraments, especially the Eucharist (as will be discussed later). In short, God's inner power and presence helps Christians become better people who are more able and willing to do the right things in life, and this brings personal fulfillment and true joy.

God offers each of us an abundant life of inner joy, love, and friendship if we just turn to him. As C. S. Lewis also declared, "God cannot give us a happiness and peace apart from Himself, because it is not there. There is no such thing."[60] This is also expressed well in the following prayer traditionally attributed to St. Augustine: "God our Father, we find it difficult to come to you, because our knowledge of you is imperfect. In our ignorance we have imagined you to be our enemy; we have wrongly thought that you take pleasure in punishing our sins; and we have foolishly conceived you to be a tyrant over human life. But since Jesus came among us, he has shown that you are loving, and that our resentment against you was groundless."[61]

Being a Christian is much more than believing certain doctrines and following specific precepts and commandments. *Being a Christian is first and foremost a personal relationship with Jesus Christ, the very source of life and love.* Jesus made it clear that he wants to be our friend when he stated to his followers, "I no longer call you servants, but friends" (see Jn 15:15). What is unique to Christianity is that God is offering us a loving and caring friendship through Jesus Christ. Our relationship—our friendship—with God is one of love, trust, loyalty, faithfulness, compassion, mercy, encouragement, support, and strength.[62]

God is light and love and truth who brings order and

meaning and serenity to our lives. Only in God will we find the true happiness and deep joy we seek in this life and glory in the eternal life to come. Joy is the lasting happiness we are actually searching for. As Peter Kreeft writes:

> Joy is more than happiness, just as happiness is more than pleasure. Pleasure is in the body. Happiness is in the mind and feelings. Joy is deep in the heart, the spirit, the center of the self.
>
> The way to pleasure is power and prudence. The way to happiness is moral goodness. The way to joy is sanctity, loving God with your whole heart and your neighbor as yourself.
>
> Everyone wants pleasure. More deeply, everyone wants happiness. Most deeply, everyone wants joy.[63]

However, we often do not realize that joy is what we are truly seeking. How often do we instead seek to satisfy the happiness hole in our hearts with worldly pleasures? As St. Thomas Aquinas wrote in the thirteenth century, "Man cannot live without joy. That is why one deprived of spiritual joys goes over to carnal pleasures."[64] Again, why do we look for lasting happiness and joy in all the wrong places? Truly, our hearts are restless until they find their rest in God, Jesus, and his Church.

When we humbly and sincerely turn to God, God can free us from the griping power of fear and the selfishness and pride that can block our experience of God's love and joy in our lives. Actively belonging to a community of Christians—the Church—can help free us from loneliness, isolation, and rejection, as well as any hope-lessness or despair that hamper God's power to heal life's hurts.

Being active in the Church can also provide the grace needed to forgive others from the depth of our hearts, as Jesus did and still does, when things don't go as well as we'd like. In this way, we have access to the treasure that God offers us and that no amount of money can buy if we but turn to God.

Though not always easy, life becomes a fulfilling journey when we trust God with both our joys and our sorrows. Our joys are multiplied and our sorrows are reduced when we accept that God is with us. God's grace is sufficient, and his love for each of us is strong. No one and nothing can ever surpass God's love, forgiveness, and generosity.

If you seek God with trust and expectant faith, God will not disappoint you and will lavish his true love upon you. God will meet you more than half way and give you what you truly need. The moment we turn toward God, God will guide us through any mess we have made of our lives and bring us home to "the road that leads to life" (Mt 7:14).

As you continue reading through this book, we invite you to consider surrendering your doubts and fears, your pride and guilt, to God and trust in God's saving pres-ence and healing love. God never refuses anyone who sincerely puts his or her trust in him.

Just like the father in Jesus's parable of the prodigal son (see Lk 15:11–32), God is always ready to welcome us with open arms and a loving embrace when we turn to him in humility and repentance. God is constantly waiting for us, running after us. He never relents, never gives up. The more we run from God, the more God runs after us; the more we resist, the more God persists. We know no matter how many times we fail that God's love for us is everlasting and his patience with us endures forever.

God fully respects our freedom and patiently waits for an invitation. But we are often too preoccupied with our everyday lives and worries to consciously invite God in and experience God's love in our lives. We are, however, not free of the consequences of our choices. Our choices will either lead us on the path of abundant life and union with God or the path that leads to emptiness and separation from God. As Pope Francis challenged over a million young people gathered at the 2016 World Youth Day in Poland:

> So I ask you: Are you looking for empty thrills in life, or do you want to feel a power that can give you a lasting sense of life and fulfillment? Empty thrills or the power of grace? What do you want: deadening thrills or the power of fullness? What do you want? To find fulfillment, to gain new life, there is a way, a way that is not for sale, that cannot be purchased, a way that is not a thing or an object, but a person. His name is Jesus Christ.[65]

Intellectual Questions and Searching Faith

We have looked at the joys and benefits the active Christian life has to offer and that make available a life truly worth living. But we realize before you or anyone else can make the choice to live such a life, there are certain intellectual doubts and questions that need to be addressed.

For example, how can we know that Jesus was a real historical person who is truly divine and who really rose from the dead? Is there any evidence that heaven and the afterlife are actually real? If so, how are we saved to eternal life in heaven? Why should we bother going to Mass, and are the Catholic Church and the sacraments even relevant today?

It is completely normal to have intellectual doubts and questions about religion as we grow older. There is nothing wrong with these doubts and questions. In fact, honest doubts and sincere questions can be a launching point to a deeper and more committed faith.

Intellectually questioning and testing what we have been taught about our faith has been called "searching faith."[66] Searching faith usually begins during late adolescence and often continues in earnest during young adulthood. This is when "religion of the head" becomes as important as "religion of the heart." God gave us inquisitive minds and expects us to honestly explore questions about religion and faith.

A personal experience from college illustrates the reality of searching faith. As was common on weekends, the music was blaring at a party I was attending in a dorm room. We were all engaged in different conversations and having a good time. Then another student and I began discussing whether or not God exists. Before long, the music was turned off and everyone in the room was actively engaged in discussing the existence of God. This is searching faith in action.

Searching faith is important because it is only by questioning and internalizing what we have been taught during childhood that we can come to personally accept and maturely commit to these teachings as adults, to make them our own. It is now our own faith and not merely the faith of our family or friends. Those who "own" their faith are willing and able to stand up for their beliefs and strive to witness the faith in both word and deed as committed disciples (followers) of Jesus Christ. Thus, addressing our personal doubts and questions is vital if we are to maturely "own" and commit to the faith.

Brian's Story

My friend Brian is one such person who experienced this questioning in his life. Here is his story:

> I remember as a young boy going to Mass on Sundays with my brother and parents. During elementary school, I started attending religious education classes (CCD) at my parish on Sunday evenings. But this was not the way I wanted to wind down my weekend before heading off to school on Monday morning.
>
> When I was in first grade, I was baptized in the Catholic Church, and I remember having the water poured on my head and thinking how silly I probably looked in front of my classmates. I went through First Communion the following year, but

was just "going through the motions." After a con-
flict with a classmate, I stopped attending CCD in
the sixth grade. Even though I felt like I did not get
anything out of Mass, our family did keep going to
Mass—when it didn't interfere with soccer.

In college, I went to Mass only on the "big days,"
such as Christmas and Easter. I felt if I was a good
person, then I didn't really need Mass. Even though
I did pray every night when I went to bed, for some
reason I didn't feel the need to go to Mass. Looking
back, it was probably because I worried about being
judged for how little I knew. I always avoided religious conversations, and I felt like religion was my
own private thing between myself and God. I never
felt comfortable asking other people questions and
always felt like understanding Catholicism was too
big of a mountain to climb at that stage in my life.

During my senior year, I started dating Kim
from my broadcasting class. Religion came up in
one of our early conversations, and I could tell it
was important to her. As our relationship grew,
I started to realize that me being Catholic was
important to her if we were going to get married
and someday start a family.

After college, Kim and I did get married. She
was good about attending Mass but never pushed
me to go. There were times that I would go bik-
ing with my brother and friends instead of making
time for Mass, mostly because none of my friends
went to church.

Early in our marriage, I was intimidated by my

wife's knowledge in this area, and I was embarrassed to ask for her help even though deep down I wanted to. I also felt like the Church was not a safe place to seek answers and that I would be judged if people knew how little I understood about our faith.

When we had kids, I kept telling myself that I needed to "get all in" so our kids could come along to Mass with both their mother and me. I tried for several years to focus on the readings in Mass as we dragged our three young children and all that goes with them to the cry room. I knew we were doing the right thing, but if there was the opportunity to miss Mass, I would take full advantage of it.

As the kids got a little older, things got much easier and we could actually have conversations on the way home from Mass about what was discussed. Most of the time, my wife led the conversations with a few questions and I listened to see what our kids learned and to make sure I was learning too. Watching our kids start to grow in the Faith and knowing I wasn't able to help them brought feelings of low self-worth and inadequacy. So I started searching for ways to grow in my faith.

I have always heard that teaching something is a great way to learn it, so I started taking the lead in asking our children what they learned from CCD and Mass. It helped me make sure I was getting spiritually fed at Mass and was ready to discuss it afterwards. I don't know if our children realize how much they and their mom have helped me grow and become a committed Catholic.

I recently completed the Rite of Christian Initiation of Adults (RCIA) program at our parish. I received the Sacrament of Confirmation as an adult since I had stopped going to CCD in the sixth grade. I was excited to be doing this a year before my oldest child was confirmed because it was important for me to know that I can be there for our children as they have questions.

I did not feel like I could fully lead my family if I was not a leader in this area, because I started to realize that everything our children are going to do will be built on a solid foundation of their faith. Looking back, I realize how foolish some of my earlier thoughts were. And now after talking with several people around my parish, I have come to find it is indeed a safe place to seek answers and that the strongest men I know have the strongest faith. I used to look at Mass as the end of the week and something my parents made me do. But now I look at Mass as the beginning of my week and it equips me for what lies ahead.

Addressing the Big Questions

Like Brian, we may have questions and doubts about core beliefs of the Catholic Christian faith tradition. These questions should be sincerely encouraged and doubts earnestly explored if we are to ultimately find true happiness with Jesus in his Church. The rest of this book, therefore, clearly and concisely addresses "big questions" about Jesus, salvation, and the Church that are of interest to anyone who wants to earnestly explore the truth of the Catholic faith.

We are asked by Jesus to love God with all our heart, with all our soul, and with all our *mind* (see Mt 22:37). But we cannot love what we do not know. Some people, therefore, use reason and logic to find God, then gradually discover God's love and the love of other Christians. Other people first experience the love of God in their family or a Christian community and then use reason and logic to learn more about their faith. In either case, it is vitally important to earnestly explore and rationally address "big questions" about the Catholic Christian faith.

Our look at these questions will be of interest to those who believe that God exists but do not regularly attend church, and who may consider themselves "spiritual but not religious." This includes those who were raised Catholic and who, like Brian, stopped practicing the faith but are now interested in exploring more deeply the faith of their childhood. This book will also strengthen the faith of practicing Catholics and provide valuable information for discussion with family and friends who have questions about Jesus, salvation, and the Catholic Church.

In the following chapters, we will clearly and concisely address important questions about the Catholic faith as well as common objections to the most basic tenets of Christianity. We will not, however, deal with the foundational question, "Does God exist?" or with the related question, "Which is true: evolution, creation, or both?" Both of these questions are addressed in my earlier book, *The Reality of God: The Layman's Guide to*

Scientific Evidence for the Creator.[67] Let's start by exploring how we can know that Jesus is truly God incarnate (God in human form) who really rose from the dead.

Part 2

THE TRUTH OF JESUS

Chapter 4

IS JESUS TRULY GOD?

The New Testament of the Bible provides many details about the life and teachings of Jesus Christ, especially the Gospels of Matthew, Mark, Luke, and John. These four Gospels all claim that Jesus of Nazareth was a Jew who lived in first-century Palestine and was crucified under the Roman governor Pontius Pilate. Credible references to Jesus in ancient texts written by Roman and Jewish enemies of Christianity support the truth of these claims. This "enemy attestation" is significant because opponents of Jesus had no reason to acknowledge that he was a real person who was crucified by the Romans if it was not true.

For example, Cornelius Tacitus—a Roman senator and the most important Roman historian of the first century—referred to Jesus Christ and his crucifixion by Pontius Pilate in his *Annals*, which was written about AD 115.[68] Writing about Emperor Nero's persecution of Christians after the Great Fire that devastated Rome in AD 64, Tacitus states:

> Nero fastened the guilt and inflicted the most exquisite punishments on a class hated for their

disgraceful acts, called Christians by the populace. Christ, from whom the name had its origin, suffered the extreme penalty [crucifixion] during the reign of Tiberius at the hands of one of our procurators, Pontius Pilatus, and a most mischievous superstition, thus checked for the moment, again broke out not only in Judea, the first source of the evil, but even in Rome, where all things hideous and shameful from every part of the world find their center and become popular. Accordingly, an arrest was first made of all who pleaded guilty; then, upon their information, an immense multitude was convicted, not so much of the crime of firing the city, as of hatred against mankind. Mockery of every sort was added to their deaths. Covered with the skins of beasts, they were torn by dogs and perished, or were nailed to crosses, or were doomed to the flames and burnt, to serve as a nightly illumination, when daylight had expired.[69]

It is very significant that Tacitus—who was clearly anti-Christian—provides an unsympathetic historical account of the existence of a movement based on a real person who had been crucified under Pontius Pilate.[70] There are other ancient, non-Christian historical references that Jesus of Nazareth was an actual person and not just a mythological figure.[71] There is little reason to doubt that Jesus of Nazareth was a real historical person who was actually crucified by the Romans.

But Christianity, unlike other religions, makes a more radical claim about its founder. Namely, that Jesus Christ is the divine Son of God who became human in order to redeem humankind from our sins and failings and to accomplish our salvation. In other words, Jesus Christ is God incarnate who became truly man while remaining truly God. Jesus is the fully human and fully divine Son of God.

But how do we know Jesus himself made that claim of divinity, and how can we know if it is true? There are several places in the New Testament recording Jesus's claims of divinity, including:

- "I am the bread of life. . . . I came down from heaven. . . . For this is the will of my Father, that everyone who sees the Son and believes in him may have eternal life. . . . The living Father sent me" (Jn 6:35, 38, 40, 57).
- "Why do you say that I'm dishonoring God because I said, 'I am the Son of God'? God set me apart for this holy purpose and has sent me into the world" (Jn 10:36 GW).
- "Again the High Priest questioned him, 'Are you the Messiah, the Son of the Blessed God?' 'I AM,' answered Jesus" (Mk 14:61–62 TEV).

As we see from Scripture, Jesus claimed to be the Son of God. This means Jesus has the same nature and essence as God. But how can we know this is true? Since Jesus claimed to be divine, he was either a deliberate liar (he knew his claim was false), sadly mistaken and delusional (he thought he was the Son of God, but was not), or he was telling the truth.[72]

As C. S. Lewis noted in *Mere Christianity*, for Jesus to have talked as he talked, lived as he lived, and died as he died, he was either a boldfaced liar, an insane lunatic, or truly our Lord and God.[73] In other words, anyone who spoke about God and himself in the way that Jesus did was either a deliberate liar, or was completely deluded, or was profoundly right. The claims of Jesus suggest either conspiracy, insanity, or divinity. So let's next examine the first two options; namely, was Jesus a liar or a lunatic?

Was Jesus a Liar?

Liars do not speak with audacity. Liars want to be seen as credible, so they do not make outlandish claims and tell audacious lies. But Jesus made some very audacious claims, as in the following:

- "I am the way and the truth and the life. No one comes to the Father except through me" (Jn 14:6).
- "No one knows the Son except the Father, and no one knows the Father except the Son and anyone to whom the Son wishes to reveal him" (Mt 11:27).
- "Amen, amen, I say to you, unless you eat the flesh of the Son of Man and drink his blood, you do not have life within you" (Jn 6:53).
- "My teaching is not my own but is from the one who sent me" (Jn 7:16).

The Jewish leaders at the time took Jesus's incredibly audacious claims seriously. They did not dismiss him as a liar or a lunatic. In fact, they considered him to be a blasphemer whose audacious claims showed clear disrespect for God, and thus they wanted him killed.

Furthermore, what would Jesus have gained by willingly dying for a lie? The Gospels tell us that Jesus went willingly to his death. For example, Jesus said, "I lay down my life in order to take it up again. No one takes it from me, but I lay it down on my own" (Jn 10:17–18). And when on trial before the Jewish Council, Jesus made some astonishing statements that unquestionably hastened his death for blasphemy against God, as follows:

> Then the high priest said to him, "I order you to tell us under oath before the living God whether you are the Messiah, the Son of God." Jesus said to him in reply, "You have said so. But I tell you: From now on you will see 'the Son of Man seated at the right hand of the Power' and 'coming on the clouds of heaven.'" Then the high priest tore his robes and said, "He has blasphemed! What further need have we of witnesses? You have now heard the blasphemy; what is your opinion?" They said in reply, "He deserves to die!" (Mt 26:63–66)

A common counter-argument is that Jesus himself did not claim to be divine, but these words were later "put in his mouth" by his overzealous followers. If that was the case, how do we explain why Jesus was crucified? For if Jesus was not crucified for claiming to be God (blasphemy), then why did the Jewish leaders want him killed?

Jesus was not killed because he was an anti-Roman political zealot, as is sometimes claimed. There is no evidence in the four Gospels or in any other historical record that Jesus worked to put an end to Roman political rule in Palestine. Jesus had no interest in being a political or military leader and did not try to foment a rebellion against the Roman occupation. In fact, he did just the opposite, as when he said, "Blessed are the peacemakers," (Mt 5:9) and, "Put your sword back into its sheath, for all who take up the sword will perish by the sword" (Mt 26:52). Moreover, Jesus implicitly supported Roman rule when he said, "Repay to Caesar what belongs to Caesar" (Mt 22:21, Mk 12:17, Lk 20:25).

The main reason most Jews at the time did not accept Jesus as the Messiah was because he did not liberate them from the oppressive rule of pagan Rome, which was their Messianic expectation at the time.[74] The Jews believed that the Messiah would come as their king and would free them from foreign tyranny and domination. But during his entire public career, Jesus resisted when the crowds hailed him as the Messiah or wanted to make him a king. He sternly ordered them to be silent (see Mt 12:16, Lk 9:21), and he slipped away when they wanted to take him by force to make him king (Jn 6:15). Clearly, Jesus was no ordinary king, and he was not the type of Messiah that they expected. They expected their Messiah to be a warrior king, not a crucified carpenter.

Furthermore, the Gospel of John specifically records that the Jewish leaders wanted Jesus put to death for claiming to be the Son of God when they stated: "We have a law, and according to that law he ought to die, because he made himself the Son of God" (Jn 19:7). Even the Roman centurion at the foot of the cross acknowledged that Jesus was crucified for claiming to be divine when he said, "Truly this man was the Son of God!" (Mk 15:39). It is difficult to explain Jesus's crucifixion, which is a well-attested historical fact, if he did not actually claim to be God.

What could have been the motive of Jesus's apostles and disciples for proclaiming Jesus as the Son of God if they knew full well that this was nothing but a lie? What person would suffer torture and death for what they know to be a lie? This makes no sense. Instead, the apostles and many of Jesus's early followers proved their sincerity by their martyrdom.

Paul was beheaded in Rome. We are told that Mark was put to death in Alexandria, Egypt, after being cruelly dragged through the streets of that city and that Luke was hanged in Greece.[75] Only the apostle John died a natural death in old age. All of the remaining ten original apostles (Judas committed suicide after betraying Jesus) were martyred for their beliefs. According to ancient tradition, they died as follows:

- Peter was crucified upside down in Rome.
- James the Greater (son of Zebedee) was beheaded in Jerusalem.
- Bartholomew (Nathanial) was flayed alive and crucified upside down.
- James the Lesser (son of Alphaeus) was thrown from a pinnacle of the Temple in Jerusalem and then, after surviving the fall, was beaten to death with clubs.

- Andrew was crucified by being bound to an X-shaped cross with ropes (not nailed) in order to prolong his suffering.
- Thomas was thrust through with a spear and then burned to death in India.
- Phillip was crucified.
- Matthew was killed with a halberd in Ethiopia.
- Jude (Thaddeus) was either killed with arrows or beaten to death with a club.
- Simon the Zealot was either crucified or sawed in half.[76]

It is hard to believe that all these men would have suffered such painful deaths if they were just telling a made-up story about Jesus being the Son of God who had risen from the dead. It is not very likely that either Jesus or his followers would have endured all that pain and suffering if they knew what they were proclaiming was nothing but a lie.

If Christianity was a hoax and the apostles had taken it too far, one would think that they would "fess up" and stop the endless martyrdom, not just of themselves, but also of other Christians. They didn't "fess up" and they couldn't, because they knew what they proclaimed was the truth. Again, people do not die or let many other people be killed for what they know to be a lie. So it is reasonable to conclude that Jesus and his followers were not deliberately lying about his divinity, nor about his resurrection (as we shall see in the next chapter).

Was Jesus a Lunatic?

However, could the apostles and his followers have been deceived by a delusional Jesus? In other words, could Jesus have been a lunatic who sincerely believed he was divine but was not? After all, there are many lunatics in asylums who sincerely believe they are God.

The character traits of the "divinity complex" are well known: egotism, narcissism, inflexibility, dullness, and an inability to understand and love others.[77] Would thousands of people follow such a person, many to their deaths? Would you?

The madness of megalomania is essentially selfish. Such a person seeks nothing but his own glory and prestige. But Jesus spent his whole life unselfishly doing good things for others. He healed the sick, comforted the sorrowful, and fed the hungry. So the deeds of Jesus were not the deeds of a madman.

Moreover, the words of Jesus were not the words of a madman. Insane people do not speak the way Jesus spoke. Jesus's teachings have resonated with billions of people over the last two thousand years. Men and women throughout the centuries have judged the teachings of Jesus to be a source of hope and inspiration in a sometimes-crazy world. Here are two examples that show the appeal of his teachings and character:

- They came and said to him, "Teacher, we know that you are a truthful man. . . . You . . . teach the way of God in accordance with the truth" (Mk 12:14).

- The Sermon on the Mount is the ultimate presentation of Christ's teaching. "When Jesus finished these words, the crowds were astonished at his teaching, for he taught them as one having authority, and not as their scribes" (Mt 7:28–29).

Even so, some people at the time thought that Jesus was indeed crazy and even possessed by evil spirits. But many others did not think that Jesus's words and deeds were those of a crazy person. For example, "Again there was a division among the Jews because of these words. Many of them said, 'He is possessed and out of his mind; why listen to him?' Others said, 'These are not the words of one possessed; surely a demon cannot open the eyes of the blind, can he?'" (Jn 10:19–21).

Just as the words and deeds of Jesus were not those of a madman, so too his effect on others was not that of a lunatic. The undeniable fact is that the lives of his followers, including billions of people throughout the past twenty centuries, have been radically transformed by the power and presence of Jesus Christ. The bad have become good, the weak have become strong, the worried have become serene, and the selfish have become selfless. It is not madness that fosters such positive changes, but wisdom and sanity.

Furthermore, what caused the twelve apostles to suddenly leave their families and everyday lives behind and follow Jesus after he made the simple request, "Come and follow me"? The apostles were mostly fishermen, and some, such as Peter, were married and their families lived on the income from their fishing. Imagine you saw a man you did not know who said, "Leave your job, leave your family, and come follow me." Would you do it? Logic says no way! But these twelve men did.

The Gospels tell us that Jesus was walking by the Sea of Galilee when he saw two brothers, Simon who was called Peter and his brother Andrew, catching fish with a net. Jesus said to them, "Follow me, and I will make you fishers of men" (see Mt 4:18–20; Mk 1:16–18). Simon Peter and Andrew immediately left their nets and followed Jesus.

A little farther along the seashore, Jesus saw two other brothers, James and John, in a boat with their father, Zebedee. Jesus called them, and immediately they left the boat and their father, and they followed him (see Mt 4:21–22, Mk 1:19–20). The other apostles similarly left everything and followed Jesus when he asked them to join him.

What inspired the apostles to just leave everything and follow Jesus? Why would they have done this, especially if Jesus was nothing but a madman? Most of these men had not yet witnessed the miracles of Jesus or heard his teachings. One can only assume that being in the presence of the Son of God and being touched by God's unfathomable grace could have led these uneducated men to immediately follow Jesus and go on to change the world forever. For as Jesus later said to them, "With people it is impossible, but not with God; for all things are possible with God" (Mk 10:27).

Indeed, how could the apostles have been so successful in gaining followers and fostering the transformed lives of so many people, from so many different places, if they were just naive fools who had been deceived by a delusional Jesus? Is it realistic to expect that all of the apostles would have been continually deceived for so long? But not one of them ever denied what they believed to be true.

It is unrealistic to expect that the apostles and many other people throughout the centuries would willingly suffer torture and death if what they believed was indeed a false deception or delusion. Insane or delusional people just are not this widely successful for so long. It is hard to expect that a deliberate lie or false delusion would have "withstood the test of time" for two thousand years without being exposed as such.

If Jesus was a self-promoting liar or delusional Messiah, he would have tried to garner favors and royal treatment for himself. Yet Jesus did none of those things. Rather, he mostly traveled and taught among the humble masses and the downtrodden, not among the rich and powerful upper classes of his society.

Furthermore, some people believe that Jesus was not divine but only a great moral teacher. C. S. Lewis addresses that claim in *Mere Christianity*:

> I am trying here to prevent anyone saying the really foolish thing that people often say about Him: "I'm ready to accept Jesus as a great moral teacher, but I don't accept His claim to be God." That is the one thing we must not say. A man who was merely a man and said the sort of things Jesus said would not be a great moral teacher. He would either be a

lunatic . . . or else he would be the Devil of Hell. You must make your choice. Either this man was, and is, the Son of God; or else a madman or something worse. You can shut Him up for a fool, you can spit at Him and kill Him as a demon; or you can fall at His feet and call Him Lord and God. But let us not come with any patronizing nonsense about His being a great human teacher. He has not left that open to us. He did not intend to.[78]

Since Jesus claimed to be God, he could not have been just a great moral teacher. That's because great moral teachers do not deceive others by falsely claiming to be God.

Even non-Christians agree that Jesus was a good and wise person. Jesus talked about loving others, healed the sick, defended the poor, and cared for the outcast. Who but a good and wise person does that? However, a liar is not a good person. A liar is the opposite of good. And a lunatic is the opposite of wise. So we can reasonably conclude that Jesus, being a good and wise person, was not a liar or a lunatic. Jesus did not bring a deluded madness into the world but the perfect sanity of God.

Is the Divinity of Jesus a Legend?

But there is another possibility. Could the divinity of Jesus have been neither a deliberate lie nor a lunacy but a mythical legend that developed and grew over time? In other words, could exaggerated fictitious elements have been added by Jesus's overzealous followers to the actual historical reality of his life? After all, overdone hero worship can tend to divinize the hero.[79]

It is true the Gospels show that the apostles gradually came to realize Jesus was the divine Son of God. They did not have this belief when they initially started following him. For example, the Gospels record it was only after following Jesus for a while that Peter first came to realize his divinity. Matthew states:

> When Jesus went into the region of Caesarea Philippi he asked his disciples, "Who do people say that the Son of Man is?" They replied, "Some say John the Baptist, others Elijah, still others Jeremiah or one of the prophets." He said to them, "But who do you say that I am?" Simon Peter said in reply, "You are the Messiah, the Son of the living God." Jesus said to him in reply, "Blessed are you, Simon son of Jonah. For flesh and blood has not revealed this to you, but my heavenly Father." (Mt 16:13–17)

The Church has long held that God's revelation of himself becomes clearer over time through the work of the Holy Spirit. Jesus alluded to the ongoing nature of divine revelation when he spoke to his disciples about the gift of the Holy Spirit that would be given to them at Pentecost. He said, "The Advocate, the Holy Spirit, whom the Father will send in my name, *will teach* you all things and will remind you of everything I have said to you" (Jn 14:26, emphasis added).

However, just because the apostles came to gradually understand and deepen their belief in the divinity of Jesus, especially after his resurrection, does not mean this belief was false or simply an exaggeration of the early Church. There are at least seven reasons why claims of the divinity of Jesus could not have been a fictitious myth or legend that developed over time.

New Testament Books Written Before a Legend Could Develop

First, the Gospels and other books of the New Testament were written within a few decades of the death of Jesus, and this is too quick for a new mythical legend about the divinity of Jesus to develop and be taken as fact.[80] Peter Kreeft and Ronald Tacelli write:

> If Jesus' divinity is a myth invented by later gen-
> erations ("the early Christian community," often a
> code word for "the inventors of the myth"), then
> there must have been at least two or three gener-
> ations between the original eyewitnesses of the
> historical Jesus and the universal belief in the new,
> mythic, divinized Jesus; otherwise, the myth could
> never have been believed as fact because it would
> have been refuted by eyewitnesses of the real Jesus.
> Both disciples and enemies would have had rea-
> sons to oppose this new myth. However, we find
> no evidence at all of anyone ever opposing the
> so-called myth of the divine Jesus in the name of
> an earlier merely human Jesus. . . . No competent
> scholar today denies the first-century dating of vir-
> tually all of the New Testament—certainly Paul's
> letters, which clearly affirm and presuppose Jesus'

divinity and the fact that this doctrine was already universal Christian orthodoxy.[81]

Most scholars date the death of Jesus around the year AD 30 and hold that many of the letters written by Paul were composed in the decade of the 50s, making them the earliest New Testament texts.[82] The vast majority of scholars believe that Mark was the first of the New Testament Gospels to be written, sometime around AD 70.[83] The scholarly consensus is that the Gospels of Matthew and Luke are based on Mark and were composed sometime in the 80s or 90s, followed by the Gospel of John around the end of the first century.[84]

The Acts of the Apostles in the New Testament is attributed to the same author as the Gospel of Luke, which is believed to have been written before Acts.[85] The book of Acts is very concerned with the persecution and death of early Christian leaders (e.g., Acts 8:1; 12:1–2). However, Acts makes no mention of the brutal persecution of Christians in Rome by the Emperor Nero in AD 64–65, which greatly impacted the early Church and likely included the martyrdom of Saints Peter and Paul.[86] The book of Acts also fails to mention the destruction of Jerusalem and its Temple by Roman armies in AD 70. The best explanation for these major omissions is that those tragic events had not yet occurred. Some scholars, therefore, believe that the Gospel of Luke and the Acts of the Apostles were written *before* the destruction of Jerusalem in AD 70.

In any case, it can be safely accepted that the first Gospel was written within forty years of the death of

Jesus. This is well within the lifetime of many eyewitnesses to the words and deeds of Jesus, and they would have refuted what was being written if it was not true.

By comparing the Gospels to other ancient biographies, such as those of Alexander the Great and the Roman Emperor Tiberius, the rate at which legend was added can be measured.[87] Scholars have concluded there was not enough time between the death of Jesus and the writing of the Gospels for added mythological elements to be mistakenly taken as fact.

For example, historian A. N. Sherwin-White concluded that the time between the death of Jesus and the writing of the Gospels was too short for legend to accrue that would corrupt the main message of the life of Jesus. He writes, "Herodotus enables us to test the tempo of myth-making and the tests suggest that even two generations are too short a span to allow the mythical tendency to prevail over the hard historic core of the oral tradition."[88]

Ancient Non-Christian Historians Stated Early Christians Believed Jesus Was Divine

Second, several ancient non-Christian historians stated that the early Christians believed Jesus was divine. Pliny the Younger was the Roman governor of Bithynia-Pontus, which is in modern Turkey. Around AD 112, Pliny wrote a letter to Emperor Trajan asking for advice on how to deal with Christians.[89] The letter describes how Pliny conducted trials of suspected Christians who appeared before him as a result of anonymous accusations. He asked the emperor for guidance on how they should be treated if they did not recant their Christian beliefs and worship the emperor and other Roman gods (as some did). Pliny wrote (emphasis added):

> I asked them whether they were Christians or not. If they confessed that they were Christians, I asked them again, and a third time, intermixing threats with the questions. If they persevered in their confession, I ordered them to be executed. . . . Others of them that were named in the libel, said they were Christians, but presently denied it again; that indeed they had been Christians, but had ceased to be so, some three years, some many more; and one there was that said he had not been so these twenty years. All these worshipped your image, and the images of our gods; these also cursed Christ. However, they assured me that the main of their fault, or of their mistake was this: That they were wont, on a stated day, to meet together before it was light, and to *sing a hymn to Christ, as to a god.* . . . These examinations made me think it necessary to inquire by torments what the truth was; which I did of two servant maids, who were called Deaconesses: but still I discovered no more than that *they were addicted to a bad and to an extravagant superstition.*[90]

Here we have a Roman official, who was no friend of Christianity, affirming that early Christians worshipped Jesus as divine and believed in his resurrection, which he and other Roman non-believers called a "superstition."[91] Lucian of Samosata (a second-century Greek satirist) wrote that the early Christians "deny the gods of Greece, and worship the crucified sage."[92] Thus, we find objective historical evidence that belief in the divinity of Jesus was common in the early Christian Church and did not arise in later centuries.

New Testament Writers Did Not Have a Motive for Proclaiming a Legend

Third, the New Testament writers did not have a good motive for proclaiming an exaggerated legend about the divinity of Jesus. Both the Romans and Jews were hostile to the message of Jesus's divinity. The Romans viewed the deity of Jesus as politically subversive to the Roman Empire. Therefore, they routinely persecuted and killed Christians who would not worship the emperor.

While the message of Jesus's divinity and resurrection brought the early Christians hope, it also brought them a "giant target on their foreheads" from the political and religious culture in the first century.[93] The early Christians clearly risked persecution and death by testifying to Jesus's divinity. What could have been the motive of Jesus's apostles and disciples for proclaiming Jesus as the divine Son of God if this was just an exaggerated myth?

It is understandable that Jesus's grieving disciples would commemorate his life and teachings. But it makes no sense that they would emerge just weeks after his gruesome death on the cross full of confidence and joy, boldly proclaiming his resurrection from the dead. There was nothing to be gained financially, socially, or otherwise from promoting such a myth. Besides, it makes no sense that the apostles would, as a group, all proclaim the exact same mythological message and then endure brutal persecution and even death if what they were proclaiming was just a myth.

If their proclamations about Jesus's divinity and resurrection had been made-up exaggerations, wouldn't even one of the apostles have recanted to save his life? Recall that Peter had earlier denied Jesus three times to "save his skin" (see Mk 14:66–72). As noted earlier, all but one of the remaining eleven original apostles suffered horrific and torturous deaths without ever once denying even a single word of what is now written in the New Testament. It is most unlikely they would have endured all this suffering if what they were proclaiming was something other than what they had actually witnessed.

The Bible Is Historically Reliable

Fourth, the Bible has a very good track record when it comes to historical reliability. For example, in just one verse, Luke mentions fifteen specific historical details that have been confirmed.[94] He writes, "Now in the [1] fifteenth year of the reign of [2] Tiberius Caesar, when [3] Pontius Pilate was [4] governor of [5] Judea, and [6] Herod was [7] tetrarch of [8] Galilee, and his [9] brother [10] Philip was [11] tetrarch of the region of [12] Ituraea and Trachonitis, and [13] Lysanias was [14] tetrarch of [15] Abilene" (Lk 3:1).

The modern science of archaeology has confirmed—not denied—much of what is written in the Bible. This led world renowned scholar Gleason Archer to write, "As I have dealt with one apparent discrepancy after another and have studied the alleged contradictions between the biblical record and the evidence of linguistics, archaeology, or science, my confidence in the trustworthiness of Scripture has been repeatedly verified and strengthened by the discovery that almost every problem in Scripture that has ever been discovered by man, from ancient times until now, has been dealt with in a completely satisfactory manner by the biblical text itself—or else by objective archaeological information."[95]

New Testament Writers Stated They Were Writing About Actual Events

Fifth, the New Testament writers knew the difference between myth and history, and they stated they were writing eyewitness descriptions of actual historical events, not myth or legend.[96] Luke, for example, states that he had carefully investigated everything and wrote an accurate and truthful testimony about Jesus. At the beginning of his Gospel, he states, "Since many have undertaken to compile a narrative of the events that have been fulfilled among us, just as those who were eyewitnesses from the beginning and ministers of the word have handed them down to us, I too have decided, after investigating everything accurately anew, to write it down in an orderly sequence for you, most excellent Theophilus, so that you may realize the certainty of the teachings you have received" (Lk 1:1–4).

Luke tells us his account is totally believable because it comes from firsthand witnesses who knew Jesus personally, heard him teach, saw his miracles, and witnessed his agonizing death on the cross and resurrection from the dead. Luke wants his friend Theophilus and all who read his account to know the factual truth concerning Jesus of Nazareth.

Likewise, the Gospel of John states, "An eyewitness has testified, and his testimony is true; he knows that he is speaking the truth" (Jn 19:35). This same Gospel concludes with the definitive statement: "It is this disciple who testifies to these things and has written them, and we know that his testimony is true" (Jn 21:24).

Similarly, St. Peter wrote, "We did not follow cleverly devised myths when we made known to you the power and coming of our Lord Jesus Christ, but we had been eyewitnesses of his majesty" (2 Pt 1:16). The style of the New Testament is not the style of myth but is the style of eyewitness description of real events and factual beliefs, including the Resurrection and divinity of Jesus.[97]

The Gospel authors wrote from either firsthand experience or the personal testimony of eyewitnesses they knew well. That was because people in the first century valued eyewitness testimony.[98] Matthew and John were both apostles who personally followed and lived with Jesus for several years. They were personal eyewitnesses to events recorded in their Gospels. Papias, an early second-century Church Father, tells us that Mark was a disciple of Peter and wrote his Gospel based on Peter's eyewitness testimony.[99] As noted earlier, the Gospel of Luke is the first volume of Luke-Acts and was composed by "Luke the beloved physician," who was a traveling companion of the apostle Paul (see Col 4:14).[100]

Trivial Details Recorded in the Gospels

Sixth, there are trivial details recorded in the Gospels that distinguish them from myth. For example, John 1:38–39 states, "Jesus turned and saw them following him and said to them, 'What are you looking for?' They said to him, 'Rabbi' (which translated means Teacher), 'where are you staying?' He said to them, 'Come, and you will see.' So they went and saw where he was staying, and they stayed with him that day. It was about four in the afternoon."

Why would the trivial detail about it being four o'clock in the afternoon be included in a mythical legend about Jesus? That would serve no purpose. Rather, this detail is surely a personal recollection of an actual eyewitness to this event. The life-changing significance of the day when Jesus called some of his apostles to follow him was so vividly etched in the memory of this eyewitness (John) that he could even recall the specific time of day that it occurred.

Since the Gospels were written relatively soon after the actual events, other eyewitnesses—especially those who were hostile to the early Christians—could have refuted them. But they did not. Jesus's followers and enemies alike accepted the Gospels, including claims of the divinity and resurrection of Jesus, as truthful eyewitness testimony.

Unfavorable Elements In Eyewitness Testimonies

Seventh, the authors of the four Gospels carefully put down in writing an oral tradition that preserved these eyewitness testimonies—"warts" and all. If the Gospel authors were just trying to market or sell Christianity, why would they have included Jesus's difficult sayings (those stories, events, or phrases that were controversial then just as they are now) and embarrassing facts, especially about their leaders?

If the early Church wanted to make up a propaganda piece about its leaders, they would not have painted Peter and the other disciples as cowardly and even clueless! Imagine you were trying to concoct a story that you wanted others to follow you in believing, would you portray yourself as dim-witted, uncaring, and doubting cowards?[101] Of course not. But that is exactly what we find in the New Testament.[102] If the Church intended to distort fact or fabricate stories in support of their efforts, as critics often claim, why didn't it?

The authors of the New Testament did not change the story even when it would have benefited the leaders of the early Christian Church. They wrote that the apostles and disciples were unintelligent (see Mk 9:32; Lk 18:34), uneducated (see Acts 4:13), uncaring (see Mk 14:37), cowardly (see Mt 26:56; Mk 14:50–51; Lk 22:54–60), and doubtful (see Mt 28:17; Jn 20:24–27). In fact, Peter was even called "Satan" by Jesus in the biography that he helped author—the Gospel of Mark (Mk 8:33).

Why would the New Testament authors have said these types of derogatory things about their leaders if they were not true? It would have been far easier for the Gospel authors to simply leave these details out of their accounts. But they were so committed to telling the truth that they didn't tamper with the facts—even when these facts were embarrassing to the early Church leaders. This is evidence of the reliability and trustworthiness of the Gospels.

Moreover, the early Christians had a number of disputes and disagreements with one another. They disagreed about the importance of circumcision (Acts 11:2-3; 15:1-2), obeying the Jewish Law (Gal 5:3-4), speaking in tongues (1 Cor 14:23), and the relationship between Jews and Gentiles in the Church (Gal 2:11-14). If the Gospel authors were inventing details or exaggerating their stories, imagine how tempting it would have been for them to simply add a made-up teaching or two from Jesus to help settle these controversial matters. And yet Jesus, in all four Gospels, is strangely silent on these controversies. The Gospel authors clearly did not feel at liberty to invent some teachings from Jesus to help resolve these controversial issues. This indicates they only wrote what they knew to be true and factual.

These are seven rational reasons why we can trust that the Gospels are an authentic representation of fact written by or containing the testimony of sane and reliable eyewitnesses who were not exaggerating their claims, including about Jesus's divinity and resurrection. We can reasonably conclude that neither Jesus nor his followers were deliberate liars or delusional lunatics, nor that belief about his divinity is a mythical legend. That leaves the final option; namely, that Jesus is indeed our Lord—the fully human and fully divine Son of God.

Positive Evidence that Jesus Is Lord and God

Unique among all major world religions, only Jesus claimed to be the divine Son of God. Unlike Moses, Mohammed, Confucius, or Buddha, Jesus did not claim to be merely a teacher of the truth but to be "the truth" (Jn 14:6). In Christianity, the teacher himself—not just his teachings—is all-important.

Of course, anyone claiming to be divine must have some pretty solid evidence to back up this claim in order to be taken seriously. What reasons are there that caused Jesus's claim of divinity to be taken seriously, including by those who wanted him crucified? There are several good reasons to take his claim seriously.

Jesus's Miracles

First, Jesus's many miracles are evidence of his divinity. For example, "Jesus stood up and commanded the wind, 'Be quiet!' and he said to the waves, 'Be still!' The wind died down, and there was a great calm. . . . But they were terribly afraid and began to say to one another, 'Who is this man? Even the wind and the waves obey him!'" (Mk 4:39, 41).

Some of Jesus's other miracles include:

- Changing water into wine (Jn 2:6–10)
- Healing diseases (Mt 4:23–25; 8:1–16; Mk 1:29–34; Lk 17:12–14)
- Healing the paralyzed (Mk 2:3–12, 3:1–5)
- Curing the mute and deaf (Mt 9:32–33; Mk 7:32–37)

- Restoring sight to the blind (Mt 9:27–30; Mk 8:22–25; Lk 18:35–43; Jn 9:1–7)
- Feeding the crowds (Mt 14:15–21; 15:32–38)
- Raising the dead (Mt 9:18–26; Lk 7:11–15; Jn 11:38–44)
- Walking on water (Mk 6:45–51)
- Commanding nature (Mk 4:35–41)

Today, we might be a bit skeptical that these miracles actually occurred. But it is hard to deny that Jesus was known at the time as a healer and a miracle worker. There is abundant evidence that Jesus's frequent miracles were a major reason why he drew such large crowds. If these miracles did not actually happen, why would so many people have been drawn to him?

The miracles that Jesus performed were a direct fulfillment of what the Jewish prophets had foretold many centuries earlier. For example, Isaiah had prophesied that the coming of the Messiah would bring new life for those who were oppressed by afflictions, infirmities, fear, and hopelessness (see Is 29:18–19; 35:5–6; 61:1). Jesus's many miracles confirmed his divine power and signaled the coming of God's kingdom in his own person.

Jesus's Divine Actions

Second, Jesus's divine actions also confirm that he is who he said he was. Some examples: "I give you a new commandment: love one another" (Jn 13:34) and "All power in heaven and on earth has been given to me" (Mt 28:18). Who but God issues "commandments" and has "power in heaven"? Thus, Jesus talked and acted as if he was God.

In addition, who but God can forgive sins? As stated in the Gospels:

> And there people brought to him a paralytic lying on a stretcher. When Jesus saw their faith, he said to the paralytic, "Courage, child, your sins are forgiven." At that, some of the scribes said to themselves, "This man is blaspheming." Jesus knew what they were thinking, and said, "Why do you harbor evil thoughts? Which is easier, to say, 'Your sins are forgiven,' or to say, 'Rise and walk'? But that you may know that the Son of Man has authority on earth to forgive sins"—he then said to the paralytic, "Rise, pick up your stretcher, and go home." He rose and went home. (Mt 9:2–6, see also Mk 2:1–12, Lk 5:17–26)

By healing the cripple of his physical ailment and by forgiving his sins, Jesus revealed his divine authority over both the physical world and the spiritual world. C. S. Lewis puts this in perspective when he states in *Mere Christianity*:

> Now comes the real shock. Among these Jews there suddenly turns up a man who goes about talking as if He was God. He claims to forgive sins. He says He has always existed. He says He is coming to judge the world at the end of time. Now let us get this clear. Among Pantheists, like the Indians, anyone might say that he was a part of God, or one with God: there would be nothing very odd about it. But this man, since He was a Jew, could not mean

that kind of God. God, in their language, meant the Being outside of the world, who had made it and was infinitely different from anything else. And when you have grasped that, you will see that what this man said was, quite simply, the most shocking thing that has ever been uttered by human lips.[103]

However, why did Jesus typically refer to himself as the "Son of Man" instead of the "Son of God"? Doesn't this mean that Jesus didn't think of himself as the divine Son of God? Not at all. This term comes from the Old Testament book of Daniel. The relevant passage (Dn 7:13–14) reads: "As the visions during the night continued, I saw coming with the clouds of heaven One like a son of man. When he reached the Ancient of Days and was presented before him, he received dominion, splendor, and kingship; all nations, peoples and languages will serve him. His dominion is an everlasting dominion that shall not pass away, his kingship, one that shall not be destroyed."

The eternal lordship and final judgment authority that the Son of Man receives is an attribute of God. Thus, in the title Son of Man we have a human being who exercises divine kingship and authority. We see in one person a combination of both humanity and divinity. This combination of humanity and divinity in one person is why Jesus called himself the "Son of Man" and why that title supports his claim of divinity. By using this title, Jesus revealed that he is both fully human and fully divine.

The Son of Man is also a Messianic title for God's anointed King. Since the beginning, Christians have proclaimed that God the Father did not send the Son to establish a political kingdom on earth, but to bring us into God's heavenly kingdom—an eternal kingdom of truth, justice, peace, and joy. The Greek word for "Messiah" is *Christos*. Both words mean the same thing, which is the "Anointed One" or the "Anointed King." That is why Jesus of Nazareth came to be called "Jesus Christ"—meaning Jesus the Christos, Jesus the Messiah, or Jesus the Anointed King.

The Originality, Creativity, and Authority of Jesus's Teachings

Third, the originality, creativity, and authority of Jesus's teachings, especially his parables, is further evidence of his divinity. Jesus was a masterful storyteller who gained his listeners' keen interest and involved them in the drama of the story. In his many parables, Jesus used images and characters from everyday life to create a short drama that illustrated his message and helped people understand who God is and what the kingdom (or reign) of God is like. The parable of the sower in Luke 8:4–15 is one example.

Parables were Jesus's most common way of teaching. His stories appealed to the young and old, poor and rich, as well as to the learned and unlearned, since they enabled each person to find himself in the story. But Jesus's parables are much more than engaging stories from the past and about things from long ago. The parables of Jesus reveal profound insights about God and call us to a deeper conversion, even today.

St. Cyril of Alexandria, an early Church Father,

described the purpose of Jesus's parables as follows: "For parables we may say are the images not of visible things, but rather of things of the mind and the spirit. For that which it is impossible to see with the eyes of the body, a parable will reveal to the eyes of the mind, beautifully shaping out the subtlety of things intellectual, by means of things perceivable by the senses, and which are as it were tangible."[104]

What other person in history has told so many profoundly insightful stories, in such an impromptu manner, which are still strongly relevant over two thousand years later? Anyone hearing the parables of Jesus back then or reading them today cannot help but marvel at the "superhuman" creativity and wisdom of their author.

For instance, many people who first heard Jesus speak in his hometown of Nazareth "were astonished" and remarked, "Where did this man get all this? What kind of wisdom has been given him?" (Mk 6:2; see also Mt 13:54; Lk 4:22). The Gospels also record that people were "utterly amazed" after Jesus delivered one of the most famous one-liners in history, "Repay to Caesar what belongs to Caesar and to God what belongs to God" (Mk 12:17; see also Mt 22:22; Luke 20:26).

Jesus spoke and taught as nobody had spoken or taught before. Those who heard Jesus speak were astonished by the authority of his speech. For example, the Gospel of Mark declares, "The people were astonished at his teaching, for he taught them as one having authority and not as the scribes" (Mk 1:22; see also Mt 7:28–29; Lk 4:32).

The people who heard Jesus speak knew they were in the presence of a teacher far greater than any other teacher in Jewish history. This wasn't merely because Jesus spoke with conviction and enthusiasm. Rather, it was because Jesus did not trace his authority back to Moses, as did the other Jewish teachers.

Jewish teachers had always supported their statements with quotes from other authorities, especially the teachings of Moses. But Jesus needed no other authorities to back up his teachings, and his listeners knew it. Jesus went, as it were, over the head of Moses. Unlike the Old Testament prophets who spoke with delegated authority from God ("Thus says the Lord"), Jesus spoke with personal authority.

For example, when speaking about the Ten Commandments and the Law of Moses at the beginning of the Sermon on the Mount, Jesus repeatedly stated, "You have heard that it was said [quoting a Commandment] . . . but I say" (see Mt 5:21–22, 27–28, 31–32, 33–35, 38–39, 43–44). This is evidence that Jesus was authority incarnate—the Word of God made flesh.[105] For when he spoke, God spoke.

Jesus's Resurrection

The fourth and most important evidence of Jesus's divinity is his resurrection from the dead. This claim is central to the faith of Christians. The Resurrection is the be-all and end-all of the Christian faith. For as St. Paul wrote, "If Christ has not been raised, then empty [too] is our preaching; empty, too, your faith" (1 Cor 15:14).

Many other men at the time of Jesus claimed to be the Messiah. Some of these men were quite popular and had a very large following. But we hear nothing about them today. Jesus was just a poor carpenter from a small town in Galilee. While he did draw large crowds, Jesus had only a small group of close followers—most of whom abandoned him when he was crucified. So why do we still hear about Jesus of Nazareth today? Because his followers boldly and courageously continued to proclaim—even when faced with persecution and death—that Jesus had risen from the dead. Without the Resurrection, then, Jesus would have been just another failed Messiah, and his life and death would be a forgotten footnote of history.

The gospel, which literally means "good news," proclaimed since the beginning of Christianity is essentially the wonderful news of the resurrection of Jesus Christ. This "good news" is that a man who claimed to be the Son of God and savior of the world has risen from the dead. And if Jesus rose from the dead, that validates everything he said and did, including his claim to be divine and not merely human, because rising from the dead is beyond human power.

It comes down to this: if Jesus did not rise from death, Christianity is a fraud and a joke, and all the bishops and priests should go home and the Christian faithful should immediately leave their churches. But if Jesus was indeed raised from the dead, then Christianity is truly the fullness of God's revelation, and Jesus must be the absolute center of our lives. Given the centrality of the Resurrection in Christian belief, how can we know that it really happened? This is what we will explore next.

Chapter 5

DID JESUS REALLY RISE FROM THE DEAD?

Since the beginning, Christians have proclaimed the resurrection of Jesus Christ. No other major religion claims that its founder rose from the dead. The bodily resurrection of Jesus was one of the most controversial claims made by the early disciples of Jesus. They claimed that Jesus was now alive again in the same body that had been crucified and that he would never die again. In other words, the apostles did not preach just the immortality of Jesus's soul. Rather, they also proclaimed the resurrection of his body from the dead.

The resurrection of Jesus was, however, not simply a return to this life. In John 11:38–44, we read how Lazarus was raised from the dead. When Lazarus came forth from the tomb, he was still wearing his grave clothes. He still belonged to the earthly realm and later died again. That is not what happened with the resurrection of Jesus.

When Jesus rose from the dead, he left his grave clothes behind in the tomb (see Lk 24:12; Jn 20:3–7). He

89

passed through locked doors (see Jn 20:19) and came and went as he pleased. His relationship with space and time was completely altered. The post-Resurrection Jesus now lives at an entirely different and more spiritual realm of existence.

The Christian proclamation is that Jesus is the first fruit of a higher and more spiritual way of life that awaits each of us after our death. This is truly good news because this new life is what God intends for each of us. God wills that we share in the risen and glorified life of Jesus Christ.

But how can we know that the Resurrection really happened, especially since Jesus is said to have appeared to only a few people after the Resurrection? Why was this? Would it not make more sense for Jesus to have risen from the dead very publicly and be seen by lots of people? For Jesus to have publicly and visibly risen from the dead would be an event that would never be forgotten. Surely this would draw many to faith, would it not?

And yet none of this is what happened. Not only did Jesus appear to relatively few people after his resurrection, but the actual moment of the Resurrection seems to have been witnessed by nobody at all. Instead of dramatically emerging from the tomb in broad daylight to a fanfare of trumpet blasts, the risen Jesus seems to have come forth before dawn, and this event was not witnessed by anyone.

In short, there is a hidden quality to the Resurrection. St. Peter affirms the hidden quality of the post-Resurrection appearances of Jesus when he said, "God raised Jesus from the dead on the third day and granted that he be visible, not to all people, but to us, the witnesses chosen by God in advance, who ate and drank with him after he rose from the dead" (Acts 10:40–41).

But why was the Resurrection such a hidden event, and why were the post-Resurrection appearances of Jesus witnessed by just a few people? We cannot definitely know why. But there is a reasonable explanation, and this explanation is rooted in the nature of God and our free will. Monsignor Charles Pope of the Archdiocese of Washington, DC, writes in his blog, "God is love (1 John 4:16). Love is not merely something God does, nor is it just one of his many attributes. Scripture says God is love. And it is in the nature of true love to woo the beloved, to invite, not to overwhelm or importune, not to force or coerce. For the lover wants to be loved. But to force the beloved to love or to overwhelm the cherished into a fearful love is not to receive true love in return."[106]

True love cannot be forced, and God desires our true love. God seeks our free and faithful response. God whispers; God quietly calls us; God gently draws us in. God supplies grace and evidence but does not overwhelm our freedom with awesome events that would compel us to believe.[107] Thus, the gentle and hidden nature of the Resurrection is actually another example of God's love.

Faith that needs to see is not real faith. For no one needs faith to believe what can be plainly seen with our eyes. That is why Jesus did not publicly rise from the dead. Jesus did, however, appear to his close disciples, and he sent out these eyewitnesses to proclaim the reality of his resurrection.

God also provides evidence and rational reasons to help us believe. But this is done in a way that does not overwhelm our freedom or force us to believe. We have a choice. Given that we have a free choice as to whether or not we will believe in the Resurrection, let's look at some credible evidence and logical reasons to believe that Jesus Christ really did rise from the dead.

The Empty Tomb

The starting point for our discussion of the reality of the Resurrection is the empty tomb. The empty tomb itself does not prove the Resurrection. But we cannot have a resurrection without an empty tomb. So how can we know that the tomb into which the body of Jesus was placed after his crucifixion was indeed found empty several days later? There are several good reasons.

First, all four Gospels tell us that Jesus was buried in the tomb of Joseph of Arimathea. He was a prominent member of the Jewish Sanhedrin—the very court that had condemned Jesus to death. Yet Joseph risked his reputation and his life to make sure Jesus received a proper burial. The embarrassing and awkward nature of Joseph's presence in all the accounts of Jesus's burial shows that this is a historically reliable account of what actually happened. It could not have been made up. As William Lane Craig states in *The Case for Christ*:

> It is highly unusual to find that the person who alone has the courage to go to Pilate and give Jesus an honorable burial is not members of family or faithful disciples who followed him to the end. Instead, it is a member of Jewish Sanhedrin, the

very high court, all of whom (Mark says), had condemned Jesus of Nazareth to the cross. The fact
that it is Joseph of Arimathea who is the person
responsible for giving Jesus an honorable burial
was an awkward and embarrassing fact for the
early Church and yet this tradition is faithfully preserved in almost all of the traditions that we have
about the burial of Jesus.[108]

Because Joseph of Arimathea was a public figure and
well-known person, it would have been clear where his
tomb was located. There would have been no question
where Jesus was buried. After hearing claims of Jesus's
resurrection, people could easily investigate whether or
not that tomb was indeed empty.

Second, as recorded in the Gospel of Matthew (28:11–
15), even the chief priests acknowledged that the tomb
in which Jesus was buried was empty. They even bribed
the Roman guards to say that the body of Jesus had been
stolen from the tomb. Their claim that the body was stolen confirms that Jesus's enemies acknowledged the tomb
was indeed empty. For if Jesus's body was not actually
missing, they would have just produced his corpse from
the well-known tomb of Joseph of Arimathea to clearly
refute claims that he had risen from the dead.

Alternatives to the Resurrection

Even though the tomb was empty, how do we know that
Jesus really rose from the dead? The best way to discover
the truth about the Resurrection is to rationally examine

other possible alternatives that could explain the empty tomb or the post-Resurrection appearances of Jesus. These alternatives are:

- The claim of the resurrection of Jesus could have been a deliberate lie and conspiracy by the apostles. They could they have stolen the body, as asserted by the Jewish leaders, and then falsely proclaimed that Jesus rose from the dead.
- Jesus could have not died on the cross but merely passed out and later revived in the tomb, thus appearing to have risen from the dead.
- The Resurrection could be just a myth or legend that developed over time.
- Jesus's post-Resurrection appearances could have been nothing more than hallucinations.

These are several possible alternatives to the good news of Christ's resurrection from the dead. Let's look in more detail at each of these four possible alternatives— conspiracy, swoon, legend, and hallucination.

The Stolen Body Theory

In order to examine the truth of the Resurrection, let's first answer the question: Could the Resurrection have been a deliberate lie and conspiracy to deceive by the disciples of Jesus? The "stolen body theory" holds that the disciples stole Jesus's body from the tomb and then promoted a deliberate lie and conspiracy that he rose from the dead. As noted above, this is what the Jewish leaders claimed at the time (see Mt 28:11-15).

However, such a bold action is contrary to all the evidence we have about the character of the apostles and disciples of Jesus.[109] We are told the male followers of Jesus denied, betrayed, and deserted him (except for John) when he was dying on the cross. They went into hiding and were afraid for their lives. It is very hard to envision how such fearful and cowardly men would have been able to muster up the courage and risk their lives to take on the Roman guards, raid the tomb, and steal the body.

Besides, what would the apostles have had to gain by planning and promoting a lie that Jesus rose from the dead? What could possibly have been their motive? They all faced persecution and death by proclaiming that Jesus rose from the dead. Yet not one of them ever denied their claim of Jesus's resurrection, even when faced with torture and death. Again, people do not give their lives for what they know is a lie.

Unlike in real conspiracies, none of the apostles recanted under duress. Chuck Colson, who was an aide to President Richard Nixon and who went to prison because of the Watergate scandal, compared his experience to the apostles when he wrote:

> Watergate involved a conspiracy to cover up, perpetuated by the closest aides to the President of the United States—the most powerful men in America, who were intensely loyal to their president. But one of them, John Dean, turned state's evidence, that is, testified against Nixon, as he put it, "to save his own

skin"—and he did so only two weeks after inform-
ing the president about what was really going on—
two weeks! The real cover-up, the lie, could only be
held together for two weeks, and then everybody
else jumped ship in order to save themselves. Now,
the fact is that all that those around the President
were facing was embarrassment, maybe prison.
Nobody's life was at stake.

But what about the disciples? Twelve powerless
men, peasants really, were facing not just embarrassment or political disgrace, but beatings, ston-
ings, execution. Every single one of the disciples
insisted, to their dying breaths, that they had physically seen Jesus bodily raised from the dead.

Don't you think that one of those apostles
would have cracked before being beheaded or
stoned? That one of them would have made a deal
with the authorities? None did. You see, men will
give their lives for something they believe to be
true—they will never give their lives for something
they know to be false.

The Watergate cover-up reveals the true nature
of humanity. Even political zealots at the pinnacle
of power will, in the crunch, save their own necks,
even at the expense of the ones they profess to
serve so loyally. But the apostles could not deny
Jesus because they had seen Him face to face, and
they knew He had risen from the dead.[110]

The Swoon Theory

Let's next ask: Did Jesus really die? The "swoon theory" is that Jesus did not die on the cross but later revived while in the tomb and thus seemed to have risen from the dead. It is highly unlikely, however, that Jesus could have survived the crucifixion. Roman execution procedures did not allow that to happen. Roman law even proscribed death to any soldier who bungled a crucifixion and allowed a capital prisoner to escape.[111] By piercing Jesus's side with a spear and not breaking his legs, which was done to hasten death by asphyxiation, the soldiers established that Jesus was dead. They would not have left the scene of such a public crucifixion, especially of an individual who was so disliked by the Jewish leaders, until they were absolutely sure he was dead.

Even if Jesus did survive his crucifixion and later revived in the tomb, how could he have moved the large stone at the entrance of the tomb and overpowered the Roman guards given that he would have been in a very weakened condition and had nail holes in his hands? It is also unlikely he would have been able to walk very far with pierced feet.

And if Jesus did revive and get past the Roman guards, he would have been a battered, bleeding pulp of a man who would have been pitied by his followers, not worshiped as divine.[112] There is no way that Jesus's disciples would have boldly proclaimed his resurrection if he had merely struggled out of a swoon, badly in need of medical treatment. A half-dead, staggering man who

had narrowly escaped death would not be fearlessly proclaimed the conqueror of death!

The Legend Theory

Let's continue by looking at the next possible alternative:
Is the Resurrection just a mythological story or legend
that developed over time?

The main reason that the Resurrection could not be
a myth is that there was not enough time after the actual
event for a myth to have developed. There is not a single
example in recorded history of a great myth or legend
based on a historical figure developing so soon after that
person's death. As noted in the previous chapter, several
generations must pass before added mythological elements can be mistakenly taken as fact.

Furthermore, several of the recorded details distinguish the Gospel accounts of Jesus's resurrection from
myth. A prime example is the claim that the first witnesses to the Resurrection were women (see Mt 28:1–10;
Mk 16:1–8; Lk 24:1–12; Jn 20:1, 11–18). If the Resurrection was a legend, the proponents of this legend would
not have had the empty tomb be discovered by women.
That's because women were second-class citizens in the
patriarchal societies of the ancient Jewish and Roman
worlds. Women could not even testify in a court of law
because their testimony was considered unreliable.[113]
If the apostles were proclaiming a false or embellished
story about Jesus's resurrection, they would have made
themselves—not women—the first eyewitnesses of the
empty tomb.

There is no way the first Christians or any of the

Gospel authors would have proclaimed a story that relied primarily on the testimony of women unless the women really were eyewitnesses and what they said had actually happened. As early as the second century, the Roman pagans were sneering at the accounts of the resurrection of Jesus because it was based on the testimony of "hysterical" women. But the early Christians stuck to their story. They stuck with the women. They said this is how it was. They just never would have made that up.

The Hallucination Theory

Let's look at the final alternative: Could Jesus's post-Resurrection appearances have been nothing more than hallucinations? The "hallucination theory" holds that Jesus's appearances to his followers after the Resurrection were not real but just hallucinations. However, this is quite unlikely for at least three reasons.

First, if the Resurrection was an hallucination of the apostles, the Jewish leaders could have produced the corpse of Jesus to refute their claim that he had risen from the dead. But they could not do so. Thus, the "hallucination theory" also requires the "stolen body theory" (along with all its difficulties) to explain the empty tomb. Isn't this is a bit much to expect of the apostles if they were only hallucinating?

Second, hallucinations do not happen to large groups of people who all "see" the same thing at the same time.[114] Hallucinations happen privately and only to individuals. Numerous people do not simultaneously experience the same hallucination. However, the apostles and other disciples saw the risen Jesus many times when together as a group.

Third, hallucinations usually last only a few seconds or minutes.[115] Numerous people do not simultaneously experience the same lengthy hallucinations over a long period of time, especially not over a period of forty days as was the case with the post-Resurrection appearances of Jesus.

Summary of Alternatives to the Resurrection

Let's summarize what we have discussed so far about possible alternatives to Jesus's actual resurrection from the dead:

- First, the Resurrection could *not* have been a deliberate lie or conspiracy because the apostles had no motive to promote such a lie and none of them recanted under duress. All they got for their efforts was suffering and death. Nobody dies for what they know is a lie.
- Second, the expertise of the Romans and the evidence shows that Jesus really died on the cross and did not later revive in the tomb. There is no way that a half-dead, staggering man who had narrowly escaped death would be worshipped as divine and fearlessly proclaimed as the conqueror of death by his followers.
- Third, stories about the Resurrection could

not be just a myth or legend because there was not enough time for such a legend to develop and recorded details distinguish the accounts of Jesus's resurrection from myth.

- Fourth, the post-Resurrection appearances of Jesus could *not* have been mass hallucinations because groups of people do not simultaneously experience the same lengthy hallucinations over a long period of time.

Positive Evidence of the Resurrection of Jesus

In order to further examine the truth of the Resurrection, let's look at the positive evidence of the Resurrection, starting with the numerous eyewitness accounts of the risen Jesus. Perhaps the most interesting is Paul's statement in 1 Corinthians 15:3–6: "For I handed on to you as of first importance what I also received: that Christ died for our sins in accordance with the scriptures; that he was buried; that he was raised on the third day in accordance with the scriptures; that he appeared to Cephas [St. Peter], then to the Twelve. After that, he appeared to more than five hundred brothers at once, most of whom are still living."

St. Paul reports that over five hundred people witnessed the risen Jesus—many of them still alive at the time of his writing and able to affirm or dispute the accuracy of his statement. There are many other recorded eyewitness accounts, including:

- Guards at the tomb: Matthew 28:11–15.

- Mary Magdalene and other women, outside the tomb: Matthew 28:1–10, Mark 16:1–8, Luke 24:1–12, and John 20:1, 11–18.
- The disciples while in hiding: John 20:19–23.
- "Doubting" Thomas touching the wounds of Jesus: John 20:26–29.
- Simon Peter and six other disciples while fishing in the Sea of Galilee: John 21:1–14.
- Two disciples on the road to Emmaus: Luke 24:13–35.
- Jesus showing his wounds and teaching: Luke 24:36–49 and Acts 1:3.
- The Ascension: Luke 24:50–51 and Acts 1:9.

By far the most compelling evidence of the truth of the Resurrection is the radically transformed lives of Jesus's followers afterwards. Before the Resurrection, they were cowards in hiding. Afterwards, they were bold proclaimers of the good news of Jesus's saving death and resurrection. How can this radical transformation from fearful cowards to fearless witnesses be explained if Jesus did not truly appear to them after he rose from the dead? To quote from *The Case for Easter* by Lee Strobel:

> When Jesus was crucified, his followers were dis-couraged and depressed. So they dispersed. The Jesus movement was all but stopped in its tracks. Then, after a short period of time, we see them abandoning their occupations, re-gathering, and committing themselves to spreading a very specific message—that Jesus Christ was the Messiah of God

who died on a cross, returned to life, and was seen alive by all of them.

And they were willing to spend the rest of their lives proclaiming this, without any payoff from a human point of view. They faced a life of hardship. They often went without food, slept exposed to the elements, were ridiculed, beaten, imprisoned. And finally, most of them were executed in torturous ways. For what? For good intentions? No, because they were convinced beyond the shadow of a doubt that they had seen Jesus Christ alive from the dead.[116]

One thing is certain, if Jesus had not risen from the dead and appeared to his disciples, we would never have heard of him today. Nothing else could have changed this sad and despairing group of men and women into people radiant with joy and courage. The apostles knew that torture and death would be their fate if they did not stop preaching about the Risen Jesus Christ. But they could not stop.

Unlike us, who have only our faith, the apostles personally experienced first-hand the Risen Jesus and acted accordingly. As Peter and John said to the Jewish leaders who commanded them not to speak about Jesus, "It is impossible for us not to speak about what we have seen and heard" (Acts 4:20). Just put yourself in their shoes. Wouldn't you have done the same if you actually saw Jesus alive and well after his crucifixion? Like them, you could not help but exclaim: "My God, he is God!"

The public courage and boldness of the apostles after

Jesus's crucifixion, especially compared to their earlier fearfulness and timidity, was recognized from the beginning as evidence of the truth of their claims about Jesus and his resurrection. It has long been recognized that something big, really big, profoundly influenced and dramatically transformed the apostles, and this was Jesus rising from the dead. For example, St. John Chrysostom stated in a homily on St. Paul's First Letter to the Corinthians in the late fourth century:

> St. Paul had this in mind when he said: *The weakness of God is stronger than men.* That the preaching of these men was indeed divine is brought home to us in the same way. For how otherwise could twelve uneducated men, who lived on lakes and rivers and wastelands, get the idea for such an immense enterprise? How could men who perhaps had never been in a city or a public square think of setting out to do battle with the whole world?
>
> That they were fearful, timid men, the evangelist makes clear; he did not reject the fact or try to hide their weaknesses. Indeed he turned these into a proof of the truth. What did he say of them? That when Christ was arrested, the others fled, despite all the miracles they had seen, while Peter, who was leader of the others, denied him!
>
> How then account for the fact that these men, who in Christ's lifetime did not stand up to the attacks by the Jews, set forth to do battle with the whole world once Christ was dead—if, as you claim, Christ did not rise and speak to them and

rouse their courage? Did they perhaps say to themselves: "What is this? He could not save himself but he will protect us? He did not help himself when he was alive, but now that he is dead he will extend a helping hand to us? In his lifetime he brought no nation under his banner, but by uttering his name we will win over the whole world?" Would it not be wholly irrational even to think such thoughts, much less to act upon them?

It is evident, then, that if they had not seen him risen and had proof of his power, they would not have risked so much.[117]

All of the apostles maintained to the very end that Jesus had indeed risen from the dead. Why didn't they recant under duress? The only plausible explanation is that they were absolutely certain they had seen Jesus Christ risen from the dead. Their bold courage and steadfast witness confirm that their testimony about the Resurrection is true. And that makes it, even for us today, a truth worth living for.

Summary and Key Points

Let's summarize what we learned in these chapters about Jesus truly being the divine Son of God who really rose from the dead. The following evidence makes the case that Jesus Christ is indeed our Lord:

1. Jesus's many and varied miracles confirm

that he had divine power and demonstrate God's love and mercy for all of us.

2. Jesus's divine actions testify that he is who he said he was. For example, who but God can forgive sins and issue new commandments?

3. Jesus's profoundly insightful parables and "superhuman" teachings, which were told in such an impromptu manner and are still relevant two thousand years later, also support his claims.

4. The reality of the Resurrection is the central belief of the Christian faith and is powerful evidence that Jesus is more than just a normal human being. St. Paul wrote about why the Resurrection is so important in 1 Corinthians 15:12–19 (New Living Translation):

But tell me this—since we preach that Christ rose from the dead, why are some of you saying there will be no resurrection of the dead? For if there is no resurrection of the dead, then Christ has not been raised either. And if Christ has not been raised, then all our preaching is useless, and your faith is useless. And we apostles would all be lying about God—for we have said that God raised Christ from the grave. But that can't be true if there is no resurrection of the dead. And if there is no resurrection of the dead, then Christ has not been raised. And if Christ has not been raised, then your faith is useless and you are still guilty of your sins. In that case, all who have died believing in Christ are lost!

And if our hope in Christ is only for this life, we are more to be pitied than anyone in the world. But in fact, Christ has been raised from the dead. He is the first of a great harvest of all who have died.

Referencing the writings of St. Thomas Aquinas, Dr. Peter Kreeft and Fr. Ronald Tacelli have this to say in their *Pocket Handbook of Christian Apologetics*: "If the Incarnation [God becoming a man in the person of Jesus Christ] did not really happen, then an even more unbelievable miracle happened: the conversion of the world by the biggest lie in history and the moral transformation of lives into unselfishness, detachment from worldly pleasures and radically new heights of holiness all by a mere myth."[118]

The evidence provided in these chapters strongly supports that Jesus is indeed the risen Lord and Son of God—both true God and true man. This evidence should be enough to convince anyone willing to believe. But there must be some ambiguity so as not to compel those who are unwilling to believe.[119]

Thus, there can be no irrefutable proof of the divinity of Jesus. That is because such proof would take away our voluntary choice to believe and invalidate our free will. Since we have been endowed by God with the gift of free will, we must have the freedom to reject the divinity of Jesus. The evidence in support of belief is necessarily imperfect. There must be a gap that needs to be filled by our "leap of faith."

The gift of free will means that we each must personally answer Jesus's question to Peter, "Who do you say that I am?" Peter's response was, "You are the Messiah, the Son of the living God" (Mt 16:16). We, too, are each asked this question by Jesus: "Who do you say that I am?" How will you answer?

It seems that some people reject Christ not because of the evidence but because they do not want to accept the responsibilities and implications of accepting him as Lord of their life. Peter Kreeft and Ronald Tacelli address this in their book: "The reluctance is usually moral. To admit that Jesus is divine is to admit his absolute authority over your life, including your private life, including your sex life. . . . There may also be simple pride, refusal to lose control of the reins of our lives."[120]

Acknowledging the Lordship of Jesus means realizing your life is not about you and that it must change. For many, this can be a threat. If Jesus is Lord of my life, my ego and self-centered desires cannot be lord. Could this be a motive for not fully accepting and practicing the Christian faith? This is a key question we need to honestly answer for ourselves.

The resurrection of Jesus means that God is truly the Lord of history, that all of the suffering, anxiety, and injustice in the world have been conquered, and that a new, transformed life is being offered to us. Our response is clear and simple: start living life in accord with the risen Lord Jesus Christ. Some of the responsibilities and implications of accepting Jesus as Lord of our lives are:

1. If Jesus really rose from the dead, then he is alive today and available for us to encounter on a personal basis through prayer,

Scripture, the sacraments (Baptism, Confirmation, Eucharist, etc.), and friendship with other Christians.

2. If Jesus is truly the divine Son of God, then his teachings and the teachings of his Church are more than just good ideas from a wise teacher. Rather, they are God's own insights upon which we can confidently build our lives.

3. If Jesus is who he said he is, then he deserves my unconditional allegiance without worrying about what my friends or family may think of my witness and lifestyle.

4. If Jesus has indeed conquered death, then he can open the door of eternal life in heaven for each of us.

It is not enough that we merely know about Jesus or discuss his claims and teachings. Each of us are called to meet Jesus in prayer and in the sacraments and come to know him personally and intimately. Through the power of the Resurrection, we can encounter the living Christ who loves each of us and wants to share his glory with us. The resurrection of Jesus is the foundation of our hope that we will see God face-to-face and share in the eternal glory and joy of heaven. As St. Peter states, "Although you have not seen him you love him; even though you do not see him now yet believe in him, you rejoice with an indescribable and glorious joy, as you attain the goal of your faith, the salvation of your souls" (1 Pt 1:8–9).

This is what we will explore in the next several

chapters; namely, how are we saved to eternal life in heaven? As part of this discussion, we will look at why Christ's passion and death were needed for our salvation. After all, there must have been some really good reasons for God to have become human in Jesus Christ. *Christianity proclaims that God became a man out of true love and offered his life for each of us so that we could be saved to eternal life in heaven.*

But there is no need to be concerned about being saved if heaven and the afterlife are not in fact real. So before looking at how we are saved, let's first investigate if scholarly studies of the many reported near-death experiences affirm the reality of heaven and the afterlife.

Part 3

THE HOPE OF HEAVEN

Chapter 6

DO NEAR-DEATH EXPERIENCES REVEAL THE REALITY OF HEAVEN AND AN AFTERLIFE?

If heaven, hell, and the afterlife are indeed real, then it would be most prudent to seriously consider Church teachings on how we are saved to eternal life in heaven. After all, nobody wants to spend eternity in hell. So we will now look at whether the thousands of reported near-death experiences provide compelling evidence of heaven, hell, and the afterlife.

Many people who have come close to dying report having had a near-death experience (NDE). An NDE is a lucid experience associated with perceived consciousness apart from the body occurring at the time of actual or threatened imminent death.[121] NDEs typically encompass several possible sensations, including being outside of one's physical body, feelings of levitation, peace and joy, and the presence of a loving light.

I personally know several reasonable people who

report having had an NDE. You may know such people too. You may have even had such an experience yourself.

Surveys taken in the United States, Australia, and Germany reveal that between 4 and 15 percent of the total population report having had an NDE.[122] That's over nine million Americans.[123] Thus, NDEs are not exceedingly rare.

Many books have been written by people about their NDE or the NDE of someone they love. The number one *New York Times* best-selling book and popular movie *Heaven is for Real* is a good example.[124] Another is the best-selling book *Proof of Heaven* by the neurosurgeon Dr. Eben Alexander.[125] These and other personal testimonies are usually quite fascinating and captivating.

However, individual reports from a single person—no matter how sincere and credible he or she may be—can be viewed as merely anecdotal evidence. In this chapter, therefore, we will look at what several well-respected scholarly studies, involving in-depth interviews with thousands of patients, have revealed about NDEs and the reality of heaven and the afterlife.

Scientific Studies of Near-Death Experiences

Scholarly interest in this field of study was originally spurred by the research in the 1960s and 1970s of pioneers such as psychiatrist Elisabeth Kübler-Ross and Dr. Raymond Moody, who has a PhD in Philosophy and an MD in Psychiatry. In the years since then, over sixty-five scholarly studies of more than 3,500 NDEs have been performed by various researchers.[126]

In 2014, scientists under the direction of Dr. Sam Parnia at the University of Southampton in the United Kingdom completed the largest ever medical study into near-death and out-of-body experiences. The results of this study were published in the medical journal *Resuscitation.*[127] These scientists spent four years examining 2,060 people who suffered cardiac arrest at fifteen hospitals in the United Kingdom, United States, and Austria. Nearly 40 percent of those surveyed who survived cardiac arrest experienced conscious awareness during the time while they were clinically dead, and 9 percent reported having an NDE, even after their brain had completely shut down.[128]

One man reported leaving his body and watching his resuscitation from the corner of the room. Despite being unconscious and clinically dead, the fifty-seven-year-old man recounted the actions of the nursing staff in detail. "We know the brain can't function when the heart has stopped beating," stated Dr. Sam Parnia when announcing the results of their study.[129] He continued, "But in this case, conscious awareness appears to have continued for up to three minutes into the period when the heart wasn't beating, even though the brain typically shuts down within 20–30 seconds after the heart has stopped. The man described everything that had happened in the room, but importantly, he heard two bleeps from a machine that makes a noise at three-minute intervals. So we could time how long the experience lasted for.

He seemed very credible and everything that he said had happened to him had actually happened."

This recent study supports other medical studies that have indicated consciousness may be present even while a person is clinically dead with no brain function.[130] For example, another important study of NDEs was performed by world-renowned cardiologist Dr. Pim van Lommel and his team in the Netherlands. As a cardiologist, van Lommel was struck by the number of his patients who claimed to have had an NDE as a result of their heart attack. As a scientist, this was difficult for him to accept. But he could not ignore these repeated and consistent stories.

Therefore, Dr. van Lommel and his fellow researchers decided to undertake a large, long-term study of NDEs in cardiac arrest patients to investigate the NDE phenomenon under the controlled environment in a cluster of hospitals with a medically trained staff. In 2001, van Lommel and his fellow researchers published the results of their study in one of the most prestigious medical journals in the world, *The Lancet*.[131]

For more than twenty years, van Lommel and his team systematically studied near-death experiences in patients who survived a cardiac arrest. In their study of 344 patients who were successfully resuscitated after suffering cardiac arrest, they found that 18 percent reported experiencing an NDE.[132] These patients recounted vivid details of their NDE despite being clinically dead with flat-lined brain stem activity at the time. After resuscitation, they spoke of being very much alive somewhere else and had experienced something that was very real, astounding, and life changing.[133]

One reason this study is so important is that van Lommel and his team interviewed patients in the Netherlands, which is a very secular country where the vast majority of people do not believe in life after death.[134] Thus, these patients' NDEs could not have been a case of wish-fulfillment or prompted by religious expectation. Besides, their brain was inactive (flat EEG) and their physical body totally unconscious at the time of their NDE, so they should have been incapable of having the conscious experience that they later recounted in detail.

According to van Lommel and other NDE researchers, the current view on the link between the brain and consciousness held by most physicians and psychologists is inadequate to properly understand NDEs. In his book *Consciousness Beyond Life: The Science of the Near-Death Experience*, van Lommel argues that human consciousness does not always coincide with brain function and that, remarkably and significantly, consciousness can even be experienced separate from the physical body.[135] As concluded by van Lommel in his article in *The Lancet*: "How could a clear consciousness outside one's body be experienced at the moment that the brain no longer functions during a period of clinical death with flat EEG? . . . NDE pushes at the limits of medical ideas about the range of human consciousness and the mind-brain relation."[136]

Common Elements of Near-Death Experiences

Even though not all of the following elements are found in any single NDE, the various core experiences typically reported by those who have an NDE include:[137]

- A sense or awareness of being dead.

- An out-of-body experience, which is a separation of consciousness from the physical body and often includes perceiving one's lifeless body from above and sometimes observing doctors and nurses performing medical resuscitation efforts.

- Feeling positive emotions, including a sense of peace, joy, well-being, and painlessness.

- Passing into or through a dark tunnel or entering a deep darkness.

- Meeting deceased relatives and other deceased persons.

- Encountering angelic "beings dressed in white," "guardian spirits," or similar.

- A rapid movement toward and/or sudden encounter with a mystical and very bright light (usually described as "a Being of Light," "God," or "Jesus Christ"), which has a definite personality and often communicates with the dying person.

- Being embraced by and absorbed into the bright light, which conveys intense feelings of absolute love, total acceptance, unconditional forgiveness, universal knowledge, and complete perfection.[138]

- Receiving a life review, commonly referred to as "seeing one's life flash before one's eyes."
- Encountering celestial ("heavenly") realms, often very beautiful and manifesting extremely brilliant colors and pleasing sounds.
- Receiving special knowledge, such as about one's life and the nature of the universe.
- Approaching a border, limit, or boundary, and/or a decision by oneself or others to return to one's physical body, often accompanied by a reluctance to return back to this life.
- Suddenly finding oneself back inside one's earthly body.

These experiences were first described in Raymond Moody's groundbreaking and best-selling book *Life After Life*, which was initially published in 1975.[139] Moody includes in his book many gripping personal stories from those who have had an NDE. Here is one example:

I got up and walked into the hall to get a drink, and it was at that point, as they found out later, that my appendix ruptured. I became very weak, and fell down. I began to feel a sort of drifting, a movement of my real being in and out of my body, and to hear beautiful music. I floated on down the hall and out the door onto the screened-in porch. There, it almost seemed that clouds, a pink mist really, began to gather around me, and then I floated right straight on through the screen, just as though it weren't there, and up into this pure crystal clear light, an illuminating white light. It was beautiful and so bright, so radiant, but it didn't hurt my eyes. It's not any kind of light you can describe on earth. I didn't actually see a person in this light, and yet it has a special identity, it definitely does. It is a light of perfect understanding and perfect love.

The thought came to my mind, "Lovest thou me?" This was not exactly in the form of a question, but I guess the connotation of what the light said was, "If you do love me, go back and complete what you began in your life." And all during this time, I felt as though I were surrounded by an overwhelming love and compassion.[140]

However, studies show that more than 10 percent of NDEs are reported to be frightening and distressing experiences, akin to biblical descriptions of hell.[141] For example, here is an account of a negative NDE reported by van Lommel in his book *Consciousness Beyond Life*:

Suddenly I stopped in this dark tunnel and began to fall at enormous speed, faster and faster and faster. Like I was literally hurled down, head-first, into this black hole. It was pitch-dark; I couldn't see a thing. And as I was falling, I began to hear screams, shrieks, heartrending, dreadful, terrible laughter, and the most disgusting stench you can imagine, and then the blackness changed to fire. . . . And there were all kinds of ghastly looking and

terrifying creatures, some worse than others, who
were snatching at me. . . . I begged for God's mercy.
. . . And suddenly I was woken up by the voices of
female ER doctors who had resuscitated me.[142]

Studies have shown that religious beliefs and prior
knowledge do not influence the experience of negative
NDEs.[143] There are also reported cases of NDEs with
both pleasant and frightening components.

Studies also show that no one type of person is more
likely to have an NDE. Those having an NDE cut across
race, gender, age, education, marital status, and social
class. Researchers also found that religious orientation
was not a fact affecting either the likelihood or the depth
of an NDE.[144] An atheist was just as likely to have an NDE
as was a devoutly religious person.

How Can We Know Near-Death Experiences Are Real?

Some scientists and researchers have attempted to
develop a naturalistic explanation of NDEs based on
psychological and physiological factors. In other words,
could NDEs be hallucinations or dreams, be induced by
certain medical drugs, or be a defense mechanism produced by a dying body? While these scientific investigations should be encouraged, it is important to note that
most primary NDE researchers have found them to be
inadequate explanations of the NDE phenomenon.[145] For
example, many researchers have concluded that NDEs
are not hallucinations or dreams, since hallucinations

and dreams are rambling, unconnected, often unintel-
ligible, and vary widely, whereas reported NDEs have
many consistent elements in a clear, connected pattern.

For an extensive treatment of whether or not NDEs
have a naturalistic explanation, see *Science and the Near-
Death Experience: How Consciousness Survives Death*
by Chris Carter.[146] The book *Near-Death Experiences as
Evidence for the Existence of God and Heaven* by J. Steve
Miller is another good reference on this subject.[147] Using
evidence from scientific studies, these and other books
show that consciousness does not depend upon the brain
but can exist independently of the physical body.

There are several ways we can know that NDEs are
indeed real and not just based on psychological and/or
physiological factors. Some compelling evidence for the
validity of NDEs includes: (1) confirmed observations
of the physical world when unconscious or during clinical death, (2) blind people seeing during an NDE, (3)
meeting previously unknown deceased relatives during
an NDE, (4) shared death experiences, and (5) the dramatically changed lives of people who have had an NDE.
Each of these is difficult to reconcile with the various psychological and physiological explanations of NDEs and
reveal that consciousness can survive bodily death and
that NDEs may provide a glimpse of an awaiting afterlife.

Confirmed Observations of the Physical World When Unconscious or During Clinical Death

Some patients find themselves outside of their unconscious physical bodies and are able to visually observe
earthly events or objects—sometimes hundreds of miles

away—that were later verified by third parties to actually be true. This phenomenon is called "veridical perception" and is highly indicative that consciousness can exist apart from the physical body. Veridical NDEs occur when a patient has an out-of-body experience when near death and describes unusual events or objects that he or she could not have known about by normal means, and which are later confirmed to be accurate.[148] Raymond Moody reports in his book *Life After Life*, "The description of events witnessed while out of the body tend to check out fairly well. Several doctors have told me, for example, that they are utterly baffled about how patients with no medical knowledge could describe in such detail and so correctly the procedure used in resuscitation attempts, even though the events took place while the doctors knew the patients involved were 'dead.'"[149]

There are several notable and widely documented cases of veridical near-death experiences. Following are three such accounts. First, in his article in *The Lancet*, van Lommel quotes from a Dutch coronary-care-unit nurse who reported on the veridical out-of-body experience of a resuscitated patient:

> During a night shift an ambulance brings in a 44 year-old cyanotic, comatose man into the coronary care unit. . . . When we went to intubate the patient, he turns out to have dentures in his mouth. I remove these upper dentures and put them onto the "crash car." Meanwhile, we continue extensive CPR. After about an hour and a half the patient has sufficient heart rhythm and blood pressure, but he

is still ventilated and intubated, and he is still coma-
tose. He is transferred to the intensive care unit to
continue the necessary artificial respiration. Only
after more than a week do I meet again with the
patient, who is by now back on the cardiac ward. I
distribute his medication. The moment he sees me
he says: "Oh, that nurse knows where my dentures
are." I am very surprised. Then he elucidates: "Yes,
you were there when I was brought into hospital
and you took my dentures out of my mouth and
put them onto that cart, it had all these bottles on it
and there was this sliding drawer underneath and
there you put my teeth." I was especially amazed
because I remembered this happening while the
man was in deep coma and in the process of CPR.

When I asked further, it appeared the man had
seen himself lying in bed, that he had perceived
from above how nurses and doctors had been busy
with CPR. He was also able to describe correctly
and in detail the small room in which he had been
resuscitated as well as the appearance of those present like myself. At the time that he observed the situation he had been very much afraid that we would
stop CPR and that he would die. And it is true that
we had been very negative about the patient's prog-
nosis due to his very poor medical condition when
admitted. The patient tells me that he desperately
and unsuccessfully tried to make it clear to us that
he was still alive and that we should continue CPR.
He is deeply impressed by his experience and says

he is no longer afraid of death. Four weeks later he left the hospital as a healthy man.[150]

Second, in her book *After the Light: What I Discovered on the Other Side of Life That Can Change Your World*, Kimberly Clark Sharp reports the famous case of Maria's shoe.[151] Sharp was a social worker in Harborview Hospital in Seattle when Maria was brought in unconscious, suffering from a severe heart attack. After successful resuscitation, Sharp visited Maria the following day in her hospital room. During the visit, Maria told Sharp about her out-of-body experience, including detailed observations of her resuscitation. Maria also described her consciousness passing outside and floating above the hospital. Desperate to prove that she had indeed left her body and was not crazy, Maria described seeing, on the ledge outside a third-story window on the far side of the hospital, a man's well-worn, dark-blue tennis shoe, which was scuffed on the left side over the little toe and with a shoelace caught under the heel. Not believing her but wanting to help, Sharp looked from the ground all around the hospital but did not see anything. She then went systematically window-to-window on the hospital's third floor looking out at the ledges. Pressing her face against one window, she saw a tennis shoe on the ledge that perfectly matched the details Maria had described. Sharp carefully opened the window and retrieved the shoe. She later showed the shoe to Maria, who was ecstatic at having been proven right in her observation.

Third, in his book *Light and Death: One Doctor's Fascinating Account of Near-Death Experiences*, cardiologist

Michael Sabom reports the case of singer Pam Reynolds.[152] In order to remove a life-threatening aneurysm deep in her brain, Pam Reynolds underwent a rare surgical operation called a "standstill" in which her body temperature was lowered to sixty degrees, her heartbeat and breathing stopped, her brain waves flattened, and the blood drained from her head. In everyday terms, she was dead. Pam was fully anesthetized and had sound-emitting earplugs installed before her surgery began. Dr. Spetzler, her surgeon, was sawing into her skull when Pam suddenly heard the saw and began observing the surgical procedure from a vantage point over his shoulder. She also heard what the nurses said to the doctors. Upon returning to consciousness, she was able to accurately describe the unique surgical instrument used and report the statements made by the nurses.

There have been several published studies on veridical perception during NDEs. A comprehensive study of veridical NDEs was performed by Dr. Janice Holden, who is a professor of counseling at the University of North Texas and is a licensed certified mental health professional. The results of her studies are reported in the book *The Handbook of Near-Death Experiences: Thirty Years of Investigation.*[153]

In her study, Holden compiled all of the out-of-body accounts in which veridical experiences had been reported in all of the scholarly books and studies published about NDEs. This included thirty-nine studies by thirty-seven authors. She determined that of the 107 veridical perception cases in NDE literature, 92 percent were independently verified and completely accurate, 6 percent were accurate with some erroneous elements, and only one case was completely erroneous.[154]

Holden was a stickler for accuracy and used a most stringent criterion in this study. She classified a case as inaccurate if only one detail of the observations was found to not correspond to reality during later investigations. As recounted by Dr. Jeffrey Long, "So if NDE observations were fully 99% accurate, the one percent that was inaccurate would lead the NDE observations overall to be labeled as inaccurate in this study."[155]

Because veridical perceptions during an NDE can be corroborated, they can help establish whether NDEs are real. Since the vast majority of perceived observations did in fact occur and accurately conveyed previously unknown information, it can be reasonably concluded that veridical NDE perceptions are not just hallucinations or dreams.

It is difficult to believe that this high degree of verifiably accurate reporting, which typically occurred at a time when there was no electrical activity in the brain cortex, can be attributed to psychological and physiological factors. Since the self-consciousness that accompanied these veridical perceptions was independent of bodily function, it is reasonable to conclude that this self-consciousness (our soul) remains alive after bodily death.[156]

Blind People See During a Near-Death Experience

In 1997, psychology professor Dr. Kenneth Ring and Sharon Cooper published the results of a landmark study of blind persons, including those blind from birth, who actually "see" during an NDE or during an out-of-body experience (OBE) not associated with a near-death incident.[157] During this study, they interviewed thirty-one blind and sight-impaired persons, including fourteen who were born blind, most of whom reported visual experiences during their near-death and/or out-of-body episode. In their article, they present several in-depth case studies in scrupulous detail and carefully analyze them to evaluate these astounding claims. The results of this study are also included in their book *Mindsight: Near-Death and Out-of-Body Experiences in the Blind.*[158]

One such case study involved Vicki Umipeg. She has been completely blind since shortly after birth because of damage to her optic nerves caused by receiving too much oxygen in an incubator. Vicki related that following an automobile accident, she found herself floating above a body in a hospital emergency room. She was up near the ceiling watching a male doctor and a female nurse working on the body. Vicki had a clear recollection of how she came to realize that this was her own body below her:

> I knew it was me. . . . I was pretty thin then. I was quite tall and thin at that point. And I recognized at first that it was a body, but I didn't even know that it was mine initially. Then I perceived that I was up on the ceiling, and I thought, "Well, that's kind of weird. What am I doing up here?" I thought, "Well, this must be me. Am I dead? . . ." I just briefly saw this body, and . . . I knew that it was mine because I wasn't in mine.[159]

Vicki was married and wearing wedding rings at the time of her NDE, but she had never seen them. Here is her recollection of how these rings also helped her determine that the body she was observing below was her own: "I think I was wearing the plain gold band on my right ring finger and my father's wedding ring next to it. But my wedding ring I definitely saw. . . . That was the one I noticed the most because it's most unusual. It has orange blossoms on the corners of it."[160]

There is something quite remarkable about Vicki's recollection of these visual images, especially because she had not previously understood the concept of vision. "This was," she said, "the only time I could ever relate to seeing and to what light was, because I experienced it."[161]

Ring and Cooper's study found that blind persons, including those totally blind since birth, do report classic NDEs of the kind common to sighted persons, that the great preponderance of blind persons claim to see during an NDE or OBE, and that several claims of visually-based knowledge which could not have been obtained by normal means (veridical perception) were independently verified.[162] As they state in their article on whether blind persons can see during an NDE or OBE, "Overall, 80 percent of our [blind] respondents reported these claims, most of them in the language of unhesitating declaration, even when they had been surprised, or even stunned, by the unexpected discovery that they could in fact see. Like sighted experiencers, our blind respondents described to us both perceptions of this world and otherworldly scenes, often in fulsome, fine-grained detail, and sometimes with a sense of extremely sharp, even subjectively perfect, acuity."[163]

Ring and Cooper conclude that a form of vision

without physical sight, which they call "mindsight," occurs during these experiences. It is medically inexplicable how a blind person, especially one blind since birth, could have a vividly visual NDE or OBE. These experiences offer compelling evidence of the afterlife, since blind people are obviously not "seeing" with their useless physical eyes, but through the upgraded "eyes" of a spiritual body that does not have the limitations of the physical body they left behind.[164]

Meeting Previously Unknown Deceased Relatives During a Near-Death Experience

Many people, including children, report meeting deceased relatives during an NDE, including relatives they had not known before but are able to later identify (e.g., from old family photographs). By contrast, studies show that dreams and hallucinations are much more likely to be about people who are still living, not deceased relatives as with NDEs.[165]

One such case of meeting unknown deceased relatives during an NDE is reported in the popular movie and bestselling book *Heaven is for Real*.[166] This book and movie are about the NDE of Colton Burpo, which occurred in 2003 when he was just four years old. Colton reported meeting his grandfather, called "Pop," who had died in 1976, twenty-three years before Colton was born.[167] What is interesting about this account is that Colton did not recognize his grandfather from photos taken when he was older, but he recognized "Pop" in a photo taken when he was much younger—a photo taken more than a half-century before Colton was born and that he had never seen before.[168]

Even more astounding is when, about seven months after his NDE, Colton unexpectedly and spontaneously told his parents, Todd and Sonja, that in heaven he had met his other sister who had died of a miscarriage before he was born—a miscarriage Colton was never told about before. As recounted by Colton's father Todd:

> "Mommy, I have two sisters," Colton said. I put down my pen. Sonja didn't. She kept working. Colton repeated himself, "Mommy, I have two sisters." Sonja looked up from her paperwork and shook her head slightly. "No, you have your sister, Cassie, and . . . do you mean your cousin, Traci?" "No." Colton clipped off the word adamantly. "I have two sisters. You had a baby die in your tummy, didn't you?" At that moment, time stopped in the Burpo household, and Sonja's eyes grew wide. . . . "Who told you I had a baby die in my tummy?" Sonja said, her tone serious. "She did, Mommy. She said she died in your tummy."[169]

There are many other published accounts of people meeting deceased relatives during an NDE, including accounts from other children. For example, van Lommel recounts the story of a person who, when five years old, had fallen into a coma after contracting meningitis and had an NDE:

> I saw a little girl of about ten years old. I sensed that she recognized me. We hugged and then she

told me, "I'm your sister. I died a month after I was born. I was named after your grandmother. Our parents called me Rietje for short." She kissed me, and I felt her warmth and love. "You must go now," she said. . . . In a flash I was back in my body. I opened my eyes and saw the happy and relieved looks on my parents' faces. When I told them about my experience, they initially dismissed it as a dream. . . . I made a drawing of my angel sister who had welcomed me and repeated everything she'd told me. My parents were so shocked that they panicked. They got up and left the room. After a while they returned. They confirmed that they had indeed lost a daughter called Rietje. She had died of poisoning about a year before I was born. They had decided not to tell me and my brother until we were old enough to understand the meaning of life and death.[170]

Several studies have shown that the reported elements of childhood NDEs are similar to adult NDEs (e.g., out-of-body experience, dark tunnel, bright light, meeting others). But how is this possible when these children have never heard of a near-death experience and may be too young to read? As noted by van Lommel, "It seems inconceivable that children without any prior knowledge could fabricate a story that is entirely consistent with the NDE reports of adults."[171] This is especially true when reported details not previously known, such as Colton's miscarried sister, are verified by others.

Van Lommel also notes that children are much more

likely to report meeting a deceased grandparent than a living parent. He states that if an NDE was merely based on wishful thinking, we would expect children to meet living relatives, such as their father or mother.[172]

Adults also report meeting deceased blood relatives during their NDE who they did not know at the time but were able to later identify. Van Lommel shares the following testimony: "During my NDE following a cardiac arrest, I saw both my dead grandmother and a man who looked at me lovingly but whom I didn't know. Over ten years later my mother confided on her deathbed that I'd been born from an extramarital affair; my biological father was a Jewish man who'd been deported and killed in World War II. My mother showed me a photograph. The unfamiliar man I'd seen more than ten years earlier during my NDE turned out to be my biological father."[173]

The fact that many more people who have an NDE report meeting deceased relatives instead of persons still alive is strong evidence that NDEs are real and not just a dream or hallucination. This is especially true when these relatives are unknown at the time of the NDE but are able to be identified afterwards (e.g., from old family photographs).

Shared Death Experiences

Sometimes, those who are gathered at the bedside of a dying person experience the same NDE elements and have the same visions of the afterlife that the dying person experiences. In these shared death experiences, family, friends, and medical personnel may themselves be lifted up out of their own body and go along with the dying person through a dark tunnel and toward a loving light. They also describe seeing deceased relatives of the dying person and may even empathically participate in the life review of the person who is passing on. They sometimes do not know the friends or relatives of the dying person they see but are able to later identify them. One such person looked in a yearbook afterward and recognized persons first seen in the shared life review.[174]

Dr. Raymond Moody calls these "empathic death experiences," and he shares scores of firsthand accounts in his book *Glimpses of Eternity: Sharing a Loved One's Passage from This Life to the Next.*[175] Moody also discusses shared death experiences, including his own, in the excellent *Afterlife* DVD.[176]

For example, Moody recounts in *Glimpses of Eternity* the following shared death experience, corroborated by all who were present:[177]

> Five members of the Anderson family in metro Atlanta were at their mother's bedside as she was dying. Since this was the end of an extended illness, none were especially psychologically distraught at the time. As one of the daughters reported, "Suddenly a bright light appeared in the room." The appearance of the light was unlike "any kind of light on this earth. I nudged my sister to see if she saw it too, and when I looked at her, her eyes were as big as saucers. . . . I saw my brother literally gasp. Everyone saw it together and for a little while we were frightened."
>
> They next saw lights that shaped themselves

into an entranceway. Her mother left her body and departed through the passage, ushering in a feeling of ecstatic joy. They all agreed that the entranceway resembled the Natural Bridge in the Shenandoah Valley.

Moody reports that persons present at the bedside of a dying person may themselves experience one or more of the following elements of a shared death experience:

1. Room is distorted and changes shape.
2. Mystical light in the room.
3. Music or musical sounds.
4. Leaving their own body and rising up with the loved one.
5. Co-living the life review of their loved one.
6. Traveling partway toward the light and seeing "heavenly" realms.
7. Mist rising from the body at death.

These reports of shared death experiences are a significant addition to near-death literature and provide more compelling evidence of the afterlife. In his book *Glimpses of Eternity*, Moody concludes that accounts of shared death experiences represent the best evidence to date for the continuation of consciousness after death.

Since these experiences come unexpectedly to people who are not dying, they cannot be attributed to wish fulfillment. And since multiple people experience the same events, they cannot be a hallucination, since multiple people do not simultaneously experience the same hallucination. They cannot be a dream since the healthy participants are awake and fully conscious.

Shared death experiences also provide compelling evidence that NDEs are not the biological result of a brain in the process of shutting down. A shared death experience cannot be attributed to a lack of blood flow, lack of oxygen, buildup of carbon dioxide, etc., in the dying brain, since those sharing the death experience are healthy and do not have dying brains.

Transformed Values and Changed Life After a Near-Death Experience

Studies show that almost all those who have an NDE report that their lives, religious beliefs, values, and behaviors are significantly changed afterward. As Dr. Raymond Moody writes, "There is one common element in all near-death experiences: they transform the people who have them. In my twenty years of intense exposure to NDErs, I have yet to find one who hasn't had a very deep and positive transformation as a result of his experience."[178]

Many people say that their NDE has transformed their views of what really matters in life and that they have lost their fear of death. They have a much stronger belief in the afterlife because they are convinced they were there. Research has also found a myriad of other aftereffects following an NDE, including increased belief in the sacredness of life and a deeper sense of God's presence, as well as a greater appreciation for the meaning and purpose of life.[179] They also report having less interest in material things, such as a lot of money, big house, or expensive car, following an NDE.

Those who had an NDE also express stronger feelings of self-acceptance and a greater compassion for other people. They feel a greater need to help others, and this can even result in a career change in favor of the healing and caring professions, such as nursing. Many of those having an NDE, especially those NDEs that include a panoramic life review, think a lot afterward about "what might have been" and what they should do differently now. For example, in his book *Life After Life*, Moody shares the following testimony from a person who had an NDE: "Since then [my NDE], it has been on my mind constantly what have I done with my life, and what will I do with my life. . . . But since I died, all of a sudden, right after my experience, I started wondering whether I had been doing the things I had done because they were good, or because they were good for *me*. . . . I want to do things because they are good, not because they are good for me."[180]

Several studies have documented the transformational life changes after an NDE. These studies reveal the following:

- Nearly 100 percent of those who had an NDE report no fear of death afterward, far more than the general population.[181]
- At least 90 percent of those who had an NDE now believe that there is life after death.[182]
- Spiritual growth, a loving attitude, knowing a Higher Power/God, inner peace, and a sense of purpose in life characterize the

changes most meaningful to those who had an NDE.[183]

- Over 80 percent of those who had an NDE express a strong increase in their concern for others and that life has meaning or purpose.[184]

Two studies of cardiac arrest survivors, including van Lommel's, found that it is primarily the NDE and not the close brush with death that caused these life-changing aftereffects.[185] Both of these studies found that cardiac arrest survivors who had an NDE describe many more transformative life changes than cardiac arrest survivors who did not have an NDE.

Studies also show that these life changes after having an NDE are permanent and long-lasting. For example, van Lommel and his colleagues conducted follow-up studies of cardiac arrest survivors who had an NDE as well as cardiac arrest survivors who did not have an NDE. They found that profound and transformational life-changes lasted many years afterward for cardiac arrest survivors who had an NDE. They concluded that eight years afterward,

> People with an NDE scored significantly higher in the following areas: showing emotions; less interest in the opinions of others; accepting others; compassion for others; involvement in family; less appreciation of money and possessions; increase in the importance of nature and environment; less interest in a higher standard of living; appreciation of ordinary things; sense of social justice; inner

meaning of life; increased interest in spirituality; less fear of death; less fear of dying; and increase in belief in life after death. These different levels of change are a consequence of the NDE and not of surviving a cardiac arrest.[186]

People who have an NDE are quite adamant that what they experienced was absolutely real and has changed them. They often choose who they will and will not disclose their experience to because they don't want to deal with people who will not consider the possibility that what they experienced was real.

Indeed, many NDE researchers are convinced that reported NDEs are absolutely authentic experiences. They note that the transformed lives of those who had an NDE are powerful testimonies to the reality of what they experienced. As reported by Dr. Jeffery Long in his book *Evidence of the Afterlife*, "Those who manifest substantial changes may seem to have become completely different people to their friends and family."[187]

If the NDE is not real, what could explain these profound and long-lasting life changes, especially when the person is unconscious or clinically dead at the time? As noted by van Lommel, "Is there any scientific explanation for comprehensive and permanent life changes after a two-minute cardiac arrest?"[188]

What Can Be Learned From Near-Death Experiences?

What lessons can be learned from scholarly studies of thousands of NDEs? In summary, compelling evidence for the validity of NDEs includes: (1) confirmed (veridical) observations of the physical world when unconscious or during clinical death, (2) blind people seeing during an NDE, (3) meeting previously unknown deceased relatives during an NDE, (4) shared death experiences, and (5) the dramatically transformed lives of people who have had an NDE. It is virtually impossible to explain this intensely studied evidence of NDEs unless human consciousness actually survives clinical (bodily) death. It is especially difficult to explain how blind people, particularly those blind since birth, are able to see things during their clinical death that are later verified by others as being completely accurate.

The combined weight of all this evidence affirms that there is a component of human beings that is not reducible to our mere physical body. In his book *Consciousness Beyond Life*, Dr. van Lommel states, "Death merely marks the end of our physical aspect. In other words, we *have* a body, but we *are* consciousness. Free from our body, we are still capable of having conscious experiences, we are still sentient beings. Recently somebody with an NDE wrote to me: 'I can live without my body, but apparently my body cannot live without me.'"[189]

This immaterial and spiritual part of our being has traditionally been called our soul and is linked to our human consciousness.[190] *The scientific evidence from these scholarly studies of NDEs affirm longstanding philosophical and religious traditions that human beings are composed of both a body and a soul, and that the soul lives on after death of the body.*[191]

Many ancient cultures and religions recognized an immaterial and immortal aspect of human life corresponding to the soul. Ancient Greek philosophers further developed the concept of the immaterial soul as being distinct from the physical body, and many Greek philosophers, notably Socrates and Plato, accepted the immortality of the human soul.[192]

In early Christian theology, St. Augustine spoke of the immortal soul as a "rider" on the mortal body, making clear the distinction between the material and the immaterial.[193] In the Middle Ages, St. Thomas Aquinas expanded upon the Greek philosophers' concept of the soul as the animating principle of the body and that human beings are an integral unity of both body and soul. Building on these traditions, the *Catechism of the Catholic Church* (366) states, "The Church teaches that every spiritual soul is created immediately by God— it is not "produced" by the parents—and also that it is immortal: it does not perish when it separates from the body at death."

NDEs also support the reality of the afterlife and that death is merely a transition from one state of existence to another. *NDEs reveal a continuing life that transcends physical death and is usually a very pleasant and most wonderful experience, much like what has traditionally been called heaven. However, some NDEs also point to the existence of a hellish afterlife.*

NDEs also affirm the existence of a vastly loving intelligence that guides the universe.[194] The typical experience of a "Being of Light" provides compelling evidence for the existence of a personal God—a God who is unconditionally loving and infinitely good.[195] The life reviews during many NDEs also reveal that God knows each of us intimately and cares about our personal moral choices in life.[196]

The love of the "Being of Light," the joy of being with departed loved ones, and the perception of a heavenly paradise during NDEs all affirm traditional Church teaching about a loving and just God who wants to fulfill our greatest desire; namely, experiencing unconditional love and joy with God for all eternity in heaven. Therefore, in the next two chapters we explore what the Scriptures and the Catholic Church teach about how we can be saved to eternal life in heaven, beginning with a look at why Jesus Christ's passion and death were needed for our salvation.

Chapter 7

WHY WERE CHRIST'S PASSION AND DEATH NEEDED FOR OUR SALVATION?

Have you ever been asked by a friend or relative, "Are you saved?" If so, how did you respond? Or was the question so confusing that you did not know how to respond? In the next chapter, we will learn an appropriate Catholic response to this question. However, we will first examine the general question of how we are saved from our sins and moral failings to the joy of eternal life with God in heaven.

Being saved to eternal life in heaven is the most important issue in this life. This is highlighted in the following excerpt from the *Pocket Handbook of Christian Apologetics* by Peter Kreeft and Ronald Tacelli:

> Salvation is the ultimate reason for your existence: your end, goal, point, purpose, hope, meaning. The difference between success and failure at life's first task—becoming who you were meant to be—is not

the difference between riches and poverty, fame and obscurity, health and sickness, pleasure and pain, or niceness and nastiness, but between salvation and damnation. . . . [For as] Jesus said, "What does it profit a man if he gains the whole world but loses his soul." No one in history ever asked a more practical question than that one. In other words, don't get all A's but flunk life.[197]

Therefore, a most important part of this life is believing and acting as necessary to enter the joy of heaven. For what good does it do if we achieve success in this world but are eternally lost in the next?

Will Everyone Be Saved?

We must come to know our need for a Savior in order to be saved. Some of us come to this knowledge through our feelings, the perception of an inner emptiness, a feeling that something is never right no matter what one does; others come to this knowledge thinking their way to the truth. Whatever road we take, we must come to know our need for a Savior and then set out to find him.

However, many people today do not feel a need for a Savior since they think everything is fine in their life. When things do go wrong, they may ask God to heal their sickness, deliver them from addiction, fix broken relationships, and generally bring them peace and happiness. But if these are the main reasons to follow Jesus, then those without such issues will not feel the need for him. And those who do turn to Jesus for these reasons may eventually turn away from him because their motivation for being a Christian is flawed. The truth is we need Jesus because he is our Savior. Jesus Christ came to earth to save us from the eternal consequences of our sins and failings. The other stuff is incidental.

Many people, however, do not think of themselves as a sinner in need of a Savior. They believe if they are a "good person," they will go to heaven. Many believe that just being nice and kind to others is enough to be saved and enter heaven. They essentially believe that God is like the children's character Barney: "I love you, you love me"—and this alone makes everything all right. Since God loves everyone, everyone will enter heaven, right?

But is this what Jesus Christ actually taught? Did Jesus say that everyone will enter heaven no matter what and that just being nice and kind is enough to be saved? Not at all. Even though God desires salvation for all, God is not Barney and not everyone will be saved—by their own choice. For as Jesus warned, "Enter through the narrow gate; for the gate is wide and the road broad that leads to destruction, and those who enter through it are many. How narrow the gate and constricted the road that leads to life. And those who find it are few" (Mt 7:13–14).

Jesus also warned that we need to openly and publicly confess the Christian faith when he stated, "Everyone who acknowledges me before others I will acknowledge before my heavenly Father. But whoever denies me before others, I will deny before my heavenly Father" (Mt 10:32–33).

However, Jesus also warned that our words must be backed by action when he stated, "Not everyone who says to me, 'Lord, Lord,' will enter the kingdom of heaven, but only the one who does the will of my Father in heaven" (Mt 7:21). God expects more of us than just being nice and kind to one another. We are to do all that God wills, especially as found in the teachings of Jesus and his Church.

The *Catechism of the Catholic Church* makes clear that those who knowingly and deliberately reject God are not going to be saved when it states, "God predestines no one to go to hell; for this, a willful turning away from God is necessary, and persistence in it until the end" (1037). In other words, no amount of being nice to others will overcome a resolute rejection of God in one's own life (see also Mt 13:41–43; 13:47–50, where Jesus teaches that we will each be judged and not everyone will be saved).

Thus, our time on earth is a test.[198] The test is: will we choose to know, love, and serve God, or not? When we die, God essentially says to each of us, "I love you very much. I will give you forever what you love the most." Can we say we love God the most? Could we show that by how we spend our time every day? Could we show that we love God above all else because we never just fit God into our day but build our entire day around God? And so the question is: do we want God more than anything else? For when we die, God gives us what we want the most. Let's now look at how we can have what we truly want—eternal life with God in heaven.

Jesus Died for Us

What do these Bible verses say is needed for our salvation?

- "Indeed, only with difficulty does one die for a just person, though perhaps for a good person one might even find courage to die. But *God proves his love for us in that while we were still sinners Christ died for us*" (Rom 5:7–8, emphasis added).
- "All have sinned and are deprived of the glory of God. They are justified freely by his grace through the *redemption in Christ Jesus*, whom God set forth as an expiation, through faith, *by his blood*" (Rom 3:23–25, emphasis added).

From these New Testament passages and many others, we see that God's love made manifest by Christ's death on the cross was needed for our salvation. Since the beginning, Christians have proclaimed that Jesus Christ died so we could be saved to eternal life in heaven.

Even though we humans are capable of doing good and wonderful things, our tendency to also do the wrong thing can taint and even undo the good things we do. Due to our inclination to do what we know is wrong, we need a redeemer who will forgive our sins and bring God's grace to help us do better.

For this reason, the Father sent his Son into the world to become human like us in all things but sin and to suffer and die on our behalf so that we might have access to eternal life in heaven. As revealed in the Gospel of John,

"For God so loved the world that he gave his only Son, so that everyone who believes in him might not perish but might have eternal life" (3:16).

This is the core proclamation of the Christian gospel ("good news"). It is truly good news that Jesus Christ saved us from the consequences of our sins and saved us for eternal life and happiness with God in heaven!

But why did Jesus have to suffer and die on the cross for our sins? Why couldn't God just be merciful and simply forgive our sins without Jesus enduring such a torturous and brutal death? Why was it necessary, as St. Paul says, that Jesus humble "himself, becoming obedient to death, even death on a cross" (Phil 2:8)?

The cross was meant to terrify people, and the fear it provoked in the populace was key to the power of Rome. If someone ran afoul of the Roman state, they would fix him naked to this terrible instrument of torture and allow him to hang there until he slowly and painfully died. They would then leave his dead body on the cross for the birds and beasts to devour. Being crucified was designed to be the most agonizing, painful, and humiliating death possible.

This point is vividly brought home in Mel Gibson's popular movie *The Passion of the Christ*.[199] This powerful movie provokes a range of different feelings. Some feel gratitude that Jesus suffered so much on our behalf. Many others feel guilt and deep sadness that Jesus endured this terrible suffering and death because of our own sins.

However, we may also come away from this movie trying to understand more fully why such brutality would be the will of a loving and merciful God. Many times we have heard it said, "Christ died for our sins." But after seeing such a realistic depiction of Christ's scourging and crucifixion, we may ask ourselves why was all that needed for our salvation. This massive suffering seems more like what would be done to appease an angry and vengeful God, not a loving and merciful God.

A key realization to better understand the need for and purpose of Christ's passion and death is to recognize that even though God is *perfectly loving*, God is also *perfectly just*. Since God is perfectly just, God cannot merely "sweep our sins under the rug."

What criminal court judge would let all sincerely contrite felons who come before his bench go free without any imprisonment or punishment at all? That would make a mockery of our legal justice system and would not be tolerated.

Similarly, God's justice cannot be a mockery. We all deserve punishment because of our sins. None of us deserve, on our own, the reward of heaven. *We will never fully feel the love of God until we realize the seriousness of our sins and the justice of the punishment we are due.*

Yet, instead of acknowledging the seriousness of our sins, we often minimize our own faults and tend to regard our sins as "small." Christ's horrific passion and death reveal the fallacy of that attitude. The cross testifies how much God despises sin. If the Son of God willingly chose to suffer such a torturous death on our behalf, then our sins cannot be "small."

The Purpose of Christ's Passion and Death

Because of the original sin of the first humans (Adam and Eve) and the sins of humans ever since, we owed a massive debt to God that could not possibly have been repaid by our efforts alone. In our legal justice system, however, someone else can repay a debt on behalf of another. When payment of what is due to another is made either by the indebted person or someone else, it is legally called "satisfaction" of the debt.

Satisfaction is also repairing or restoring the harm done after an injury or injustice due to the fault of another. If I damage or destroy something of yours, I am obligated to pay to have it fixed or replaced. That is satisfaction, which is also called reparation. Satisfaction or reparation can go beyond money. It is about setting things right with the injured party. Satisfaction is payment or performance of what is due to another. If no such satisfaction is forthcoming, however, then the only alternative is punishment.

As Cardinal Christoph Schönborn (general editor of the *Catechism of the Catholic Church*) states in his book *God Sent His Son*:

> Satisfaction or "atonement" is something done as compensation, through which both parties can agree amicably and through which the injured, aggrieved party indicates his readiness to forgive, and the guilty party his readiness to ask and to accept forgiveness by an appropriate sign (the reparation). There can be only one or the other, either

satisfaction or punishment; once satisfaction has been made the punishment thereby become superfluous. Being freed from the burden of punishment goes along with the satisfaction. The social relationship has then truly been restored, and there is no need to do anything more.[200]

Applied to the effects of human sin, God was the injured party whom humanity offended because of our sins. There can be no other alternative for restoring our sinful world besides satisfaction or the eternal punishment we deserve. As Cardinal Christoph Schönborn also states in *God Sent His Son*, referencing the writings of St. Anselm, bishop of Canterbury and Doctor of the Church, "God's goodness cannot mean that God does something unworthy of himself. Yet it would be unworthy of him if he did something unjust or disordered. Since, however, sin is a "disorder," it would then be unworthy of God not to punish the sinner. Anselm concludes from this that, in view of God's justice and honor, there remains only the dilemma: either satisfaction or punishment."[201]

In order to avoid punishment for our sins, we humans needed to make satisfaction to God for our offenses against him. But we humans could not possibly have made this satisfaction, as an infinite reparation is needed when the offended party is the infinite God. Only God can achieve something like that. But God is not the one who owes it. Man alone must, but cannot, make amends. If you or I died on a cross, it would not bring salvation to the world. Only God has the power to restore humanity to a right relationship to himself.

This is why, in God's wonderful plan of salvation, God became man in Jesus. It was so that, as a man, he could offer to God and give to mankind what we needed but could not achieve by ourselves—the reparation for our sins. This is what Jesus Christ, the God-man, achieved by freely and obediently suffering and giving up his own life on our behalf. Because Jesus Christ is both fully human and fully divine, his sacrificial death on the cross offered the one supreme act of self-giving that can reconcile all of us to God.[202] As stated in *My Way of Life: The Summa Simplified for Everyone*, which summarizes the teachings of St. Thomas Aquinas:

> Christ suffered for men because this was the will of God. God willed that His only-begotten Son should become man to suffer and die for the salvation of men. This divine decision manifests both the justice and the mercy of God. It manifests His justice, because it shows that God has actually demanded satisfaction for the sins of men against Him. It manifests His mercy, because no one but a God-man could have offered a suitable satisfaction for the sins of men. Because He was God, Christ could offer God an infinite satisfaction for the infinite malice of sin. Because He was man, Christ could offer a man's satisfaction for man's sins.[203]

By willingly suffering on our behalf out of love and obedience, Jesus made satisfaction to God as reparation for the sins of all humanity. By lovingly substituting his obedience for our disobedience, Christ's passion and death set things right with God. His passion and death are the source of our salvation not because of the awfulness of his suffering but because of the greatness of his love and obedience to the will of the Father.[204]

It is just for God to remit the debts of mankind if the price paid is more than the debt owed and if this price is given to God with the appropriate love. Thus, Jesus, out of perfect love for his Father and for us, obediently suffered on our behalf to obtain God's pardon for our sins. The debt was paid. His love paid the price.

In short, if God was not *just*, there would be no need for his Son to suffer and die. And if God was not *loving*, there would be no willingness for his Son to suffer and die. But *God is both just and loving. Therefore, God's love is willing to satisfy the needs of his justice.* It is not to work out anger issues that the Father sent the Son but that the justice of the world might be restored by Jesus's love and obedience to the Father's will. As Cardinal Christoph Schönborn also states in *God Sent His Son*, again referencing the writings of St. Anselm:

> Sin has confused the order of God's works and has thereby injured God's honor. God's justice leaves only two possibilities open—either the order that has been destroyed is repaired, or the just punishment ensues. Since, however, Christ has made reparation for sins and for the disorder they have brought about, the punishment no longer applies. Hence, for Anselm, Jesus' death is certainly not God's punishment; rather, Jesus' obedience is putting right what sin destroyed. . . . Jesus' obedience is the satisfaction for the disobedience of

sin and by that very fact renders the punishment superfluous.[205]

From a human perspective, it is inconceivable that the God of perfect holiness would subject himself to such suffering at the hands of sinful, selfish creatures like ourselves. Yet that is exactly what happened! God loves each of us so much that he lovingly and mercifully chose to rescue us at the cost of his own Son's life.

Jesus's death on the cross was both a complete offering to God and the perfect sacrifice of atonement for our sins and the sins of the entire world. As stated in the *Catechism of the Catholic Church*, "By his obedience unto death, Jesus accomplished the substitution of the suffering Servant, who 'makes himself an offering for sin,' when 'he bore the sin of many,' and who 'shall make many to be accounted righteous,' for 'he shall bear their iniquities.' Jesus atoned for our faults and made satisfaction for our sins to the Father" (615).

Jesus freely and obediently accepted the cruelest of human sufferings to reconcile us to God and win for us the possibility of eternal life with God in heaven. *Christ paid the highest price possible to give us the greatest gift possible.* Jesus willingly offered his life on the cross—not only out of obedience to his Father's will but also out of a merciful love for each one of us—in order to set us free from sin and throw open the gates of heaven. This is what the Prophet Isaiah wrote about the "Suffering Servant" over seven hundred years before Christ's passion and death: "But he was pierced for our sins, crushed for our iniquity. He bore the punishment that makes us whole, by his wounds we were healed. We had all gone astray like sheep, all following our own way. But the Lord laid upon him the guilt of us all" (Is 53:5–6).

In the death of Jesus Christ, we see the wondrous plan of God in giving us a Savior who would bring us grace (the gift of God's favor) and freedom from the power of sin and the fear of death. The God who put the stars in the heavens longs for us to be with him and came running to help us. The plain truth is that God wants us to be with him in heaven. God wants this so much that the Father sent the Son who suffered and died on our behalf so this could happen. God our heavenly Father created us in his own image and likeness to be his sons and daughters, and God did what was needed for us to be able to have true happiness in this life and access to eternal life in heaven. It has been said, "Natural life came by God's breath and eternal life comes by Christ's death."

God's Love in Action

The act of God the Father sending Jesus Christ to redeem us was done out of pure mercy and love. Neither the Father nor Jesus were obligated to do what they did for us. God's mercy and love are the motive of God's plan for our salvation. In this plan, God tempered the needs of his justice with mercy and sent his Son to save us from everlasting damnation. By Christ's passion and death, God made clear how much he loves each of us and how much God wants us to spend eternity in his love and presence.

Jesus Christ—who is God's love incarnate—does not

merely love us abstractly or from a distance. It was not enough for Jesus to remain in heaven and merely hope that we would turn back to God. It was not even enough for Jesus to take on human flesh so that he might show us the way back to God. Rather, Jesus took a more significant step forward on our behalf. Jesus knew that the cross was the Father's way for us to be saved from our sins. Jesus counted the cost and said yes to his Father's will. Through the passion and death of Jesus Christ, God showed the whole world that he would spare nothing, not even his own Son, to bring us back to a right relationship of peace and friendship with himself.

Jesus Christ, the only-begotten Son of God, became a man, dwelt among us, and rescued us from certain eternal damnation, and it cost him his life. Jesus willingly gave up his glorious place in heaven and assumed a human body so that he could save us from our sinful human state. As St. Paul wrote, "Though he was in the form of God, [Jesus] did not regard equality with God something to be grasped. Rather, he emptied himself, taking the form of a slave, coming in human likeness; and found human in appearance, he humbled himself, becoming obedient to death, even death on a cross" (Phil 2:6–8).

The eternal Son of God became incarnate as a vulnerable, helpless baby and chose to identify with our human condition, going all the way down so to speak. By taking on a human body, he submitted to our physical limitations. God in Jesus Christ experienced life from an earthly perspective, including facing temptation, hunger, fatigue, weakness, suffering, and death. As a man, he felt pain (just like the rest of us) and was misunderstood,

despised, ridiculed, and rejected and finally suffered a
most horrendous death on a cross.

In Christ, God entered the world of human suffering
and now has the scars to prove it. Only the purest and
most sacrificial love would accept all this just to redeem
a people lost in sin. It is for this reason that Jesus can
bring us all the way up to heaven, so to speak. As noted
in a daily Scripture reflection in *The Word Among Us*:
"Jesus gave up everything—and he did it for us. He came
from heaven to earth so that we could go from earth to
heaven. He was hated so that we could know love. He was
condemned so that we could be pardoned. He died so
that we could have eternal life. In every way, he emptied
himself so that we could be filled."[206]

There is no greater proof of God's love for us than
sending his Son to become one with us in our humanity
and to lay down his life for our sake. For as Jesus said—
foreshadowing his death on the cross—there is no greater
love than "to lay down one's life for one's friends" (Jn
15:13). Jesus gave himself completely out of love for us.
He willingly laid down his life out of selfless love for our
sake and for our salvation. True love is costly because it is
willing to sacrifice all for the sake of the beloved.

Jesus Christ humbled himself and suffered so that we
could experience God's true nature: love. In Jesus, we see
what God is like. Jesus is the perfect revelation of God.
In Jesus, we see the perfect love of God, a God who cares
intensely for and who yearns for each one of us, loving us
to the point of laying down his life for us upon the cross.

Jesus came to earth as a man because he wanted to
show how much God loves each and every one of us and

how valuable we are to God. For the love that moved Jesus Christ to embrace our humanity is the same love that moves God to embrace each of us, imperfect though we are.

God loves us so much that he sent his only-begotten Son to free us from the eternal consequences of our unruly desires and sinful habits. The very reason the Son of God took on flesh and became a man for our sake was to redeem us from bondage to sin and eternal damnation as well as to give us new life as adopted children of God. Jesus Christ came to unite earth with heaven and to raise those on earth to the glory of heaven.

God showed his deep love for us by sending his Son, the Lord Jesus Christ, who willingly offered up his own life as an atoning sacrifice for our sins. As the apostle John wrote in his first letter, "In this way the love of God was revealed to us: God sent his only Son into the world so that we might have life through him. In this is love: not that we have loved God, but that he loved us and sent his Son as expiation for our sins" (1 Jn 4:9–10).

God's act of tender mercy and infinite love shows how precious we are in God's sight and that God's deep love for each and every one of us knows no bounds. As stated in the *Catechism of the Catholic Church*, "It is love 'to the end' that confers on Christ's sacrifice its value as redemption and reparation, as atonement and satisfaction. He knew and loved us all when he offered his life" (616).

The Christian "good news" is that the all-powerful God of the universe became a helpless baby and died on the cross in order to reconcile us with himself and save us. *Isn't it truly "good news" that God loves each of us so much that the only-begotten Son of God left his heavenly home, took on a human body, and endured the agony of the cross so that we could experience God's love and be able to live a new life with God both now and eternally in heaven?*

God's Gracious Gift

The sobering reality is that we could not save ourselves from the consequences of our sins and wrongdoing. But the "good news" is that we have been offered salvation through the gracious love of God in Jesus Christ. When we were dead in sin, God sent his Son to restore us to life. When we could not save ourselves, Jesus rescued us by his passion and death on the cross.

Wondrously, the cross of Christ is not the end of the story. Rather, the cross is when heaven and earth met in a momentous event that changed our world and opened the doors to heaven. The cross is the sign of sin's defeat. The "good news" of the cross is basically, because Jesus suffered, died, and now lives, we have the hope of salvation and eternal life in heaven. *The "good news" of Christianity also offers us peace, hope, truth, promise, and immortality, as well as salvation.* Don Schwager elaborates on this in a daily Scripture reflection:

> It is the good news of *peace*—the Lord comes to reconcile and restore us to friendship with God. The good news of *hope*—the Lord comes to dwell with us and to give us a home with him in his heavenly kingdom. The good news of *truth*—the Lord

Jesus sets us free from the lies and deception of Satan and opens our mind to understand the truth and revelation of God's word (John 8:32). The good news of *promise*—Jesus fulfills the promise of God to reward those who seek him with the treasure of heaven. The good news of *immortality*—Jesus overcomes sin and death for us in order to raise our lowly bodies to be like his glorious body which will never die again. And the good news of *salvation*—the Lord Jesus delivers us from every fear, every sin, and every obstacle that would keep us from entering his everlasting kingdom of righteousness, peace, and joy.[207]

Of course, we did nothing to earn this undeserved and gracious manifestation of God's love in Christ Jesus. It has been said, "Grace is an unearned blessing to unworthy sinners." The *Catechism of the Catholic Church* emphasizes, "The grace of Christ is the free gift that God makes to us of his own life" (1999).

How does this realization make us feel? We can be profoundly grateful for the marvelous gift of a new and eternal life that Jesus Christ lovingly won for us on the cross. By stretching out his arms on the cross, Jesus beckons us to lift up our hearts in gratitude and know how much God desires to forgive us, heal us, and save us. Devout Christians are indeed a deeply thankful and grateful people. *This gratitude, and not fear of damnation, is the prime motive for our response and actions as Christians.*

God has already done so very much for us. Now God

is asking that we each take a few steps toward him. Seeing how much God loves each of us, we are called in return to love God more deeply and follow Christ more completely. The more we feel God's deep love for each of us, the more we will want what God wants and reject what is contrary to God's will.

God loved us first, and our love for God and others is a response to God's mercy and kindness toward us. God, in his mercy, offers us the grace and help of the Holy Spirit so we can love as he loves, pardon as he pardons, and treat others with the same mercy and kindness that God has shown to us. If we turn to God and gratefully follow Jesus Christ as our Lord and Savior, we will find every grace and blessing we need to be truly happy in this life and in the eternal life to come.

God's most precious gift in the saving life, death, and resurrection of Jesus Christ was given out of the depth of God's love for us, not because we earned it and certainly not because we deserved it. God loves us so much that he wants to be fully reconciled with us through the gift of his Son, Jesus Christ. God is now offering each of us the precious gift of a new life and eternal salvation through Jesus Christ. However, we are totally free to accept or reject this gift. The choice is ours. But how can we accept God's gracious gift of salvation? This is what we will look at next.

Chapter 8

HOW ARE WE SAVED?

We are saved by God's grace through the atoning sacrifice of Jesus Christ on the cross. Since Jesus suffered and died for all, God desires the eternal salvation of everyone. Salvation is a gracious gift from God that is available to each and every one of us. A gift, however, may be accepted or rejected. But a gift is beneficial only when it is accepted.

Being made in God's image and likeness means we have intelligence, the knowledge of right and wrong, and a genuinely free will. As such, we are each able to make a real choice to either accept or reject God's gift of salvation.[208] Each of us is invited to personally, freely, and fully accept the gift of salvation that Jesus won for us on the cross.

In accepting God's gracious gift, we are called to repentance and to do the will of God in our daily lives. We are saved by God's grace, but we need to cooperate with that grace by living as a disciple of Jesus Christ. As stated by St. Augustine, "God created us without us: but he did not will to save us without us."[209] In other words, God expects our cooperation in order to be saved.

For example, we cannot ignore God and the teachings of the Church and still expect that the door to heaven will be opened wide for us. We cannot just take our salvation for granted. God has much higher expectations. If religious faith has no bearing whatsoever on our daily lives, our salvation is not guaranteed.

Accepting God's Gift of Salvation

But how do we accept God's gift of salvation? When the rich young man asked Jesus what else, beyond observing the Ten Commandments, was necessary to inherit everlasting life, Jesus responded that he must "come and follow me" by living a life of discipleship (see Mt 19:16–22).

Followers of Jesus are called to live a life of Christian discipleship in three specific ways. Just like a tripod needs three legs to be stable, Catholics are called to a three-fold response to accept God's gracious gift of eternal salvation.

Faith and Conversion

What do these Bible verses say is needed for our salvation?

- Jesus said, "And just as Moses lifted up the serpent in the desert, so must the Son of Man be lifted up, so that everyone who *believes* in him may have eternal life. For God so loved the world that he gave his only-begotten Son, so that everyone who believes in him might not perish but might have eternal life" (Jn 3:14–16, emphasis added).

- Jesus said, "Whoever hears my word and *believes* in the one who sent me has eternal life and will not come to condemnation, but has passed from death to life" (Jn 5:24, emphasis added).
- "[The Jailer] asked for a light and rushed in and, trembling with fear, he fell down before Paul and Silas. Then he brought them out and said, 'Sirs, what must I do to be saved?' And they said, '*Believe in the Lord Jesus* and you and your household will be saved'" (Acts 16:29–31, emphasis added).

These Bible verses show that belief in Jesus Christ as the Son of God and our Redeemer is needed for salvation. As stated in the *Catechism of the Catholic Church*, "Faith is necessary for salvation" (183). We are justified by faith because faith is the beginning of human salvation. Faith is the foundation and root of our justification, without which it is impossible to please God.[210] Thus, faith is the first thing we are called to do to accept God's gracious gift of salvation. Faith is the first "leg of the tripod." Faith is letting God into our soul, and eternal salvation is having God in our soul forever.

Christian faith includes belief in a *personal* God, not an impersonal force, made manifest in the persons of the Father, Son, and Holy Spirit. One of the greatest truths of the Christian faith is that our knowledge of God is not simply limited to knowing something about God, but we can know God personally. The essence of Christianity, and what makes it different from other religions, is our being able to have a personal and prayerful relationship with the one God in the three persons of Father, Son, and Holy Spirit.

Faith is both a free gift of God and the free and full assent to the whole truth about God as revealed in Jesus Christ. Our faith, however, must be more than mere intellectual assent to the existence of the triune God and acceptance of Church teachings. This intellectual acceptance may be the first step, but by itself is not sufficient for salvation.[211] As stated in the *Catechism*, "Faith is a personal adherence of the whole man to God who reveals himself. It involves an assent of the intellect and will to the self-revelation God has made through his deeds and words" (176).

The *Catechism* also states, "*By faith, man completely submits his intellect and his will to God*" (143, emphasis added). The faith that leads to salvation includes acknowledging our complete dependence upon God and entrusting our whole life to God. Faith is an attitude of trust in the presence and power of God. To trust in God means to root the whole of our life in God, and not to ground our concerns in the things of this world, in wealth, power, pleasure, or prestige.

Faith is being open to and accepting what God will reveal, do, and invite. It should be obvious that in dealing with the infinite, all-powerful person who is God, we are not in complete control. Rather, we are part of God's great plan and purpose for life. We must repent of our sins, reject our selfish ways, and seek a deep, prayerful, growing, and trusting relationship with God. This is conversion.

Conversion is much more than believing certain truths and doing certain good acts.[212] This is emphasized by Fr. Thomas White and Fr. Desmond O'Donnell in their book *Renewal of Faith*:

> Full acceptance of Jesus implies a very radical change in our lives. It is not at all certain that every person who is baptized, who says he is a Christian or who acts like a Christian has really made this change. In English we use the words "conversion" and "repentance" for two aspects of this deep change which is essential if one is to be a true Christian.
>
> Have we ever converted, changed, turned ourselves completely toward Jesus? Perhaps some of us thought that we could follow Jesus satisfactorily just by believing certain truths and by doing certain good acts. Following Jesus demands that, but it demands *much more*; it calls for a deep change, a radical turning about, a total commitment of our lives to Jesus.
>
> But this is not easy; it implies a total surrender to God's will. We are not trying any longer to make God fit into our ideas; we are rather making ourselves fit into God's ideas.
>
> Conversion is a free, personal and radical offering of one's whole self to God. Have we ever done this? Have you ever done it? Or have you perhaps drifted along since your childhood doing Christian things? Have you ever given yourself completely to Jesus?

> So, we cannot spend our lives merely *thinking*
> about Jesus, *wondering* about his claims, debat-
> ing about his existence, *discussing* his demands.
> He does not call for mere interest or admiration
> or study of his life; he calls for *decision* about his
> claims and *conversion* to him as a real living and
> loving person.[213]

How often do we hear this? How often should we hear
it? Jesus encourages us to think about the consequences
of our choices, especially the choices and decisions that
matter not just here and now but also for all eternity. The
decisions we make now will affect and shape our future,
both on earth as well as in the life to come. Please take a
few minutes to prayerfully reflect if you have ever made a
deliberate, adult decision to personally accept Jesus Christ
as your Lord and Savior and put God first in your life.

Fr. Donald L. Gelpi, in his book *The Conversion Experience*, explains that conversion is fostered by embracing
the liberating conviction that our worth and value are
given as our birthright because we are children of a loving God.[214] We experience *initial* conversion to Christ
through repentance when we candidly acknowledge
and confront the pride and emotional barriers that may
inhibit our consent of faith and look to God as the source
of emotional healing.

Repentance involves changing our way of thinking,
our attitudes, disposition, and choices in life so that
Jesus Christ is the Lord of our life rather than sin and
selfishness. If we are only sorry for the consequences of
our sins, we will most likely keep repeating the sin that is

controlling us. True repentance requires a sincerely contrite heart, a deep sorrow for our sins, and a firm resolution to avoid them in the future.

We know our life has gone "off the rails" in a number of ways and we want to get back on track. So the time for repentance is now. As Don Schwager advises:

> Jesus gives a clear warning—take responsibility for your actions and moral choices and put sin to death today before it can destroy your heart, mind, soul, and body as well. Unrepentant sin is like a cancer which corrupts us from within. If it is not eliminated through repentance—asking God for forgiveness and for his healing grace—it leads to a spiritual death which is far worse than physical destruction.
>
> God is patient, but for those who persistently and stubbornly rebel against him and refuse to repent and change their course, there is the consequence that they will lose both their soul and body to hell. God, in his mercy, gives us time to get right with him, but that time is now. We must not assume that there is no hurry. A sudden and unexpected death leaves one no time to prepare to settle one's accounts when he or she must stand before the Lord on the day of judgment. Jesus warns us that we must be ready at all times. The Lord in his mercy gives us both grace (his gracious help and healing) and time to turn away from sin, but that time is right now. If we delay, even for a day, we

may discover that grace has passed us by and our time is up.[215]

Repentance and initial conversion mean that we renounce everything that separates us from the love of God. It is when we realize that God, who from all eternity has known and loved us, invites us to partnership in our life's mission and purpose.

Initial conversion is, therefore, primarily a conscious commitment to Jesus Christ and a mature decision to give one's life completely to him in discipleship. In this context, initial conversion is not necessarily the profoundly emotional event experienced by many evangelical Christians. For many Christians, initial conversion is simply a low-key discovery of an owned faith that has developed over time, coupled with a conscious commitment to actively live out that faith in our own life.

Conversion has been called "the Achilles' heel of Catholicism" because too often Catholics have simply presumed it has happened or will happen. In the early Church, adult conversion came first, then catechesis (religious education), and finally baptism. Today, this order is usually reversed. Infant baptism is first, then catechesis, and finally conversion. But when *is* this conversion? When was *your* conversion?

While Catholic teaching recognizes the importance of initial conversion and mature commitment to Jesus Christ, the Church also emphasizes that conversion is a gradual process and way of life. Conversion is more than a major decision that happens once, twice, or a few times in our life. Conversion is a lifelong process of moving from a world-centered perspective to a God-centered perspective. It means letting go of the passing things of this world and resolutely relying on God's help and grace to grow in holiness and live out our faith in Jesus Christ every day.

The only conversions that count are those confirmed by a life of discipleship. There is discipline involved in discipleship. Our faith cannot save us if we deny that faith by how we live. True faith will express itself in the way we actually live. Christian faith involves understanding the demands of Christ and seeking, by the grace of God, to live according to the Church's moral teachings. It is when the primary goal of our life becomes not, "What do I want?" but rather, "What does God want?"

Jesus asks his followers to believe in him, to be obedient to his will, and to trust that God will always be with us. For as stated in Hebrews 5:8–9 about Jesus, "Son though he was, he learned obedience from what he suffered; and when he was made perfect, he became the source of eternal salvation for all who *obey* him" (emphasis added). Don Schwager writes, "The Gospel demands a response of faith and obedience to God's gift of salvation. In announcing the good news, Jesus makes two demands: repent and believe! Repentance requires a change of course—a turning away from sin and disobedience and a turning towards the Lord with faith and submission to his word of truth and righteousness (right living according to God's truth and moral goodness)."[216]

Christian faith includes rejecting sin and seeking to live in obedience to the will of God as expressed in Scripture and the teachings of the Church. For our faith to be effective, it must include trust and obedience, including our active submission to God and a willingness to do whatever God commands. For as the apostle John writes, "The way we may be sure that we know Jesus is to keep his commandments. Whoever says, 'I know him,' but does not keep his commandments is a liar, and the truth is not in him. But whoever keeps his word, the love of God is truly perfected in him" (1 Jn 2:3–5).

However, God does not want us to merely do what he commands, as if we were robots. God wants to be our loving Father, not just a boss or commanding officer. The commands of Jesus and the Church are not burdensome or hard for those who trust in God's love and mercy. God wants to form us, not just command us. When we yield to Jesus Christ, our lives are transformed by the gift of the indwelling Holy Spirit and we are empowered to live more fully as God wills.

It is not enough that we just know about God in Jesus; we must come to know him personally. It is not enough to learn about the Lord; we must meet him personally in prayer, the sacraments, and the Scriptures. And so God invites us to listen carefully and grow in our personal relationship with the Father, Son, and Holy Spirit through frequent prayer, receiving the sacraments, studying the Bible, and learning the teachings of the Church, especially as found in the *Catechism of the Catholic Church*.

By God's grace and the power of the Holy Spirit, especially as received in the sacraments, Christians are able to move from self-centeredness toward doing God's work in the world. Lifelong conversion involves re-centering our passions and re-aligning our affections toward a vocation of service in partnership with God. Reaching out in loving service to others and seeking God's will in our life becomes primary. This brings us to the second "leg of the tripod."

Loving Service to God and Others

What do these Bible verses say is needed for our salvation?

- "There was a scholar of the law who stood up to test Jesus and said, 'Teacher, what must I do to inherit eternal life?' Jesus said to him, 'What is written in the law? How do you read it?' He said in reply, *'You shall love the Lord, your God, with all your heart, with all your being, with all your strength, and with all your mind, and your neighbor as yourself.'* He replied to him, 'You have answered correctly; do this and you will live." (Lk 10:25–28, emphasis added).

- Jesus said, "When the Son of Man comes in his glory ... [he] will say to those on his right, 'Come, you who are blessed by my Father. Inherit the kingdom prepared for you from the foundation of the world. For I was hungry and you gave me food, I was thirsty and you gave me drink, a stranger and you welcomed me, naked and you clothed me, ill and you cared for me, in prison and you visited me.' Then the righteous will answer him and say, 'Lord, when did we see you hungry and feed you, or thirsty and give you drink?

When did we see you a stranger and welcome you, or naked and clothe you? When did we see you ill or in prison, and visit you?' And the king will say to them in reply, 'Amen, I say to you, *whatever you did for one of these least brothers of mine, you did for me.*' Then he will say to those on his left, 'Depart from me, you accursed, into the eternal fire prepared for the devil and his angels. For I was hungry and you gave me no food, I was thirsty and you gave me no drink, a stranger and you gave me no welcome, naked and you gave me no clothing, ill and in prison, and you did not care for me. . . . Amen, I say to you, what you did not do for one of these least ones, you did not do for me.' And these will go off to eternal punishment, but the righteous to eternal life" (Mt 25:31–46, emphasis added).

- "What good is it, my brothers, if someone says he has faith but does not have works? Can that faith save him? If a brother or sister has nothing to wear and has no food for the day, and one of you says to them, 'Go in peace, keep warm, and eat well,' but you do not give them the necessities of the body, what good is it? So also *faith of itself, if it does not have works, is dead*" (Jas 2:14–17, emphasis added).

Thus, the second "leg of the tripod" and our second

response needed to accept the gift of salvation is loving service to God and others. Genuine faith requires an active response. This active response includes acts of charity done out of love of God and love of others. The love of God and love of neighbor are inextricably bound together. If we love God but hate our neighbor, we are wasting our time. The love of God and love of others are tightly connected because it is impossible to love God without loving the humans that God created and embraced in the humanity of Jesus Christ, the God-man.

Being a Christian means we are called to love God and to love others as we love ourselves (Mt 22:36–39; Mk 12:29–31). When we love God, we want to develop a deeper personal relationship with the Lord through our prayers and actions. The more we grow in our relationship with God, the more the Holy Spirit works in us to make us the person that God wants us to be. The more we allow the Holy Spirit to work in us, the more we will lovingly serve God and others.

We share in God's kingdom by laying down our lives in loving service of others as Jesus laid down his life on the cross for our sake. An early Church father summed up Jesus's teachings with the expression "to serve is to reign with Christ."[217]

However, Christians do not do charitable good deeds to try to earn or merit our salvation. We cannot work our way into heaven. Christians do good deeds to demonstrate our love for God and others, not because we are expecting something in return. Our charitable acts of loving service flow from a heart full of gratitude for the abundant mercy and grace that God has given us. We are called to show our gratitude for what Christ did for us on the cross by seeking, with God's grace and help, to live a life that will bring joy to God and other people.

Faith is vital, but without charitable acts of love, it proves nothing (see 1 Cor 13). St. James says that "faith without works is dead" and that we are to demonstrate our faith by our actions.[218] As the *Catechism of the Catholic Church* states, "Living faith works through charity" (1814).

Faith calls us to do charitable good works by lovingly serving God and others. Both faith and works are essential for our salvation.[219] It is not a matter of one or the other. C. S. Lewis noted that any discussion about which is more important—faith or works—is as senseless as "asking which blade of a pair of scissors is most necessary."[220] Both are important. Both are necessary.

The *Joint Declaration on the Doctrine of Justification*, which has been endorsed by the Catholic, Lutheran, Methodist, Presbyterian, Reformed, and Anglican Churches, affirms the need for both faith and works.[221] This joint declaration states that Christian "faith is active in love and thus the Christian cannot and should not remain without works."[222]

Our faith is made perfect in love because love orients us to the supreme good which is God himself as well as the good of our neighbor who is created in God's image and likeness. Our loving service to God and others flow as the fruit of our faith. St. Paul calls this "faith working through love" (Gal 5:6).

As Christians, we are commanded by Jesus to love others as he has loved us (see Jn 13:34). But what does this mean? In today's culture, love is usually associated with romantic feelings and sexual relationships. Clearly, this is not the type of love Jesus meant we should have for everyone! Also, we often think of love as a feeling. But since we cannot consciously decide what we feel, how can we have feelings of love for everyone? Love is, however, not primarily an emotion. Love is an act of the will. It is willing the good of the other person.

To better understand Jesus's command to love one another, it helps to look at the Greek word for love most often used in the New Testament. For in the Greek language, unlike in English, there are four different words used for four different types of human love. These Greek words are *storge*, *philia*, *eros*, and *agape*. C. S. Lewis expands upon these in his book *The Four Loves*.[223]

Storge is the Greek word for the natural affection and love between family members. Storge is most clearly evident in the love of parents for their children. Most parents are so devoted to their children's welfare that they are willing to sacrifice and do most anything, even unto death, for the good of their children. Storge is also the love children feel for their parents, as well as the love between siblings and relatives in an extended family. Storge is a committed, often sacrificial love. It does not expect too much, usually revives after quarrels, is relatively unconditional, often overlooks the other's faults, and frequently forgives. We often take the storge love of our family members for granted. Storge is the love where we can be comfortable and secure just being in the presence of one another. Just being together in comfortable closeness is often enough.

Philia is the love between good friends. Philia is also called "Platonic" love. Philia is a chosen love because we choose whom we will befriend—usually on the basis of shared interests. Philia is more conditional and less sacrificial than storge. Philia is less willing to continually overlook faults and frequently forgive the other person. If they upset us too much, we may choose to no longer be their friend.

Eros is the Greek word for romantic love and is the root of the English word *erotic*. Eros is the passionate feeling of romantic attraction. It is also associated with infatuation and lust. Unlike friends who stand side-by-side, absorbed in some common interest, eros lovers are normally face-to-face, absorbed with each other. Since eros is a passionate feeling and because we cannot consciously decide what we will feel, we usually do not choose this type of love. That is why we say a man and a woman "fall in love." Eros ("being in love") usually just happens. Of course, this does not mean we must always give in to the desires of these passions. While we cannot decide what we feel, we can and should control what we do in response to our feelings.

The final type of love is *agape*. Agape is the word used most often in the New Testament to describe Christian love. Agape is a self-giving, sacrificial love that acts only for the good of another. Agape is made manifest in our acts of charity and service for others, including those we may not even know or like. Agape is unconditional in that it does not expect anything in return. Agape only desires what is best for the other person.

Unlike eros, agape is not a feeling that just happens.

Rather, like philia, agape is a deliberately chosen love. Agape takes a decision of our free will, a commitment to act for the good of another. Like storge, agape can be a sacrificial and unreciprocated love. Agape is the self-giving and sacrificial love seen in the charitable actions of St. Teresa of Calcutta and that Jesus made manifest for us on the cross.

While storge, philia, and eros all have their rightful place, they are prone to selfishness and possessiveness in and of themselves. It is only in submission to agape that these dangers can be avoided. Agape enables us to love and care for our family, our friends, and our spouses for their own sake and not just for what they give us or do for us.

Agape is a joyful and spiritual love that grows in our lives by the grace of God. The Holy Spirit is the source of agape love. Agape flows from the abundant, over-flowing, and unconditional love of God. After all, God is love—agape love (see 1 Jn 4:8). God's love is uncondi-tional agape love and is wholly directed toward the good of others.

Agape is God's love made visible in our works of charity and service for others. Charity is the virtue by which we love God above all things and our neighbor as ourselves. Agape is the type of love that all Christians are called to manifest in their lives by unconditional acts of charity for others, especially the poor and disadvantaged.

In Matthew 25:31–46, the nature of Christian love (agape) is specified. Agape is not primarily a feeling, an attitude, or a conviction, but rather is expressed through concrete acts of charity on behalf of those in need—the

hungry, the homeless, the hurting, the lonely, the imprisoned, the confused, the forgotten. Christian love both
embraces and lifts the burdens of others.

Acts of charity to help meet the physical and bodily
needs of others are traditionally called the "*Corporal
Works of Mercy.*" These include feeding the hungry, giving drink to the thirsty, clothing the naked, offering hos-
pitality to the homeless, caring for the sick, and visiting
the imprisoned.[224]

The "*Spiritual Works of Mercy*" are another way
to actively demonstrate our Christian love by helping
others with their spiritual and emotional needs. They
include counseling the doubtful, educating the unin-
formed (including those confused about what the Church
teaches), admonishing the sinner, comforting the sorrowful, forgiving offenses willingly, bearing wrongs patiently,
and praying for others.[225]

In short, Christian love is the active bearing of another's burden, whether physical, emotional, or spiritual.
Such is our calling.

The Sacraments

Let's now consider the third and final "leg of the tripod"
for how we can accept Christ's gift of salvation. What do
these quotes from Jesus say is needed for our salvation?

- "Whoever believes and is *baptized* will be
  saved; whoever does not believe will be condemned" (Mk 16:16, emphasis added).
- "Jesus answered, 'Amen, amen, I say to
  you, no one can enter the kingdom of God

without being *born of water and Spirit*. What is born of flesh is flesh and what is born of spirit is spirit. Do not be amazed that I told you, "You must be born from above""" (Jn 3:5–7, emphasis added).

- "Jesus said to them, 'Amen, amen, I say to you, unless you eat the flesh of the Son of Man and drink his blood, you do not have life within you. *Whoever eats my flesh and drinks my blood has eternal life, and I will raise him on the last day*'" (Jn 6:53–54, emphasis added).

Thus, the third "leg of the tripod" required for salvation, Catholics believe, are the sacraments—notably Baptism and the Eucharist. The sacraments and the life of Christ experienced in the Church are the necessary basis and foundation of our entire life as Catholics. That is because a committed and active faith and all the charitable good deeds we are called to do (the first two "legs of the tripod") would be difficult, if not impossible, without the grace and divine help we receive from the sacraments. They truly make possible our life as disciples of Jesus Christ. Edward Sri writes, "Jesus actually wants to reproduce his love in us through sending his Spirit into our hearts so that we can live like him. Jesus does this work in us most especially through baptism and the other sacraments of the Church. Through the sacraments, Christ fills us with his Spirit, deepens our union with God, and enables us to love far beyond what we could do by our own natural power."[226]

The sacrament of Baptism heals the wounds of sin and gives the indwelling of the Holy Spirit. The *Catechism of the Catholic Church* states, "Through Baptism we are freed from sin and reborn as sons of God; we become members of Christ, are incorporated into the Church and made sharers in her mission" (1213). The *Catechism* has this to say about Baptism and salvation:

> The Lord himself affirms that Baptism is necessary for salvation. He also commands his disciples to proclaim the Gospel to all nations and to baptize them. Baptism is necessary for salvation for those to whom the Gospel has been proclaimed and who have had the possibility of asking for this sacrament. The Church does not know of any means other than Baptism that assures entry into eternal beatitude; this is why she takes care not to neglect the mission she has received from the Lord to see that all who can be baptized are "reborn of water and the Spirit." (1257)

Interestingly, the *Catechism* also has this to say, "Every person who is ignorant of the Gospel of Christ and of his Church, but seeks the truth and does the will of God in accordance with his understanding of it, can be saved. It may be supposed that such persons would have desired Baptism explicitly if they had known its necessity" (1260).

While the rite of Baptism is necessary for the salvation of Christians, it is not by itself sufficient for the salvation of adults. As discussed in the preceding two "legs of the tripod," we adults cannot say that we are saved just by the rite of our Baptism alone.

In addition, Jesus clearly revealed the importance of what we now call the sacrament of the Eucharist for our eternal salvation when he said, "Whoever eats my flesh and drinks my blood has eternal life." As Jesus stated in John 6:48–58:

> "I am the bread of life. Your ancestors ate the manna in the desert, but they died; this is the bread that comes down from heaven so that one may eat it and not die. I am the living bread that came down from heaven; whoever eats this bread will live forever; and the bread that I will give is my flesh for the life of the world."
>
> The Jews quarreled among themselves, saying, "How can this man give us his flesh to eat?" Jesus said to them, *"Truly, truly, I say to you, unless you eat the flesh of the Son of Man and drink his blood, you do not have life within you. Whoever eats my flesh and drinks my blood has eternal life, and I will raise him on the last day.* For my flesh is true food, and my blood is true drink. Whoever eats my flesh and drinks my blood remains in me and I in him. Just as the living Father sent me and I have life because of the Father, so also the one who feeds on me will have life because of me. This is the bread that came down from heaven. Unlike your ancestors who ate and still died, whoever eats this bread will live forever." (emphasis added)

These statements were extremely objectionable

language for a Jew of Jesus's time. To eat someone's flesh was a term of contempt, and the drinking of animal blood is expressly forbidden throughout the Old Testament—much less the drinking of a man's blood. So it is not surprising that people began to quarrel and object to Jesus's statements. But when they objected, Jesus did not soften his language. Rather, he intensified it and repeated it several times.

Not surprisingly, many of those who heard Jesus repeatedly make these astonishing statements could not accept that they were to literally eat his flesh and drink his blood. As reported in John 6:60–61: "Then many of his disciples who were listening said, 'This saying is hard; who can accept it?' Since Jesus knew that his disciples were murmuring about this, he said to them, 'Does this shock you?'"

Many of Jesus's followers then rejected him and walked away. As recorded in John 6:66–68: "As a result of this, many of his disciples returned to their former way of life and no longer accompanied him. Jesus then said to the Twelve, 'Do you also want to leave?' Simon Peter answered him, 'Master, to whom shall we go? You have the words of eternal life.'"

Remarkably, Jesus did not seek to bring them back by saying they misunderstood his meaning or that he was only speaking symbolically.[227] Jesus did not attempt to clarify or "water down" his statements at all. Jesus obviously meant what he said about literally eating his body and drinking his blood. In fact, he meant it so much that he let many of his followers who heard it walk away. He let them go.

Jesus even turned to his twelve apostles and asked if they wanted to leave him too. He was prepared to also let them go, instead of trying to clarify or change one word in what he had said about eating his flesh and drinking his blood.

At no time during this entire "Bread of Life" discourse recorded in chapter 6 of the Gospel of John did Jesus say that he was speaking symbolically or metaphorically, as is the belief of many Protestant Christians. No, Jesus literally meant what he said that we are to "eat the flesh of the Son of Man and drink his blood." This is what Catholics do whenever receiving the sacrament of the Eucharist, also called Holy Communion, primarily at Mass.

In Holy Communion, we partake of Jesus Christ himself truly and completely, body and blood, soul and divinity under the appearance of bread and wine. Jesus's presence is not simply symbolic, but rather real, true, and substantial. But how can this be? It is certainly not easy to understand how what still looks like bread and wine can actually be the body and blood of Jesus Christ.

But this is so because Jesus is God and what God says, is. Thus, when Jesus's words at the Last Supper ("This is my body," "This is my blood") are spoken by the priest at Mass, the bread and wine are mysteriously changed into what Jesus's words say they are. By God's word and divine action, the bread and wine become really, truly, and substantially the body and blood of our Lord and Savior Jesus Christ.

We have been given the precious gift of the Holy Eucharist as spiritual nourishment for our growth in holiness. The Eucharist is sustenance, food for the journey, nourishment to get us through each day. How strong would we be if we never ate or ate only on special occasions? Not very. So in the spiritual life, we must eat and drink or we will not have strength.

As Pope St. John Paul II stated, "In the humble signs of bread and wine, changed into his body and blood, Christ walks beside us as our strength and our food for the journey, and he enables us to become, for everyone, witnesses of hope."[228] And, Pope Francis wrote, "The Eucharist is not a prize for the perfect but a powerful medicine and nourishment for the weak."[229]

There is no getting around the reality that just as the body needs physical nourishment, the spirit needs spiritual nourishment. Just as bodily nourishment replenishes our strength, so in the Eucharist we become more firmly rooted in and strengthened by the love of God, which helps us break with disordered attachments to the world and become more like Jesus Christ himself in our thoughts, words, and deeds. St. Thomas Aquinas has this to say about the Eucharist:[230]

> He shed his blood for our ransom and purification, so that we might be redeemed from our wretched state of bondage and cleansed from all sin. But to ensure that the memory of so great a gift would abide with us forever, he left his body as food and his blood as drink for the faithful to consume in the form of bread and wine.
>
> O precious and wonderful banquet, that brings us salvation and contains all sweetness! Could anything be of more intrinsic value? Under the old law

it was the flesh of calves and goats that was offered, but here Christ himself, the true God, is set before us as our food. What could be more wonderful than this? No other sacrament has greater healing power; through it sins are purged away, virtues are increased, and the soul is enriched with an abundance of every spiritual gift.

In the sacrament of the Eucharist, we are more deeply united with Jesus Christ and intimately partake of his divine life so as to have access to eternal life with God in heaven. Jesus graciously offers us the abundant supernatural life of heaven itself in the Eucharist. But we can miss it or even refuse it. We will further explore the gift of the Holy Eucharist when we look at why we go to Mass in chapter 10.

Conclusion

In closing, let's look at the question raised at the beginning of this chapter on how we should respond if asked, "Are you saved?" An appropriate answer for Catholics to give to this question is "*I hope to be saved and I am being saved.*"[231]

What do we mean by the first part, "I *hope* to be saved"? Evangelical Christians usually believe in "one moment of salvation" (normally when you "accept Jesus Christ as your Lord and Savior") and "once saved always saved." Many Evangelicals claim they "have been saved" once and for all and there is nothing they can do to lose that salvation.

When Catholics speak of being saved, however, we have in mind more than one moment of a person's initial conversion to Jesus Christ or the reception of any single sacrament. Nevertheless, we could say to an Evangelical Christian who asks if we have been "saved" that at our confirmation we made a formal commitment of our life to Christ and this is when we essentially "accepted Jesus as my Lord and Savior." That's because the sacrament of Confirmation is a formal opportunity to publicly reaffirm and confirm the faith in which we have been baptized, most often as an infant. We could also tell them that we make a public faith commitment to Jesus Christ whenever we renew our baptismal promises at Mass.

However, unlike Evangelicals who claim with absolute certainty that they are saved, Catholic teaching recognizes that we are not the best judge of our own spiritual condition. Jesus told many parables about people who thought they were ready for heaven but were not. A person's salvation is God's call to make, not his or hers alone. That is why Catholics do not say that we are "saved" once and for all.

Jesus stated that "whoever endures to the end will be saved" (Mt 10:22). We cannot presume to know ahead of time that we will persevere in our faith in God and obedience to God's will until the very end of our lives.[232] It is possible that we could turn away from God at any point in life and thereby lose the hope of heaven.

As Jesus stated in John 3:36, "Whoever believes in the Son has eternal life, but whoever *disobeys* the Son will not see life, but the wrath of God remains upon him" (emphasis added). In order to be saved, we must, therefore, continually seek to obey the moral teachings of Jesus as found in the Bible and in his Church (see 1 Cor 6:9–10; Gal 5:19–21).

Although we cannot know with absolute certainty that we will be saved, faithful Catholics possess our salvation in *confident hope* (see Rom 5:2; 8:24–25). As stated in the *Catechism*, "We can therefore hope in the glory of heaven promised by God to those who love him and do his will. In every circumstance, each one of us should hope, with the grace of God, to persevere 'to the end' and to obtain the joy of heaven, as God's eternal reward for the good works accomplished with the grace of Christ" (1821).

While we do not presume to pass a final judgment on ourselves or others in advance, we do have great confidence that God will give us the grace needed to persevere in faithful discipleship so that we will be saved. As St. Paul wrote about hope and his eternal salvation in Philippians 3:11–14:

> In the *hope* that I myself will be raised from death to life. I do not claim that I have already succeeded or have already become perfect. I keep striving to win the prize for which Christ Jesus has already won me to himself. Of course, my friends, I really do not think that I have already won it; the one thing I do, however, is to forget what is behind me and do my best to reach what is ahead. So I run straight toward the goal in order to win the prize, which is God's call through Christ Jesus to the life above. (GNT, emphasis added)

If the great St. Paul had only "hope" for his salvation, how can we expect more certainty than that? Like St. Paul, we can have confident hope of our salvation. This does not mean we need to worry or be anxious about our eternal destiny. Rather, this hope enables us to be more aware of and continually rely on the mercy and grace of God to help us persevere in faith until the end.

Let's now look at the second part of the answer Catholics can give when asked if we are saved; namely, "I am being saved." As St. Paul wrote, "The message of the cross is foolishness to those who are perishing, but to us who *are being saved* it is the power of God" (1 Cor 1:18, emphasis added). He also wrote, "For we are the aroma of Christ for God among those who *are being saved*" (2 Cor 2:15, emphasis added). St. Paul clearly did not believe that those to whom he was writing had already been saved. Rather, they "are being saved"—just like each of us. But what do we mean by "I *am being* saved"?

We recognize that God, through Jesus Christ, lovingly did his part to enable our salvation. However, salvation is a two-way street and a lifelong process. God will do his part if we do ours. We need to do our part by accepting God's gracious gift of salvation. We do this by living a life of Christian discipleship and by seeking an ever deeper conversion to Christ. Catholics believe we accept God's gift of salvation by living as a follower of Jesus Christ through a life of:

1. faith, including our commitment, surrender, and trust in God;

2. Christian charity and loving service to God and others;
3. and the sacraments, especially Baptism and regular reception of the Holy Eucharist.

We also know that we must persevere in our faith and love for God until the end of our lives. As St. Paul also wrote, "Work out your salvation with fear and trembling" (Phil 2:12). We continue to look to God for the grace to fully "work out" our salvation as we live our daily life here on earth and strive, like St. Paul, to reach the prize of everlasting life made available to us by Christ's redemptive sacrifice on the cross.

Those who accept the gift of salvation that Jesus won for us on the cross have entered into a relationship with God that even death does not end. Death has lost its finality. Those who love and follow Jesus do not go from life to death, but from life to life. Death is only the introduction to a closer presence with God and a fuller experience of divine love and eternal joy.

In summary, salvation is a process in which we participate by forming ourselves in the Word of God through prayer, contemplation, and study; by faithfully fulfilling with love the duties of our state of life; by doing any charitable good works we are able to perform; and by returning regularly to the fountains of grace available in the sacraments of the Church.

We cannot simply rely on ourselves for salvation (e.g., by trying to be a morally good person). Rather, God's help and grace found in the sacraments is essential for our salvation. A recent Vatican document, *On Certain*

Aspects of Christian Salvation, states, "Both the individu-
alistic and the merely interior visions of salvation contra-
dict the sacramental economy through which God willed
to save the human person. The participation, in the
Church, in the new order of relationships begun by Jesus
occurs by means of the sacraments, of which Baptism is
the door, and the Eucharist is the source and the summit.
In this, the inconsistency of the claims to self-salvation
that depend on human efforts alone can be seen."[233]

In short, salvation is not a purely private and personal matter. This Vatican document also highlights
that "salvation is found in the relationships that are born
from the incarnate Son of God and that form the communion of the Church."[234] Thus, we will next look at why
the Catholic Church matters and why we should bother
going to Mass.

Part 4

THE COMMUNITY OF THE CHURCH

Chapter 9

WHY DOES THE CHURCH STILL MATTER TODAY?

We all have a need to belong. We need a sense of community in our lives. This is especially evident during the hard times when we naturally tend to seek the comfort of God and the companionship of others.

This was quite apparent after the horrific events of September 11, 2001. Early that September, my wife took our eldest son to boarding school in Virginia. On the evening of September 11, she was scheduled to fly out of Washington, DC's Reagan National Airport to rejoin myself and our other two children in the Middle East. She clearly didn't make it and instead stayed with her brother in northern Virginia.

While there, my wife went to Mass the following Sunday at a local Catholic church. She was astonished to find that the church was absolutely full—standing room only—and that people were even standing in the doorway and outside on the sidewalk. This was typical at churches all across the country. Why was that? Why is it that people who say they only want to have a "personal relationship" with God outside the Church seek the Church community for comfort when bad things happen? And why is it common for people to say that they will keep others "in their prayers" when bad things happen?

Jesus knows that we have an ongoing need to belong and experience the support and companionship of others, and not just during the hard times. This is one reason why he left us his Church—the community of his followers. So let's explore why it is important to follow Jesus in the Church, not just by ourselves. We will look at some key reasons why active involvement in the life of the Church, especially regularly attending Mass, is Christ's will for his followers.

Christ Willed the Church

Many people today see no practical need to attend Mass regularly—thinking it is not necessary in order to practice their faith—and may perceive the Church's teachings as a set of beliefs that have little relevance to modern life. Many believe they can go it alone and just follow their own conscience and personal beliefs. But is this what Jesus Christ wills for his followers?

We see many instances in the New Testament where Christ willed the formation of the Church to be the community of his followers. When Jesus called the twelve apostles, this action showed that he intended to establish a supportive and active Christian community (see Mk 1:16–20; 3:13–19). In addition to the apostles, this community included many other disciples and followers of Jesus (see Lk 10:1–2).

Like those first followers of Jesus, the Church is the community where we meet Jesus, discover his love for us, and learn to love and follow him in return. As Jim Auer writes regarding why Jesus formed a community:

> Jesus didn't tell his followers, "Go your separate ways and think religious thoughts." He told them to preach the gospel, to baptize, to guard the truth, to heal, to worship together, and to make the love of God visible—in other words, to be an active sign of his continuing presence and work among us. Try getting millions of people to do these things without any organization whatsoever.
>
> In establishing a community, Jesus was building on human nature. We learn, grow, and receive support—for virtually anything and everything—through other people in communities. (Try learning to play soccer with nothing but yourself, a soccer ball, and a rulebook . . . to say nothing of playing it!)[235]

The Church is not a club to which only a few good people are invited. Rather, everyone is warmly welcome. We all need forgiveness and healing, and that is just why the Church exists. Why would we want to turn away from the help, healing, and support found within the community of his followers?

Catholics come together at Mass and during other parish activities to pray and worship God together, as well as to celebrate joys, mourn losses, serve others, provide support, and receive strength for our daily lives as Christians. Catholics recognize the importance of walking together with others in our journey of discipleship. Pope Francis, in an interview published in *America* magazine, stressed the importance of the Church as the people of God when he said, "In the history of salvation, God has saved a people. There is no full identity without belonging to a people. No one is saved alone, as an isolated individual, but God attracts us looking at the complex web of relationships that take place in the human community. God enters into this dynamic, this participation in the web of human relationships."[236]

And after knocking Paul to the ground on the road to Damascus (where he was going to arrest followers of Jesus), what did Jesus mean when he asked Paul, "Why are you persecuting *me*?" (Acts 9:4, emphasis added). By this statement, Jesus plainly equates himself with the Church. Bishop Robert Barron addresses this in his book about Catholicism: "Paul had never met Jesus and was confident that the leader of this rebellious band of followers was safely in his grave. Yet this mysterious Christ insisted that Paul was harassing him personally—"I am Jesus, whom you are persecuting"—a claim that makes sense only on the condition that Jesus has identified himself with his followers in a manner so vivid and incarnate that when they suffer, he suffers."[237]

After coming to understand this reality on the road to Damascus, St. Paul often taught that the Church is the bride of Christ, that the Church is the body of Christ, and that Christ and the Church are one and inseparable. Christ loves his Church as a bridegroom loves his bride (see Ephesians 5:31–32). And, as St. Paul stated in Colossians 1:18, "Christ is the head of his body, the Church."

Jesus Christ wills that all his followers be active members of and contribute to the building up of his body the Church. Pope Francis also emphasized the unity of Christ with his Church when he stated:

> Likewise inseparable are Christ and the Church; the salvation accomplished by Jesus cannot be understood without appreciating the motherhood of the Church. To separate Jesus from the Church would introduce an "absurd dichotomy," as Pope Paul VI stated in his Apostolic Exhortation, *Evangelization in the Modern World*. He wrote that it is not possible "to love Christ but without the Church, to listen to Christ but not the Church, to belong to Christ but outside the Church." For the Church is herself God's great family, which brings Christ to us. . . . Without the Church, Jesus Christ ends up as an idea, a moral teaching, a feeling. Without the Church, our relationship with Christ would be at the mercy of our imagination, our interpretations, our moods.[238]

While the Church is a community of Jesus's followers, this does not mean it is perfect. It never has been and never will be, at least not here on earth. The Church in this world has always been full of imperfect and sinful humans—ever since the betrayals of Peter and Judas.

As Abigail Van Buren, more commonly known as Dear Abby, famously stated, "The Church is a hospital for sinners, not a museum for saints." And as Jesus declared,

"Those who are well do not need a physician, but the
sick do. I did not come to call the righteous but sinners"
(Mk 2:17). Receiving help and healing are major reasons
for regularly attending Church. *Abandoning the Church
because it is full of imperfect people is like abandoning a
gym because it is full of out-of-shape people or not going to
the doctor because sick people are there.*

Because the Church is full of imperfect people, it has
always been a flawed, sinful, human institution filled
with both light and darkness. Scandals in the Church,
such as the terrible and tragic clerical sex abuse scandal,
occur not because of the Church's teachings but because
individual Catholics fail to follow these teachings.[239] To
sexually abuse children while acting as a representative
of Christ and for shepherds of the Church to cover up
such abuse are horribly heinous sins for which these
priests and bishops will ultimately be held accountable
by God. For as the Lord spoke through the prophet Jere-
miah, "Woe to the shepherds who mislead and scatter the
flock of my pasture" (Jer 23:1).

Throughout its history, the Church has been in contin-
ual need of renewal and restoration. As such, the Church
continues to respond to the clerical sex abuse scandal
by taking proactive steps to eradicate these wrongs and
help the victims. For example, dioceses around the world
have created offices of safe environment and child protection that have trained millions of adults to recognize
and report child abuse. The Church has also instituted
widespread zero tolerance policies that require immedi-
ate reporting of alleged child abuse to law enforcement
agencies.[240]

While not ignoring or excusing those who commit such horrible crimes, even when perpetrated by priests and bishops, most Catholics do not leave the Church, because they know it is the original church founded by Jesus Christ and guided by the Holy Spirit for over two thousand years. Despite the failings of individuals who make up the Church, be they clerical or lay, it is the Holy Spirit who continually builds and renews the Church, even today.

Pentecost (see Acts 2:1–13) has long been called the "Birthday of the Church," as that is when Christ's community of disciples were empowered by the Holy Spirit to begin their courageous public proclamation of the message of hope and salvation in Jesus Christ. The Church today and throughout the centuries is the public and visible manifestation of the work of the Holy Spirit.

It is also quite significant that the Church has lasted for two thousand years in spite of many challenges, difficulties, and persecutions. The power and presence of God in the early Church was recognized by the respected Jewish leader and teacher Gamaliel, as we read in Acts 5:27–39:

> When they had brought them [Peter and the apostles] in and made them stand before the Sanhedrin, the high priest questioned them, "We gave you strict orders to stop teaching in that name [Jesus]. Yet you have filled Jerusalem with your teaching and want to bring this man's blood upon us." But Peter and the apostles said in reply, "We must obey God rather than men. The God of our ancestors

raised Jesus, though you had him killed by hanging
him on a tree. God exalted him at his right hand
as leader and savior to grant Israel repentance
and forgiveness of sins. We are witnesses of these
things, as is the Holy Spirit that God has given to
those who obey him."

When they heard this, they became infuriated
and wanted to put them to death. But a Pharisee
in the Sanhedrin named Gamaliel, a teacher of the
law, respected by all the people, stood up, ordered
the men to be put outside for a short time, and said
to them, "Fellow Israelites, be careful what you are
about to do to these men. Some time ago, Theudas
appeared, claiming to be someone important, and
about four hundred men joined him, but he was
killed, and all those who were loyal to him were
disbanded and came to nothing. After him came
Judas the Galilean at the time of the census. He also
drew people after him, but he too perished and all
who were loyal to him were scattered. So now I tell
you, have nothing to do with these men, and let
them go. *For if this endeavor or this activity is of
human origin, it will destroy itself. But if it comes
from God, you will not be able to destroy them;
you may even find yourselves fighting against God."*
(emphasis added)

As Gamaliel postulated, the early Church obviously
did not destroy itself, and the historical fact that the
Catholic Church still exists two thousand years later is
evidence of its divine origin and purpose. Thus, Christ

willed and has supported his Church, the community of his followers, for the past twenty centuries.

Christ Expects Us to Do What He Wills

As we see from the preceding discussion, Jesus Christ specifically willed the formation of his Church for the benefit of his followers and the entire world. In his book *Love Unveiled: The Catholic Faith Explained*, Edward Sri addresses why it is best if we follow Jesus within the community of his Church instead of just by ourselves:

> One danger, however, of seeking God all on our own, apart from the Church, is that we make God in our own image and likeness; it's too easy to tailor a spirituality and morality that suits our own comforts, lifestyles, and interests. After all, being "spiritual but not religious" would be a very appealing option for someone who still wants to have some sense of God in his life—someone whose conscience is uneasy about rejecting God entirely—but who wants to keep God at arm's reach and still do his own thing.
>
> In such a case, it's easier to create my own religious and moral values—values that are comfortable for me—than it is to accept the revelation of Jesus Christ and the teachings of a Church that calls me to ongoing conversion. Rather than follow a moral standard outside myself—one that calls me on to greater responsibility, commitment to others, generosity, and sacrificial love—I can determine

for myself what is right and wrong. I can craft my
own beliefs and values that conveniently justify my
current way of living. In the world of being "spiritual but not religious," I can make myself my own
pope in my own religion: the Church of Me.

But Jesus invites us to something greater. He
calls us out of ourselves. . . . Jesus calls us out of our
limited perspectives and selfish pursuits, so that
we can go beyond ourselves and experience the joy
that comes from living for God and for others, the
joy that comes from living like him in total self-
giving love.

We can't separate Jesus from his Church. In
other words, we can't say that we love the king but
don't accept his kingdom, or that we love Christ but
reject his Church. When we willfully separate ourselves from Christ's Church, we separate ourselves
from Christ himself. When we pick and choose
which teachings of the Church *we* want to follow,
we're in the end picking and choosing what we
want to do instead of fully allowing Christ's teachings to shape our lives.[241]

We know that Christ expects us to do what he wills
(e.g., be active in the Church and seek to follow Church
teachings) when he explicitly stated:

- "If you love me, you will do what I command" (Jn 14:15).
- Jesus said to his disciples, "Whoever listens
  to you listens to me. Whoever rejects you

rejects me. And whoever rejects me rejects the one who sent me" (Lk 10:16).

Jesus's second statement above means if we reject today's successors of Peter and the apostles—the pope and bishops respectively—that we are rejecting Jesus Christ himself, as well as God the Father. That's because the authority of the popes and bishops is God's own authority, given to them by Jesus Christ himself and passed on from the apostles to their successors down through the ages.[242]

Christ Willed the Church's Leadership Structure

The Church provides the leadership structure and authoritative teaching to help us be true and faithful followers of Jesus Christ. The leadership structure that Jesus intended for his Church became clear when he said, "You are Peter and upon this rock I will build my church" (Mt 16:18).

We repeatedly see in the Acts of the Apostles that Peter, the "rock" of Christ's Church, was widely acknowledged to be their central leader. Chapter 15 of the Acts of the Apostles is a case in point showing how the authority of Peter and the apostles was called upon to resolve a major disagreement in the early Church. According to Acts 15:24, this problem was caused by people "who went out without any mandate from us" (i.e., Peter and the apostles). This shows that having a "mandate" from the authority of Peter and the apostles was important in the early Church, right from the beginning.

Furthermore, it is hard to believe that Jesus would

go through the trouble of establishing such a leadership structure—teaching the apostles for three years and
endowing them with his authority to lead and teach—
if all this was to become obsolete in a few decades after
the original apostles died. It seems more reasonable to
believe that Jesus intended the apostolic leadership to be
continued through their successors.

Indeed, this is precisely what we see in the New Testament itself. In Acts 1:15–26, the eleven remaining apostles appointed Matthias to replace Judas as his successor.
The Bible says that Matthias "was added to the group of
eleven apostles" (Acts 1:26). Matthias was considered
equal to the other apostles even though he was not an
original apostle. He possessed the same authority that
they all did. This is the first instance of what has come to
be called "Apostolic Succession."[243]

Thus, we see from Scripture that the Church founded
by Jesus Christ under the leadership of Peter and the
apostles was meant to have a visible leadership structure
that would endure throughout time. All central leaders
of the Catholic Church, a position we now call the pope,
descend in a direct and unbroken line from St. Peter.
As such, today's pope traces his authority directly back
through all the previous popes to the authority that Jesus
first gave to Peter.

The same is true of the bishops as successors of the
original apostles. Every bishop in the Catholic Church
today has been ordained in a direct line from the original apostles. This direct and unbroken Apostolic Succession of Church leaders through the generations is a
historical reality.

However, this does not mean the leadership of the Catholic Church is perfect. The Church, just like any organization, is lead by imperfect people. But that is simply because all human beings are imperfect. Catholics, however, are comforted by the fact that the Church's leaders, despite their imperfections, are linked through Apostolic Succession to Jesus and the apostles under the continuing guidance of the Holy Spirit. As such, the Church has repeatedly shown throughout its history the willingness and ability to reform itself and adapt its methods to the needs of the times (e.g., the councils of Trent and Vatican II).

But some people wonder why we need this leadership structure, especially if it is imperfect. Many people believe that we have Jesus and the Bible, and we don't need anyone telling us what to believe or how to act. Yet because Jesus is not physically present to tell us how to interpret his teachings, we need to rely on some sort of authority. This authority could be anyone, even yourself. However, the authority of the Catholic Church, and subsequently its interpretations, is directly linked through Apostolic Succession to the will of the apostles. Without the leadership structure of the pope and bishops, everyone could make their own interpretation of Jesus's teachings and we would have as many denominations as there are Christians. Monsignor Charles Pope expanded upon this point when he wrote:

> At the heart of the office of the papacy is the uniting of the faithful around a visible vicar (or representative) of Christ. Denominations and groups

that left the Church and severed their ties to the pope demonstrate this very fact by their subsequent disunity.

The fact is that thousands of denominations have emerged in the wake of the Protestant movement that broke from Catholic Church and rejected the pope's authority. And though they claim that Christ and Scripture are the only sources of authority and unity, the remarkable disunity among these denominations belies their claim. Simply put, if no one is pope, everyone is pope.

It is not enough to say, "the Bible clearly teaches 'A,'" because too easily another person will say, "No, Jesus and the Bible actually say 'B.'" Both camps are invoking the Bible and what they sense Jesus and the Holy Spirit are saying to them. So now what?

What usually happens is just what has happened among Protestants: divisions into new denominations or branches of denominations. They all claim the authority of the Bible and the inspiration of the Holy Spirit but cannot agree even on essentials, such as how one is saved, and if once saved, are they always saved? Protestants also have serious divisions regarding the moral issues of our time: abortion, same-sex unions, euthanasia, etc. These are very serious divisions, and there is no real way for Protestant denominations to resolve them. They say Scripture alone is an adequate source of authority. But without an authentic and authoritative interpreter, their own history shows that Scripture can divide as often as it unites. A text, even a sacred text, needs an interpreter that all agree who can authoritatively deal with differences.

And this is a central reason of why we need the pope.[244]

Talk of religious authority, however, can be troubling to many people today. The prevailing attitude in today's culture is, "What right does anyone have to impose his or her beliefs on others?" Regarding religious authority, Bishop Robert Barron writes:

> I realize that this talk of apostolic authority runs counter to many of our cherished assumptions, at least in the West, about democracy, the free play of ideas, freedom of expression, and so on. Why doesn't the Church democratize itself and accept the authority of the majority of its people? Again, it is most important to note that the apostolic Church is not a debating society that endlessly bats around ideas or a democratic polity whose direction is simply a function of popular choice. The Church is grounded in the revelation personally granted to a chosen few, who in turn passed it on to others and so forth.[245]

And as stated in the *Youth Catechism of the Catholic Church* (YOUCAT): "Democracy operates on the principle that all power comes from the people. In the Church, however, all power comes from Christ. That is why the Church has a hierarchical structure."[246]

In this sense, the Catholic Church is organized much like a modern business corporation or military organization with hierarchical lines of authority. Today's corporations and military organizations are structured this way to best accomplish their mission and meet the external and internal challenges they face. Imagine how chaotic and relatively ineffective these organizations would be if they were set up as democracies with every-one having an equal vote.

The same holds true with the Catholic Church. We see in 1 Corinthians 12:28 a description of the hierar-chical nature of the very early Church. Catholics trust that Jesus and the Holy Spirit have guided the Catholic Church throughout its two-thousand-year history to be as effective as possible in proclaiming the good news of salvation and fostering a missionary community of his followers.

Jesus Founded the Catholic Church on the "Rock" of Peter and the Apostles

It is important to note that the Catholic Church has been present in every century, in every generation, from the present time all the way back to the time of the apostles. In other words, since the time of Christ there has never been a time when the Catholic Church was not. As stated by Patrick Madrid in his book *Why Be Catholic? Ten Answers to a Very Important Question*, "When I reflect on the Reformation, I take solace in knowing that, alone among all other Christian groups, the Catholic Church was always there, always on the scene, always present and accounted for, since the days of the apostles."[247]

As we look back in time, however, all of today's other Christian churches and denominations begin to disappear. For example, when we look back to the early 1700s, we do not find the Methodist, Jehovah Witness, Seventh Day Adventist, or Pentecostal churches, nor any of today's nondenominational mega-churches. In fact, no Protestant churches at all, including Anglican (Episcopal), Calvinist (Presbyterian), Lutheran, or Baptist, existed before Martin Luther initiated the Protestant Reformation in the early sixteenth century. And the Church of Latter-day Saints (Mormon) was not founded until the early nineteenth century by Joseph Smith.

While reforms in the Catholic Church have obviously been needed throughout its history, this does not negate the historical reality that it can trace its formation directly back to Jesus Christ himself. *Unlike the post-Reformation Christian churches, only the Catholic Church can credibly claim that it was established by Jesus Christ himself with Peter as its first leader (pope).*

Some claim that the Roman Emperor Constantine, not Jesus, established the Catholic Church. Constantine did indeed legalize the practice of Christianity in the Roman Empire with the Edict of Milan in AD 313. The number of Christians in the Roman Empire had grown significantly in the previous three centuries, despite Christianity being illegal and subject to frequent and brutal persecutions. When Constantine legalized Christianity, he merely recognized its unstoppable growth and significant presence in the Roman Empire. He did not establish the Catholic Church. It existed before. What we now call the Catholic Church has existed since Pentecost, when Peter and the apostles began publicly proclaiming the good news of salvation in Jesus Christ and gathering believers together in communities to pray and break bread. This is what Catholics still do at Mass today.

Some also declare that no Christian community has maintained a true continuity with the early Church.[248] They often claim that the essence of true Christianity was lost after it was legalized by Constantine.[249] If that is so, why did no Church Father (e.g., St. Augustine) or Christian leader at that time write about such a disturbing change if it had in fact occurred?

Just the opposite is the case. Many early Christian writers affirmed that the Catholic Church, led by an unbroken line of bishops, priests, and deacons going back to the apostles, is indeed the true community of disciples established by Jesus Christ. For example, St. Ignatius of Antioch (who was a disciple of the apostle John) wrote in his letter to the Trallians around AD 107, "Correspondingly, everyone must show the deacons respect. They represent Jesus Christ, just as the bishop has the role of the Father, and the presbyters (priests) are like God's council and an apostolic band. *You cannot have a church without these.* I am sure that you agree with me in this" (emphasis added).[250]

The following quote of St. Ignatius of Antioch from his letter to the Philadelphians has convinced some people to convert to Catholicism:[251]

> Make no mistake, my brothers, if anyone joins a schismatic he will not inherit God's Kingdom. If anyone walks in the way of heresy, he is out of

sympathy with the Passion. Be careful, then, to observe a single Eucharist. For there is one flesh of our Lord, Jesus Christ, and one cup of his blood that makes us one, and one altar, just as there is one bishop along with the presbytery and the deacons, my fellow servants. In that way whatever you do is in line with God's will.[252]

The Church founded on the rock of St. Peter has been called "catholic" from very near the beginning. The Greek root of the word *catholic* means "according to the whole" or "universal."[253] Around AD 107, St. Ignatius used the term to refer to the visible and authoritative Church in his letter to the early Christians in Smyrna, "Where the bishop is present, there let the congregation gather, just as where Jesus Christ is, *there is the Catholic Church*."[254]

St. Cyril of Jerusalem also stated the following about the Catholic Church around AD 350, "The Catholic, or universal, Church gets her name from the fact that she is scattered through the whole world from the one end of the earth to the other, and also because she teaches universally and without omission all the doctrines which are to be made known to mankind, whether concerned with visible or invisible things, with heavenly or earthly things.[255]

He continues, "And if ever you are sojourning in cities, inquire not simply where the Lord's House is, nor merely where the Church is, but where is the Catholic Church. For this is the peculiar name of this Holy Church, the mother of us all, which is the spouse of our Lord Jesus Christ, the only-begotten Son of God. . . . In this Holy

Catholic Church receiving instruction and behaving ourselves virtuously, we shall attain the kingdom of heaven,
and inherit eternal life."[256]

The Catholic Church was founded by Jesus Christ
and is grounded in the people who were most privileged
to live in close company with him for several years.[257]
Since the beginning, the Catholic Church's leaders have
been a succession of bishops in an unbroken line back to
Peter and the apostles. This is attested to by many early
Christian writers, including the historian Eusebius and
the Church Fathers. This Apostolic Succession of bishops has continued in the Catholic Church through the
present day.

Without an unbroken and formal line of succession
going directly back to Peter and the apostles, anyone could
just step up and claim religious authority for themselves
independent of the "rock" established by Jesus Christ—
sometimes with dangerous consequences (e.g., Jim Jones
leading more than nine hundred of his followers to their
deaths in a mass suicide).[258] Without Apostolic Succession, what is to ensure that such self-proclaimed Christian leadership is legitimate?

Catholics take comfort in knowing that the Church
and its leadership are the chosen leaders of the sole
religious organization established by Jesus Christ and
the apostles. The Catholic Church is the only post-
Reformation Christian organization that can trace its
leaders and their authority directly back to Jesus and
the apostles in an unbroken line of succession for over
twenty centuries. This makes the Catholic Church an
authority we can rely upon.

Christ Willed the Church's Teaching Authority

Just before ascending into heaven after the Resurrection, Jesus made clear his desire that the Church is to have a lasting teaching authority when he stated to the apostles, "Go, therefore, and make disciples of all nations, baptizing them in the name of the Father, and of the Son, and of the Holy Spirit, *teaching them to observe all that I have commanded you*. And behold, I am with you always, *until the end of the age*" (Mt 28:19–20, emphasis added).

Why would Jesus promise that he would be "with you always, until the end of the age" if this "Great Commission" was meant only for the first apostles? This promise demonstrates that the apostles' mission as leaders of the Church was not meant for them alone but was to last throughout future generations. As apologist Frank Sheed explains, "You will observe that the mission Our Lord gave to the apostles was to last until the end of the world, so that he was speaking to them not as themselves only, but as officials in his kingdom who should have successors until the end of time. . . . What he was doing [with the apostles] was establishing the framework of his kingdom, a kingdom of which there would be no end."[259]

It is also important to note that Jesus's words in the "Great Commission" just before his ascension empowered the leaders of his Church with the authority to teach others to obey his commands (see Mt 28:20). Jesus also alluded to the work of the Holy Spirit in helping the leaders of his Church more fully understand and correctly teach divinely inspired truth when he told the apostles, "The Advocate, the Holy Spirit, whom the Father will send in my name, *will teach* you all things and will remind you of everything I have said to you" (Jn 14:26, emphasis added).

Catholics believe Sacred Scripture is the Word of God and is inspired by the Holy Spirit for the good of the whole Church and each person who ponders its message. The Bible is not just a historical artifact or set of rules for our lives. Rather, God reveals himself to us in Sacred Scripture, and God speaks to us as we prayerfully reflect on what we read in the Bible.

Moreover, Catholics believe the Holy Spirit continues to make God's revealed truth more explicit over time and enlightens the successors of the apostles (the pope and bishops) to "faithfully preserve, expound, and spread" this truth throughout the centuries.[260] This "living transmission of the message of the Gospel in the Church" is called Sacred Tradition (with a capital *T*).[261]

This Sacred Tradition is firmly rooted in the apostles and is Christ's gift to them, as well as to us through Apostolic Succession. Sacred Tradition is the active presence of Christ applying his teachings through the Church in each age by the work of the Holy Spirit. This reality of the divine action of the Holy Spirit within the Church is essential to understanding this living Tradition, including as contained in the doctrinal and moral teachings of the *Catechism of the Catholic Church*.

For Catholics, Sacred Tradition is not in opposition to Sacred Scripture. They complement and confirm one another. As stated in the *Catechism of the Catholic Church*, "Both Scripture and Tradition must be accepted and honored with equal sentiments of devotion and reverence"

(82). Thus, the full "deposit of faith" is conserved and handed on in both the Scriptures and the Tradition of the Catholic Church.[262] There is an immeasurable wealth of wisdom available to us through the inspired Scriptures and the apostolic Tradition of the Church.

The pope and the bishops, as successors of the apostles, form the Magisterium—the teaching authority of the Catholic Church. Catholics believe that the Magisterium is guided by the Holy Spirit in faithfully teaching us what to believe and how to live our faith.[263] Catholics hold that Christ established his Church as an institution blessed with divine authority to reliably teach God's revelation.

If we accept only beliefs consistent with our own experience, we are not accepting them on faith in their divine authenticity but rather on mere human analysis. Thus, Jesus wills that his followers know and obey the formal moral and doctrinal teachings of the Magisterium as contained and conveyed in the living Tradition of his Church, especially as found in the *Catechism of the Catholic Church*.

Most Catholics understand the wisdom of Jesus establishing a lasting and legitimate source of human authority in his Church. Just relying on Scripture alone ("sola scriptura" in Latin) as the only source of divine truth is not enough. Otherwise, people will interpret the Bible differently and do whatever they please. As mentioned earlier, the thousands of different Protestant denominations today show what happens when there is no central human authority in religion.

It is also worth noting that Jesus did not establish a Bible, but he established a Church founded on the "rock" of St. Peter and endowed with his teaching authority. Monsignor Charles Pope makes this point: "The Lord founded the Church; he did not write a book. And he gifted the Church, the apostles and their successors, with the Holy Spirit to remember what he had taught, understand it, authentically hand it on, and bind and loose based on that understanding. It was the Church that collected the New Testament in written form and authorized it."[264]

Islam is another example that highlights the wisdom of Jesus establishing a legitimate human authority in his Church. There is no central hierarchical authority structure in most of Islam that could universally condemn and stop acts of terrorism done in the name of Islam.[265] To understand this difference, just imagine how the pope and bishops would react if some Catholics today did these sorts of things in the name of Catholicism. This would simply not be tolerated, and that would be made abundantly clear by the words and actions of Church leadership. We saw this when the bishops in Ireland publicly condemned the actions of the Irish Republican Army (IRA).[266]

Thus, we see the wisdom of Jesus providing legitimate human authority figures to properly guide the application of the Christian faith in the lives of his followers throughout the ages. While the Church's hierarchical authority has been wrongly used in the past to control people and accomplish political objectives, especially during the Middle Ages, *Catholics trust that the doctrinal and moral teachings of the Magisterium are more reliable than the private opinion of any individual person.*

Catholics who earnestly seek to follow Jesus Christ usually come to understand and accept the wisdom of the Church's moral and doctrinal teachings, especially as found in the *Catechism of the Catholic Church*. Those who are seeking to live a truly Christian life typically do not see the Church's authoritative teachings as burdensome but welcome them as definitive aids and guides on how to faithfully live as a follower of Jesus Christ.[267]

Could this be the crux of the "spiritual but not religious" preference? Could it be that some people do not like to think of themselves as religious simply because they do not want to follow the "rules" of the Church? Could being "spiritual" mean not having to commit ourselves to following any rules or beliefs that we feel are too uncomfortable to keep? But does Jesus really want his followers to ignore the traditional moral and doctrinal teachings of his Church? That is highly unlikely.

The moral and doctrinal teachings of the Church provide the specific instructions and guidance we need for how to be truly spiritual in accord with what God wants. They are like the rules for a game or the map for a journey. As Fr. Dwight Longenecker writes in his blog, "Saying you're spiritual but not religious is like saying you love sports but you don't play a sport and don't watch it on TV or go to any games, because once you tried to play the sport or even go to the games you would have to be taking part in the rules that make sport actually happen."[268]

Catholics trust the Church's moral and doctrinal teachings because they are based on a two-thousand-year heritage of helping people achieve true happiness in this life and in the eternal life to come. Human nature does not change over the generations, and neither does what is needed for us to be fully human and fully alive.

The Church's moral teachings, in particular, are not some arbitrary "rules" and restrictions concocted by old men in the Vatican to make us unhappy. Rather, they are the owner's manual for the human soul, handed down from God himself, and based on an accurate understanding of human nature and what is actually best for our own good.[269] As St. Cyprian wrote way back in the third century, "The commands of the Gospel, most beloved brethren, are nothing else than God's lessons, the foundations on which to build up hope, the supports for strengthening faith, the food that nourishes the heart. They are the rudder for keeping us on the right course, the protection that keeps our salvation secure. As they instruct the receptive minds of believers on earth, they lead safely to the kingdom of heaven."[270]

To a devout Christian, therefore, being religious and spiritual do not represent an either/or proposition. Rather, to a believer in the God of the Bible and God's plan for our salvation, religious and spiritual represent a both/and proposition. They exist together since religion puts substance in the spiritual. Religion defines the beliefs, worship, and morality needed for happiness in this life and salvation in the next. For a believer, the words *spiritual* and *religious* overlap so much that they are interchangeable.

Faithful Catholics understand that only with the Church can they find the support and guidance needed to fully love and truly live as a disciple of Jesus Christ. As Patrick Madrid writes in his book *Why Be Catholic?*:

The voice of our conscience warns us against doing things we know deep down are bad and wrong, and, after we've done them, it reminds us of our guilt and also prods us to repent and turn away from sin. This is true for everyone, everywhere. It is a universal human condition, because our innate awareness of good and evil and that we should do what is good and avoid doing what is evil is written on our hearts. In other words, God hardwired us for virtue and moral integrity. Serious sin is like a rogue electrical surge, a voltage spike of passion or malice that will thoroughly fry the circuits of your soul if you give in to it.

The Catholic Church offers the solution to the problem of sin—a divinely designed surge protector of truth—in its moral teachings. To use a different analogy, Catholic moral teachings are akin to flashing lights and warning signs on a highway (Bridge Out! Slow Down! Flooding Ahead! Turn Around—Don't Drown!), and its sacraments repair and restore the damage we inflict on ourselves when we don't heed those warning signs and get ourselves into everything from fender-benders to high-speed, head-on collisions.

This is why I am Catholic and why you should be, too. The Catholic Church, with all its problems and sinful members, teaches the truth that will set us free, even though not every Catholic obeys those teachings.[271]

Fortunately, the sacraments are available through the

Catholic Church to "repair and restore the damage we inflict on ourselves" and bestow God's power and presence—divine grace that actually helps us grow in holiness and live an authentic Christian life.

Holiness, not just "being nice," is what God desires for us. Since God is absolute holiness, he can accept nothing less in his presence. In order to be with God in heaven, we need to be perfect as God is perfect. For as Jesus said, "You must be perfect, just as your Father in heaven is perfect" (Mt 5:48). As Scripture also states, "Nothing unclean shall enter it [heaven], nor anyone who does abominable things or tells lies" (Rv 21:27). Anyone who has not been completely freed from the tendency to sin is, to some extent, "unclean."

The divine grace and power we need to grow in holiness—which the Lord calls us to, offers us, and requires of us—are found in the Church, especially the sacraments. Once we realize that my goodness or niceness is wholly insufficient without the grace of Christ perfecting it, life in the Church, warts and all, becomes not merely possible but the only possibility.

Christ Willed the Sacraments

A truly religious person relates to and worships God through both the physical and the spiritual dimensions of life. Christ knew that, which is why he left us the seven sacraments—Baptism, Confirmation, Eucharist, Reconciliation, Matrimony, Holy Orders, and the Anointing of the Sick.[272]

The seven sacraments of the Catholic Church are when and how God spiritually feeds us, heals us, and strengthens us.[273] They are the primary means by which the Holy Spirit makes God's grace and power available to us today. The *Catechism of the Catholic Church* states, "Sacraments are 'powers that come forth' from the Body of Christ, which is ever-living and life-giving. They are actions of the Holy Spirit at work in his Body, the Church" (1116).

Patrick Madrid addresses the purpose of the sacraments when he writes:

> Because God loves us and created us for happiness and freedom, through the sacraments He provides the remedies to heal and repair our self-inflicted wounds of sin. You can say that He is the Divine Physician. He's got the cure for what ails you. The cure is found in the sacraments of the Church.
>
> Just as our bodies need nourishment to flourish, so, too, do our souls. The sacraments are to the soul what food, water, and medicine are to the body.
>
> Three key effects are accomplished in the soul of one who receives the sacraments. First, the soul is further purified, cleansed from those base things that pose a barrier to God's holiness. Second, the soul is strengthened and inured against the corrosive effects of sin. And third, the soul's capacity for grace—in a sense, similar to the lungs' capacity to breath in air—is expanded.[274]

Christ willed the sacraments for our benefit through

the gift of the Holy Spirit at work in his Church. *The sacraments are gifts of God available to us only through the Church.* As per the *Catechism*: "It is in the Church, in communion with all the baptized, that the Christian fulfills his vocation. From the Church he receives the Word of God containing the teachings of 'the law of Christ.' From the Church he receives the grace of the sacraments that sustains him on the 'way'" (2030).

But why did Christ will that God's grace be made available to us through the sacraments? The answer lies in how we humans relate to each other through our physical bodies and our five senses. When "the Word became flesh and dwelt among us" (Jn 1:14), God began a new way of relating to humans. In Jesus, God became human and made himself present to our bodily senses. As the incarnation of Christ makes clear, God desires to relate to us in the fullness of our human experience, including both the physical and spiritual dimensions.

Catholics have an incarnational faith because God not only shares his life with us in an invisible or "spiritual" way but also through the physical realities that we experience with our five senses in the sacraments. We see, hear, taste, touch, and smell God's divine presence and power though the sacraments. They are God's "incarnational" way of relating to us.

Just as we relate to each other through our bodily senses, the sacraments are how we relate to God through our bodily senses. The sacraments express a spiritual reality though a physical reality—water, oil, bread, wine, incense, etc. It is the physical component that leads us to a deeper experience of the grace and love of God.

Thus, the sacraments are outward physical signs of an inner spiritual reality. As Patrick Madrid writes, "The sacraments are composed of tangible elements like water and bread, but because Christ is working in them, they are vastly more than just symbols or metaphors for getting clean, satisfying hunger, and becoming strong and healthy. They actually *do* what they symbolize."[275]

Through the physical reality of the sacraments, we reach up to God and God reaches down to us. They are God's "channels" for sharing divine grace and power with us and our way of relating to and worshipping God through our bodily senses. And they are available to us only in the Church. This is affirmed by the *Catechism*: "Seated at the right hand of the Father and pouring out the Holy Spirit on his Body which is the Church, Christ now acts through the sacraments he instituted to communicate his grace. The sacraments are perceptible signs (words and actions) accessible to our human nature. By the action of Christ and the power of the Holy Spirit they make present efficaciously the grace that they signify" (1084).

The sacraments are signs and instruments of grace, instituted by Christ and entrusted to the Church, by which the transforming power of the Holy Spirit is truly encountered.[276] Those with the required dispositions are empowered by this divine grace and power to bear the fruit necessary for salvation by means of persevering in loving service to God and others.[277] The required dispositions for fruitful reception of the sacraments include a sincere willingness to awaken faith, experience a conversion of heart, and adhere to God's will in our life.[278]

Through the sacraments, God gives us the grace to say yes to God's will and to reject whatever is contrary to his loving plan for our lives.

Jesus Christ comes to us in the sacraments and gives us the grace we need to truly live our life as his disciple and help us in our daily walk as Christians. All the sacraments offer a direct encounter with Jesus Christ. When we become weak, frightened, hurt, or uncertain, we can draw upon God's power and grace through the sacraments, particularly the Eucharist. Why wouldn't we want that help and support, which is found only in the Church?

Christ Willed the Eucharist

We also know Jesus specifically willed that we regularly celebrate the sacrament of the Eucharist, or Holy Communion, when he said at the Last Supper after breaking bread and blessing the cup of wine, "Do this in remembrance of me" (Lk 22:19; 1 Cor 11:23–25). Jesus made clear that his followers are called to regularly gather together in community to remember and celebrate what he did for us on the cross and to realize that he continues to be present with us for all time. We are asked to remember not only who Jesus is but also how and why he died for us. In this celebratory gathering, he wants to strengthen his followers and bring them closer to each other and to him.

The *Catechism of the Catholic Church* calls the Eucharist the "source and summit of the Christian life" (1324).

The Mass being the "source and summit" of our faith means that our faith has its beginning and finds its highest expression in the celebration of the Holy Eucharist. It is the "source" of our faith since we partake of the very source of our lives—Christ himself—and we encounter the goal or "summit" of our lives—Christ himself. Thus, Christ wills that the Mass, when we receive the Eucharist, be central in our lives as Christians.

Following are some quotes on what previous generations of Catholics have said about the Mass.[279] As you read them, please note which of these quotes you find to be the most striking.

- "The Mass is the most perfect form of prayer." Pope Paul VI
- "The celebration of Holy Mass is as valuable as the death of Jesus on the cross." St. Thomas Aquinas
- "If we really understood the Mass, we would die of joy." St. John Vianney
- "For each Mass we hear with devotion, Our Lord sends a saint to comfort us at death." Revelation from Christ to St. Gertrude
- "Put all the good works in the world against one Holy Mass; they will be as a grain of sand beside a mountain." St. John Vianney
- "It would be easier for the world to survive without the sun than to do without Holy Mass." St. Padre Pio
- "When Mass is celebrated, the sanctuary is filled with countless angels who adore the

divine victim immolated on the altar." St. John Chrysostom

- "Without doubt, the Lord grants all favors which are asked of him in Mass, provided they be fitting for us." St. Jerome
- Once St. Teresa was overwhelmed with God's goodness and asked Our Lord, "How can I thank you?" He replied, "Attend one Mass."
- "I believe that were it not for the Holy Mass, as of this moment the world would be in the abyss." St. Leonard of Port Maurice
- "A single Mass offered for oneself during life may be worth more than a thousand celebrated for the same intention after death." St. Anselm
- "What graces, gifts and virtues the Holy Mass calls down." St. Leonard of Port Maurice

Which of these quotes are the most striking? Is there a disconnect between the typical experience of Mass and what these quotes say about the Mass? If so, why? Maybe we need to learn more about what really happens at Mass and some good reasons to regularly and actively participate in the Mass. This is what we will explore next.

Chapter 10

WHY GO TO MASS?

Not every Mass is going to be a deeply moving experience. Even lifelong Catholics may have grown so used to the ritual that they aimlessly go through the motions and find their minds wandering. So why bother going to Mass? The following are several important reasons for regularly attending and actively participating at Mass. These reasons are not presented in order of importance but are listed roughly along the lines of how they are experienced during the flow of the Mass.

To Gather Together in Christian Community

One reason we go to Mass is to gather together in Christian community. When we gather together, we are able to enjoy and benefit from one another's company. We are able to give each other support, encouragement, and affirmation when we gather together. The Mass originated when early Christians gathered together, shared a meal, and supported one another through the joys and difficulties of living a Christian life. Living a truly Christian life is not easy, and a supportive community is vitally important. We cannot live as Christians just by ourselves. We are, rather, called to enter into relationships with others on our Christian journey through this life. As it says in the New Testament, "We should not stop gathering together with other believers, as some of you are doing. Instead, we must continue to encourage each other even more as we see the day of the Lord coming" (Heb 10:25, GWT).

Without fellow Christians, our faith would be stunted, fade away, and die. An example illustrates this: Imagine a fire made up of glowing embers. It burns. It gives out light. It gives out heat. Remove one ember from the rest and, on its own, that single ember will soon lose its fire and stop glowing. The fire within it will die. So it is with the faith of those who stay apart from the community of the followers of Jesus—the Church.

But it is more than that. Jesus Christ is really and truly present in the community of his followers that gather together at Mass. As Jesus said, "For where two or three are gathered together in my name, there am I in the midst of them" (Mt 18:20). This means that God is more fully present with us when we worship together with other people. By participating in Mass, we become part of the Catholic community, together with Jesus and the saints, where we live or where we happen to be.

The Mass has many other names, and each gives a clue to its rich meaning. These include Liturgy, Eucharist, Lord's Supper, and Holy Communion. The word *liturgy* comes from a Greek word meaning "the work of the people." This word emphasizes that the Mass is an action (not a thing) that we all (not just the priest) have an important role in doing. In fact, for the first several centuries of Christianity, the word *mass* was a verb and not a noun. The early Christians gathered to do liturgy, not just go to the Liturgy. So it should be with us today.

To Celebrate With Song

Congregational singing has always been one of the most powerful ways for the Christian community to pray together. In the words of St. Augustine, "Singing is praying twice."

Whether one listens to Handel's "Messiah," Newton's "Amazing Grace," or any one of thousands of other hymns, all good liturgical music has one thing in common: it inspires us in a way that nothing else can. There is something uplifting in singing along with a choir and the congregation. Many people find liturgical music quite inspiring and an important part of worshipping God in a community of believers.

Just as Christianity has inspired some of the greatest music ever written, there is no denying the importance that liturgical music plays in worship. It is no secret that having a good choir and music program at Mass increases attendance. But liturgical music cannot be mistaken as entertainment. We do not go to Mass to be entertained. It is much more than that.

Music in worship is a means incline you toward prayer, contemplation, and reflection. Liturgical music is carefully selected to reinforce the central message of the Word of God, to unite our many prayers into one, to draw into union with each other, and to be an expression of contemplative praise that words alone do not offer. Truth set to music, embodied in a singing community, can seep into our souls and convince us when spoken words may fall short, and can unite us into the one holy People of God, the Spouse of Christ.

To Worship God and Pray Together

We are all spiritual and religious people. That is how God made us. We can surely pray by ourselves. And we should. As a Christian, however, that is not enough. Jesus established the pattern for his disciples to pray together, to be in community together, and to go out in the world and live the Christian life together. Jesus taught the apostles to gather together in prayer, and we continue this tradition today with the Mass. From the first days after the Resurrection, the apostles set Sunday aside to gather for Eucharist. This has always been a part of who we are.

If we love God, we will spend time with God in the way he wants. And God wants us to give ourselves to him in frequent communal worship, not just for God's own sake but for ours as well. From the earliest days of Christianity, men and women have brought their needs to the table of the Lord, confident they will be joined to Christ's great act of intercession before the Father. Thus, we can bring our deepest desires to the table of the Lord at Mass, confident they will be heard.

We come together at Mass to join our prayers of adoration, contrition, thanksgiving, and supplication, the acronym "ACTS," with other members of the faith community. Supplication is asking God for something we need (prayers of petition) or something someone else needs (prayers of intercession). In prayers of petition, we are called to acknowledge that we are dependent upon God, and "when we share in God's saving love, we understand that every need can become the object of petition" (CCC 2633). Whereas in prayers of intercession, we "look not only to our own interests, but also to the interests of others" (CCC 2635). We should also remember the needs of others in our supplications, especially at Mass. It does not matter if these others are separated from us by distance or death. The Mass brings us all together as the Body of Christ and unites those of us on earth with the communion of saints already in the glory of heaven.[280]

At Mass, we speak to God through our singing, in our personal prayers, and in our communal responses and prayers. It has been said that just like we have two lungs, there are two lungs of prayer; namely, private prayer and liturgical prayer. St. John Vianney said of liturgical prayer, "Private prayer is like straw scattered here and there: If you set it on fire, it makes a lot of little flames. But gather these straws into a bundle and light them, and you get a mighty fire, rising like a column into the sky; public prayer is like that."[281]

To Receive God's Help and Healing

We can receive God's help and healing in our lives at Mass. It is hard to do difficult things alone. Following Jesus can be hard work. We need God's help to keep going in life, to live as Jesus and his Church call us to live. We go to Mass to receive the help we need to live a truly Christian life.

At Mass, we are assured we are not alone in our efforts. Going to Mass gives us a special sense that there are other people who are also struggling to live better lives, and maybe we can all make it together. We do not go to Mass to proclaim our holiness. Rather, we go to humbly seek God's help and healing.

We need God's help and the support of others to change our lives, to repent, and to convert. At Mass, we acknowledge our mistakes and admit that we have sinned in thought, in word, and in deed, in what we have done and in what we have failed to do, and we seek God's forgiveness for our sins. God then mercifully displays his patience with our shortcomings by wiping away our everyday (venial) sins.[282] Every Mass is, therefore, a healing celebration.

To Receive the Word of God

A fifth reason to regularly attend Mass is so we can receive the Word of God during the first of the two main parts of the Mass—the Liturgy of the Word. During the Liturgy of the Word, we hear God speak to us in the readings from Scripture as the Church feeds the People of God from the table of his Word.[283] As the world's Catholic bishops stated in the Second Vatican Council's *Constitution on the Sacred Liturgy*, it is Christ himself "who speaks when the holy scriptures are read in the Church" (7). Christ is truly present in the Word of God proclaimed at Mass.

We also hear Christ's voice in the homily when the priest applies the inspired words of Scripture to our lives. Catholics believe at Mass that Christ is also truly present in the person of the priest. In the homily, the priest focuses on the Scripture texts or some other texts from the liturgy, drawing from them lessons that may help us to live better lives and be more faithful to Christ's call to grow in holiness.[284] The homily is for everyone, but Christ places a personal message for each of us in every homily. We know that if we listen in the right frame of mind, asking Jesus to open our hearts and minds, we will receive a message, a personal message.

In his Apostolic Exhortation *Sacrament of Charity*, Pope Benedict XVI wrote, "By the preaching of God's Word, faith is nourished and grows in the grace-filled encounter with the Risen Lord which takes place in the sacraments: faith is expressed in the rite, while the rite reinforces and strengthens faith" (13).

God speaks to each of us in a special way through the Word of God, the homily, and the various prayers spoken during the Mass. By attentively listening to the revealed Word of God in the Liturgy of the Word, including reflecting on its meaning for our lives in the homily, we are prepared to enter into Christ's ultimate act of love for us—his sacrificial death on the cross—in the second main part of the Mass, the Liturgy of the Eucharist.

To Re-Present Christ's Sacrifice on the Cross

A major reason to go to Mass is to share in Christ's sacrifice on the cross at Calvary, as he asked us to do at the Last Supper. During the second main part of the Mass—the Liturgy of the Eucharist—God makes present and available to us, with lavish generosity, the saving power of the cross.

Jesus established the Eucharist at the Last Supper when he said, "This is my body given for you," and, "This is my blood poured out for you." The language Jesus used was clearly sacrificial when he said that his body would be "given for you" and his blood would be "poured out for you." The Last Supper made present in anticipation what was to happen the very next day on the altar of the cross at Calvary. Only in light of these words of Jesus at the Last Supper is Calvary's meaning understood. At Calvary, the meaning of Jesus's words and the link between the Last Supper and his sacrifice on the cross became clear.

In the same way, every single Mass is a unique and marvelous sacrifice. It is the mystical reality where the very same sacrifice of Christ on Calvary is re-presented (not represented, or symbolic). The Eucharist makes present for us here and now Christ's once-for-all sacrifice so that we might praise and thank God for this great act of love done for our salvation and forgiveness of sins.

The Greek word *eucharistein* means "to give thanks." The Holy Eucharist is the sacramental celebration of the Paschal Mystery, which is Christ's saving work of redemption brought about by his crucifixion, death, and resurrection. At every Mass, we give thanks for and participate in Jesus Christ's one and abiding sacrifice on the cross for the salvation of the world.

Christ willed that his sacrificial death be perpetuated through the ages. At the Last Supper when Jesus said "do this," he made clear that he wanted to perpetuate, for all time, this sacrificial meal and his sacrificial death on the altar of Calvary. He did this so that we and the people of all places, all times, and all ages could enter into it and so that we could offer our lives in union with his perfect sacrifice, as well as partake of the fruits of that sacrifice offered for our salvation and for building up the body of Christ.

At every Mass, we join in a special way with the event of the crucifixion, and we offer to God the same sacrifice that Jesus offered to the Father on the cross. We also offer our lives and ask the Father to accept everything we have—our joys, our talents, our sorrows, our all.

When we participate in the Mass, everything we do is given eternal value. At Mass, we participate in Christ's redeeming of the world when we unite our sufferings and trials with those of Christ on the cross. As St. Paul wrote, "Now I rejoice in my sufferings for your sake, and in my flesh I am filling up what is lacking in the afflictions of Christ on behalf of his body, which is the Church" (Col 1:24). At Mass, our lives (struggles, good deeds, etc.) are offered through the sacrifice of Jesus to God the Father. With and like Christ, at the Mass we learn to overcome fear, discouragement, and anxiety so as to live in the freedom of God's children.

In short, the Mass is much more than just a symbolic memorial. In the Mass, we participate in the act by which divinity and humanity are reconciled, and we eat the sacrificed body and drink the poured-out blood of Jesus Christ, the Lamb of God. Jesus left us the gift of the sacrament of the Holy Eucharist because it was not enough for him that his followers should merely hear about his saving death and resurrection. Rather, Jesus wanted all of his followers, through every generation until the end of time, to "take and eat" and have a direct encounter with his very body, blood, soul, and divinity that is fully present in the Eucharist.

To Be Filled With and Become More Like Jesus Christ

Unquestionably, a major reason Catholics go to Mass is to be filled with and become more like Jesus Christ by receiving his body and blood in the sacrament of the Eucharist. When Jesus blessed the bread and wine at the Last Supper—saying "This is my body" and "This is my blood"—he meant it literally (see Jn 6:51–67 and chapter 8 herein).

Today, the priest at Mass speaks the same words to signify that the bread and wine really and truly become the body, blood, soul, and divinity of our Lord and Savior Jesus Christ. At the consecration during the Liturgy of the Eucharist, the priest asks God the Father to send the power of the Holy Spirit upon the gifts of bread and wine so they become Jesus Christ himself.

The consecration of the bread and wine at Mass changes the substance but not the physical appearance of the bread into Christ's body and the substance of the wine into Christ's blood. This is not a mere symbol, but Jesus's real flesh and real blood under the appearance of bread and wine. The Eucharist is the most intimate and real presence of Our Lord and Savior Jesus Christ on this earth. As stated in the *Catechism of the Catholic Church*, quoting the Council of Trent:

> Because Christ our Redeemer said that it was truly his body that he was offering under the species of bread, it has always been the conviction of the Church of God, and this holy Council now declares again, that by the consecration of the bread and wine there takes place a change of the whole substance of the bread into the substance of the body of Christ our Lord and of the whole substance of the wine into the substance of his blood. This change the holy Catholic Church has fittingly and properly called transubstantiation. (1376)

The Real Presence of Christ's body and blood in the Eucharistic bread and wine has been the constant teaching of the Church since the very beginning. It is not some medieval invention.

Belief in the Real Presence was a cornerstone of Christian worship in the early Church. This belief was so widely held that the early Christians were even accused of being cannibals.[285] One of the reasons that Christians were persecuted by the Roman Empire was because it was thought that they actually ate human flesh and drank human blood during their gatherings.

Many of the early Church Fathers, including Saints

Ignatius of Antioch (35–107), Irenaeus of Lyons (130–202), and Clement of Alexandria (150–215), wrote about the Real Presence with a vigor and clarity that is most impressive.[286] For example, St. Ignatius of Antioch wrote in his letter to the Romans around AD 105, "I have no delight in corruptible food, nor in the pleasures of this life. I desire the bread of God, the heavenly bread, the bread of life, which is the flesh of Jesus Christ, the Son of God, who became afterwards of the seed of David and Abraham; and I desire the drink of God, namely His blood, which is incorruptible love and eternal life.[287]

Clearly, he held the Eucharist to be the real body and blood of Jesus Christ and not a mere symbol. And St. Justin Martyr wrote around AD 150, "This food we call the Eucharist. . . . For we do not receive these things as common bread or common drink; but as Jesus Christ our Savior being incarnate by God's Word took flesh and blood for our salvation, so also we have been taught that the food consecrated by the Word of prayer which comes from him, from which our flesh and blood are nourished by transformation, is the flesh and blood of that incarnate Jesus."[288]

St. Cyril of Jerusalem taught in the middle of the fourth century, "Do not, then, regard the Eucharistic elements as ordinary bread and wine: they are in fact the Body and Blood of the Lord, as he himself has declared. Whatever your senses may tell you, be strong in faith. You have been taught and you are firmly convinced that what looks and tastes like bread and wine is not bread and wine but the Body and the Blood of Christ."[289]

So we see that belief in the Real Presence of Christ's

body and blood under the appearance of Eucharistic bread and wine was present from the very beginning of Christianity. But the question is why? Why did Christ wish to leave us his body and blood in this manner?

It is because the Eucharist is spiritual food for our eternal soul. The Eucharist is spiritual food for spiritual life. We need the spiritual strength that comes from Holy Communion to pray, develop our virtues, and resist temptation. Without physical food, we will die physically. In the same way, without spiritual food, we will die spiritually. This supernatural food heals our body and soul and gives us strength for our journey heavenward.

But it is even more than that. It has been said, "*We are what we eat.*" Receiving Holy Communion helps to spiritually transform us into Christ's likeness because it is Jesus Christ himself whom we receive. As Fr. Tom Washburn writes in his blog:

> The Eucharist is true food and drink but at the same time it is very different from every other food and drink. The great difference lies in these words of Christ which St. Augustine heard in prayer, "You will not change me into yourself as you would food of your flesh; but you will be changed into me." We transform ordinary food into our own bodies but the food of the Eucharist transforms us into the body of Christ.
>
> When we regularly eat, that food becomes energy for our bodies, but when we eat this bread and drink this cup, the food of the Eucharist transforms us into the body of Christ. We become what

we receive. We receive the Body of Christ in the Eucharist so that we may become the Body of Christ in the world. "You will not change me into yourself . . . you will be changed into me!"

God does not force transformation on us, He invites us into it. You are today, and at every Eucharist, invited into the transformation. Open the eyes of your heart, open your soul, to let Jesus, really, truly, physically present today in this Eucharist, change you, shape you, mold you to more closely resemble the same Lord we receive.[290]

By thoughtfully participating in the Holy Eucharist, Christ gradually changes our values, our thoughts, our words, and our actions to become more like his own. This enables us to become a better person and a better Christian. By receiving Holy Communion, we receive the graces needed to become more like Jesus Christ. Pope Francis addressed this when he taught:

Each time we receive Communion, we resemble Jesus more; we transform ourselves more fully into Jesus. As the Bread and the Wine are converted into the Body and Blood of the Lord, so too those who receive it with faith are transformed into a living Eucharist. You reply "Amen" to the priest who distributes the Eucharist saying "the Body of Christ"; that is, you recognize the grace and the commitment involved in becoming the Body of Christ. Because when you receive the Eucharist, you become the Body of Christ. This is beautiful; it is very beautiful. As it unites us to Christ, tearing us away from our selfishness, Communion opens us and unites us to all those who are a single thing in him. This is the wonder of Communion: we become what we receive![291]

This is not a new understanding of the Eucharist, but has been the constant teaching of the Catholic Church since the beginning. For example, Pope St. Leo the Great stated in the fifth century, "For the effect of our sharing in the body and blood of Christ is to change us into what we receive."[292] And Bishop St. Hilary of Poitiers wrote about AD 360:

> We believe that the Word became flesh and that we receive his flesh in the Lord's Supper. How then can we fail to believe that he really dwells within us? When he became man, he actually clothed himself in our flesh, uniting it to himself forever. In the sacrament of his body he actually gives us his own flesh, which he has united to his divinity. This is why we are all one, because the Father is in Christ, and Christ is in us. He is in us through his flesh and we are in him. With him we form a unity which is in God.
>
> Christ himself bore witness to the reality of this unity when he said: He who eats my flesh and drinks my blood lives in me and I in him. No one will be in Christ unless Christ himself has been in him; Christ will take to himself only the flesh of those who have received his flesh.[293]

The principal fruit of receiving the Eucharist,

therefore, is a deeper and more intimate union with Jesus Christ himself. This is why Catholics are called to receive Holy Communion regularly and reverently.

Amazingly, Jesus is still here with us two thousand years later in the Eucharistic bread and wine. Jesus has chosen to stay with us in a truly special and humble way. When we see Jesus hidden in the Sacred Host, we can begin to see him in all human beings. By his continuous presence, Jesus reminds us that we are not alone in our earthly struggles and that he will mend our human weaknesses and help us grow in love and holiness.

The Eucharist is very important because in the words of Jesus, "Whoever eats my flesh and drinks my blood has eternal life." The Eucharist, as the eternal presence and power of God, eternalizes those who consume it by making us ready to spend an eternity with God in heaven. What could be more important in life?

To Strengthen Us for Our Mission

An additional reason to regularly attend Mass is to strengthen us for our mission here on earth. This mission is to go forth to love and serve the Lord and one another. Jesus summed up our mission in Matthew 22:37–39 when he said, "You shall love the Lord, your God, with all your heart, with all your soul, and with all your mind. This is the greatest and the first commandment. The second is like it: You shall love your neighbor as yourself."

The most challenging effect of the Mass is living afterwards with the same self-giving love that the Eucharist celebrates. In our daily lives, we are called to live as Christ lived and act as Christ would act. We are to be "Christ with skin on."

Fortunately, the Mass not only gives us a sense of what we ought to do but also strengthens us for accomplishing it. Our Lord does not send us as orphans. Rather, Jesus equips us for the journey. The Christ we receive as food in the Eucharist truly enables us to go forth and do God's work in the world.

Let us always be mindful of the strength and grace we receive from our encounter with Christ in the four forms of his Real Presence at Mass. Catholics believe Christ is truly present at Mass in the forms of the:

1. community gathered in his name,
2. the Word of God,
3. the person of the priest,
4. and the Eucharist.

The word *mass* is an English translation of the Latin term *missa*, which means "to send." At one time, the people were dismissed with the Latin words "Ite, missa est," meaning "Go, you are sent." The celebration takes its name from the sending forth that occurs at the end of every Mass. The word *missa* comes from the word *missio*, which is the root of the English word *mission*.[294]

The Mass does not simply come to an end, but has an inherently missionary dimension. Those assembled are sent forth to bring the fruits of the Eucharist to the world. The Mass is a dismissal or commissioning to go forth as his disciples and make Christ present to others and to the world. We go forth from the church building empowered to live the Word of God and bear witness to the risen and saving Christ in our daily lives.

Just as our Lord walked the streets of Jerusalem, so now Jesus is more fully within each of us to help us live as his disciples. Together with Christ we can make a positive difference in our world. So the final test of whether the Mass "works" is: "By their fruits shall you know them" (Mt 7:16). And our fruit must be the loving service of God and others.

To Develop and Express Our Faith Commitment

Another reason to attend Mass at least once each week is because this helps us develop and express our faith commitment. The Mass can sometimes seem boring. We don't always want to go to Mass, and we certainly don't always seem to have the time. We sometimes think to ourselves, "I really don't have time for this. Why am I doing this?"

But like any other major commitment, our spiritual life involves developing self-discipline and motivation. Nothing in life that is taken seriously exists without self-discipline and perseverance. We should think of our commitment to regularly attend Mass as the same sort of commitment we make for any personal relationship that matters to us. We can surely give God just one hour of our time each week. After all, one hour is only 0.6 percent of a week's time.

Human beings ordinarily develop by forming habits, some good and some bad. Regularly going to Mass helps develop the good habit of worshiping and glorifying God.

The discipline of regularly worshiping God helps us grow into being habitual "adorers of God," even when we do not feel like it. Thus, active participation in the Mass is an opportunity to express our commitment to Jesus Christ and to help fulfill our role in the Church.

At Mass, we have the opportunity to stand up and publicly proclaim that we believe in God, Jesus Christ, the Holy Spirit, the Catholic Church, the communion of saints, the forgiveness of sins, and life everlasting. Proclaiming these beliefs publicly at Mass is a powerful statement of our allegiance and an opportunity to recommit ourselves to the truths of the Christian faith.

Children and young people, however, often wonder why the Mass can't be more fun and exciting. But instead of asking, "What should I get out of Mass?"; the better question is, "What should I put into the Mass?" We are there to pray, worship, and thank God. God is not there to entertain us. It helps to remember the words of St. John Vianney: "If we really understood the Mass, we would die of joy." Bill Dunn, who returned to the Catholic Church many years after losing his faith to atheism, writes:

> If you ask people why they no longer go to Mass, by far the most common answer you will hear is, "Because I don't get anything out of it." Literally millions of American Catholics stay home each and every Sunday because they, quote, "Don't get anything out of Mass."
>
> Is going to Mass similar to going to a movie or a ball game, or going out to a restaurant, where

the whole reason for going is to get some personal enjoyment or entertainment? No, of course not.

Mass is not a show; it's not a party; it's not entertainment. Mass is community worship where believers gather to offer praise and thanksgiving to the God who created them, and to enter into a mystical communion with the Almighty Lord by receiving the body and blood, soul and divinity, of Jesus Christ in the Eucharist.

Many people think of Mass as a show. The priest is the performer; God is the prompter, who whispers to the priest what to say; and the people in the pews are the audience, who sit back and expect to be entertained. And if the priest does not entertain the audience, either with inspirational or humorous comments, then the show is a flop. By this standard, virtually every Mass is a flop.

But in reality, here are the correct roles: The people in the pews are the performers; the priest is the prompter who guides the pace of the performance; and the audience is God. When we go to Mass, we're not going as audience members to be entertained. We're going as performers to put on a presentation of prayer and worship and gratitude for our audience of One: God Himself.

In yet another amazing Christian paradox, when we forget about trying to "get something" out of Mass, and instead focus on putting something into Mass, that's when we discover that we truly do get something out of it after all. When we go to Mass determined to give God our best performance of prayer and devotion and thanksgiving, we are filled with His joy and peace and love. We enter into a personal relationship with the Eternal Being who knows us and loves us and has prepared a heavenly dwelling for us. And that is a whole lot better than any Broadway show or ball game.[295]

To Follow the Commands of God, Jesus, and the Church

The final of these "Top Ten" reasons to go to Mass is to obey the commands of God, Jesus, and the Catholic Church. The third of the Ten Commandments given to Moses by God is, "Remember to keep holy the Sabbath day" (see Ex 20:8; Dt 5:12–15). The "Sabbath rest" is meant to be a time to remember and celebrate God's goodness and the goodness of God's work of creation and his saving actions on our behalf.

Since the earliest times, and in keeping with the spirit of this commandment, Christians have observed Sunday as the Lord's Day to commemorate God's work of redemption accomplished through Christ's death and resurrection, which occurred on the Roman day of the sun (Sunday). Taking our "Sabbath rest" on Sunday is a way to honor God and thank him for all he has done for us.

Jesus instituted the Eucharist at the Last Supper when he took bread, blessed it, broke it, and gave it to the disciples, saying, "This is my body, which will be given for you. Do this in remembrance of me" (see Lk 22:14–20; 1 Cor 11:23–25). When we celebrate the Mass, we follow

Jesus's command to "do this" and remember his great act of love for us on the cross, and so that we—if we follow his commandments—can live with him forever in heaven.

Therefore, the Church teaches that we must fulfill the command of Jesus to "do this" by regularly attending Mass. The *Catechism of the Catholic Church* (2042) explains that attending Mass on Sundays and Holy Days of Obligation is the first of the five Precepts of the Church. Deliberately and willingly disobeying this precept without a valid reason is seriously sinful.[296]

However, participating in the Mass is more than a mere obligation. Rather, properly understood, Mass is the most important thing we do in life. We live in an increasingly secular society, and going to Mass at least weekly helps us remain focused on God and spiritual matters. *At Mass, Christ strengthens us in his community, forms us by proclaiming and preaching God's Word, and nourishes us in our Holy Communion with him.* The strength, formation, and nourishment we receive at Mass leads us nearer to God, spurs us on in our struggles against sin, and empowers us to serve God and help others. What could be more important?

Summary and Key Points

In the preceding chapter, we saw that Christ willed his Church and the sacraments, including the Eucharist. Jesus wants us to thank him and celebrate the gift of eternal life that he made possible for us by his sacrificial death on the cross by remembering and receiving him at Mass.

In short, Mass is about getting together, thanking and celebrating what Jesus did for us, and knowing that he is still here with us and helping us live a truly Christian life.

We are reminded at Mass that we are children of God, brothers and sisters in Christ, and that we are in relationship with one another. It is about belonging to a community that cares for one another and who shares common values. The prayers we pray together at Mass, the readings from Scripture, the fullness of the body, blood, soul, and divinity of Jesus Christ that we receive all help us be who we are really meant to be. We all fail and we make mistakes, but Mass is where we come to more fully experience that we are unconditionally loved by God and invited into a deeper union with him so that we can live in a more fulfilled, loving way every day.

By gathering with our fellow Christian brothers and sisters at Mass, we celebrate God's love for us and receive the Lord Jesus Christ. We are transformed by him and allow him to meet our needs. We receive special graces by worshipping God, by hearing God's Word proclaimed in the Scriptures, and by being nourished by the Lord's Body and Blood in the Holy Eucharist.

The strength we receive from the true presence of Jesus Christ at Mass and the support we experience from belonging to the community of his followers help us meet the challenges and struggles we all experience in life. Jesus really does love each of us, and he wants to be truly present with us and help us, especially during the hard times. As such, following Jesus in the Church can help us find meaning and purpose in life and put us on the path to true happiness.

Chapter 11

WHAT'S NEXT?

God longs for us to fully devote ourselves to seeking him and doing what he wills, including being an active member of the People of God in his Church. It is our sincere hope and prayer that after reading this book you are motivated to become more active in living out your Christian faith within a local Catholic faith community. The United States Conference of Catholic Bishops (USCCB) provides a good explanation of what a parish community is and why it is important: "The parish is where the Church lives. Parishes are communities of faith, of action, and of hope. They are where the Gospel is proclaimed and celebrated, where believers are formed and sent to renew the earth. Parishes are the home of the Christian community; they are the heart of our Church. Parishes are the place where God's people meet Jesus in word and sacrament and come in touch with the source of the Church's life."[297]

A vibrant parish community also provides many other opportunities to grow closer to God and other Christians in the service of God and others. These activities, based on your interests and talents, enable you to experience the fulfillment and joy found in the highest levels of human happiness.

In his book *Finding True Happiness*, Fr. Robert Spitzer describes the four levels of happiness that have been recognized since the time of Plato and Aristotle.[298] The first level of happiness—physical/sensual happiness—is found in the gratification we get from satisfying our most basic desires for bodily comfort and pleasure (food, drink, sex, clothing, shelter), including our desire for excitement and fun. However, this Level One Happiness is not fulfilling since it quickly fades and leaves us feeling empty and wanting more once the desire is met.

The second level of happiness—ego-comparative happiness—is found in the enhanced self-esteem we get from personal achievement and success. However, this Level Two Happiness is also not fulfilling because we can never get enough fame and fortune, for example. Our Level Two ego needs can even become detrimental to our happiness when we become obsessed with being better than others—with winning, status, and popularity.[299]

Levels One and Two Happiness usually become the dominant view of happiness for most people, in part because our culture embraces and promotes them with great enthusiasm.[300] However, in chapter one of this book, we discussed how seeking happiness in only the first two levels (e.g., fun, fame, and fortune) is not ultimately fulfilling because this type of happiness is superficial and always leaves us wanting more in life.

The third level of happiness—contributive happiness—is found when our central focus in life is *to give*, not to get. This happiness is experienced when we lovingly serve others and seek to make a positive difference in the world around us. Though more satisfying than Levels One and Two, even the altruistic Level Three Happiness is not fulfilling if we ignore the spiritual aspect of our nature. While Level Three Happiness moves us to bring goodness into the world, Level Four stirs within us the sense that we are destined for a goodness that goes beyond this world, that transcends it.

Only with the fourth level of happiness—transcendent happiness—will we be truly fulfilled and our "restless hearts" satisfied. As discussed in my first book, *The Reality of God*, we all experience desires for perfect truth (knowledge), love, justice (goodness), beauty, and home.[301] Because these desires are so universal, they rise above (or "transcend") cultural differences and make us aware that there is something greater out there. This "awareness of the more" moves us to realize that true happiness is not found in this world alone but in God himself—who is perfect truth, love, justice, beauty, and home.

If we want to be truly happy and live the fullest life possible, we should focus our lives on Level Three Contributive Happiness and Level Four Transcendent Happiness, while not neglecting the lower levels. Both Levels Three and Four are necessary for pervasive, enduring, and deep happiness. A person who is very generous to others but doesn't have faith will eventually feel empty. A person striving for a close relationship with God without helping others will have a superficial faith.

In the Level Four transcendental desires, God is

inviting us to experience true happiness by growing closer to God within the community of his Church. We can best be truly happy and live the fullest life possible by growing closer to God in holiness and virtue and by lovingly serving God and others.

Growing Closer to God

All Christians, of whatever age, are called to become more like Jesus by seeking the holiness and virtue that only God provides. This lifelong process of growing in holiness and virtue is called sanctification. The good news is that we do not strive alone. God is with us, and God's grace, especially in the sacraments, is sufficient!

The Holy Spirit is the source and giver of all holiness. As we allow the Holy Spirit to work in our lives, especially through prayer and the sacraments, we grow in personal holiness and grow closer to God. Following are some ways to grow closer to God in the Church:

- Prayer. We grow closer to God by deepening our personal relationship with the Father, Son, and Holy Spirit through frequent prayer. We can communicate with God in both structured and formal prayer (such as the Breviary and Rosary) as well as by spontaneous and conversational prayer throughout the day. Prayer, like any communication, is a "two-way street." We tell God what is on our heart and then listen for God to share what is on his. In our heartfelt prayers of adoration, contrition, thanksgiving, and supplication (the acronym ACTS), we communicate with God, who always hears us. Then, when we pause to reflect and listen, we can discern what God may be trying to say to us, usually in a "gentle whisper" (as God spoke to the Prophet Elijah in 1 Kings 19:12). Although setting aside time for prayer can be difficult in today's fast-paced society, we can start with a small offering— even five minutes per day—to speak with God. There are several fine guides to personal prayer readily available, including on the internet.[302]

- The sacraments. The gift of the sacraments of the Catholic Church, especially frequent Holy Communion and confession, are wonderful ways to receive the divine grace and help we need to grow in personal virtue and holiness. If you are not already doing so, actively participating at Mass every week at your local parish is a great place to start.

- Bible reading and study. If we are to grow in holiness, it is essential that we develop the habit of prayerfully and regularly reading and reflecting upon the inspired Word of God—the Holy Bible. We must be steeped in God's Word if our faith is to grow and mature, especially in our culture that often undermines the biblical worldview. By spending a little time each day immersed in

Scripture and setting aside time to talk with God in prayer, we get to know God better and deepen our commitment to follow the way of Jesus. We can read the Bible on our own, assisted by many good guides.[303] However, we can even more deeply experience the power of the God's Word in our lives by joining or forming a Bible Study or small faith sharing group at your church. The friendships and close-knit community experienced by joining with other committed Christians who are trying to grow closer to God is invaluable in our walk with Christ.

- Theological studies. We can also learn a lot about the Catholic faith tradition by reading the *Catechism of the Catholic Church* or, if younger, the *Youth Catechism of the Catholic Church* (YOUCAT), as well as other theological books, Catholic websites, and classes/seminars.[304] There are several good resources listed in the bibliography near the end of this book. These resources are excellent ways to grow in understanding and living our faith. Theology is simply "faith seeking understanding," as noted by St. Anselm.[305] But how many of us—who do not hesitate to deepen our understanding of technology, finance, science, literature, art, gardening, sports, etc.—allow our understanding of religion to remain at an elementary grade level? On the other hand, when

we seek to learn more about God and our
faith, a light shines in the darkness and our
path becomes more clearly illuminated.

All these are valuable ways to grow closer to God
and allow God to make us more like Jesus Christ in our
character and attitudes. However, the gradual process of
becoming more like Christ is not automatic. Some people grow older without growing up.

Personal and spiritual growth requires intentional
commitment. We must want to grow, decide to grow,
make an effort to grow, and persist in growing. We eventually reach whatever we stay committed to, especially
with the grace and help of God. God does not leave us
orphans. Rather, through prayer and the sacraments,
especially the Eucharist and confession, God comes to us
and helps us grow in holiness. If you want true happiness
and joy, then allow the Lord Jesus to transform every area
of your life, your home, your work, your relationships,
and your possessions so that he may truly be the Lord
and Giver of abundant life.

Experiencing God's Forgiveness

Confession is often a first step Catholics take when
seeking anew to discover God's love—the only kind of
love that truly satisfies the human heart. Jesus came to
remove every obstacle that keeps us from fully experiencing God's love, especially the obstacle of sin. That is why
Jesus Christ left us the gift of divine forgiveness available
in his Church through the sacrament of Reconciliation.

Catholics who go to confession for the first time in many years are very often moved to tears and are tremendously grateful to receive God's complete forgiveness for past failings. But we need to be open to this experience of God's mercy and forgiveness. Pope Francis addresses this:

> When we feel in our hearts: "I would like to be a better man, a better woman. . . . I regret what I have done. . . ." That is the Lord knocking. He makes you feel this: the will to be better, the will to be closer to others, to God. If you feel this, stop. That is the Lord! And go to prayer, and maybe to confession, cleanse yourselves. . . . This will be good. But keep well in mind: if you feel this longing to be better, He is knocking: don't let Him pass by![306]

Sometimes it is difficult to admit that we do wrong. But we all do. Sin is a natural part of our fallen human condition. Sin is a misuse of the God-given free will with which we have been blessed. Jesus addressed the source of human sin and moral evil when he said, "It is from within, from the human heart, that evil thoughts come, as well as sexual immorality, stealing, murder, adultery, greed, wickedness, cheating, shameless lust, envy, slander, arrogance, and foolishness. All these evils come from within and make a person unclean" (Mk 7:21–23).

However, this does not mean things are hopeless and we can never improve. We should never think that we are beyond redemption or can never change—quite the contrary. Jesus came, suffered, and died out of love for each and every one of us. He offered his life for ours so that we might experience God's forgiveness of our sins and be empowered by sacramental graces and the Holy Spirit to overcome sin and live more righteously.

Far from being a means of judging or condemning us, the sacrament of Reconciliation is how God heals and restores us. God is not out to get us. God wants to help us and reunite us to himself. In the sacrament of Reconciliation, God brings us home and grants us peace.

Frequent confession can be a real help in the necessary and ongoing conversion of our hearts, minds, and lives. God's grace and forgiveness that are available in this sacrament enable our reconciliation to be a true joy and enable our lifelong conversion and growth in holiness.

Of course, only God in Jesus Christ can forgive sins. However, Jesus granted the power to forgive sins in his name to the apostles and their successors—the bishops and priests of the Church. The first thing Jesus did after the Resurrection was to establish the sacrament of Reconciliation. Jesus did this when he said to the apostles, "Receive the Holy Spirit; whose sins you forgive are forgiven them, and whose sins you retain are retained" (Jn 20:22–23). These words of Jesus are the foundation of the sacrament of Reconciliation, which has existed in the Church from that moment until today as the privileged vehicle of receiving God's mercy and forgiveness.

Some people wonder why we should tell our sins to a priest. Why not just confess our sins directly to God? We can look at the analogy of a medical doctor for an answer. When we are sick, a doctor does what he or she can to heal us. It is not prudent to rely only on prayer and expect our bodies to be healed. Rather, God works through the human instrument of a doctor to grant us physical healing. Similarly, God works through the human instrument of a priest to grant us spiritual healing and forgiveness of sins.

Even though it may be difficult, we should not be afraid to approach Jesus in the sacrament of Reconciliation and tell him our sins through the human instrument of a priest. This sacrament is his gift to us through the Church.

Besides, as any psychologist will attest, there is tremendous emotional benefit in sharing our deepest burdens and shortcomings with another human being, especially someone whom we can trust will keep what we share in total confidence. This sacramental sharing, as well as hearing Christ's compassionate and merciful words of forgiveness through the priest, greatly helps us to deal effectively with feelings of guilt for our past failings—no matter how grave.

The Next Step

Depending upon your talents and interests, there are many ways to get involved and share your gifts with your local parish community. If you like singing and enjoy music, please consider joining a choir or music group. If you like working with children or youth, please consider getting active in your parish's religious education or youth ministry programs. If you are interested in social justice or helping the poor, please ask what your parish has available (e.g., the St. Vincent DePaul Society). Many parishes also have active young adult groups.

There are many other options for getting involved and sharing your gifts in the Catholic Church. Please check your parish's weekly bulletin or talk with the parish staff about additional opportunities. Your fellow parishioners will surely welcome you and will be there to help and support your efforts. The first step, however, is yours.

Here are some additional suggestions for getting involved in the Catholic Church, depending upon your specific situation:

- If you have *never been baptized* in any Christian church, please consider participating in the Rite of Christian Initiation of Adults (RCIA) program at a nearby Catholic parish. RCIA is the Catholic Church's path for new converts who have never been baptized in any Christian denomination. RCIA is an excellent program that helps inquirers learn more about the faith within a small group of others who are seeking full initiation into the Catholic Church. Those who have never been baptized are normally welcomed into the Catholic Church by reception of all three sacraments of Christian Initiation— Baptism, Confirmation, and Eucharist—at an Easter Vigil service the evening before Easter.

- If you were *baptized in a non-Catholic Christian church*, your baptism is recognized by the Catholic Church. However, to be in full communion with the Church requires that baptized Protestants receive the other two sacraments of Christian Initiation—Confirmation and Eucharist. Thus, please consider joining the RCIA program at a nearby parish if you were baptized in another church and are interested in possibly becoming a Catholic.

- If you were baptized in the Catholic Church (e.g., as an infant) but have not received either First Communion or Confirmation, please consider attending the RCIA program at a nearby parish. In most parishes, RCIA is open to those who were baptized Catholic but have *not been fully initiated* into the Catholic Church by reception of both of the other two sacraments of Christian initiation (Eucharist and Confirmation).

- If you have already been *fully initiated* into the Catholic Church by reception of all three sacraments of Christian Initiation (Baptism, Confirmation, and Eucharist), you may also attend RCIA meetings at a nearby parish. In most parishes, the RCIA program is open to any adult Catholic who wants to deepen his or her knowledge of and commitment to the Faith. This invitation includes "reverts" who may have not been active in the Catholic Church for many years (e.g., since childhood).

In addition to RCIA, most parishes have Bible studies and other faith sharing or prayer groups. As when joining any new organization, it is imperative that you get to know and befriend others in the parish to help you feel more welcome and at home there. These small groups are a wonderful way to fellowship with others in your parish and to grow in faith.

Closing Thoughts

Knowing we long for the kind of love that truly satisfies, Jesus was born, lived, died, and rose again to offer us true happiness in this life and salvation in the eternal life to come. Heaven is where we, God's beloved sons and daughters, will fully share in the divine love of the Father, Son, and Holy Spirit in a life that goes well beyond our wildest imagination—a life of everlasting joy, peace, and happiness.

So ask the Lord Jesus to fill you with the Holy Spirit and to renew in you the gifts of faith, hope, and love. God will then give you his peace and joy as you seek to know, love, and serve him. If you put seeking God's will first in your life, then God will give you everything you need in this life and let you enjoy being with him forever in the next.

What God has in store for us is more breathtaking than anything we can imagine. We are asked to take a journey into the unknown and to trust that we are going somewhere good. The Christian journey is never dull and is truly satisfying. Is there anything holding you back from giving God your complete trust and seeking God's will for your life?

It is when we live our everyday lives with a focus on growing in personal holiness and lovingly serve God and others that we discover the keys to true happiness and our life becomes a prayer offering to God. For as the Danish proverb says, *"What you are is God's gift to you, what you become is your gift to God."*[307] When we focus our lives on serving God and others and seeking to grow closer to God and to become more like Christ, we are on our way to finding true and lasting happiness—the higher levels of happiness.

May God bless you as you seek to grow closer to God as an active disciple of Jesus Christ within the community of his followers in the Catholic Church. *For it is in union with Jesus and his Church that we find true happiness and fulfillment of heart's deepest desires.* Spending time with God's people and in God's presence, especially at the Mass, enables us to more powerfully serve God and others and to more fully reflect God's wondrous love in the world. When we have that kind of life and love, we become truly rich and fully alive. And wouldn't it be wonderful if God is able to say of each of us at the end of our life on earth, "Well done, my good and faithful servant" (Mt 25:21)?

KEY POINTS IN EACH CHAPTER

Chapter 1: Why Aren't We Happier?

- Worldly pleasures, such as fun, fame, and fortune, will always leave us with a sense of wanting more.
- Worldly pleasures cannot bring us sustained happiness, and so we are left with a "happiness hole in our hearts."
- True happiness and joy that lasts can only come from God, by learning to master our passions and making God central in our lives.

Chapter 2: How Does Being a Christian Bring True Happiness?

- Being an active Christian enables us to meet our five core needs of identity, security, belonging, purpose, and competence.

- Christians know that our identity is not based on what we look like, what we do, or what we have, but instead our self-worth is rooted in that we are each a beloved child of God.
- We can find security in Jesus Christ, who is with us in our moments of triumph and our times of hardship.
- Christians know that not only does God want us but we also belong to his people—our fellow brothers and sisters in the Church.
- We also know that our purpose in life is not merely to be happy but to serve God and others through our abilities and thus find true and lasting happiness.
- Christians realize that we each have the competence to do the work which God has made us to do because God will give us everything we need.

Chapter 3: Why Turn to God?

- In order to make sense of our lives, we must first turn to God through prayer and by attending Mass.
- God expects us to have intellectual questions about religion and go through "searching faith" as we internalize and make our own what we have learned as children.
- If we truly seek lasting happiness, we must

turn to God in everything we do by talking with God, even if we do not yet fully believe, because our hearts will be restless until they find rest in God.

Chapter 4: Is Jesus Truly God?

- There are many instances in the New Testament where Jesus Christ claims his divinity.
- Jesus Christ's claim to be the Son of God would have only been made by a liar, a lunatic, or truly our Lord and God.
- If Jesus Christ's claim was a lie, he would not have spoken so audaciously, and his followers would not have died terrible deaths willingly for a lie.
- Jesus Christ's words and deeds in life are not those of a liar or a lunatic but rather someone of wisdom and compassion.
- If the divinity of Jesus Christ was a legend devised soon after his death, it would have been refuted by eyewitnesses to the real Jesus.
- The divinity of Jesus Christ is also evident through his miracles, divine actions, timeless parables, and, most importantly, his resurrection.

Chapter 5: Did Jesus Really Rise From the Dead?

- The resurrection of Jesus Christ was not witnessed directly by anyone.
- However, positive evidence for the resurrection of Jesus can be found in the historical accounts of the empty tomb and the eyewitness accounts of the apostles.
- Despite the evidence, belief in the resurrection of Jesus Christ ultimately comes down to an act of faith.

Chapter 6: Do Near-Death Experiences Reveal the Reality of Heaven and an Afterlife?

- Near-death experiences (NDEs) are not rare, even in the US.
- Studies have shown that people from various ethnic and religious backgrounds have experienced NDEs.
- Reports of out-of-body experiences, meeting unknown or deceased relatives, and of "mind-sight" of the blind are all examples providing evidence for NDEs.
- NDEs affirm the existence of the human soul that can live without the body and the existence of the afterlife.

Chapter 7: Why Were Christ's Passion and Death Needed for Our Salvation?

- Jesus Christ taught that not everyone will be saved, but only those who do "the will of my Father in heaven" (Mt 7:21).
- Jesus Christ's passion and death were needed for our salvation because God is perfectly loving and perfectly just.
- Jesus Christ willingly offered up his own life as the atoning sacrifice for our sins, and his death satisfied, or was atonement for, the infinite debt of our sins.
- This act by God was done out of perfect mercy and love for each one of us so that we would be able to join him in heaven for eternity.

Chapter 8: How Are We Saved?

- The gift of salvation is only beneficial to us if we accept that gift, and thus live our lives doing God's will.
- There are three ways in which we are called to accept the gift of salvation.
- The first way is faith, or "conversion," in which someone completely submits their intellect and will to God.
- The second way is loving service to God and

others expressed through unconditional, charitable, "agape" love.

- The third way is receiving the sacraments, especially Baptism and the Holy Eucharist.

Chapter 9: Why Does the Church Still Matter Today?

- Jesus Christ willed the creation of the Church.
- Even though the Church here on Earth is imperfect and full of sinners, it is still inseparable with Jesus Christ, who willed it to last throughout the ages.
- If we want to do what Jesus Christ wills for us, we must seek to follow the teachings of the Church rather than trying to seek God all on our own.
- Jesus Christ willed the leadership of the pope and the structure of the Church, beginning with Peter and the other eleven apostles.
- Unlike the post-Reformation Christian churches, only the Catholic Church can credibly claim that it was established by Jesus Christ himself with Peter as its first leader (pope).
- Jesus Christ willed that the Church would have teaching authority and that divine revelation would come to us through Sacred Scripture and Sacred Tradition.

- Jesus Christ willed the seven sacraments so that we may relate with God, spiritually and physically, through our human senses.
- The seven sacraments found in the Catholic Church are Baptism, Confirmation, Eucharist, Reconciliation, Matrimony, Holy Orders, and the Anointing of the Sick.
- The seven sacraments of the Catholic Church are when and how God spiritually feeds us, heals us, and strengthens us.
- The sacraments are gifts of God available to us only through the Church.
- The sacraments are God's "channels" for sharing divine grace and power with us, and our way of relating to and worshipping God through our five senses.
- Jesus specifically willed that we regularly celebrate the sacrament of the Eucharist when he said at the Last Supper after breaking bread and blessing the cup of wine, "Do this in remembrance of me."
- The Holy Eucharist is the "source" of our faith, since we partake of the very source of our lives and we encounter the goal or "summit" of our lives—Christ himself.

Chapter 10: Why Go to Mass?

- The "Top Ten" reasons to attend Mass are:

- ➤ To gather together in Christian fellowship
- ➤ To celebrate with song
- ➤ To worship God and pray together
- ➤ To receive God's help and healing
- ➤ To receive the Word of God
- ➤ To re-present Christ's sacrifice on the cross
- ➤ To be filled with and become more like Jesus Christ
- ➤ To strengthen us for our mission
- ➤ To develop and express our faith commitment
- ➤ To follow the commands of God, Jesus, and the Church

- The Real Presence of Christ's body, blood, soul, and divinity under the appearance of bread and wine has been the constant teaching of the Church since the very beginning.

- In Holy Communion, we receive the graces we need to become more like Jesus Christ.

- The Eucharist, as the eternal presence and power of God, eternalizes those who consume it by making us ready to spend an eternity with God in heaven.

- The strength we receive from the true presence of Jesus Christ at Mass and the support we experience from belonging to the community of his followers helps us meet the challenges and struggles we all experience in life.

Chapter 11: What's Next?

- Parishes are communities of faith, of action, and of hope where believers are formed and sent to renew the earth, and the place where God's people meet Jesus in word and sacrament.
- The Rite of Christian Initiation of Adults (RCIA) is for:
  - ➤ New converts who have never been baptized in any Christian denomination.
  - ➤ People who were baptized in another Christian denomination and are interested in being fully initiated into the Catholic Church.
  - ➤ Baptized Catholics who have not been fully initiated into the Catholic Church by reception of both of the other two sacraments of Christian initiation (Eucharist and Confirmation).
  - ➤ Any adult Catholic who wants to deepen his or her knowledge of and commitment to the Faith.
- It is in union with Jesus and his Church that we find true happiness and fulfillment of our heart's deepest desires.

PERSONAL REFLECTION AND DISCUSSION QUESTIONS

Chapter 1: Why Aren't We Happier?

1. Do you agree that we can never have enough pleasure, prestige, popularity, power, possessions, and prosperity because we always want more? Why or why not?
2. Do you believe "our hearts are restless until they find their rest in God"? Why or why not?

Chapter 2: How Does Being a Christian Bring True Happiness?

1. In your experience, have you noticed that highly religious people seem happier than non-religious people? If so, why do you think that is the case?
2. How does being an active and committed Christian meet our five core needs in life?

Chapter 3: Why Turn to God?

1. Do you agree that intellectual questions and doubts about religion can be a good thing? Why or why not?
2. What "big questions" about Jesus, salvation, and the Church that are addressed in the remaining chapters of this book are of the most interest to you and why?

Chapter 4: Is Jesus Truly God?

1. Do you believe Jesus is the divine Son of God? Why or why not?
2. Do you believe the divinity of Jesus is a legend that developed over time? Why or why not?

Chapter 5: Did Jesus Really Rise From the Dead?

1. Do you believe Jesus really rose from the dead? Why or why not?
2. What lessons are to be learned from the transformed lives of the apostles?

Chapter 6: Do Near-Death Experiences Reveal the Reality of Heaven and an Afterlife?

1. Do you believe near-death experiences are real? Why or why not?
2. Do you believe in heaven and the afterlife? Why or why not?

Chapter 7: Why Were Christ's Passion and Death Needed for Our Salvation?

1. Do you believe Christ's passion and death were needed for our salvation? Why or why not?
2. Do you believe that everyone will be saved? Why or why not?

Chapter 8: How Are We Saved?

1. What specific steps can you take to deepen your conversion and your faith?
2. What are some specific acts of loving service to God and others that you can do?

Chapter 9: Why Does the Church Still Matter Today?

1. Do you believe the Catholic Church still matters today? Why or why not?
2. Do you agree that the Catholic Church can credibly claim that it was established by Jesus Christ himself with Peter as its first leader? If so, how does this Apostolic Succession impact your view of the Catholic Church?

Chapter 10: Why Go to Mass?

1. What motivates you or others you know to go to Mass? What keeps you or them away?
2. Which of the "Top Ten" reasons to go to Mass do you find most compelling? Why?

Chapter 11: What's Next?

1. If you are not Catholic, are you considering joining the Rite of Christian Initiation of Adults (RCIA) program at a nearby parish? Why or why not?
2. What other opportunities to get involved in your parish are you interested in pursuing? When and how do you plan to pursue these opportunities?

NOTES

Chapter 1

1   Ravi Zacharias, *The End of Reason: A Response to the New Atheists* (Grand Rapids, Michigan: Zondervan, 2008), 40–41.

2   See http://dailyscripture.servantsoftheword.org/readings/2016/dec21.htm.

3   For example, see http://www.chnetwork.org/story/everything-thought-wanted-isnt-enough/.

4   Rick Warren, *The Purpose Driven Life: What On Earth Am I Here For?* (Grand Rapids, Michigan: Zondervan, 2002), 239.

5   See http://catholicquotations.com/god-and-humanity.

6   See http://liturgy.co.nz/reflection/632b.html.

7   C. S. Lewis, *Mere Christianity* (New York: HarperCollins, 2001), 49.

8   C. S. Lewis, *The Weight of Glory* (New York: HarperCollins, 2001), 26.

9   See https://www.shmoop.com/augustine-confessions/sin-quotes.html.

10   See http://www.catholicherald.com/stories/A-narrow-gate-leading-to-life,32167.

11   See http://www.catholic365.com/article/4400/gods-way-of-freeing-a-catholic-man-from-all-his-sexual-addictions-forever.html.

12   See http://www.crisismagazine.com/2016/hook-culture-done-women.

13   See http://qz.com/685852/hookup-culture/.

14   See http://www.crisismagazine.com/2016/hook-culture-done-women.

15   Ibid.

16   George Cardinal Pell, *Test Everything: Hold Fast to What Is Good* (San Francisco: Ignatius Press, 2015), 325.

17   See https://cruxnow.com/commentary/2017/03/01/catholic-rules-sex-arent-party-pooping-theyre-wisdom/.

18   *Catechism of the Catholic Church* (CCC), Second Edition (Washington, DC: United States Catholic Conference, 2000), 2361–63.

19   See http://www.ewtn.com/library/MARY/DOMINIC.htm.

20   See http://www.cam.org.au/vocations/The-Call/What-is-a-Vocation-.

21   Note: Unless otherwise noted, quotations from the Bible are taken from *The New American Bible, Revised Edition* (NABRE), which may be found on the website of the United States Conference of

Catholic Bishops (USCCB) at: http://www.usccb.
org/bible/books-of-the-bible/index.cfm.

Chapter 2

22 See https://w2.vatican.va/content/john-paul-ii/
en/speeches/2000/jul-sep/documents/hf_jp-ii_
spe_20000819_gmg-veglia.html (no. 5).

23 See http://www.pewforum.org/files/2016/04/Reli-
gion-in-Everyday-Life-FINAL.pdf, p. 19.

24 See http://www.washingtonpost.com/news/acts-
of-faith/wp/2015/08/14/want-sustained-happi-
ness-get-religion-study-suggests.

25 Kathy Koch, *Finding Authentic Hope and Wholeness: 5 Questions That Will Change Your Life* (Chi-
cago: Moody Publishers, 2005), 14.

26 Koch, *Finding Authentic Hope and Wholeness*,
20–21.

27 Koch, *Finding Authentic Hope and Wholeness*, 67.

28 Koch, *Finding Authentic Hope and Wholeness*, 78.

29 See http://www.catholicwebphilosopher.
com/2010/04/god-so-loved-world-that-he-gave-
his.html.

30 See http://dailyscripture.servantsoftheword.org/
readings/2016/may13.htm.

31 *The Upper Room: Where the World Meets to Pray*,
March-April 2017, p. 70.

32 Warren, *The Purpose Driven Life*, 235.

33 See https://aleteia.org/2017/06/14/pope-francis-
there-is-a-remedy-for-your-unhappiness/.

34 See http://dailyscripture.servantsoftheword.org/readings/2016/aug19.htm.

35 See CCC 253–55.

36 *The Word Among Us*, Easter 2015 (Volume 34, Number 4), 62.

37 See http://dailyscripture.servantsoftheword.org/readings/2016/oct15.htm.

38 See https://www.brainyquote.com/quotes/quotes/o/oscarwilde107108.html.

39 Koch, *Finding Authentic Hope and Wholeness*, 49.

40 Koch, *Finding Authentic Hope and Wholeness*, 50.

41 Malcolm Gladwell, *David and Goliath: Underdogs, Misfits, and the Art of Battling Giants* (New York: Little, Brown and Company, 2013), chapter 8, and "How I Rediscovered Faith," *Relevant Magazine*, 2014. See http://www.relevantmagazine.com/culture/books/how-i-rediscovered-faith (original post), and http://www.breakpoint.org/2014/12/malcolm-gladwells-tipping-point-3/.

42 Ibid.

43 See http://dailyscripture.servantsoftheword.org/readings/2016/sep20.htm.

44 See http://www.goodreads.com/quotes/601956-the-church-is-a-hospital-for-sinners-not-a-museum.

45 Christian Smith et al., *Young Catholic America: Emerging Adults In, Out of, and Gone from the Church* (New York: Oxford University Press, 2014), 228.

46 Koch, *Finding Authentic Hope and Wholeness*, 121.

47 Koch, *Finding Authentic Hope and Wholeness*, 122.

48 See http://www.goodreads.com/quotes/64541-the-purpose-of-life-is-not-to-be-happy-it.

49 See http://thinkexist.com/quotation/those_who_are_not_looking_for_happiness_are_the/146493.html.

50 See http://dailyscripture.servantsoftheword.org/readings/2016/aug19.htm.

51 See http://dailyscripture.servantsoftheword.org/readings/2016/nov29.htm.

52 See http://dailyscripture.servantsoftheword.org/readings/2016/aug28.htm.

53 Warren, *The Purpose Driven Life*, 148.

54 See http://dailyscripture.servantsoftheword.org/readings/2016/aug28.htm.

55 Koch, *Finding Authentic Hope and Wholeness*, 137.

56 Koch, *Finding Authentic Hope and Wholeness*, 139.

57 Smith et al., *Young Catholic America*, 230.

Chapter 3

58 *The Upper Room: Where the World Meets to Pray*, September-October 2015, p. 50.

59 Lewis, *Mere Christianity*, 92.

60 Lewis, *Mere Christianity*, 50.

61 See http://dailyscripture.servantsoftheword.org/readings/john1244.htm.

62 See http://dailyscripture.servantsoftheword.org/readings/2016/jul19.htm.

63   See http://www.peterkreeft.com/topics/joy.htm.

64   See https://en.wikiquote.org/wiki/Thomas_Aquinas.

65   See http://m.ncregister.com/daily-news/pope-francis-challenge-are-you-looking-for-empty-thrills-or-the-power-of-gr/.

66   John H. Westerhoff, III, *Will Our Children Have Faith?* (Harrisburg, Pennsylvania: Morehouse Publishing, 2000), 87–103.

67   Steven R. Hemler, *The Reality of God: The Layman's Guide to Scientific Evidence for the Creator* (Charlotte, North Carolina: St. Benedict Press, 2014).

Chapter 4

68   Lee Strobel, *The Case for Christ: A Journalist's Personal Investigation of the Evidence for Jesus* (Grand Rapids, Michigan: Zondervan Publishing House, c. 1998), 81–83.

69   See http://www.princeton.edu/~achaney/tmve/wiki100k/docs/Tacitus_on_Christ.html.

70   Strobel, *The Case for Christ*, 83.

71   Ralph O. Muncaster, *Evidence for Jesus: Discover the Facts That Proved the Truth of the Bible* (Eugene, Oregon: Harvest House Publishers, 2004), 114–27.

72   Peter J. Kreeft and Ronald K. Tacelli, *Pocket Handbook of Christian Apologetics* (Downers Grove, Illinois: InterVarsity Press, 2003), 64.

73   Lewis, *Mere Christianity*, 52.

74   Peter J. Kreeft and Ronald K. Tacelli, *Handbook of Catholic Apologetics: Reasoned Answers to Questions of Faith* (San Francisco: Ignatius Press, 2009), p. 172.

75   See http://www.orgsites.com/ky/jesusfirst/_pgg6.php3.

76   See http://www.apostles.com/apostlesdied.html and http://www.about-jesus.org/martyrs.htm.

77   Kreeft and Tacelli, *Pocket Handbook of Christian Apologetics*, 65.

78   Lewis, *Mere Christianity*, 52.

79   Kreeft and Tacelli, *Handbook of Catholic Apologetics*, 170.

80   See http://www.evidenceunseen.com/theology/lord-liar-lunatic-or-legend/.

81   Kreeft and Tacelli, *Handbook of Catholic Apologetics*, 171.

82   See http://www.bc.edu/schools/stm/c21online/resources/birthofjesus/intro/the_dating_of_thegospels.html.

83   Ibid.

84   Ibid.

85   See http://en.wikipedia.org/wiki/Gospel#Dating.

86   Ibid.

87   See http://www.evidenceunseen.com/theology/lord-liar-lunatic-or-legend/.

88   A. N. Sherwin-White, *Roman Society and Roman Law in the New Testament: The Sarum Lectures 1960-1961* (Oxford: Oxford University Press, 1963), 195.

89   See http://en.wikipedia.org/wiki/Pliny_the_ Younger_on_Christians.

90   See http://www.pbs.org/wgbh/pages/frontline/ shows/religion/maps/primary/pliny.html.

91   Strobel, *The Case for Christ*, 84.

92   See http://www.neverthirsty.org/pp/historical-secular-quotes-about-jesus/lucian-of-samosata.html.

93   See http://www.evidenceunseen.com/theology/ lord-liar-lunatic-or-legend/.

94   See http://www.evidenceunseen.com/theology/ lord-liar-lunatic-or-legend/.

95   Gleason L. Archer, *Encyclopedia of Bible Difficulties* (Grand Rapids, Michigan: Zondervan, 1982), 12.

96   See http://www.evidenceunseen.com/theology/ lord-liar-lunatic-or-legend/.

97   Kreeft and Tacelli, *Handbook of Catholic Apologetics*, 172.

98   See https://www.osv.com/OSVNewsweekly/ Faith/Article/TabId/720/ArtMID/13628/ArticleID/20710.

99   See http://www.newadvent.org/cathen/09674b.htm.

100 See http://www.catholicnewsagency.com/ resources/bible/introduction-to-the-new-testament/gospel-of-luke/.

101 Norman Geisler and Frank Turek, *I Don't Have Enough Faith to be an Atheist* (Wheaton, Illinois: Crossway Books, 2004), 276.

102 Ibid.

103 Lewis, *Mere Christianity*, 51.

104 See http://www.tertullian.org/fathers/cyril_on_luke_04_sermons_39_46.htm (Sermon 41).

105 See http://dailyscripture.servantsoftheword.org/readings/2016/aug30.htm.

Chapter 5

106 See http://blog.adw.org/2014/04/why-was-the-resurrection-such-a-hidden-event/.

107 Ibid.

108 Quoted in: *The Case for Christ* DVD (La Mirada, California: La Mirada Films, 2007).

109 Kreeft and Tacelli, *Pocket Handbook of Christian Apologetics*, 73.

110 See http://www.breakpoint.org/2002/03/an-unholy-hoax/.

111 Kreeft and Tacelli, *Pocket Handbook of Christian Apologetics*, 71.

112 Geisler and Turek, *I Don't Have Enough Faith to be an Atheist*, 305.

113 Kreeft and Tacelli, *Pocket Handbook of Christian Apologetics*, 77.

114 Geisler and Turek, *I Don't Have Enough Faith to be an Atheist*, 302.

115 Kreeft and Tacelli, *Pocket Handbook of Christian Apologetics*, 75.

116 Lee Strobel, *The Case for Easter* (Grand Rapids, Michigan: Zondervan, 2003), 87.

117   See https://www.crossroadsinitiative.com/media/
      articles/the-apostles-timid-men-who-won-the-
      world-john-chrysostom/.

118   Kreeft and Tacelli, *Pocket Handbook of Christian
      Apologetics*, 64.

119   Geisler and Turek, *I Don't Have Enough Faith to be
      an Atheist*, 31.

120   Kreeft and Tacelli, *Pocket Handbook of Christian
      Apologetics*, 67.

Chapter 6

121   See http://www.nderf.org/NDERF/Articles/
      NDE%20Overview.htm.

122   See http://iands.org/about-ndes/key-nde-facts.
      html?start=1.

123   J. Steve Miller, *Near-Death Experiences as Evi-
      dence for the Existence of God and Heaven: A Brief
      Introduction in Plain Language* (Acworth, Georgia:
      Wisdom Creek Press, 2012), 25.

124   See http://heavenisforreal.net.

125   See http://www.ebenalexander.com/books/proof-
      of-heaven.

126   Miller, *Near-Death Experiences*, 23.

127   Sam Parnia et al., "AWARE—AWAreness during
      REsuscitation—A Prospective Study," *Resuscita-
      tion: Official Journal of the European Resuscitation
      Council* (Volume 85, Issue 12, December 2014),
      1799–1805.

128 See http://www.resuscitationjournal.com/article/
S0300-9572(14)00739-4/fulltext.

129 See http://www.telegraph.co.uk/sci-
ence/2016/03/12/first-hint-of-life-after-death-in-
biggest-ever-scientific-study.

130 Robert J. Spitzer, *The Soul's Upward Yearning:
Clues to Our Transcendent Nature from Experience
and Reason* (San Francisco: Ignatius Press, 2015),
182.

131 Pim van Lommel, Ruud van Wees, Vincent Mey-
ers, Ingrid Elfferich, "Near-Death Experience in
Survivors of Cardiac Arrest: A Prospective Study
in the Netherlands," *The Lancet* (Volume 358,
December 15, 2001), 2039–45.

132 van Lommel et al., "Near-Death Experience",
2040–41.

133 Miller, *Near-Death Experiences*, 21.

134 Miller, *Near-Death Experiences*, 22.

135 Pim van Lommel, *Consciousness Beyond Life: The
Science of the Near-Death Experience* (New York:
HarperOne, 2010).

136 van Lommel et al., "Near-Death Experience", 2044.

137 Jeffery Long, *Evidence of the Afterlife: The Science
of Near-Death Experiences* (New York: HarperOne,
2010), 6-17. See also Pim van Lommel, *Consciousness Beyond Life*, Chapter 2, "What is a Near-
Death Experience."

138 See http://www.neardeathsite.com/experts31.php.

139 Raymond A. Moody, *Life After Life: The Investigation of a Phenomenon–Survival of Bodily Death*
(New York: HarperOne, 2001), 10–77.

140   Moody, *Life After Life*, 53–54.

141   Miller, *Near-Death Experiences*, 186.

142   van Lommel, *Consciousness Beyond Life*, 30.

143   Miller, *Near-Death Experiences*, 186.

144   See http://www.near-death.com/experiences/
      experts04.html.

145   Miller, *Near-Death Experiences*, 31.

146   Chris Carter, *Science and the Near-Death Experi-
      ence: How Consciousness Survives Death* (Roches-
      ter, Vermont: Inner Traditions, 2010).

147   Miller, *Near-Death Experiences*, especially chapter
      4, "Naturalistic Explanations."

148   Kenneth Ring and Madelaine Lawrence, "Further
      Evidence for Veridical Perception During Near-
      Death Experiences," *Journal of Near-Death Studies*
      (Volume 11, Summer 1993), 228.

149   Moody, *Life After Life*, 93.

150   van Lommel et al., "Near-Death Experience", 2041.

151   Kimberly Clark Sharp, *After the Light: What I Dis-
      covered on the Other Side of Life That Can Change
      Your World* (New York: William Morrow and
      Company, 1995), 8–15.

152   Michael B. Sabom, *Light and Death: One Doctor's
      Fascinating Account of Near-Death Experiences*
      (Grand Rapids, Michigan: Zondervan Publishing
      House, 1998), 37–41.

153   Janice Holden, Bruce Greyson, Debbie James (Edi-
      tors), *The Handbook of Near-Death Experiences:
      Thirty Years of Investigation* (Santa Barbara, Cali-
      fornia: Praeger Publishers, 2009).

154 Janice Holden, "Veridical Perception in Near-Death Experiences," *The Handbook of Near-Death Experiences,* 196–97.

155 Jeffery Long, *Evidence of the Afterlife,* 72.

156 See http://magisgodwiki.org/index.php?title=The_ Human_Soul#The_van_Lommel_et_al_Study.

157 Kenneth Ring and Sharon Cooper, "Near-Death and Out-of-Body Experiences in the Blind: A Study of Apparent Eyeless Vision," *Journal of Near-Death Studies* (Volume 16, Winter 1997), 101–47.

158 Kenneth Ring and Sharon Cooper, *Mindsight: Near-Death and Out-of-Body Experiences in the Blind* (Palo Alto, California: William James Center for Consciousness Studies, Institute of Transpersonal Psychology, 1999)

159 Ring and Cooper, *Mindsight,* 25.

160 Ring and Cooper, *Mindsight,* 46–47.

161 Ring and Cooper, *Mindsight,* 41–42.

162 Ring and Cooper, *Journal of Near-Death Studies,* 101.

163 Ring and Cooper, *Journal of Near-Death Studies,* 125.

164 Miller, *Near-Death Experiences,* 72–73.

165 Long, *Evidence of the Afterlife,* 49, 123.

166 Todd Burpo, *Heaven is for Real: A Little Boy's Astounding Story of His Trip to Heaven and Back* (Nashville, Tennessee: Thomas Nelson, 2010).

167 Burpo, *Heaven is for Real,* 86–90, 155.

168 Burpo, *Heaven is for Real,* 120–23.

169   Burpo, *Heaven is for Real*, 94.

170   van Lommel, *Consciousness Beyond Life*, 72.

171   van Lommel, *Consciousness Beyond Life*, 71.

172   van Lommel, *Consciousness Beyond Life*, 74.

173   van Lommel, *Consciousness Beyond Life*, 32–33.

174   Miller, *Near-Death Experiences*, 67.

175   Raymond Moody, *Glimpses of Eternity: Sharing a Loved One's Passage from This Life to the Next* (New York: Guideposts, 2010).

176   See *Afterlife* DVD (Los Angeles: Vanguard Cinema, 2011)

177   Moody, *Glimpses of Eternity*, 13–14.

178   Raymond Moody, *The Light Beyond* (New York: Bantam Books, 1988), 33.

179   Long, *Evidence of the Afterlife*, 177.

180   Moody, *Life After Life*, 83–84.

181   van Lommel, *Consciousness Beyond Life*, 55.

182   Ibid.

183   See http://iands.org/about-ndes/key-nde-facts.html?start=4.

184   Ibid.

185   Long, *Evidence of the Afterlife*, 179.

186   van Lommel, *Consciousness Beyond Life*, 67–68.

187   Long, *Evidence of the Afterlife*, 178.

188   van Lommel, *Consciousness Beyond Life*, 45.

189   van Lommel, *Consciousness Beyond Life*, 300.

190   Robert J. Spitzer, *In the Beginning: Evidence for God from Physics, Study Guide* (Irvine, California: Magis Publications, 2012), 67.

191 See CCC 382.

192 See https://www.britannica.com/topic/soul-religion-and-philosophy.

193 Ibid.

194 Long, *Evidence of the Afterlife*, 202.

195 Miller, *Near-Death Experiences*, 83–85.

196 Miller, *Near-Death Experiences*, 86.

Chapter 7

197 Kreeft and Tacelli, *Pocket Handbook of Christian Apologetics*, 113.

198 See *What More Could He Do For You?* DVD (Erie, Pennsylvania: The Reason For Our Hope Foundation).

199 See http://www.yidio.com/movie/the-passion-of-the-christ/22266?utm_source=Bing&utm_medium=Search&t_source=64&utm_campaign=465.

200 Christoph Cardinal Schönborn, *God Sent His Son: A Contemporary Christology* (San Francisco: Ignatius Press, 2010), 270.

201 Schönborn, *God Sent His Son*, 269.

202 Edward Sri, *Love Unveiled: The Catholic Faith Explained* (San Francisco: Ignatius Press, 2015), 92.

203 Walter Farrell and Martin J. Healy, *My Way of Life: The Summa Simplified for Everyone* (Brooklyn: New York, Confraternity of the Precious Blood, 1952), 497–98.

204 Sri, *Love Unveiled*, 89.

205   Schönborn, *God Sent His Son*, 287.

206   *The Word Among Us*, Lent 2016 (Volume 35, Number 3), 65.

207   See http://dailyscripture.servantsoftheword.org/readings/2016/jan4.htm.

Chapter 8

208   Alan Schreck, *Catholic & Christian: An Explanation of Commonly Misunderstood Catholic Beliefs* (Cincinnati, Ohio: St. Anthony Messenger Press, 2004), 23.

209   See https://www.osv.com/TheChurch/Eternal-Life/Article/TabId/738/ArtMID/13694/ArticleID/20068/.

210   See John 3:16, 3:34–36, 5:24, 6:28–29, 11:25–27, 20:30–31; Mark 16:16; Acts 16:29–31; Romans 3:22–26, 5:8–11; Ephesians 2:8–10; and 2 Thessalonians 2:13.

211   Schreck, *Catholic & Christian*, 24.

212   See Luke 18:9–14.

213   Thomas White and Desmond O'Donnell, *Renewal of Faith: Adult Instruction in the Catholic Faith* (Notre Dame, Indiana: Ave Maria Press, 1974), 29–33.

214   Donald L. Gelpi, *The Conversion Experience: A Reflective Process for RCIA Participants and Others* (New York: Paulist Press, 1998).

215   See http://dailyscripture.servantsoftheword.org/readings/2016/oct22.htm.

216 See http://dailyscripture.servantsoftheword.org/readings/2016/jan4.htm.

217 See http://dailyscripture.servantsoftheword.org/readings/luke2224.htm.

218 See Matthew 7:21–23, 16:27; Luke 18:18–22; John 5:29; Romans 2:6–8; 2 Corinthians 5:10; Ephesians 5:1–5; 1 Peter 1:17; and especially James 2:14–26.

219 See https://www.catholic.com/magazine/online-edition/why-james-says-faith-without-works-is-dead.

220 Lewis, *Mere Christianity*, 148.

221 See https://www.osv.com/TheChurch/Article/TabId/563/ArtMID/13751/ArticleID/23411/Yearning-for-unity-as-the-Reformation-hits-500.aspx.

222 See http://www.vatican.va/roman_curia/pontifical_councils/chrstuni/documents/rc_pc_chrstuni_doc_31101999_cath-luth-joint-declaration_en.html.

223 C. S. Lewis, *The Four Loves* (San Diego: Harcourt Brace Jovanovich Publishers, 1960).

224 *Compendium of the Catechism of the Catholic Church* (Washington, DC: United States Conference of Catholic Bishops, 2006), 193.

225 Ibid.

226 Sri, *Love Unveiled*, 59.

227 Patrick Madrid, *Why Be Catholic? Ten Answers to a Very Important Question* (New York: Image, 2014), 67.

228 See http://www.vatican.va/holy_father/special_features/encyclicals/documents/hf_jp-ii_enc_20030417_ecclesia_eucharistia_en.html (no. 62).

229   See http://w2.vatican.va/content/francesco/en/
      apost_exhortations/documents/papa-francesco_
      esortazione-ap_20131124_evangelii-gaudium.
      html (no. 47).

230   See http://catholicfaithwarriors.blogspot.
      com/2012/06/writings-of-st-thomas-aquinas.html.

231   Schreck, *Catholic & Christian*, 41–42.

232   Schreck, *Catholic & Christian*, 36, 42.

233   See http://www.vatican.va/roman_curia/con-
      gregations/cfaith/documents/rc_con_cfaith_
      doc_20180222_placuit-deo_en.html.

234   Ibid.

Chapter 9

235   Jim Auer, *Handbook for Today's Catholic Teen*
      (Liguori, Missouri: Liguori Publications, 2004),
      48-49.

236   See http://www.americamagazine.org/pope-inter-
      view.

237   Robert Barron, *Catholicism: A Journey to the Heart
      of the Faith* (New York: Image, 2011), 145.

238   See http://en.radiovaticana.va/news/2015/01/01/
      homily_for_the_solemnity_of_mary_the_
      mother_of_god/1116647.

239   Madrid, *Why Be Catholic?*, 13.

240   Trent Horn, *Why We're Catholic: Our Reasons for
      Faith, Hope, and Love* (El Cajon, California: Cath-
      olic Answers Press, 2017), 131.

241 Sri, *Love Unveiled*, 134-135.

242 See CCC 77, 862.

243 See CCC 77, 1087.

244 See https://www.osv.com/OSVNewsweekly/Perspectives/Columnists/Article/TabId/797/ArtMID/13632/ArticleID/18150/Necessity-of-the-pope.aspx.

245 Barron, *Catholicism*, 168–69.

246 *YOUCAT: Youth Catechism of the Catholic Church* 87.

247 Madrid, *Why Be Catholic?*, 29.

248 See http://www.catholic365.com/article/2858/12-early-church-quotes-that-will-challenge-protestants.html.

249 Rod Bennett, *The Apostasy That Wasn't: The Extraordinary Story of the Unbreakable Early Church* (San Diego: Catholic Answers Press, 2015).

250 See http://www.ccel.org/ccel/richardson/fathers.vi.ii.iii.iii.html (no. 3).

251 See https://churchpop.com/2015/09/01/this-one-quote-convinced-me-to-convert-to-catholicism/.

252 See http://www.ccel.org/ccel/richardson/fathers.vi.ii.iii.v.html (nos. 3, 4).

253 See https://www.catholic.com/magazine/online-edition/apologetics-with-st-ignatius-of-antioch.

254 See http://www.ccel.org/ccel/richardson/fathers.vi.ii.iii.vi.html (no. 8).

255 See http://site.catholicxybr.com/main/3124/index.asp?pageid=123896&t=office-of-readings&newsid=19161.

256 See http://www.newadvent.org/fathers/310118. htm (nos. 26 & 28).

257 Barron, *Catholicism*, 167.

258 See http://www.biography.com/people/jim-jones-10367607.

259 Frank Sheed, *Theology and Sanity* (San Francisco: Ignatius Press, 1993), 284, 282–83.

260 See CCC 66, 81.

261 See CCC, Glossary, pg. 901.

262 Ibid.

263 See CCC 93, 2034.

264 See https://www.osv.com/OSVNewsweekly/ ByIssue/Article/TabId/735/ArtMID/13636/Arti-cleID/22105/Divinity-of-Jesus.aspx.

265 See the second pillar of prayer at: http://www.sau-diembassy.net/about/country-information/Islam/ understanding_Islam.aspx.

266 For example, see https://news.google.com/ newspapers?nid=1129&dat=19871116&id=YM-5RAAAAIBAJ&sjid=620DAAAAIBAJ&p-g=6520,5063327&hl=en.

267 Schreck, *Catholic & Christian*, 34.

268 See http://www.patheos.com/blogs/standingonmy-head/2015/07/spiritual-but-not-religious-how-do-you-do-that.html.

269 See http://jenniferfulwiler.com/2012/04/contra-ception-the-discussion-has-begun/.

270 See http://companionscross.org/articles-blogs/dai-ly-reflection/effective-prayer.

271 Madrid, *Why Be Catholic?*, 17–18.

272 See CCC 1210.

273 Madrid, *Why Be Catholic?*, 37.

274 Madrid, *Why Be Catholic?*, 37, 41, 42.

275 Madrid, *Why Be Catholic?*, 40.

276 See CCC 1131, 1127, 1129.

277 See CCC 1131, 1128, 1133, 1134.

278 See CCC 1098.

279 See https://www.youtube.com/watch?v=CJtRXzy-Wul8.

Chapter 10

280 See CCC 1370.

281 See http://www.americancatholic.org/Features/Saints/saint.aspx?id=1097.

282 See CCC 1394.

283 See http://www.usccb.org/about/media-relations/backgrounders/structure-and-meaning-of-the-mass-backgrounder.cfm.

284 Ibid.

285 See http://www.patheos.com/blogs/albertlittle/so-you-think-youre-smarter-than-the-early-church-fathers/.

286 Madrid, *Why Be Catholic?*, 58–59.

287 See http://www.newadvent.org/fathers/0107.htm (chapter 7).

288 See http://www.therealpresence.org/eucharst/father/a5.html#justin.

289   See https://www.crossroadsinitiative.com/
      library_article/383/Real_Presence_of_Christ_in_
      the_Eucharist_in_the_Early_Church__St._Cyril_
      of_Jerusalem.html.

290   See http://afriarslife.blogspot.com/2008/05/you-
      will-be-changed-into-me.html.

291   See http://w2.vatican.va/content/francesco/
      en/audiences/2018/documents/papa-fran-
      cesco_20180321_udienza-generale.html.

292   See http://www.vatican.va/spirit/documents/
      spirit_20010427_leone-grande_en.html.

293   See https://www.crossroadsinitiative.com/media/
      articles/eucharist-and-the-incarnation-st-hilary/.

294   See http://www.usccb.org/about/media-relations/
      backgrounders/structure-and-meaning-of-the-
      mass-backgrounder.cfm.

295   See http://www.catholic365.com/article/337/i-
      dont-get-anything-out-of-mass.html.

296   See CCC 2181.

Chapter 11

297   See http://www.usccb.org/beliefs-and-teachings/
      how-we-teach/parish-life/.

298   Robert J. Spitzer, *Finding True Happiness: Satis-
      fying Our Restless Hearts* (San Francisco: Ignatius
      Press, 2015).

299   Spitzer, *Finding True Happiness*, 71–85.

300   Spitzer, *Finding True Happiness*, 72.

301 Hemler, *The Reality of God*, chapter 10.

302 For example, see http://www.holyspiritinteractive. net/columns/aneelaranha/personalprayer/preface. asp.

303 For a popular Bible study guide based on the daily Mass readings, see http://wau.org/subscribe/.

304 For example, see http://www.cdu.edu/.

305 See http://americamagazine.org/issue/100/ what-theology-and-not.

306 See http://w2.vatican.va/content/francesco/en/ angelus/2014/documents/papa-francesco_ange-lus_20141221.html.

307 See https://www.goodreads.com/author/ quotes/30796.Hans_Urs_von_Balthasar.

APPENDIX OF BIBLE ABBREVIATIONS

Bible Book Names and Their Abbreviations

Old Testament

Genesis	Gn	Esther	Est
Exodus	Ex	Job	Jb
Leviticus	Lv	Psalms	Ps
Numbers	Nm	Proverbs	Prv
Deuteronomy	Dt	Ecclesiastes	Eccl
Joshua	Jo	Song of Songs	Sg
Judges	Jgs	Wisdom of	
Ruth	Ru	Solomon	Ws
1 Samuel	1 Sm	Sirach	Sir
2 Samuel	2 Sm	Isaiah	Is
1 Kings	1 Kgs	Jeremiah	Jer
2 Kings	2 Kgs	Lamentations	Lam
1 Chronicles	1 Chr	Baruch	Bar
2 Chronicles	2 Chr	Ezekiel	Ez
Ezra	Ezr	Daniel	Dn
Nehemiah	Neh	Hosea	Hos
Tobit	Tb	Joel	Jl
Judith	Jdt	Amos	Am

Obadiah . . . . .Ob
Jonah . . . . .Jon
Micah . . . . .Mi
Nahum . . . . .Na
Habakkuk . . . . . . .Hb
Zephaniah . . . . . . .Zep

Haggai . . . . .Hg
Zechariah . . . . .Zec
Malachi . . . . .Mal
1 Maccabees . . . . .1 Mc
2 Maccabees . . . . .2 Mc

New Testament

St. Matthew . . . . . .Mt
St. Mark . . . . .Mk
St. Luke . . . . .Lk
St. John . . . . .Jn
Acts of the
   Apostles . . . . . . .Acts
Romans . . . . .Rom
1 Corinthians . . . .1 Cor
2 Corinthians . . . .2 Cor
Galatians . . . . .Gal
Ephesians . . . . .Eph
Philippians . . . . . . .Phil
Colossians . . . . . . .Col
1 Thessalonians . . .1 Thes

2 Thessalonians . . .2 Thes
1 Timothy . . . . . . .1 Tm
2 Timothy . . . . . . .2 Tm
Titus . . . . .Ti
Philemon . . . . .Phlm
Hebrews . . . . .Heb
St. James . . . . .Jas
1 St. Peter . . . . .1 Pt
2 St. Peter . . . . .2 Pt
1 St. John . . . . .1 Jn
2 St. John . . . . .2 Jn
3 St. John . . . . .3 Jn
St. Jude . . . . .Jude
Revelation . . . . . . .Rv

BIBLIOGRAPHY

DVDs

Moody, Raymond, and Jeffery Long. *Afterlife*. DVD. Directed by Paul Perry. Los Angeles: Vanguard Cinema, 2011.

Pacwa, Mitch, et al. *Did Jesus Really Rise From The Dead?* DVD. Directed by David Wright. San Francisco: Ignatius Press, 2008.

Richards, Larry. *The Mass Explained*. DVD. Erie, PA: The Reason For Our Hope Foundation.

———. *What More Could He Do For You?* DVD. Erie, PA: The Reason For Our Hope Foundation.

Strobel, Lee. *The Case for Christ*. DVD. Directed by Timothy Eaton and Michael Eaton. Santa Monica, CA: La Mirada Films, 2007.

Books

Auer, Jim. *Do I Have to Go to Church?* Liguori, Missouri: Liguori Publications, 2001.

Broussard, Karlo. *Prepare the Way: How to Overcome Obstacles to God, the Gospel, and the Church.* El Cajon, California: Catholic Answers Press, 2018.

Chacon, Frank and Jim Burnham. *Beginning Apologetics 1: How to Explain and Defend the Catholic Faith.* Farmington, New Mexico: San Juan Catholic Seminars, 2004.

———. *Beginning Apologetics 3: How to Explain and Defend the Real Presence of Christ in the Eucharist.* Farmington, New Mexico: San Juan Catholic Seminars, 2004.

Currie, David. *Born Fundamentalist, Born Again Catholic.* San Francisco: Ignatius Press, 1996.

Farrell, Walter and Martin J. Healy. *My Way of Life: The Summa Simplified for Everyone.* Brooklyn, New York: Confraternity of the Precious Blood, 1952.

Geisler, Norman L. and Frank Turek. *I Don't Have Enough Faith to be an Atheist.* Wheaton, Illinois: Crossway Books, 2004.

Horn, Trent. *Why We're Catholic: Our Reasons for Faith, Hope, and Love.* El Cajon, California: Catholic Answers Press, 2017.

Kelly, Matthew. *Rediscover Catholicism: A Spiritual Guide to Living With Passion and Purpose.* Cincinnati, Ohio: Beacon Publishing, 2010.

———. *Rediscover Jesus: An Invitation.* Cincinnati, Ohio: Beacon Publishing, 2015.

Kreeft, Peter J. and Ronald K. Tacelli. *Pocket Handbook of Christian Apologetics.* Downers Grove, Illinois: InterVarsity Press, 2003.

————. *Handbook of Catholic Apologetics: Reasoned Answers to Questions of Faith*. San Francisco: Ignatius Press, 2009.

Lewis, C. S. *Mere Christianity*. New York: HarperCollins Publishers, 2009.

Long, Jeffrey. *Evidence of the Afterlife: The Science of Near-Death Experiences*. New York: HarperOne, 2010.

Long, Jeffrey, with Paul Perry. *God and the Afterlife: The Groundbreaking New Evidence for God and Near-Death Experience*. New York: HarperOne, 2016.

Martin, Curtis. *Made for More*. Cincinnati, Ohio: Beacon Publishing, 2008.

Madrid, Patrick. *Why Be Catholic? Ten Answers to a Very Important Question*. New York: Image, 2014.

Moody, Raymond A. *Life After Life: The Investigation of a Phenomenon–Survival of Bodily Death*. New York: HarperOne, 2001.

Nelson, Matt. *Just Whatever: How to Help the Spiritually Indifferent Find Beliefs that Really Matter*. El Cajon, California: Catholic Answers Press, 2018.

Olson, Carl E. *Did Jesus Really Rise from the Dead? Questions and Answers about the Life, Death, and Resurrection of Jesus Christ*. San Francisco: Ignatius Press-Augustine Institute, 2016.

Pinto, Matthew J. and Chris Stefanick. *Do I Have to Go? 101 Questions about the Mass, the Eucharist, and Your Spiritual Life*. West Chester, Pennsylvania: Ascension Press, 2008.

Schönborn, Christoph Cardinal. *God Sent His Son: A*

Contemporary Christology. San Francisco: Ignatius Press, 2010.

Schreck, Alan. *Catholic and Christian: An Explanation of Commonly Misunderstood Catholic Beliefs.* Cincinnati, Ohio: St. Anthony Messenger Press, 2004.

———. *Catholic and Christian for Young Adults.* Cincinnati, Ohio: St. Anthony Messenger Press, 2007.

Spitzer, Robert J. *Finding True Happiness: Satisfying Our Restless Hearts.* San Francisco: Ignatius Press, 2015.

———. *The Soul's Upward Yearning: Clues to Our Transcendent Nature from Experience and Reason.* San Francisco: Ignatius Press, 2015.

———. *God So Loved the World: Clues to Our Transcendent Destiny from the Revelation of Jesus.* San Francisco: Ignatius Press, 2016.

Sri, Edward. *A Biblical Walk Through the Mass: Understanding What We Say and Do In The Liturgy.* West Chester, Pennsylvania: Ascension Press, 2011.

———. *Love Unveiled: The Catholic Faith Explained.* San Francisco: Ignatius Press, 2015.

Strobel, Lee. *The Case for Easter.* Grand Rapids, Michigan: Zondervan, 2003.

Vogt, Brandon. *Return: How to Draw Your Child Back to the Church.* Winter Springs, Florida: Numinous Books, 2015.

———. *Why I Am Catholic (And You Should Be Too).* Notre Dame, Indiana: Ave Maria Press, 2017.

White, Thomas, and Desmond O'Donnell. *Renewal of Faith: Adult Instruction in the Catholic Faith.* Notre Dame, Indiana: Ave Maria Press, 1974.

WHEN ,
Becca met him halfway. No man had ever
called her Rebecca. No man had ever made
her name sound like a prayer. No man had
ever looked at her the way Zane was looking at
her, with awe, as though she were . . . special in some way. Special to him. As if he could
see all of her, inside and out, and liked—very
much—what he saw. His look melted something inside her that she hadn't realized had
been frozen.

But trepidation wouldn't be so easily
chased away. "I'm not . . ." Becca tried looking everywhere but at him.

With a thumb to her chin, he turned her
head back. "Not what?"

Feeling all those delicious feelings fade,
she wanted to weep. "I told you—I'm not any
luckier at this than I am at anything else."

Zane heard the nerves in her voice and
reined himself in. With a deep breath he
slowly shook his head. "We're really going to
have to do something about that attitude of
yours." He placed a kiss on the turned-up tip
of her nose. "What if I told you I could prove
you wrong?"

Becca's breath caught. Possibilities blossomed. From somewhere she had the nerve to
ask, "Could you?"

Zane's smile came slowly. His eyes darkened. "Oh, darlin', just give me half a chance."

WHAT ARE *LOVESWEPT* ROMANCES?

They are stories of true romance and touching emotion. We believe those two very important ingredients are constants in our highly sensual and very believable stories in the LOVE-SWEPT line. Our goal is to give you, the reader, stories of consistently high quality that may sometimes make you laugh, sometimes make you cry, but are always fresh and creative and contain many delightful surprises within their pages.

Most romance fans read an enormous number of books. Those they truly love, they keep. Others may be traded with friends and soon forgotten. We hope that each LOVESWEPT romance will be a treasure—a "keeper." We will always try to publish

LOVE STORIES YOU'LL NEVER FORGET
BY AUTHORS YOU'LL ALWAYS REMEMBER

The Editors

Loveswept® 827

ONE
RAINY
NIGHT

JANIS REAMS
HUDSON

BANTAM BOOKS
NEW YORK · TORONTO · LONDON · SYDNEY · AUCKLAND

ONE RAINY NIGHT
A Bantam Book / March 1997

LOVESWEPT *and the wave design are registered trademarks of*
Bantam Books, *a division of Bantam Doubleday Dell Publishing Group,*
Inc. *Registered in U.S. Patent and Trademark Office and elsewhere.*

ISBN 0-553-44542-1

Published simultaneously in the United States and Canada

Bantam Books are published by Bantam Books, a division of Bantam Dou-
bleday Dell Publishing Group, Inc. Its trademark, consisting of the words
"Bantam Books" and the portrayal of a rooster, is Registered in U.S. Patent
and Trademark Office and in other countries. Marca Registrada. Bantam
Books, 1540 Broadway, New York, New York 10036.

PRINTED IN THE UNITED STATES OF AMERICA

OPM   0 9 8 7 6 5 4 3 2 1

With love and gratitude to Donita Lawrence and all the readers at Bell, Book and Candle, Del City, Oklahoma. Thanks for naming the hero of this book. When the votes were tallied, Zane Houston was born. Here he is, ladies. Enjoy!

ONE

Lightning flashed outside the window. Overhead, the kitchen light flickered off. The man at the table barely noticed, just as he barely noticed a moment later when the light flickered on again. The unopened bottle of Jim Beam was cool and sleek in his hand. Smooth, like a woman.

That was a laugh. It had been even longer since he'd had a woman than it had since he'd had a drink. The drink, he could still taste. The woman, he couldn't even remember, and that shamed him. A lot of things shamed him these days, but he was trying to put them behind him. More or less.

In his other hand he caressed the pistol, his Glock 9mm. It, too, was smooth and sleek, and promised him more peace than he'd ever found in a bottle or with a woman. He tried to think of a reason not to put the barrel in his mouth and pull the trigger. There used to be reasons. He just couldn't remember what they were these days.

Maybe later. He was too tired just then to bother ending it all. If he didn't get some sleep soon, he wouldn't have to bother doing anything, he would simply keel over dead.

But when he closed his eyes, there was no sleep. Only blood. Dead, staring eyes. A hand reaching out to him for help he couldn't give. Al's hand. Al's dead, staring eyes. Al's blood.

Zane swore and released the bottle for a moment to scrub a hand over his face. The bottle had occasionally helped block out the nightmares that haunted him, the guilt that ate at him. At least, for a time.

He reached for the bottle again, only to realize his hand was shaking.

With a deep breath he concentrated on letting go—of the tension in his shoulders, the guilt in his gut. The bottle. The gun. They would all keep.

Neither the booze nor the gun was going anywhere. They'd be around when he wanted them.

He shoved the bottle of bourbon aside. It was much too slow and humiliating a way to die. The Glock, on the other hand . . .

No, not yet. It would be rude as hell of him to splatter his brains all over his landlady's nice kitchen. The gun could wait, at least until after he'd testified next month and Buddy King was convicted and headed for death row, where the bastard belonged.

❖━━━━━❖

With a plastic tub of fudge in one hand and Clint Black wailing from the stereo downstairs, Becca Cameron leaned down to peer through the telescope in her aunt and uncle's upstairs bedroom window. She hadn't touched the telescope since that morning when she'd located the mockingbird nest in the rose of Sharon bush in front of the kitchen window of the rental house across the street. In fact, she hadn't touched the telescope then either. She'd looked through it, but hadn't touched it.

Uncle Jim had been specific. "Don't touch it, Becca. It's focused on that nest I've been watching. You can look through it, but don't touch. Got it?"

Got it. She hadn't touched. But she had looked.

What a hoot. She was really getting in to this bird-watching hobby of Uncle Jim's. If her brothers could see her now, they'd razz her clear into next week.

But the light was on in the window directly behind the nest across the street, so Becca was hoping for a glimpse of the mama bird hunkered down over the nest. She wanted to assure herself that the pounding rain just before sunset hadn't drowned the baby birds.

Lightning flashed and lit the sky. More rain was coming. Becca frowned. "Not my fault." It had been raining most of the past two weeks. Uncle Jim talked about those hatchlings across the street as if they were his own kids. If Becca had to tell him they drowned while he and Aunt Sue were off on vacation, it would break his heart. And somebody would blame Becca. They always did.

"No more rain," she begged the sky. "Please." She wasn't going to take the blame for drowning baby birds.

It had actually stopped raining earlier in the day and the sun shone for about an hour. Becca used the opportunity to get some shots with Uncle Jim's camera of a cardinal in the brush along the road out front. Jim hadn't said not to touch the camera.

At the reminder, she swore under her breath. She'd snapped a couple of mediocre shots before getting the hang of the shutter action. By the time the cardinal started flitting from branch to limb to barbed wire, she'd been able to follow, snapping shots in rapid succession. She'd even captured the bird in flight when a car came along the side road and scared it from its perch. It would have been a perfect shot except for the car.

Instead, it was a perfect shot of Mark Hammond, foreman of the Bar B down the road in Smith County, and a passenger, a white-haired man she'd never seen before, as they'd turned the corner onto the road that ran past the house.

Becca wouldn't be showing that picture to her uncle. He would only laugh at her bad luck. Although, maybe he could add a little humor to the book he was doing, *Crow County Has More Than Just Crows*. Jim could use the shot she'd taken by mistake. Hammond had been driving his go-to-town car instead of his ranch truck. The caption could read: "Although they fly through the area from time to time, Firebirds are not known to nest in Crow County."

Munching on another piece of fudge, Becca patted the roll of film in her pocket and leaned down toward the eyepiece of the telescope. On the outside chance that any of her shots were good enough for Uncle Jim to use, she would take the film to town tomorrow and drop it off for developing.

She'd meant to do it today, but made it all the way there with the film still sitting in the kitchen. She'd felt like an idiot, standing at the counter in the drugstore with empty hands. The day had gone downhill from there.

Geoff Terrill, a sheriff's deputy she'd gone to high school with, usually offered a sympathetic ear when Becca messed things up. Today, when she'd told him about the botched photographs and that she'd forgotten the film, he laughed at her. The jerk.

"Don't tell me you got a shot of Mark and that rodeo queen from down in Ardmore. You could make a fortune selling him the negatives before his wife finds out."

"Why that woman puts up with him," Becca had said, "is a mystery. But it wasn't a woman in the car with him. Just some man with snow-white hair and enough gold chains around his neck to strangle a bull moose."

"Jeez, Becca, you can't even take a decent black-mail picture."

She'd made a face at Geoff and left. When she'd come home, the kitchen faucet had sprung a leak and she'd had to replace a washer, skinning her knuckles in the process. To treat herself afterward, she made a pan of fudge. That it came out the consistency of sun-baked adobe, and with a slightly scorched flavor, proved the perfect topper to a lousy day. One peek at Uncle Jim's nest, then she would finish off Aunt Sue's apple pie and turn in.

Tomorrow had to be better.

Becca squeezed one eye shut and peered with the other through the eyepiece of the telescope. The smell of vanilla, which she'd spilled down her jeans and somehow managed to get in her hair while making fudge, teased her nose.

Through the telescope, things were fuzzier in the dark. If she turned the knob just a little, she could refocus tomorrow in the daylight. She wouldn't hurt anything by doing that.

She turned the knob just a hair. The wrong way. The dark blob that she thought was the nest grew fuzzier, while whatever that was beyond the window, inside the lighted kitchen, grew sharper.

Good grief, a gun! The man across the street had a gun in his hand. She couldn't see him, only the table, where one large, dark hand held a big, ugly gun, and the other grasped a bottle of whiskey.

A shiver of dread rushed down her spine. "What's wrong with this picture?"

The man wasn't cleaning the gun, he was caressing it. Lifting it. Pointing it . . . *at himself*!

"No!"

Becca whirled and raced down the stairs, out the front door. There was no time to call anyone for help, and no one to call. The nearest house was more than a mile to the south, the closest town, thirty miles east. If anyone was going to stop the man from . . . from . . . Lord, she couldn't even think the words.

There was no one to help. No one but her. A screwup and a jinx. Bad-Luck Becca.

The poor man didn't stand a chance.

But she had to try.

Panting in terror, she sprinted down the gravel drive, across the muddy road, up the yard of her aunt and uncle's rental house. "Don't do it, mister." She thought she'd yelled, but it came out in a whisper. "Don't you dare shoot yourself while I'm the only person around. Don't you dare!"

Sure, people called her a jinx and a screwup. Things went wrong when she was around. But not something like this! "No, no, no!"

She leapt onto the front porch and pounded on the door with her fist. "Open up! Mister? I know you're in there! Open up!" What was his name, she wondered desperately. Uncle Jim had told her, but—

The door jerked open beneath her fist.

Becca nearly sagged with relief as the big man loomed before her. She had a bad moment when she realized the gun was still in his hand. Then his name suddenly burst through her mind. "Zane Houston!"

"Who the hell are you?"

Becca stared at him, her chest heaving with exertion and the remnants of terror. "Becca Cameron," she answered automatically. He was tall, just over six feet, and menacing as the devil with that fierce frown that drew his eyebrows together over eyes as dark as day-old coffee. *And a gun in his hand.*

But those eyes. So full of torment, fatigue. Becca had the inexplicable urge to reach out to him.

"What do you want?"

I want you not to kill yourself! She couldn't say that. It didn't occur to her that he might use the gun on her. She only knew that she didn't want to do or say anything to remind him of what he'd been about to do when he'd sat alone at his kitchen table. If that's what he'd really been about to do. If that's what the pain in his eyes meant.

But what excuse could she give for barging in on a stranger after ten at night? She glanced down and realized she still held the plastic tub in her hand. Incredible. Stupid. But it would have to do.

"I, uh, made fudge. I thought you might like some."

Zane tucked his pistol into the back of his belt and shook his head, certain he'd heard wrong. Maybe he was hallucinating from lack of sleep. How else could he account for a pixie with hair shorter than his standing on his doorstep late at night offering him candy in a husky, breathless voice that slid over him like dark velvet?

He glanced beyond her into the night. No car in his driveway, none on the road. Where the hell had she come from?

Lightning flashed again. Zane's blood ran cold. The brief flash of light revealed a figure rising up out of the bar ditch that separated his yard from the road. The figure of a man. A man with a rifle.

In reflex Zane hit the light switch beside the door and darkened the hall as he jerked the woman into the house and down to the floor. She screamed.

Blue and orange fire spat three times in rapid succession from the barrel of the rifle as Zane landed half on top of her and rolled. Three *boom*s nearly covered the sound of three *splat*s as three holes appeared in the wall across from the front door. Something in the living room beyond shattered.

Son of a bitch.

Heading for the scant cover against the wall, Zane rolled again, ending up on top of the woman. In the glow of the kitchen light around the corner, he took a quick glance at her. He'd never seen her before. He was sure of that.

A strange woman knocks on his door, and less than ten seconds later someone takes a shot at him. Three shots.

Coincidence? He didn't believe it for a minute. And she looked so damned innocent. Like a little pixie. Although she didn't feel like a pixie, the way her breasts cushioned his chest and her thighs cradled his hips. She felt like a woman. And he was a stupid son of a bitch for noticing.

He braced his forearm across her neck. "Who sent you?" Damn, she even smelled like a woman—warm. Sweet. Like . . . sugar cookies. He added pressure to her throat and hated doing it.

She opened her mouth, but the only thing that came out was a choking sound. Her eyes bulged.

Zane eased the pressure on her throat and kicked the door shut. "Who sent you?" he demanded again. "Who set me up? Who's the shooter in the ditch?"

Gasping for breath, Becca gaped at the man looming over her. *Deranged*, she thought frantically. The man was deranged.

"Who sent you?" The weight of his forearm increased across her throat, cutting off her breath again.

"Nobody!" she croaked.

Her wide, frightened eyes almost made a believer out of him. Almost. "You just showed up on my doorstep and somebody started shooting? You expect me to buy that?"

"I—you—agh."

Okay, he wouldn't choke her after all. He eased up on her throat again. As he did, he whipped off his belt and used it to tie her hands behind her back.

"Hey! What are you doing?"

"Got your voice back, I see."

"Look, mister—"

"Save it. I'm going to have a look around outside. If you're as innocent as you're pretending, you won't make a sound."

"You're going to leave me here, tied up like this, so somebody can shoot me?"

"Like this? Yes. Here? No. And if I'm not mistaken, it's me he's shooting at."

Next to the front door was the coat closet. Zane pushed open the sliding door, stuffed the woman inside, and slid the door closed.

"You can't leave me in here!"

"Quiet," he commanded.

Dismissing the woman as the bait used to lure him to the door, he rolled again, this time across the hall and into the kitchen. There he hit the light switch and plunged the room—the whole house, since that had been the only light—into darkness. Careful to be quiet, he checked his pistol and let himself out the side door.

The grass was wet. Waterlogged, after two weeks of downpours. Judging by the lightning and thunder, it was going to get wetter before the night was over.

Zane circled around the back of the house and made his way carefully through the woods that edged his yard. Water dripped off branches as he ducked beneath them. Minutes before he reached the ditch, a car door slammed down the road to his left.

No need for quiet now. Zane ran the rest of the way to the ditch. When he jumped it—or, rather, when he landed on the other side—a screaming shaft of pain shot up his thigh and down his shin from the area of the steel pin just above his right knee. *Son of a bitch.* How could a metal pin hurt so bad that his vision grayed? How could steel hurt at all, dammit?

The pain cleared his head in time for him to see a car take off into the night. At that distance and through the darkness, all he could see were the tail-lights that told him the car was a late model, a full-sized sedan, dark in color.

With a grunt that was half dissatisfaction and half pain, Zane limped back to the house, careful to avoid stepping where the shooter might have. Paying no attention to the mud he tracked, he went in through the front door.

In the closet, Becca heard footsteps approach the house. It was a minor miracle that she could hear anything over the pounding of her heart. Instantly she stilled her struggles to get free of the belt binding her wrists behind her back.

Who was it? The tenant, or the man shooting at them?

Her mouth went dry.

The front door creaked open. The footsteps entered the house. Uneven footsteps, someone limping badly.

Becca held her breath and prayed.

The footsteps stopped before the closet door. "You can yell all you want now," came Zane Houston's voice.

Light filtered in through the cracks around the door. Blessed light, scant though it was, easing the tightness in her chest. Becca wilted in relief, then stiffened in outrage at his casual tone. "Let me out of here! Untie my hands!"

"In a minute."

Zane left her on the floor of the closet and went to the kitchen phone to call the county sheriff's office, knowing the sheriff himself wasn't likely to be there this time of night. Harp had a family now. He was probably snuggled up at home on his farm, surrounded by his wife and kids. But when the dispatcher answered the phone, Zane gave his name and asked, "Is Sheriff Montgomery in?"

"Hold on."

While waiting, he absently massaged the ache just above his right knee. The screaming pain had settled into a dull throb.

"Hey, Houston, ol' buddy." Harper Montgomery's familiar voice rang over the phone line. "What's up?"

"Not much. Just wanted to report a shooting."

The friendly, bantering tone disappeared, replaced by steel. "In my county?"

"In my yard."

"You do the shooting?"

"I wish. I was the target."

"I'll be right there." The line went dead.

Zane hung up the phone and reached for the flashlight he kept beneath the kitchen sink.

"Hey! Let me out of here!"

Oh, yeah. The woman in the closet. The bait to lure him to the door.

"Let me out of here!"

He really should let her out of the closet. He really should question her, shake loose a few answers. And he would. Later. First he wanted a look in the ditch before the rain returned and wiped out all signs of the shooter.

Flashlight in hand, Zane stepped back out through the front door and ignored the pounding and cursing from inside his front closet. As he approached the ditch, fat, intermittent raindrops pelted him. What Al would have called an eight-inch rain—drops eight inches wide and eight inches apart.

After more than a year, it still hurt to think of Al. They'd been partners for four years. So long that more than a year after Al's death, Zane still caught himself turning to say something to the man who was closer to him than a brother. Caught himself thinking, *I'll have to remember to tell Al that one.*

Those incidents were worse than the nightmares.

Everyone had told him that the pain would dull with time. They'd been right. It didn't help though. Dull or sharp, pain was pain. Guilt was guilt.

Three inches of runoff from earlier rains rushed along the bottom of the ditch. The shooter had left plenty of signs, none of them useful. Skids and gouges in the mud spoke of presence, but not identity. No clear footprints, no spent shells.

Using his flashlight, Zane searched in wider and wider circles, knowing it was useless. The shooter had parked his car down the road, walked back to the house, then left the same way he'd come. Zane found where the car had been parked, but there was nothing useful there either.

By the time he returned to his yard, the fat raindrops had turned into a light drizzle, the red and blue lights of the sheriff's car were flashing their way down the road from town, and Zane's leg was stiffening up.

The sheriff pulled his tan and white car into Zane's driveway while two deputies parked in the road.

Crow County Sheriff Harper Montgomery stepped out of his car and settled his Stetson against the rain. They'd never been partners, but they were old friends, Harp and Zane. They'd both worked for several years as agents for the Oklahoma State Bureau of Investigation, until a couple of years ago, when Harp retired and settled on his family farm in Crow County.

"Anybody hurt?" Harp asked.

Zane resisted the urge to rub his thigh. "No."

"You're limping."

"Yeah, so?"

"Idiot." Harper's tone was only slightly exasperated. "When are you going to get your butt back into physical therapy, where you belong?"

It was an old argument and one Zane didn't intend to pursue. The doctors had told him that his leg would never be one hundred percent again, so what was the point? "I didn't call you because of my physical shortcomings."

"Mental shortcomings, you mean," Harper retorted. "You wouldn't limp like that if you'd get back and finish that damn therapy. If it's not already too late."

"You wanna know what happened here, or not?"

With a heavy sigh Harper looked up and let the rain fall on his face. "All right." He lowered his face and wiped it with his hand. "What happened?"

Inside the front closet Becca had managed to slide the door open with her feet and was struggling futilely to free her hands. She'd heard the man call the sheriff, heard his uneven steps leave the house again. An eternity of tense silence passed before she heard the crunch and squish of tires on the mud and gravel of the driveway. Now car doors were slamming. Voices called out.

The sheriff?

She sincerely hoped so. She wanted out of this damn closet!

To that end she struggled to her knees, but getting her head out from inside the denim jacket hanging from the rod above her took a minute. Finally she stumbled out into the hall. The first thing she saw was the flashing red and blue lights of three county sheriff's cars. Her knees weakened with relief.

"Sheriff!"

Walking back from the ditch with Zane, Harper Montgomery jerked his head up at the sound of her voice. "What the—Becca? Is that you?"

Zane flinched. "You know her?"

"Hell, Zane, everybody knows Becca Cameron. I'm just surprised you do." Harp punctuated his comment with a grin and a slap on Zane's back.

"I wouldn't say I actually know her," Zane muttered. But her name tugged at a hidden memory.

Zane followed Harper to the porch, where the woman waited. Her face was pale, her eyes wide. Her short hair stood on end, like a cartoon character who'd stuck his finger in a light socket.

Becca Cameron. Becca Cameron. Why was that name suddenly so familiar?

She turned her back to him and Harp and wiggled her bound hands. "If someone would be so kind?"

Harp's mouth dropped open. "What the hell? What's going on around here?" he demanded.

Becca Cameron. Zane delved for the elusive memory. *Becca Cameron. Becca—*

"You tied up your landlord's niece?" Harp demanded.

Hell. Zane closed his eyes. "The niece." He remembered now. Jim Anderson had told him his niece would be house-sitting while Jim and Sue cruised the Bahamas for a couple of weeks. "Hell."

Becca Cameron made a low, snarling sound.

"Would someone *please* untie my hands before my fingers fall off from lack of circulation?"

"Only to you, Becca, would something like this happen." Harper reached to free her hands.

Zane waved him aside. "I'll do it."

"You're too kind," Becca said with a tight smile.

"Look, I'm sorry, all right?" Zane loosened the belt around her wrists and slipped it off. "What was I supposed to think? A strange woman comes to my door late at night—"

"I am not strange."

"—with some lame excuse about bringing me candy—"

"Which is now scattered all over your floor in pieces, thanks to you."

"—and suddenly bullets start flying."

"So naturally you blamed me."

"Naturally," Zane answered.

Wild-eyed, Becca whirled on Harp. "This was not my fault, Harper. Don't you go saying it was."

"I didn't say a word," Harp protested.

"Not yet, but you or somebody else will get around to it." She jabbed a finger in Zane's direction. "*He* already thinks it was my fault."

"I said I was sorry," Zane replied tersely.

Becca's eyes narrowed. "You didn't have to stuff me in the closet."

"You stuffed her— No." Harper held up a hand for silence. "Never mind. I don't want to know. Save it for your statement, both of you."

Becca rubbed her aching wrists. "I'll give you a statement all right."

"I expect you will. Mike," Harper called to one of the deputies standing at the end of the driveway. "Get a couple of evidence bags and come help me get the slugs. Jim, you keep an eye out."

Mike LaMott had been a deputy with the Crow County Sheriff's Department since Becca was a little girl. On his way into the house with what looked like plastic sandwich bags in his hand, he stopped and gave her the once-over from beneath bushy gray eyebrows. "You okay, girl?"

Remembering the gunfire, Becca shivered and tugged her cardigan tightly around her. "Yeah. I'm okay."

She followed Harper, Mike, and Zane Houston into the house. Using a pocket knife, Zane enlarged a hole in the Sheetrock and dug a bullet out of the wall stud there. The other two bullets had missed the stud and gone through the wall into the living room. One had taken out a table lamp and flattened itself against the fireplace. The brick there would never be the same. The third bullet had gone straight through the room and out the back window before burying itself in a post on the back porch.

Becca watched it all with a sense of detachment. Logically she knew someone had fired three bullets at her and Zane Houston, but it didn't seem real. The sting in her wrists, the pain in her shoulder from landing on the floor, the ache in her throat from a big mean arm, the memory of a man's hips settling arrogantly between her thighs—those things were real. She barely remembered the bullets.

Zane left the house and returned in a few moments with a piece of plywood. Harper and Mike helped him secure it over the broken window.

When they finished, Harper turned toward Becca. "Are you up to giving me a statement now?"

"I'm as up as I'll ever be. What do you want to know?"

He shook his head. "We'll do it at the station. I'd like both of you to come into town and give me your statements."

"Not tonight," Becca protested.

" 'Fraid so," Harper said. "While everything's fresh in your minds. You said you were up to it. It shouldn't take too long. All you'll have to do is tell me what happened so I can get it down straight. You can ride in with Zane, can't she, Zane."

"I can drive myself, thank you," Becca stated flatly.

Zane snorted. "Yeah, sure. If you don't mind ending up in the ditch. The way you're shaking, you'll probably never even get the key in the ignition."

Becca opened her mouth to protest, then snapped it shut. She couldn't argue against the obvious. It wasn't just her hands that shook. Every bone inside her was rattling, every muscle quivering in the aftermath of the terror that had gripped her.

She turned to Harper. "I'll ride with you. This man's a maniac and people are shooting at him."

"He's not a maniac," Harper protested. "Zane is an old friend. We worked together at the OSBI. You're welcome to ride with me—"

"Thanks."

"—but Tommy Carmichael got drunk and disorderly last night at the dance over at the VFW and I had to take him in. He threw up in the backseat. Nachos and beer."

"Never mind," Becca said quickly. "I guess I'll ride with him." She gestured none too graciously toward Zane.

Harper himself went with her to the house so she could get her purse and lock up. By the time she returned to the rent house across the street, her uncle's tenant had put on a denim jacket and backed his car out of the garage. He stood next to the open passenger door, waiting for her. A regular gentleman. Now that he'd decided not to strangle her.

Glancing again at the car, Becca's eyes widened. "Oh, wow." Like a sleek jungle beast poised to leap, the machine rumbled, its engine purring, ready to shake the ground at its driver's command. "Wow," Becca whispered again, her heart racing.

Zane watched, puzzled, as Becca Cameron disregarded the rain plastering her short hair against her skull and circled his car. She reached out and stroked the front fender as though it were a lover. The sudden image of those slender hands on him sent blood rushing to places that hadn't felt such a rush in more than a year. It came on so fast, so unexpectedly, it had him sucking in a sharp breath and stuffing his hands in the front pockets of his jeans.

Suddenly she turned on Zane. "Put it back."

"What?"

"Put it back in the garage. It's getting wet."

"Yeah, it does that when it rains."

"Put it back," she cried. "My God, you can't mean to drive this on these muddy roads."

"That's exactly what I mean to do, if you'll get in before we both drown."

"But—it's a *Mustang*."

"Yeah, so?"

"A 'sixty-nine Mach One. In mint condition. You can't take a car like this out on roads like that." She splayed her hands across the wet hood. "Unless I miss my guess, you've got a Cobra Jet Ram-Air 428 under here, capable of doing the quarter mile in 13.9 seconds, even though the 'sixty-nine outweighs the original model by more than a thousand pounds."

Zane blinked against the rain. It was a little like watching a two-year-old read from an encyclopedia. With those huge gray eyes in that pixie face, Becca Cameron didn't look like she had a brain in her head, yet she spouted statistics worthy of *Car and Driver* about a car built before she'd been born.

"I jinx people," she said, looking over at him.

"You what?"

"I jinx people. When I'm around, things go

wrong. Tonight is a case in point. You really don't want to drive this car with me in it. Something will go wrong."

"Nothing's going to go wrong that hasn't already. This car is in peak condition."

"You can say that again. They rated it at 335 horsepower," she said almost lovingly, "but most people thought that was conservative. 'Sixty-nine was the second major change in the Mustang body style, but it was the Mustang's best year. The Mach One was the best of the 'sixty-nine's. It's beautiful. A classic." She looked up at Zane. "Listen to it. That's a 750i Holley four-barrel carburetor with a racing manifold. You can't take it out on these roads like it was nothing more than a *car*. Especially not with me in it."

"You know cars," Zane said stupidly.

Slowly, she removed her hands from the matte black hood and narrowed her eyes to slits. Angry slits, Zane thought. "And if I do?"

"Nothing," Zane said quickly, holding his hands in the air and backing up. "Just making an observation."

She stomped around to the door he held open for her. "Let's go get this show over with. But if anything goes wrong, don't say I didn't warn you."

Puzzled by her defensive attitude, Zane closed the door after her and got in on the driver's side. A moment later they were following Harp's patrol car down the gravel road toward town with two deputies behind them.

◈────────◈

A dark gray full-sized late-model sedan had already circled the one-mile-square section of Crow County and parked just back from the intersection of the two gravel roads nearest the scene of the shooting. The driver turned off his lights and waited. A few moments later the county sheriff's car came barreling down the crossroad, headed back toward town.

Behind the sheriff's car came a classic Ford Mustang that looked slick as hell, followed by two more county sheriff vehicles.

Riley frowned, trying to decide what to do next. He wasn't about to go back to tell The Man face-to-face that he'd missed the target. He'd never missed before. Never. He still couldn't figure it. He would put his skill up against anybody, anytime, any place.

But from the outset, this job had been a disaster. He'd gotten his assignment, then headed out through the rain, and before he'd gotten within a mile of his target he'd gotten stuck in the mud. He'd been an hour getting unstuck.

Then he'd located the house and had been working his way close, when that crazy woman had come flying outside, streaking across the street and messing up his plans. Rushing him, forcing him to shoot before he was ready.

The whole night was almost as if he'd been jinxed. Even rushed, he shouldn't have missed. He was too damn good at what he did. When the front door of the small house had opened, his target had been centered smack in the middle of the rectangle of light, had loomed large and close in the scope of his rifle. He shouldn't have missed.

He'd have to tell The Man, but not in person. That's what cellular phones were for.

With a nervous twitch of his fingers, he punched in the number and waited.

"Yeah?"

"It's me."

"It is done, I presume," came the voice in his ear.

"Not yet."

"Excuse me? I'm certain I must have heard you wrong."

Cold sweat trickled down Riley's spine and gathered along the small of his back. "I, uh, mis—"

"Don't say it. I do not want to hear it. Just tell me you will take care of it."

Riley wiped the sweat from his palms one at a time and swallowed hard. The Man had been known to kill people for lesser mistakes than tonight's. "I'm going to take care of it."

"Yes, you are. Oh, and, Riley . . ." Silence stretched, filled only by a low, menacing hum over the cellular phone. "Don't come back until it's done."

Riley swallowed. "Yessir." He disconnected, then punched in another number.

TWO

The 1969 Cobra Mustang Mach One rumbled through the night as Zane followed the sheriff's car into town. Becca cocked her head. "Your timing could use some adjusting."

Zane slowed and downshifted at the hump where the gravel turned to pavement. "That's what all the women say."

Becca laughed. "Have trouble with women, do you? That's almost a lost art."

"Timing?"

"That too, but I meant shifting. Driving a stick shift. If your leg's bothering you, I'd be glad to drive."

Zane scowled and stopped rubbing his thigh, which he hadn't realized he'd been doing, and shifted into second. "There's nothing wrong with my leg."

Auburn eyebrows arched up beneath pixie

bangs. "If you say so." She ran her hand across the dash as she'd done the fender. As if stroking a lover.

Zane's blood surged again. Damn, what was it about this woman?

"Anyway," she said, "I like your car."

"So I gathered."

"Why did you think someone had sent me?"

"Because strange women don't usually show up on my doorstep late at night just as bullets start flying."

"When *do* they show up?"

Instead of answering, Zane cracked the window to let in some air.

"Are you always so suspicious?"

"Are you always so talkative?"

"So you thought someone sent me to . . . to what?"

Chagrined, Zane shrugged. "To get me to open the door, expose myself. Give the shooter a clean shot."

"Do all cops think like that? That someone's after them?"

"I'm not a cop anymore," he said tersely.

"Who would try to shoot you?"

"Any one of a number of people."

"How can you live like that?" She shivered, but he didn't think she was cold. "Always thinking someone's after you?" Suddenly her head whipped around to him. "Is that why you—"

Zane experienced a slight shiver of his own and

rolled up the window. "Why I what?" he asked when she didn't finish.

When she didn't answer, he glanced over in time to see her look quickly away. "What? Out with it."

"You thought I'd, what, set you up?"

That wasn't what she'd been about to ask. Zane would bet on it. The answer to what she did ask was so obvious that he said nothing.

"You threw me to the floor, tied my hands, and stuffed me in the closet."

"I said I was sorry."

"Tell that to my bruises."

He looked at her sharply. "Did I hurt you?"

Funny, Becca thought, but he really seemed to care. "A little." She rubbed her throat where his arm had choked her.

For the next couple of miles only the slap of windshield wipers and the swish of tires on rain-wet pavement broke the silence. Zane spent the time cursing himself. He had hurt her. He'd nearly strangled her. What kind of a lowlife was he, when a cute little thing like her came to his door, and he could treat her the way he had?

He'd had his reasons, but that didn't make his actions sit any better on his conscience. Then he thought to ask a question. "What were you doing there?"

"I'm house-sitting for my aunt and uncle."

"I mean at my door tonight."

Becca twined her fingers together on her lap.

She'd been afraid he would get around to that question, and she didn't know what to say to him.

"Answer me. Why did you come to my door tonight?"

"I was just being neighborly."

"Bull."

"I wanted to check and make sure everything was all right with the house."

"Bull."

"I wanted to introduce myself."

"Bull."

"I saw you pointing a gun at yourself."

Everything inside Zane turned to ice. Except for the heated flush that infused his face. Sickness born of shame rolled through his stomach.

It was nearing midnight when the four-car parade reached the small town of Crow Creek. The streets glistened in the rain, streetlights painting streaks down them like stripes.

This was Becca's town. She'd lived in Crow Creek, Oklahoma, all her life. Even late at night, even if she'd been alone rather than with a former OSBI agent, the county sheriff, and two deputies, Becca would have felt safe. There was nothing in Crow Creek to fear.

The streets were empty now, but not too many months ago at midnight on a hot summer night the streets of Crow Creek had been lined with five thousand people—two and a half times the population of the town—to watch and cheer as the Olympic torch passed through on its way to the Summer Games in Atlanta.

Imagine that. *The* Olympic torch passed through Crow Creek, Oklahoma. Becca got chills down her arms and a lump in her throat just remembering. The honor. The pride. The way the event had brought the whole town together, the whole county.

Yes, this was Becca's home. As a toddler she'd experienced her first Easter egg hunt on the thick emerald grass in the town square before the courthouse. In later years there had been town picnics, speeches by politicians, street dances, the crowning of Miss Crow Creek.

She'd played in the park over on Fourth, and had the scar on her left knee to prove it. She'd sat enthralled in the dark of the movie theater on Main and watched movie stars on the giant screen, back before the theater closed and was replaced by a video store. She'd slurped sodas at the old-fashioned fountain at the drugstore, and later, joined the horde of teenagers who'd spent every spare minute circling the Sonic Drive-In while sipping cherry Cokes.

She loved this town, this county. Here she had a home, family, friends. A feeling of freedom and independence, safety, and warmth.

But just a few miles the other side of the interstate, someone had shot at her uncle's tenant. She shivered.

"Cold?" Zane pulled in and parked next to Harper behind the county courthouse.

Becca forced a smile. "Nah. Last one in's a rotten egg." With her arms wrapped around her purse, she dashed from the car into the building, hitting three big puddles along the way and soaking her sneakers.

Zane watched her with a frown. Her moods changed faster than lightning.

After giving his thigh a quick rub while no one was looking, he climbed out of the car and joined Harp on the sidewalk. The rain looked like it was settling in for the duration.

The sheriff's office occupied a portion of the lower floor in the turn-of-the-century limestone building that served the citizens of Crow County as their courthouse.

Becca waited for them just inside the double glass doors. She seemed even smaller here, under the glare of fluorescent lights. More delicate. Still frightened, Zane realized now that he could see her eyes.

Part of that fright was his fault, but given the same set of circumstances, he wouldn't change what he'd done when he'd seen lightning flash along that rifle barrel. Not that that made the guilt for hurting and scaring her go down easier.

"Coffee?" Harper offered.

"Please," Becca answered.

Harper crossed to the coffeemaker in the back of the main office and filled two foam cups and one ceramic mug with what looked like the last dregs from an old crankcase. He passed the two cups to them and took the mug for himself. "Let's do this in my office."

"Lead the way." Becca's cup shook in her hand. When she walked, her sneakers squished and left wet tracks on the tile floor.

Small and cluttered, Harper's office was located at the end of a short hall that smelled of industrial strength cleaner. He motioned them to the two chairs facing a desk piled high with paperwork while he took his own chair behind it.

"Okay." He settled in, fired up the computer beside him. "Tell me what happened."

"Some lunatic shot at us," Becca said.

Harper looked from his screen to her. "Any idea who?"

"*Me?*" she squeaked. "How should *I* know? All I know is the big guy here threw me to the floor, tied my hands, and stuffed—"

"I've apologized. Twice."

Becca shot him a dirty look and took a sip of her coffee. The face she made nearly made Zane laugh. "God, you *drink* this?"

"Zane," Harp said, "let's start with you."

In succinct terms, Zane relayed everything that had happened from the moment Becca had pounded on his door.

The rapid clacking of the keyboard filled the room while Harper entered the information. After a few moments he stopped and glanced at Becca. "Do you have anything to add?"

"How can I add anything? Unless, of course, you want to know how dark it was in that closet, or what it's like to hear footsteps approaching and not know if it's him or the creep with the gun, or what it's like to fight your way out of a jacket that's attacked your head." She gave Zane a quick once-over. "That jacket, as a matter of fact."

"What were you doing there?" Harp asked.

Zane stiffened. That sick feeling rolled through his stomach again.

"In the closet?" Becca blinked like a baby owl. "Trying to get out."

Harper took a slow breath. "I mean at Zane's. What were you doing at Zane's?"

"Oh. Well." She took another sip, made another grimace, and set the cup down on the edge of Harp's desk. Somehow—Zane would have sworn it was an accident, except for the look in her eyes—the cup fell over. Coffee spilled across Harp's desk, soaking a notepad and heading for a stack of file folders.

With a sharp oath Harp jumped up and grabbed for the folders just as Becca did the same.

Zane watched closely as the two of them fumbled to save the paperwork and mop up the coffee with a pile of paper napkins from Harp's desk drawer. There was something going on here. She made all the right sounds of contrition, all the right moves, but Zane would almost swear that she spilled the coffee deliberately.

"Oh, Harper, I'm sorry. You know what they say about me. Nothing's safe when I'm around."

"I always thought that stuff about your bad luck was nonsense," Harper muttered. "Now we've got a shooting, and coffee all over the place, and no explanation for either. I'm starting to have my doubts, Becca girl."

With a smile of irony she flopped back onto her chair, hands in the air, palms up. "What can I say? These things just happen, you know?"

"Yeah, I know." Harper pitched the foam coffee cup into the wastebasket beside his desk. "Now. You were about to tell me the nature of your visit to Zane's."

"I was?" She blinked again. "Oh, okay. The visit was informational in nature."

"Beg pardon?"

"The TV conked out at the house—you know my luck. Things always go wrong when I'm around. Anyway, I wanted to catch the weather forecast."

Listen to her lie, Zane thought with wonder.

"I was going to ask him if he'd let me watch the weather."

"The weather," Harp said slowly. "You went to watch the weather."

"That's right. I wanted to know how long it was going to rain. As if the weathermen know anything," she added with disgust. "If this rain doesn't stop soon, we're going to have to build an ark. I think my feet are getting webbed."

Harper took another slow, deep breath and typed in the information. "Okay. You went to catch the forecast. Do either of you have anything else to add?"

"Not me," Becca said brightly with a shrug.

"What about you, Zane? Any idea who might have taken a shot at you?"

"I assume that's a rhetorical question. You know exactly what's running through my mind." It was odd that being shot at should reaffirm his decision to clean up his act, sober up. Something that felt like adrenaline stirred to life in Zane's chest. He hadn't felt it in more than a year. He tried to squelch it now because he wasn't sure he wanted to feel that alive. But it didn't appear to want to be squelched just yet. He shifted in his chair and tried to ignore the rush. "Buddy King's trial is next month."

Harp nodded. "I've thought of that. Which brings me to my recommendation that neither one of you go back home tonight."

"What?" Becca squawked.

"It may not be safe," Harper explained.

"You think that guy might come back?"

"It's a definite possibility."

"I'll just stay home and keep away from the doors and windows," Becca offered.

"Becca . . ." Harper rubbed a hand down his face. "If he opened fire as soon as Zane opened the door, then it stands to reason he saw you run across the street. He knows where you live. You may not have been the target, but now you're a witness."

Becca swallowed hard. "Oh."

"Yeah, oh." Harper looked past Zane and Becca toward his office door. "Geoff, what are you doing here this time of night?"

Deputy Geoff Terrill paused in the doorway. "Heard we had some excitement. Thought you might could use some extra help."

"The excitement's over," Harp said, "but you could do me a favor."

"Shoot."

Becca cringed. "Don't say that word around me."

Harp gave her a sympathetic chuckle. To Terrill he said, "Get the Wayside Inn on the phone and see if they've got a couple of rooms for the night for these two."

"Why, Sheriff." The deputy grinned and wiggled his eyebrows. "When did you start playing matchmaker?"

Becca scowled. "Blow it out your ear, Terrill. I'm not going to any motel."

"You'd rather go back to your uncle's and get shot at?" Harper asked casually.

Becca turned her scowl on him. "How long would I need to stay away? I'm supposed to be looking after Uncle Jim's dog and Aunt Sue's chickens."

"A day or two at the most. I'll have one of my

men stop by and take care of the animals. That will give us some time to check around."

She scoffed. "You have no idea who fired the shots, where he came from, where he went, but everything will be fine in a day or two? Ha!"

Harper rubbed his face again. "Just go to the motel, Becca, where you'll be safe."

"This is a really dumb idea." Becca slumped down in the seat of the Mustang and crossed her arms over her chest. "I don't trust Geoff Terrill an inch. It'll be all over town by breakfast that I'm shacked up in the motel with some man. That's just what I need."

Old habit had Zane checking his rearview mirror to make sure they weren't being followed. Becca Cameron had been talking—griping—nonstop since they'd left the sheriff's office. He wondered if she would run down anytime soon.

"Jeez, no wonder my feet are cold. My shoes are soaked." She toed off her sneakers, then propped her heels on the seat and wrapped her hands around her feet. "I can't tell if my socks are wet, or just cold."

With a shrug, she sat cross-legged with her feet tucked under her thighs. "That's better. That's all I need, to come down with a cold. If this rain doesn't stop soon, we're all going to have to grow gills."

She rattled on about the weather for another few minutes. The woman could talk more than any ten people Zane knew. He needed to tune her out. He wanted to think about what he was more and more certain had been the deliberate spilling of her coffee when Harper had first pressed for an explanation for her being on Zane's doorstep. But tuning out a voice that slid down his spine like velvet was surprisingly difficult for a man who hadn't been interested in women in a long, long time.

For that matter, he hadn't even been around a woman since he'd opted out of his physical therapy months ago. And Gerta Throckmorton hadn't even begun to light his torch. Oh, she'd had all the right equipment, more than amply supplied. But that mustache . . .

Gerta being the last woman to lay hands on him, so to speak, it was no wonder Zane was having trouble putting Becca Cameron out of his mind. That's all it was—too long a dry spell, and Becca was the first woman within range.

Why hadn't she told Harper the truth? She'd seen Zane at his table with the gun. Evidently she'd assumed the worst and rushed across the road to—to what? Try to stop him from doing the deed?

So why hadn't she told Harp?

"Jeez, I'll have to call my parents and tell them what's happened. They're going to have a fit, and my brothers will be all over me."

"All over you for what?" Zane asked as he pulled into the parking lot of the motel located halfway between town and his house. "It's not like any of this is your fault."

Business appeared brisk at the Wayside Inn, if the number of cars in the parking lot was any indication. The rain, Zane imagined. It looked like they'd been lucky to get rooms.

"Haven't you heard?" Becca said, sounding tired. "Everything is my fault."

"Everything?"

"Everything."

"Good. I've been looking for whoever's responsible for all this rain."

"Funny, mister."

"My point being, I believe you're exaggerating about everything being your fault."

"Don't I wish."

There was no covered area to park while registering at this motel. In fact, it didn't look like there was a place to park at all. Zane cruised the length of the front parking lot with no luck. At the end he turned around and headed back. Near the office he stopped behind a couple of parked cars and shifted to neutral. After he and Becca registered and got their room keys he would try the back lot for a space.

Becca leaned down to get her shoes and misjudged the distance. She whacked her head against the dashboard. "Ow!"

It had been a good, solid whack. Zane leaned down toward her. "Are you all right?"

"I don't—"

A loud *crack* echoed through the car.

Becca and Zane bolted upright, Becca still rubbing her forehead. "What the devil was— Hey!" she shouted as Zane stomped on the gas pedal and popped the clutch, shooting the car out of the parking lot and laying rubber all the way.

"Get down." Zane pushed her head down toward her knees, turned onto a side road, then shifted into second.

"I was right, you are a maniac!" She sprang up again. "What the hell are you doing?"

"He found us," Zane said grimly, one eye on the road before him, the other on the rearview mirror.

"Who . . ." She caught sight of the small hole surrounded by a startling network of spiderweb cracks in the window next to Zane's head. Beside her, her window looked the same. Her heart lurched to a stop. "What did that?"

"What do you think did it? A bullet. Fasten your seat belt."

She did, but her hands were shaking so hard that it took her three tries.

THREE

"He followed us?" Breathless, terrified all over again, Becca barely managed to croak the words.

"No," came Zane's curt reply. "I wish to hell he had."

"What's that supposed to mean?" She craned her neck to peer out through the rear window. Headlights! "Is that him?"

"No. He's two cars back."

"He had to have followed us. How else could he have been there?"

The road before them was straight, dark, and empty. The Mustang was eager. And the bad guy was coming up behind. Zane shifted into third and floorboarded it.

"He must have followed us into town, then back to the motel," Becca said, looking for sense, for an answer. A reason this terrible thing was happening. "Are you sure it's the same man?"

"You think there's more than one after me? On the same night?"

"I don't know," she cried. "You were the cop. You said it could be any one of a number of people after you. Maybe several members of your fan club got together and decided tonight was the night."

Zane didn't bother to glance at her. He merely snorted. "Yeah, right."

The Mustang's tires swished along the wet pavement. Windshield wipers slapped at the rain. Becca craned her neck again to look behind them. "Is that him?"

"That's him."

"How do you know? Did you even see where the shot came from? Maybe it was just a stray bullet, somebody playing with a gun. That sort of thing happens all the time. You were bending down. You couldn't have seen—"

"I saw the gun before he pulled it back inside the car."

"Oh."

She fell silent, for which Zane was grateful. He couldn't blame her for rattling on. A lot of people ran off at the mouth when they were scared. She was an innocent bystander, a woman who cared enough to run through a rainy night to keep a stranger from killing himself.

Now she was a target. Like him.

He wished to hell there were some safe place to stash her, but until he lost that sedan a quarter of a mile behind them, he couldn't afford to stop the car even if some likely place did present itself.

Not that any such place would pop up anytime soon. This was a section line road, and he wasn't sure where it would end. These rural county roads had the distressing habit of ending abruptly at the edge of some farmer's field.

"This isn't the way to town," Becca said.

Since that much was obvious, Zane felt no need to respond.

"Why aren't we headed for town, for the sheriff, the police, somebody to help?" She spoke so fast that her words all but ran together.

Zane shot her a look. "He didn't follow us to the motel, darlin'. Think about that."

"Don't call me darlin', sugar. And he had to have followed us. Unless you believe in bizarre co-incidence."

"He was there ahead of us."

"That's impossible," she cried.

"He was waiting for us."

"He couldn't have been," Becca protested. "The only people who knew we were going there were Harper and his deputies."

Zane clenched his jaw and flexed his fingers around the steering wheel. "And the desk clerk at the motel, but it's stretching things a bit too far for him to be in on it."

Becca tensed against the slivers of ice trickling down her spine. "You think someone tipped this guy off, told him we were headed for the motel? Someone in the sheriff's office? I don't believe it!"

"It's not an idea that thrills me either. Maybe it didn't go down that way. Maybe one of the deputies mentioned it over the radio while this guy listened in." But he wasn't betting his life on it.

Still, if Harper Montgomery was in some way involved, Zane might yet eat his own gun, because there was no more honest man on earth than Harp. Zane had to believe that. He'd known the man for years, worked with him, trusted his back to him once. It couldn't be Harp.

The deputies maybe. Two had come to the house. A third had shown up at the jail. Zane knew nothing of them. Except that they worked for Harp. If Harp thought them worthy of the job, they had to have something going for them.

But it had to have been one of them. Somehow, someone in that sheriff's office tonight had had contact with the shooter. There was no other explanation. Zane had watched his rearview mirror carefully all the way to town and back out again to the motel. There had been no one behind them. No one. Because of the rain, traffic was scarce. Zane would have spotted a tail blindfolded on a night like this, even as out of practice as he was.

Yet the man had been at the motel ahead of them. Which meant he'd known they were coming.

There was the possibility of coincidence, but Becca had put the right adjective on that thought—bizarre. Not totally out of the realm of possibility, but for the second shooting to have been coincidental, that would mean the man had come to the area to kill Zane, then, when he'd missed, gone to the nearest motel for the night.

Why? To hang around and try again? Could be, but Zane didn't buy that he would stay at the closest motel. It didn't make sense. The man had to know that any strangers in the area, especially men traveling alone, would be suspect after the shooting was reported.

Frustrated, Zane swiped at the rain hitting his neck from the hole in the window beside him. He wanted to stop the car, to call the man out, face him down. To stand out on the road like some old-time gunslinger and wait for the bastard to come after him.

But he couldn't. Not with an innocent woman along for the ride.

Zane had no choice but to lose the bastard behind them, and in the process figure out what the hell to do with a sexy-voiced pixie named Becca Cameron.

Beside him, the pixie shifted in the seat. "Where are we going?"

Good question. He wished he had an answer.

"Oh, great." Becca flopped her head back against the seat. "You don't know. That's it, isn't it? You don't know where we're going. You're just driving around in the rain because there isn't anyplace to go. Not anyplace safe, if you're right that someone in the sheriff's office set us up. Just take me back to town and drop me off at home."

"Would that I could, darlin', but—"

"I told you not to call me darlin', sugar."

"—then you'd be a sitting duck," Zane finished.

"Why would he come after me?" she cried. "You're the one with all the enemies."

"I don't have *that* many." She made it sound as though half the state were out for his hide. "He's seen us together, at my house and at a motel. He might think you'd make great hostage material to reel me in with. Sorry, but we're stuck with each other for the time being. And in answer to your previous question, we're heading for Oklahoma City."

She made a big production of peering out of each window in all directions. "Excuse me, but the last time I checked, Oklahoma City was north. Have they moved it?"

Zane shot her a scowl.

"You're driving west."

At the next crossroad a moment later, Zane turned north. "Happy now?"

"Not particularly. Are you?"

Zane watched the rearview mirror, saw the sedan turn to follow them. "Not particularly," he muttered.

Becca whipped her head around and saw the car. "Oh, no. He's still behind us. What are we going to do? Can't this thing go any faster? Never mind," she added hastily. From where she sat, it felt as if they were nearly flying already. "Forget I said that. This is fast enough. It would just be too ironic if we died in a car crash while trying to outrun a bullet, don't you think?"

"What I think," Zane said, turning on the radio, "is that you talk too much. Don't get me wrong—I like your voice. It's sexy as hell. But give it a rest, will you? I don't have time to think about sex just now."

Becca opened her mouth, but no words came out. That in itself was a rare phenomenon. But that a man found her voice sexy—it was laughable. In her entire life no one had ever said anything remotely like that to her. He was teasing her. There wasn't one damn thing sexy about her, and she knew it.

But she had been rattling like a loose screw; she just couldn't help it. She was scared. She wasn't used to being shot at, unless she counted the spitwads aimed at her from the cretin in the back row of her math class last year.

Bullets were a far cry from spitwads.

But they weren't being shot at this very minute, and bullets weren't the only things she was worried about. There was the man beside her to consider. He'd pointed a gun at himself earlier. Was she on the run with a suicidal maniac?

He didn't seem like a maniac now. He seemed . . . controlled. Confident. In charge. As if racing through a rainy night with a killer on his tail were just ordinary business. Since he'd been an OSBI agent, maybe it was.

But earlier he'd sat alone at his kitchen table with a gun in one hand and a bottle of booze in the other. And he'd pointed that gun at himself. "Would you really have done it?"

She hadn't meant to ask, to remind him, but the words spilled out before she could think to stop them.

Zane fiddled with the radio and came up with nothing but static. But he didn't turn it off. "Would I have done what?"

Becca hesitated, then blurted out, "You don't seem suicidal."

Zane flinched. The word stung. As an indication of how low he'd sunk, how self-pitying he'd become, the word shamed him. Getting shot at tonight had snapped him out of it right enough though. For the first time in more than a year he felt alive. Earlier, sitting in Harp's office, he had shied away from the feeling, but it had grown. Now he welcomed it. And it felt good. Damn good.

He wondered what it said about a man, that he felt more alive when being shot at than at any other time.

Maybe it wasn't that. Maybe it was simpler. He had something to think about, a problem to solve. The woman next to him to keep safe. Action to take.

Like turning at the next corner, which he did.

"I said, you don't seem suicidal."

"Know a lot of suicidal people, do you?"

"Not that I'm aware of. But I saw what I saw tonight."

"Which brings up the question of why you didn't tell Harp the truth about why you came to my door."

"I didn't lie. Not really."

"No, you spilled your coffee first. You were pretty convincing. I don't think he realized you did it on purpose."

Becca stiffened. "On purpose? Why do you say that?"

"The look in your eyes when you did it." Zane tossed her a tight smile. "Harper wasn't looking at your eyes. I was."

"Don't be absurd," she sputtered. "Accidents like that happen to me all the time. I'm famous for them, in fact," she added with a grimace. "Ask anybody. Bad Luck Becca, that's me. The jinx."

"No foolin'?"

"You don't have to sound so pleased about it. It's really not funny."

"Am I laughing? I'm not laughing."

Into the relative quiet of the car came a low rumble.

"Now I'm laughing." And he laughed. "Somebody's shooting at us, and your stomach's growling."

"I can't help it," she said with an injured air. "Nobody's shooting right now, and I'm hungry. All I had to eat tonight was a couple of pieces of fudge." She'd missed out on the apple pie. Just thinking of it made her stomach growl again.

"Unless you want to invite the fellow behind us to join us for a late night snack, your stomach's going to have to wait."

She waved her hand toward the miles of rain-drenched darkness. "Since there's no place to eat out here in the middle of nowhere anyway, I guess you're right."

Zane fiddled with the radio again, got more static, and swore.

"Here." Becca punched the last button on the right. Fifties rock and roll blasted out loud and clear. Fats Domino was finding his thrill on Blueberry Hill.

"I knew I should have reset that button," Zane muttered.

"Don't like oldies, huh?"

"I prefer my music much older, thank you."

"Big bands?"

"Beethoven. Tchaikovsky."

"Oh. Way old. It wouldn't have done you any good to change that button though. I have it on good authority that every 1969 Mustang in this part of the country is required to have KOMA on the radio. I don't think the cars run without oldies rock and roll."

Zane merely grunted. Then, quietly, he asked again. "Why didn't you tell Harp?"

Becca hesitated, uneasy. "I guess I thought it was too personal. I didn't figure you'd appreciate me telling him something like that. And I wasn't sure I hadn't misread the situation."

"You did. I wasn't going to kill myself." Oh, he'd thought about it, but he hadn't been able to do it. Thinking about it now, he knew that he never would have. Killing himself would make Al's death even more of a waste than it had been. Al's sacrifice had to count for something, didn't it? "You don't have to worry that you're running around in the middle of the night with some suicidal maniac," he told Becca.

"I wasn't worried."

"The hell you weren't."

She didn't answer, so the subject was dropped.

For several minutes she hummed along with Dion and the Belmonts.

At the next intersection Zane turned north again. The car in the rearview mirror followed.

Damn. He couldn't just drive around all night until he ran out of gas, hoping the guy would give up.

Unless Zane missed his guess, the county road they were on crossed a state highway soon. They couldn't be too far from a town, regardless of which direction they took. In a town he could lose the bastard. Could get to a phone and call for outside help. Get Becca someplace safe.

Then he could turn from prey to hunter. He could bait the trap and reel in that s.o.b.

Damn, but it felt good to be doing something

again instead of sitting around feeling sorry for himself.

"Zane?"

The quiver of fear that she tried to hide stabbed at him. He really shouldn't be enjoying himself quite so much when the innocent woman beside him was so scared. "Yeah?"

"You told Harper that you had an idea who might be after you."

Zane managed a casual shrug. "It was just a theory." A theory he hoped was true. If he was right and Bowen had sent someone to make sure Zane couldn't testify next month at King's trial, they'd have their connection. They would perhaps be able to prove concrete ties between the two.

"Is it someone you know?"

"The man doing the shooting? No. He's probably just a hired gun."

Becca swallowed. "A hit man."

"Yeah."

"Who would hire someone to kill you?"

Another shrug. "Maybe someone who doesn't want me to testify next month."

"Testify about what?"

"It's a murder trial," Zane said tersely. "I'm the prosecution's star witness."

Becca folded her arms and huddled in her seat. The rain was coming harder now, a true downpour. Now and then a drop found its way through the hole in the window beside her and dampened her cheek. Absently, she wiped it away.

The world closed in around them as visibility shrank. The car became a cocoon of dry warmth in a sea of cold, wet rain, lending a false air of intimacy to the night. Unwanted, inappropriate intimacy.

Becca tried to imagine what it must be like to have been an OSBI agent, to have witnessed a murder. To have someone try to kill you so you couldn't testify.

The entire situation was so foreign to her way of life that she couldn't begin to imagine . . .

She'd never known real fear before this night. She'd never tasted the coppery tang of it on her tongue, never had her heart threaten to pound its way out of her chest.

And it wasn't just being shot at that scared her. Zane Houston had her more than a little worried.

Okay, so it wasn't him, precisely, that worried her as much as it was her reaction to him. Earlier, as she ran to save him from killing himself, she must have thought he was a man to feel sorry for. In reality, he was anything but that.

He was a little on the hard side. Tough. He would have to be tough to work for the OSBI. And smart. And capable. Something in the set of his shoulders, the confident tilt of his head, assured her that he would keep her safe and get her out of this mess.

So why did she feel all jittery inside whenever she looked at him?

She remembered the shape of him, his weight settling between her thighs when they'd rolled across the floor while dodging bullets. An unintentionally intimate act during a moment of terror. She barely remembered the bullets at all. She remembered everything about Zane Houston. It was unnerving.

"You're awfully quiet over there," he said.

Becca jerked. "What?"

"You've talked nonstop most of the night. Now you're quiet. Anything wrong?"

She managed a harsh laugh. "What could possibly be wrong? Besides, you told me to be quiet."

"Are you still worried that I might try to do myself in, and maybe take you along with me?"

Becca studied his profile in the glow of the dash lights. "No. No, I'm not."

"Good." He nodded once, then glanced in the rearview mirror. "Have you got your seat belt fastened?"

"Uh-oh." Becca checked the belt and found it secure. "I don't trust a man who asks a question like that."

"What's not to trust?" He grinned at her.

Something funny happened to her breathing with that grin. Lord, Lord, he had a dimple. Right in the middle of his right cheek. She'd always been a sucker for male dimples. If that wasn't enough to shake her, he thought her bullfrog voice was sexy.

"I'm just going to see what this guy's made of. Sit tight. You'll be fine."

Becca felt the Mustang surge beneath her. "I

The darkened house on the corner ahead had an
ht-foot hedge shielding its yard from the street.
ying there was no dog to alert the neighbor-
od, Zane shut off his headlights and eased across
: driveway and behind the hedge, where he cut
the engine so the steam from his exhaust
uldn't give away their location.

Zane debated going back to the main drag,
mping his foot on the gas and speeding through
wn to attract the attention of the police, but he
carded the idea promptly. The shooter in the
rk sedan hadn't let Becca's presence stop him
m trying to kill Zane. Taking out a small-town
p or two probably wouldn't faze him as long as he
Zane in the process.

No. Zane would not involve anyone else. Not
til he could lose this guy and get to someone who
uld really help. Someone who knew him well
ough to take him at his word, because he had only
word that the man behind them was the one
o'd fired the shots.

Riley made the jog in the highway at Rock
ek at the south edge of Elmore City, then
ded north through the town. The streets were
erted. Not a moving vehicle in sight. He swore.
Mustang had turned off somewhere. Son of a
h. He'd never had such a run of bad luck as he
having this night.

lmore City was so small, it barely qualified as a

think it's only fair to remind you that my bad luck
generally extends to everyone around me."

"Meaning?"

"I told you—I'm a jinx. When I'm around,
things go wrong. Driving"—she leaned over and
peered at the speedometer. And wished she
hadn't—"eighty-five on a dark, rain-slicked road
with a bona fide jinx in the car is probably not a
good idea. Especially not after just swearing that
you aren't suicidal."

"Relax, darlin'."

"No thanks, sugar. Right now I prefer tense."

"Have it your way."

After less than a minute Becca couldn't stand
the tension. "Is he staying with us?" She would
have turned and looked, but she couldn't take her
eyes off the solid white line down the center of the
road. The solid line that she knew was not solid, but
broken. Only the speed at which they were traveling caused the dashes to run together.

"Yep. Keeping the same distance."

"I'd feel a whole lot better if you didn't all of a
sudden sound like you're enjoying this."

"Sorry. I'll try to sound properly . . . what,
morose? Shaken?"

"How 'bout if you just take the situation seriously?"

"Oh, I take it seriously." He slowed for the stop
sign up ahead. At the intersection he turned east
onto a state road—a step up and a few inches wider

than the section line road they'd been on. "I take it damn seriously."

"If you're headed for the interstate, you can't get there from here."

"I can't?"

"There's no entrance ramp from this road."

"You're sure?"

"I'm sure."

A mile later Zane turned north on State Highway 74. At the top of a rise a sign warned ROAD SUBJECT TO FLOODING.

"Oh, terrific," Becca muttered.

The road sloped down, then back up. At the low spot, water rose from the bar ditches on either side of the road and washed across the pavement. Zane slowed, but not much. The Mustang plowed through.

Headlights from behind bounced off the rear-view mirror as the dark sedan followed down the hill.

And the rain came harder.

Nearly ten miles later they'd passed through two more low spots where water crossed the road, and Elmore City came into view.

Lights. A town. Help. Relief washed through Becca. Not that she minded driving through the rain with a man who looked like Zane Houston. He was tall, around six feet, and she liked tall men. She liked the way his hair hung down over his collar. It made her want to touch it. To see if it was as thick

and lush as it looked. Not soft. Nothing ab⟨ut⟩ man was soft.

Certainly not those dark brown eyes. Sh⟨e had⟩ to see a soft expression in them. But every n⟨ow and⟩ then, when the light from the dashboard str⟨uck them⟩ so, she detected something other than hard⟨ness in⟩ them. Way in the back, behind the shield ⟨he'd⟩ raised, she detected pain. Deep, crippling p⟨ain.⟩

The Mustang flew through the rain tow⟨ard the⟩ lights of the small town ahead, faster an⟨d faster.⟩ Becca gripped the armrest so hard that he⟨r fingers⟩ went numb.

"Zane?" This time she was afraid to lo⟨ok at the⟩ speedometer.

"Yeah?"

Closer and closer came the town, yet h⟨e didn't⟩ slow. "There are two ninety-degree turn⟨s on this⟩ side of town," she warned.

"Been here before, have you?"

"My point is, you need to slow dow⟨n.⟩"

"Relax, will you?"

But he slowed down. Not enough ⟨for her⟩ peace of mind, but enough to keep t⟨he car on⟩ pavement through the two right-angle⟨ turns.⟩

In the brief time that the sedan wa⟨s out of sight⟩ Zane turned right onto a side street⟨, then left⟩ again, and again, losing himself am⟨ong the⟩ residential streets lined with tall tr⟨ees and⟩ houses.

"What are you doing?"

"Losing him, I hope."

town, no less a city, as far as Riley was concerned. It had only one main intersection. Since that made things convenient for him, he decided to stop swearing for now.

From the intersection he would be able to see which way the Mustang left town. If it left town. He parked in the lot of a convenience store that was closed for the night. The Mustang wouldn't get out of town without him seeing it.

"What are we doing?" Becca whispered.

"Waiting."

"For what?"

"For him to either leave town, or park somewhere and wait for us."

"I'm so glad I asked. I feel so much safer knowing he'll be out there somewhere waiting for us."

The Mustang's engine ticked and popped as it cooled. Large drops from the overhanging limbs of a big old pecan tree plopped on the car, jarring Becca's nerves with each *plop*.

Suddenly Zane's quiet chuckle filled the silence. "I haven't done this in a while," he murmured, a smile in his voice.

Becca hugged herself. Without the heater the air was cooling. "Done what, hidden from someone trying to shoot you?"

"Sat with a woman in the dark and fogged up the car windows."

"If this is how you did it last time, I feel sorry for whoever she was."

Zane chuckled softly again. "So tell me, before I find another man pointing a gun at me. Is there a Mr. Becca Cameron?"

Slowly Becca straightened, stunned. "Is that question supposed to make me think you're coming on to me?"

"Why do you say it like that?"

"Like how?"

"Like I'm trying to convince you the world is flat?"

"You've got about as much luck convincing me of one as you do with the other."

"Meaning?"

"Shouldn't we be going?"

"Like you said," Zane told her as he reached for the key and started the car, "my timing's off." He eased the Mustang out of its hiding place. He headed back toward the main road through town, but crossed it rather than taking it. He saw no other cars.

"You never answered my question," Zane said.

"What question?"

"Are you married?"

"No. Are you?"

"Darlin', no woman in her right mind would waste her time on me."

Becca gave an indelicate grunt. "I wish someone would have told me that before I went running to your rescue."

think it's only fair to remind you that my bad luck generally extends to everyone around me."

"Meaning?"

"I told you—I'm a jinx. When I'm around, things go wrong. Driving"—she leaned over and peered at the speedometer. And wished she hadn't—"eighty-five on a dark, rain-slicked road with a bona fide jinx in the car is probably not a good idea. Especially not after just swearing that you aren't suicidal."

"Relax, darlin'."

"No thanks, sugar. Right now I prefer tense."

"Have it your way."

After less than a minute Becca couldn't stand the tension. "Is he staying with us?" She would have turned and looked, but she couldn't take her eyes off the solid white line down the center of the road. The solid line that she knew was not solid, but broken. Only the speed at which they were traveling caused the dashes to run together.

"Yep. Keeping the same distance."

"I'd feel a whole lot better if you didn't all of a sudden sound like you're enjoying this."

"Sorry. I'll try to sound properly . . . what, morose? Shaken?"

"How 'bout if you just take the situation seriously?"

"Oh, I take it seriously." He slowed for the stop sign up ahead. At the intersection he turned east onto a state road—a step up and a few inches wider than the section line road they'd been on. "I take it damn seriously."

"If you're headed for the interstate, you can't get there from here."

"I can't?"

"There's no entrance ramp from this road."

"You're sure?"

"I'm sure."

A mile later Zane turned north on State Highway 74. At the top of a rise a sign warned ROAD SUBJECT TO FLOODING.

"Oh, terrific," Becca muttered.

The road sloped down, then back up. At the low spot, water rose from the bar ditches on either side of the road and washed across the pavement. Zane slowed, but not much. The Mustang plowed through.

Headlights from behind bounced off the rearview mirror as the dark sedan followed down the hill.

And the rain came harder.

Nearly ten miles later they'd passed through two more low spots where water crossed the road, and Elmore City came into view.

Lights. A town. Help. Relief washed through Becca. Not that she minded driving through the rain with a man who looked like Zane Houston. He was tall, around six feet, and she liked tall men. She liked the way his hair hung down over his collar. It made her want to touch it. To see if it was as thick and lush as it looked. Not soft. Nothing about this man was soft.

Certainly not those dark brown eyes. She'd yet to see a soft expression in them. But every now and then, when the light from the dashboard struck just so, she detected something other than hardness in them. Way in the back, behind the shield he kept raised, she detected pain. Deep, crippling pain.

The Mustang flew through the rain toward the lights of the small town ahead, faster and faster. Becca gripped the armrest so hard that her fingers went numb.

"Zane?" This time she was afraid to look at the speedometer.

"Yeah?"

Closer and closer came the town, yet he did not slow. "There are two ninety-degree turns just this side of town," she warned.

"Been here before, have you?"

"My point is, you need to slow down."

"Relax, will you?"

But he slowed down. Not enough for Becca's peace of mind, but enough to keep them on the pavement through the two right-angle turns.

In the brief time that the sedan was out of sight, Zane turned right onto a side street, then turned again, and again, losing himself among the quiet residential streets lined with tall trees and small houses.

"What are you doing?"

"Losing him, I hope."

The darkened house on the corner ahead had an eight-foot hedge shielding its yard from the street. Praying there was no dog to alert the neighborhood, Zane shut off his headlights and eased across the driveway and behind the hedge, where he cut off the engine so the steam from his exhaust wouldn't give away their location.

Zane debated going back to the main drag, stomping his foot on the gas and speeding through town to attract the attention of the police, but he discarded the idea promptly. The shooter in the dark sedan hadn't let Becca's presence stop him from trying to kill Zane. Taking out a small-town cop or two probably wouldn't faze him as long as he got Zane in the process.

No. Zane would not involve anyone else. Not until he could lose this guy and get to someone who could really help. Someone who knew him well enough to take him at his word, because he had only his word that the man behind them was the one who'd fired the shots.

Riley made the jog in the highway at Rock Creek at the south edge of Elmore City, then headed north through the town. The streets were deserted. Not a moving vehicle in sight. He swore. The Mustang had turned off somewhere. Son of a bitch. He'd never had such a run of bad luck as he was having this night.

Elmore City was so small, it barely qualified as a

Zane studied her as they passed beneath a streetlight. "I never thanked you for that."

"For what?"

"For caring enough about a total stranger to try to help. Not many people would have done that."

Working his way via side streets, he thought it might be time to head east toward the interstate.

The radio announcer stopped him. "Repeating, State Highway 29 east out of Elmore City has just been added to the list of roads closed due to high water. We'll update you with the entire list at the top of the hour."

So much for plan A. Zane worked his way back through town and picked up 74 again, heading north toward Maysville. He kept one eye on the rearview mirror, but no headlights appeared.

Where he should have been keeping an eye was on the gas gauge. When he noticed it sliding rapidly toward empty, he swore. Not that noticing it earlier would have helped. They hadn't passed an open gas station all night.

"What's wrong?" Becca asked with only a slight quaver in her voice.

Zane swore again. "We're about to run out of gas."

Becca let her head fall against the headrest. "I told you I was a jinx."

"Ah, so it's your fault, huh?"

"That's what Geoff Terrill figured when he took me out once when we were sixteen."

"Geoff Terrill the deputy?"

"The same."

"Pulled the ol' out-of-gas routine on you, did he?"

"Not exactly. He didn't run out of gas until after he'd taken me home."

"He blamed you for that?"

"For that, and the three flats we'd had earlier."

"Three?" Zane let out a low whistle. "Must have been some date."

Becca grunted in agreement. "At least when he ran out of gas, he only had to walk over to the station on Main. Since we can't exactly do that, what are we going to do? Stand out in the rain and hope someone other than the bad guy comes along to give us a ride to the next town?"

"What are you trying to do, cheer me up?"

"What, then? If we were at Uncle Jim's, we could fill up out at his barn."

Zane smiled. "Not a bad idea. Keep your eyes open for the next farm."

"You're kidding, right?"

"I wouldn't joke about running out of gas on a night like this."

"We can't just drive up to some farmhouse and ask for gas."

"And wake somebody up in the middle of the night? You're right. We can't do that. I knew a farmer once. If anybody knocked on his door in the middle of the night, he met them with his shotgun."

"Now who's trying to cheer up whom?"

"Whom?" Zane laughed. "I don't think I've

ever actually heard anybody use that word in real life."

"If there's a God in heaven, this is not real life," Becca retorted. "This is nothing more than a bad dream, and when we wake up, it will all be over."

Yeah, Zane thought, but would they wake up together?

Where the question came from, he had no idea. He wished it would go back though. He didn't have the time or inclination to worry about questions like that. He wasn't interested in waking up with a woman. Not even a pixie of a woman.

He drove until he spotted a tank on stilts beside a barn. Slowing, he turned into the muddy, rutted drive that led to the barn, and a hundred yards farther on, a house.

"If we're not going to steal gas, then what," Becca asked, gritting her teeth against the ruts and potholes grabbing at the Mustang's tires, "are we doing here?"

Frowning, Zane drove toward the barn. "If we're lucky, we're getting gas."

"Lucky? With me in the car? Don't count on it. I thought you just said we weren't going to—" She saw the tank and whipped her head around toward Zane. "You are! You're going to steal gasoline from some poor farmer. You, a former cop."

"I'm not going to steal anything from anybody." With his headlights off so they wouldn't shine on the house at the end of the drive, he pulled up beside the tank and got out. One whiff of the nozzle on the pump, and he cursed and climbed back in the car.

"No gas?" Becca asked.

"Diesel." He turned around and drove back to the highway.

"Now what?" Becca asked.

"We find another farm."

The rain was letting up some, increasing visibility. It was two more farms and seven miles before they spotted another large steel tank on stilts beside another barn.

"There," Becca cried out, pointing into the rain. "I see one."

Zane spotted it at the same time she did and was ~~already turning into the drive. Again he turned off~~ ...house was only fifty yards from the barn. The utility light at the corner of the barn would make them highly visible even in the rain, but the gasoline storage tank sat behind the barn, where it couldn't be seen from the house. Zane was grateful for the cover. He wasn't any too eager to find out if this farmer thought like his friend with the shotgun.

"See?" He parked next to the tank. "This time you brought us good luck."

"You're going to steal this poor farmer's gas." Sounding genuinely shocked, she shook her head.

Zane frowned. "I'm not a thief."

Becca didn't like this. She didn't like it at all. She'd been raised to be scrupulously honest. To steal, for any reason, was wrong.

Yet what choice did they have? If they ran out of gas, they would be sitting ducks. Literally, she thought, looking out at the rain gathering in puddles across the muddy ground. They had to have gasoline.

Zane got out of the car and quietly closed the door.

To Becca it sounded as loud as a gunshot.

Bad comparison, she decided with a shiver. Without Zane she felt cold inside the car. Alone. Deserted. She rammed her feet into her damp sneakers and climbed out into the drizzle. A wide back door gaped open on the barn. Becca stepped inside far enough to get out of the rain. From there she could watch as Zane stood beside the raised storage tank and filled the Mustang with gasoline.

Rain pelted the corrugated tin roof, sounding like rolling thunder over her head. She watched Zane, noticing how he favored his right leg. Because he seemed sensitive about the subject, she turned and pretended she didn't see.

From behind her came a low snarl.

The hair on the back of Becca's neck stood on end. Slowly she turned. In the deep shadows of the barn, two rows of sharp white teeth gleamed back at her.

A dog. It's only a dog, Becca.

An angry dog, judging by the growl.

She took a step backward toward the rain. "Nice doggy," she whispered, her throat dry. "Easy does it, fella. All we want is some gas."

Dry straw rustled. The growling deepened as the dog crept closer, pacing her.

The bullets had missed her—twice—and the Mustang hadn't crashed into a tree at high speed. Had she lived through those threats only to be attacked by a dog? Every muscle in her body screamed with the urge to turn and run. But she knew the dog would see that as an invitation to give chase and that run away was fair game. Lord, why had she gotten out of the car? "Nice doggy."

"Problem?" Zane called softly from beside the car.

"Yes, and it's got teeth. Big teeth."

The dog took a quick breath, then, with another low growl, lunged.

Becca shrieked.

Zane cursed.

Lightning flashed from cloud to cloud with a thunderous crash.

The dog yelped. Cringing, it tucked its tail between its legs and darted away, into the shadows of the barn.

"Quit playing with the dog and come on out of there," Zane said. "It's time to go."

Becca spared a moment to let her legs steady beneath her. She made it back to the car in time to see Zane stuff a twenty-dollar bill into the handle of the gas pump before he joined her in the car.

She was shaking so hard that once again it took her three tries to get her seat belt fastened.

"Hey," Zane said, noticing. "Are you all right?"

"Fine." The seat belt finally clicked into place. "Just fine."

But she wasn't fine. Zane saw the way she trembled. Before he realized what he was doing, he reached out to her, placed his hand on hers, where they rested on her lap. Her skin was like ice. "You're freezing."

Becca stared stupidly at the large, dark hand covering hers. His touch sent fire shooting from her hands straight up her arms. And from her thigh, where his fingers brushed, straight to her midsection. It warmed her. It teased her. It made her blood pulse and pound in secret, long-neglected places. It scared the daylights out of her.

He took his hand away to start the car. Only then was Becca able to draw a full breath.

FOUR

The rain was pounding again. It came down in thick gray sheets that sparkled silver in the headlights. In the ditches beside the road, water gathered and rose, running fast and furious, edging toward the road, crossing it in the lowest spots.

The town of Maysville came next, with still no sign of anyone following them. Everything in town was shut down for the night, but Zane located a pay phone outside a convenience store, and a place to hide the car in the alley behind the building.

"Why are we stopping?"

"I need to make a call. Why don't you stay in the car this time?"

Becca had no trouble agreeing. She had no desire to step outside and drown.

Zane made a dash for the small overhang, then circled to the phone beside the front door. It was three A.M. when he dialed Harper Montgomery's home number.

Harp answered on the fourth ring. "Montgomery."

"It's Zane."

"What's wrong?"

"He was waiting for us."

"Come again?"

While he explained, Zane stood in the glare of the store's neon window lights and wished for a power outage. He felt entirely too visible for comfort.

Harper swore. "Is he still on you?"

"We've lost him for now."

"Where are you?"

Zane paused. "No offense, Harp, but—"

"Never mind. You're right. I'd swear my phone is secure, but why take chances."

"My thoughts exactly."

"Call me tomorrow morning after ten. I'll have the office phones checked out by then. And maybe a handle on what went wrong."

"Will do."

"How's Becca?"

"She's holding up better than I expected. Only one bad minute a while ago with a dog."

"You have a dog with you?"

"Never mind. It's a long story, and I'm getting wet here."

"If you had a cell phone like the rest of the

world, you wouldn't have to stand outside in the rain to talk on the phone."

"Yeah, right."

They hung up, and Zane returned to the car. In the quick flash of the dome light as he got in, he managed a good look at Becca's face. Her color was back and the terror had left her eyes, but there was still fear there.

As he started the car, Zane cursed himself. He took full responsibility for that fear in her eyes. It was because of him that she was on the run in the middle of the night with a stranger beside her and another one out there somewhere gunning for them. She didn't deserve this. But he was damned if he could figure a way to get her out of it just yet.

Still, he had to give her credit. She was holding up all right. Better than all right. She hadn't screamed or gone all hysterical on him when the lead was flying. She talked ninety miles an hour, but he'd take her talking any day over hysterics and screams.

"Have I got something on my face?" she asked, frowning.

"No." But suddenly he couldn't look away. He'd seen beautiful women before. Becca Cameron wasn't beautiful. She was too cute for beautiful. But she was definitely cute. Pretty, even, the way her small nose tilted up at the end just so. And those eyes, huge, silver in the light, smoky in the dark. They ate up half her face, those eyes, and invited a man to fall in headfirst.

But it was her mouth that he stared at now. Ever-changing, nearly always in motion. Full, lush lips that didn't seem to go with the rest of her delicate, pixie looks, yet went with them perfectly. If her eyes invited a man to drown in them, her mouth invited much more erotic thoughts, starting with a small taste, a nibble, working up to a full feast. He wondered what that mouth would feel like against his skin.

"Then why are you staring at me?"

Zane blinked and turned away. "Just making sure you're okay. You had a pretty good scare back at that farm."

"I acted like a ninny. The dog was more scared than I was."

"Only of the storm. These old farm dogs are usually pretty damn possessive of their territory. If it hadn't been for the lightning scaring him, he could have hurt you. You were right to be afraid."

Becca smiled. "Thanks. I don't feel quite so much like an idiot now."

"I haven't seen you act like an idiot yet." He put the car in gear and eased around the building without turning on his headlights. Finding nothing more threatening coming down the street than a pickup pulling a horse trailer, Zane pulled out of the lot and in front of the pickup.

"Except," he added, "for the fudge. You have to admit that was pretty lame. Which reminds me. You never did explain how you saw me with my gun."

Becca stretched her legs out before her to ease

muscles stiff from sitting. "Through your kitchen window."

Zane frowned. "There's a bush there. Nobody can see in—or out—of that window unless they're standing right next to it. What were you doing, pressing your nose to the glass?"

Becca laughed. "Believe it or not, I was checking on a nest of baby birds."

"In my window?" he asked, incredulous.

"In your bush."

"In the dark? In the rain? Come on, you can come up with a better story than that."

"Probably, but this one happens to be the truth." She then explained how she'd ended up seeing him at his kitchen table.

The story was just dumb enough to carry the ring of truth.

Still with the intention of getting to Oklahoma City, Zane drove back to the intersection in the middle of Maysville and headed north, but not for long. The road was blocked by highway department barricades, flashing yellow lights, and a small sign that read ROAD CLOSED DUE TO HIGH WATER.

"Terrific," he muttered. He turned around and went back to the center of town. He didn't want to head back the way they'd come. Roads in that direction were probably closing too. He decided on east, toward the interstate.

No go. That road, too, was closed.

"I guess we're heading west, huh?" Becca asked.

"Looks like we don't have a choice." And they

didn't. They didn't even have the option of spending the night in Maysville in hopes that the water would recede by morning—the town had no motel, and Zane wasn't about to spend the night sleeping in the car. Driving, maybe. Sleeping, no.

They headed west, toward the town of Lindsay. Water covered several low spots on the road, deeper in each one, but the road was still open. At each flooded spot Zane held his breath and eased the Mustang through. The car was low to the ground and couldn't maneuver through high water. So far their luck was holding.

Other people must have also been trying to get out of Maysville. Traffic was picking up. That pickup and horse trailer ended up behind the Mustang, and behind them, with each mile, the line of vehicles grew. Zane wondered if their man was back there somewhere.

Oncoming traffic sprang up from nowhere. Where before they had gone miles without meeting another car, suddenly the stream of vehicles meeting them seemed endless.

"I hope they aren't planning to go far," Becca commented. "Sheesh, look at all of them. Makes me wonder what they know about what's up ahead that we don't."

It made Zane wonder, too, but speculation was useless. If he turned around and went with them, there was no place to go.

Up ahead in the oncoming eastbound lane, lights flashed red and blue in the rain. It looked like a serious accident, with an ambulance, several police vehicles, and two tow trucks.

Traffic in the westbound lane into Lindsay slowed, crawled, then, as Zane pulled up near the four-car pileup in the oncoming lane, stopped altogether.

"Looks like a bad one," Becca said, looking out at the wreck. Remembering how fast Zane had been driving earlier, she shivered.

"Looks like somebody in this lane got tired of waiting and pulled a U-turn into oncoming traffic."

Becca turned in her seat and peered out the rear window. "Do you think he's back there somewhere?"

Zane glanced in the outside mirror at the long string of vehicles behind them. "There's no telling, but I doubt it." That was a lie, but he saw no reason to worry her.

Actually, he thought the chances were pretty good that the shooter was behind them. There was no place else for him to have gone, since all the other roads were closed.

"But if all the other roads are closed," Becca said, echoing Zane's thoughts, "he'd have to be behind us. Or in front." She faced forward and shivered again.

"Are you cold?" He reached for the heater controls.

"No."

She was pale again, Zane noted. "Hey." He

reached out and rubbed her shoulder. "Don't wimp out on me now, darlin'. You're doing fine."

Her eyes narrowed. "You do that on purpose, just to get a rise out of me."

Zane blinked, feigning innocence. "Do what?"

"Call me darlin', sugar."

At least she was scowling at him now rather than worrying about where the bad guy might be. She had a cute scowl. Like a kitten attacking a ball of yarn. But he didn't think it'd be a good idea if he said so out loud.

The cars in front of them moved forward a few feet.

"Progress," Becca said. "At this rate it'll be daylight before I get to eat. Or go to the bathroom," she added with a mutter.

It took another twenty minutes to progress the next thirty yards onto the bridge leading into town. Becca refrained from grumbling about the slow progress. Since the cars heading in the other direction were not moving at all, she was actually pleased that they'd moved that far. Until she glanced toward the river.

"Oh, my God." On a normal day the Washita River went on about its business many, many feet below the bridge, way down at the base of tall, straight banks. Now, however, after two weeks of downpours, the water rushed and boiled mere inches below the bridge. The banks were invisible, hidden beneath the flood. The river was so far out of its banks that she couldn't see the edge of the water. "Oh, my God."

"It might help if you didn't look," Zane offered.

"You should have warned me sooner." She couldn't take her eyes off the terrifying sight of all that water rushing mere inches beneath them. Now and then a gust of wind slapped river water up onto the bridge. "I don't like this," she said tightly. "I don't like this at all. What was that? It felt like the car moved. Oh, God, it's the bridge! The bridge is shaking!"

Zane saw no point in lying to her. She was right—the bridge was shaking. Mother Nature was throwing hundreds of thousands of gallons of water full force at a few puny, concrete and steel pilings. Concrete and steel. Man's feeble attempt to dominate the forces of nature. Zane only hoped Becca wouldn't notice that in addition to shaking and shuddering back and forth, the bridge was also undulating up and down.

"Oh, God, it's . . . it's . . . the bridge is moving up and down. Can you feel it? It's *undulating*." She pressed one hand to her stomach, the other to her mouth. "I think I'm going to be sick."

"Don't you dare," Zane told her darkly. "Unless you do it outside."

"Outside?" she squeaked. "I'm not setting foot outside this car. *Move!*" she told the cars in front of them. "Why don't they get out of the way?"

"Why don't you take a deep breath?"

"Wha— Oh. Okay. Yeah. Sorry. You're right.

Panic won't help. But if it's all the same to you, I'd just as soon not be sitting here when this damn bridge crumbles."

"The bridge isn't going to crumble." He hoped. "It's just shifting around a little because of all the water. We'll be fine."

It was Becca's experience that whenever she was around, things were not fine. But whining wasn't going to do any good, she knew. She gripped her trembling hands tightly together on her lap, clamped her teeth together, and tried to tell herself the bridge was strong. The bridge would hold. The bridge would last.

The roaring of the river outside her window mocked her.

Zane kept one eye on Becca, the other on the bridge. Not that staring at the latter would do any good. Talk about feeling like a sitting duck. Cars were packed on the bridge like sardines in a can. The Mustang wasn't going anywhere until someone in front moved. Except into the river, if the bridge collapsed.

Zane wasn't sure keeping an eye on Becca was any more fruitful an activity. She was pale and shaking, obviously terrified. He didn't know whether to try to take her mind off the situation or leave her alone. She looked like one wrong word—or another shudder of the bridge beneath them—and she would shatter.

But she didn't shatter. They were more than an hour crossing a bridge that was no longer than an average city block. Zane felt his own tension rising as the time passed but the traffic didn't. Yet beside him, Becca, albeit pale and shaking, kept her cool.

Two car-lengths from solid ground, she grew tired of the chatter on the radio and searched for another station.

"Keep it right here on KBLP, 105 FM—Lindsay country. And if you've got a boat, start gassing it up, folks," the announcer said. "This looks like the big one. City officials report that all roads in and out of Lindsay are closed due to high water. If you're here, you're here. If you're not, you ain't gonna be. Hey, somebody throw me a life preserver!"

"Real funny," Becca muttered to the radio.

Zane glanced in the outside mirror again. "Look on the bright side," he told Becca.

"There's a bright side? If we ever get off this bridge, we won't be able to go anywhere. We'll be stuck here until the water goes down."

"Yeah, but they're not letting any more cars onto the bridge. If our man's back there in that line of cars, it won't do him any good."

Becca managed a small smile. "At least that's something."

Up ahead they finally got a glimpse of the accident that had been blocking their lane. First one wrecker, then another, hauled away smashed cars, until the road was at last cleared and traffic could move forward.

Only five cars behind the Mustang made it. The

others were stopped on the far side of the bridge, where barricades were now erected.

"We made it." Becca went limp and slumped in her seat. "If you'll pull over, I'd like to kiss the ground."

Zane felt some of the tension in his shoulders ease now that they were off the bridge. "Now we'll see if our luck holds."

"Luck? You expect good luck with Bad Luck Becca around?"

"You don't really buy that, do you?"

"Trust me. Over the years, it's become impossible to deny."

Zane shook his head. "Somebody's really done a number on you, darlin'."

"I don't see how you can think that, sugar. Since meeting me you've been shot at—more than once. You've been chased, you've nearly been washed away in a flood, and now you're stuck in a town with no way out. I don't see how you can consider those things anything but bad luck."

"I'll bet you're the type of person who looks at a glass and calls it half empty instead of half full."

"This from a man who sits alone at his kitchen table and points a gun at himself."

Her point, Zane admitted. Who the hell was he to preach against negative thinking? He was the king of negative thinkers these days. The chief wallower in self-pity and guilt.

❖———❖

"They won't have a vacancy."

"You better hope you're wrong, darlin'. It's the only motel in town, and I don't feel like spending the next day or two in a parked car."

Zane parked said car at the side of the motel, out of sight of the office. The problem with driving a hot-orange 1969 Mustang Mach One was that everyone noticed and remembered it. If he'd known he was going to be on the run, he'd have made arrangements for a different car.

He reached to open the door. Becca stopped him with a hand on his arm. Even through the fabric of his denim jacket he felt the icy trembling in her fingers. The residue from their time on the bridge. At least he hoped that's all it was.

"Wait." She licked her lips and stared at her hand on his arm for a moment before looking at him. "What if . . ."

"What if what?"

She gnawed on her lower lip. "On the outside chance that our friend in the sedan made it into town ahead of us, maybe I should check us in."

"You?"

"Yes, me." She glowered at him. "I'm not the one he's looking for. If he starts asking questions, they'll be about a man fitting your description. If the desk clerk never sees you, he can't say anything, right?"

Zane arched a brow. "You're not half bad at this being-on-the-run stuff. You'd make a good cop. Or criminal," he added with a twist of his lips.

"Thank you. I think." She rubbed her palms down the thighs of her jeans, then grabbed her purse.

The desk clerk looked exhausted but friendly. He had one room left. Becca groaned silently. She'd been looking forward to a little privacy in which to quietly collapse. It looked as though she wasn't going to get it.

"We got the last room," she told Zane back out at the car.

"Room, as in singular?"

"Room. As in singular. It was all they had."

Pictures flashed through his mind. Becca, spread out beneath him on a bed, his fingers entwined in that short hair, her big gray eyes glazed with passion. Zane shook his head. He'd never gone in for pixies. What was it about this woman that kept heating his blood?

Whatever it was, it might as well take a nap. It was the wrong time, the wrong woman, for those kinds of thoughts. He called himself a jerk and followed her to their room on the first floor. It was a typical motel, but looked like it had been redone recently. Fresh paint, new carpet. One double bed.

Zane watched as the latter registered on Becca's face.

"Okay, look." She tossed her purse on the bed and faced him with her hands on her hips. "We're stuck together for at least tonight. There's one bed and two of us. Don't get any funny ideas."

"Am I laughing?"

"You know what I mean. There'll be no hanky-panky here. We're strangers, after all."

Zane's lips quirked. He couldn't resist. "Hi." He held out a hand to her. "I'm Zane Houston. Nice to meet you."

"Let me guess. They threw you out of the OSBI for making lousy jokes, right?"

Zane lowered his hand and lost his smile. "Nobody threw me out of the OSBI."

"Oh? Well, you can tell me all about it over something to eat. I'm starving. But first . . ." Becca retrieved her purse from the bed and closed herself into the small bathroom so fast, wind gusted in her wake.

Zane waited patiently while the water in the bathroom sink ran for what seemed like forever. He wondered why women did that, turned on the faucet to cover the sound of what was really going on in there. It wasn't as though anyone was fooled.

And it wasn't as though he was fooling himself with his reaction to her comment about being thrown out of the OSBI. It had been more than a year. It had been his decision to leave. They would have retrained him for a desk job. They'd offered.

Yet let somebody innocently bring up the subject, and he got all prickly. Defensive.

Need to work on the attitude, Houston.

He shouldn't let it get to him. If he was out of a job and had nothing better to fill his days than his own sour thoughts, it was no one's fault but his.

Tonight's action told him how much he missed

his job. Which was funny, because on the job he'd never been the quarry, he'd always been the hunter. And he'd been damn good at it.

Now what good was he?

None. Less than none.

"Okay, your turn." Becca breezed out of the bathroom and waved an arm toward it. "What's wrong with your leg?"

Zane frowned. "Nothing." He hadn't realized he'd been leaning over, rubbing his thigh. It had stiffened up on him. He straightened and took a step toward the bathroom. And nearly fell flat on his face when the leg buckled.

"Zane!" Becca rushed forward and braced him with her shoulder beneath his right arm. "What's wrong?"

A flush of humiliation stung his cheeks. "Nothing's wrong," he said with a growl. Except that he was slowly growing more aware of the feel of her body against his, her hand splayed across his chest, the scent of sugar cookies, than he was of his leg or his embarrassment.

He pushed away from her and limped into the bathroom. With the door closed, he leaned his weight against the sink and allowed a grimace of pain.

Then he glared at himself in the mirror. Okay, so his libido had decided to resurrect itself for the brave, caring little pixie. So his male pride had taken a bashing, courtesy of a leg that decided not to work. He had no business taking anything out on

Becca. He shouldn't want her. He shouldn't snarl at her. None of what was eating him was her fault. Except that she existed. She was here. And he'd suddenly developed a serious fondness for big gray eyes and the smell of vanilla.

Houston, you're a real prize.

On the other side of the door, Becca was thinking the same thing about herself. She'd embarrassed him by asking about his leg. She remembered earlier in the evening when she'd asked about it and he'd denied that anything was wrong.

Male pride. Growing up with five brothers had taught her more about male pride than any woman wanted to know. Men wanted to be seen as strong, invincible. They didn't like their shortcomings pointed out, especially physical shortcomings.

She should have remembered, and not commented. Zane's leg was obviously a touchy subject, one she would studiously avoid from now on.

Fishing around in her purse for a tube of lip balm, Becca wondered darkly what else could go wrong this night. Surely there wasn't much left that she could screw up.

She'd looked through a telescope she wasn't supposed to touch, and everything had gone downhill from there. Now, after Zane had been shot at—thanks to her—then had been so patient with her all night, putting up with her endless chatter, her panic out on the bridge, she had to go and embarrass him about his leg.

Surely, she thought again, there wasn't much

left that could go wrong. All they had to do was get something to eat, then come back to this room and get some sleep.

In the same bed. Together.

Becca stared at the bed, her eyes wide, mouth dry. Being enclosed in a small car with a man for hours was one thing. Sharing a room, she could possibly—probably—maybe—manage. But sleeping in the same bed? With all that body heat, all that muscle, those long, powerful-looking legs, hard biceps . . .

Down, girl, she thought, swinging a foot at the bed. *Get a grip.*

Her toe connected painfully with the bed frame. She raised her foot, grabbed for it, hopped around on one foot until she fell butt-first onto the very thing causing her consternation—the bed.

So much for wondering what else could go wrong. Now she could limp right alongside Zane.

She sat on the edge of the bed, her aching foot resting on the opposite thigh. Holding her toe, she rocked back and forth and wondered, since her toe didn't hurt all that badly, why she felt the uncontrollable urge to cry.

Zane came out of the bathroom, then stopped abruptly. "What's wrong?" he demanded.

Becca took a swipe at her cheek, surprised to find it wet. "Nothing."

"You're crying."

"No." She sniffed. "No, I'm not."

The sight of tears on those delicate cheeks

twisted painfully inside Zane. "Ah, darlin'." He sat beside her on the bed and slipped an arm around her shoulders. "I'm sorry. This night's been rough enough without having me yell at you for no good reason. Don't cry."

His warmth and gentleness, the compassion in his voice, were Becca's undoing. All the emotion that had been pent up since she'd seen him through her uncle's telescope let loose in a flood of tears that she couldn't stop.

"I t-tol' you," she managed to say between sobs, "not to c-call me d-darlin', sug-ar. I s-stubbed my t-toe."

Zane didn't know whether to laugh or join her in a good crying jag. He wasn't a man who cried, and laughter seemed inappropriate, so he did neither. Instead, since he couldn't seem to answer her needs, he answered one of his own and pulled her onto his lap. Wrapping both arms around her, he found her more than comfortable against him. She was warm and soft in all the places a woman should be soft, firm in the places a woman should be firm. She smelled sweet, like sugar cookies. She felt good. Damn good. Like he'd feared she would.

When was the last time he'd held a woman? He couldn't remember. Not the time, not the place. Not the woman.

It shamed him, forgetting something as important as that.

Of course back then, before the shooting, he hadn't considered that holding a woman was important. He hadn't considered. Period. He'd taken things for granted. Women. The ability to walk across a room without pain. His job. His partner. His life.

No more, he vowed. Earlier, when he'd opened his door to a pixie and a hail of bullets, he'd realized he didn't want to die. He wanted to live, at least long enough to testify.

But now, holding Becca, feeling her tears hot and wet soaking his shirt, he realized there were other things to live for. There was this, the simple pleasure of holding her, the satisfaction in giving comfort, however small.

He wouldn't take this, or her, for granted. He wouldn't allow this memory to get lost to indifference. He would hold it, keep it, savor it, as he savored the feel of Becca Cameron in his arms.

He smoothed his hand up and down her back in a gesture of comfort, but suddenly wished he hadn't when he realized that all he felt beneath her sweater and T-shirt was the smooth lines of a woman. No strap across her back indicating a bra.

With a silent groan he cursed himself. This was not the time, or the woman, for his libido to awake from the dead.

Becca felt his hand on her back and wished silently that he would keep stroking her. Just keep stroking and stroking forever. His touch was so strong and warm, and felt so good.

But she was through crying now, and embarrassed that she'd ever started. And she was on his lap. How had that happened? As much as she liked the position, she feared she was hurting his leg. With a sniff she slid off his lap and sat next to him on the bed. "I'm sorry," she whispered.

"For what?"

"For crying all over you like a baby."

With his thumb he wiped the last tear from her cheek. "I didn't mean to snap at you either. Let's chalk it all up to a hell of a night and let it go, okay?"

"Okay." If her smile was a little wobbly, it was still a smile. "Now can we find something to eat?"

"You bet. As soon as we hide the car." Zane pushed himself from the bed and extended a hand. "Let's go."

Becca let him pull her to her feet, savoring the feel of his hand on hers. Together they turned toward the door, took a step, and limped. Both of them.

Zane looked down, dumbfounded, to see her favoring her right foot, him, his right leg. They looked like a Laurel and Hardy skit. For the first time since the shooting more than a year earlier that had cost him much more than just a smooth walk, Zane threw his head back and laughed.

About a half mile short of the bridge, the man called Riley fumed in impotent rage. The Mustang had to be ahead of him. All the other roads were closed. They must have come this way. If only the damn traffic would *move*.

Eventually the accident in the oncoming lane was cleared, and for a while traffic flowed past him in the opposite direction. Then there was no more oncoming traffic.

One by one the cars in front of him turned around and headed back toward Maysville. As he drew closer to the river bridge, Riley saw the barricades, the water lapping onto the bridge, the officers in rain slickers, their flashlights waving people off.

Son of a bitch. They'd closed the bridge.

The Man was going to kill him. Literally. He had to get into that town and find his target. Had to get the job done and report back. Or he was a dead man.

Instead of turning his sedan around as the officer with the flashlight indicated, Riley drove past him to the officer at the barricade. He rolled down his window and cursed the rain that pelted him.

"Sir?" The officer leaned down to peer into the car. "I'm sorry, sir, you'll have to turn around and head back. The bridge is closed."

"I can see that, officer. I don't know what to do. My wife's in town, and she went into labor a couple of hours ago. I got here as quick as I could. Is there any way . . . ?"

"Your wife's in labor?"

"Yes, sir. This is our second try. The last one

was stillborn. I just have to get through, officer. I *have* to."

"Wouldn't she have gone to Pauls Valley to the hospital?"

Riley didn't have to fake the panic that ran through him. He assumed the man meant that Lindsay didn't have a hospital. "Uh, her brother's with her. He's a doctor, and after what happened last time, he didn't want to chance the roads in her condition. It was a traffic accident last time that . . . well, you know."

The officer was young and tired and sympathetic. "I imagine the doctor's got everything he needs over at the clinic. Wait here. I'll see what I can do."

Of course, Riley thought as the young cop went over and conferred with an older one, if they checked at the clinic to see how things went, nobody will have heard of him or his wife or her brother. Riley didn't care. He just wanted across that damn bridge. His life depended on it.

FIVE

Zane and Becca drove down a side street behind the motel, then down another, and another, until they found a shed that looked abandoned on an overgrown vacant lot. Zane eased the Mustang behind the shed and parked it. This was the best he could do for now. They locked the car and started back toward the main drag on foot.

"Look at that," Becca said as she and Zane limped away from the shed. "It's down to a drizzle again."

They walked on in silence toward the lights of the convenience store down the street. Traffic was practically nonexistent now on the street, but the parking lot of the store was packed.

"We should have driven," Becca said suddenly.

Zane glanced at her, noticed her hair was getting wet. "Why?"

"Because you're obviously in pain. I'm sorry. I

know you don't want to talk about your leg, but there's no point in causing yourself more pain."

"If it's my leg you're worried about," Zane said, "walking is better. I didn't mean to snap at you earlier. I got shot. When I sit too long or put too much strain on it, it stiffens up on me. I don't like to talk about it."

Becca's heart whacked against her ribs. He got shot. He'd been an agent for the OSBI, and he got shot. Her mouth dried out at the thought of a bullet tearing through his flesh. "I'm sorry. I talk too much. I'm too nosy. Ignore me. Forget I'm here."

That, Zane thought wryly, would be impossible. He might have been able to pull it off earlier in the night, but now that he'd held her, felt her rest trustingly against him, been burned by the salty heat of her tears against his skin, he doubted he'd ever forget. Doubted that he would ever want to.

Love's Country Store, being the only apparent place open in Lindsay, Oklahoma, at 4:30 A.M., was crowded with customers. As Zane and Becca approached, Zane scanned the parking lot. There were pickups and station wagons, sports cars, and more pickups, but no dark gray sedan.

Inside, the store sold everything from motor oil to toothpaste, and everything in between. At the counter Becca ordered two hot dogs with the works; Zane settled on a ham and cheese sandwich. They managed to snare one of the few tables along the front window when a couple with a crying baby got up and left.

Becca slathered extra mustard on her first hot dog, took a big bite, then moaned in ecstasy. "Oh, this is wonderful."

Zane had a little trouble swallowing his first bite of sandwich. He'd had women in the throes of orgasm who didn't sound as pleased as Becca eating a hot dog. The notion, inappropriate though it was, heated his blood.

"Uh-oh." Becca licked mustard from the corner of her mouth. "You've got that man-confounded-by-woman look on your face."

"That what?"

"Man-confounded-by-woman. It's the look a man gets when a woman does something he can't begin to understand. Half amazement, half amusement."

"You're an expert on men, are you?"

"More or less," she said with a negligent shrug. "Growing up with five brothers and six uncles, you can't help it."

Zane's eyes widened. "Five brothers? *Five?*"

"Matthew, Mark, Luke, John, and Timothy, who gives thanks each day that he wasn't named Acts."

"I'll bet," Zane said with a chuckle. "So why aren't you Ruth?"

She grimaced. "Guilty, as charged."

Zane stared at her. "How do you get Becca out of Ruth?"

"Rebecca Ruth Cameron, at your service."

"No foolin'? Rebecca Ruth, huh? Why not Esther?"

Becca rolled her eyes. "Because my lifelong string of bad luck didn't start until I was three, when I knocked my father's pipe out of the ashtray and set the sofa on fire. Rebecca is bad enough."

"I like Rebecca," Zane said.

Becca beamed. "You do? You're the first." She took another mouthful of hot dog, then washed it down with a sip from her forty-two-ounce root beer. "So now that we know what my parents read, is it safe to assume yours read westerns?"

It was an old hurt, Zane acknowledged, one he thought he'd come to grips with years ago. That it reared its head now surprised him. He tossed it off with a negligent shrug. "I never knew my parents."

Once again Zane found humor in a situation that had never been humorous before. Becca looked as though she'd never heard of anyone growing up without knowing his parents. As though he'd just stated that his parents were from Jupiter. "It happens, you know."

She blinked, then studied her hot dog as if wondering what it was and how it came to be in her hand. "I know. I just can't imagine it, that's all. Did you have any family at all?"

"Brothers and sisters? No. My mother's cousin raised me until I was about five, then the state sent me to a foster home."

"Oh, Zane."

"Relax, will you? They were good people, treated me like one of the family."

For Becca, it didn't help that he didn't see his childhood as tragic. She did. To grow up without knowing his own parents, to be raised with no blood ties to brothers, sisters, aunts, uncles . . . Yes, she knew it happened. She just couldn't imagine what it must be like.

"I'm sorry about tonight," she said.

"What do you have to be sorry for?"

"If I hadn't come to your door, that man never would have gotten a shot at you. I'm just plain bad luck."

"Jeez, would you quit with the bad-luck bit?"

She looked troubled and fell silent. After a full thirty seconds, Zane missed the sound of her voice. "So tell me where you learned so much about cars?" he asked, hoping to get her talking again.

She made an effort to smile. "Self-defense. My father is a mechanic—not that anyone can do all that much since they started putting computers in cars. All my brothers helped him when they were growing up. I was the youngest, and I got tired of being left out. I found out quite by accident that not only do I enjoy tinkering around on old cars, but I'm good at it."

"Maybe when this is over, you can do something about my timing," Zane offered.

"Your dates are your problem, buster."

"I think I'm too tired to think of a comeback for that." They both knew he'd been talking about his car, not his love life. Zane was glad to see her mood lift enough for her to make a joke, even if it was at his expense.

"Cars," she said, "are about the only thing I have any luck with at all. I never screw up on a car."

"I'll bet there are a lot of things you don't screw up on," he offered.

The light in her eyes faded. "You'd lose, then."

When they finished eating, they bought toothbrushes, toothpaste, shampoo, deodorant, and a few other items they would need to see them through the next day or two. Since Becca had used her credit card at the motel, Zane insisted on paying for their goods himself. When she wasn't looking, he slipped a little something in with their purchases that he hoped might cheer her up and help her stop blaming herself for everything that happened.

Back in the motel a few minutes later, Becca dumped their bag of goodies on the bed and began sorting them. "What's this?"

Zane suddenly felt silly for buying it. "What's it look like?"

"It looks like a rabbit's foot key chain. Did you need a new one?"

He stuffed his hands in the front pockets of his jeans. "It's for you."

She blinked, looked down at the rabbit's foot, back up at him. "What for?"

Feeling more uncomfortable by the minute, Zane shrugged. "For luck."

Her eyes widened.

"You keep talking about your bad luck."

A smile started on her face.

"I thought . . ."

"For me? You bought this for me?"

"Well, yeah, I said so, didn't I? Just forget it. It was a dumb idea anyway. Give it here." He reached for the rabbit's foot, intending to get rid of it, but she jerked it away.

"No. I think it's sweet."

Zane stifled a groan. Sweet? Him? He couldn't remember the last time anyone thought anything about him was sweet.

"Who knows," Becca said brightly. "Maybe this will end my bad luck. Although," she added, "it doesn't seem to have been very lucky for the rabbit."

Zane's only response was a grunt. He gathered up his share of the toiletries and dumped them on the dresser at the foot of the bed. "I don't know about you, but I've had a long day." He peeled off his jacket and tossed it across the chair beside the door.

Becca's mouth went dry. She gripped the rabbit's foot in her fist and noticed not for the first time how small the bed was. Glancing up as Zane took off his jacket, she got a shock. "You're wearing a gun!"

Zane looked down at the pistol nestled beneath his left arm in his shoulder holster. "By golly, you're right." He cocked his head at her. "Is that a problem?"

"I—" She stopped and swallowed. "I guess not. I just didn't know, that's all."

"Darlin', most cops I know, even ex-cops, don't even answer the front door unarmed." He placed the gun on the bedside table, then took off his holster and draped it over the jacket.

For once Becca let his use of the word *darlin'* go unchallenged. Even the gun quickly lost its importance. She was too busy worrying about sharing this very small bed with a very large man to sweat the small stuff.

When he sat on the edge of the bed, it sagged beneath his weight. Becca, seated on the other side, felt her balance slip. "What are you doing?"

He peered at her over his shoulder. "I'm taking off my shoes."

"Why?"

"Because I usually don't sleep in them."

"Oh," she said, feeling stupid. She was a grown woman, for heaven's sake. She'd shared a bed with a man before. Sort of.

But this wasn't like that. No seduction, no fooling around. Just sleep. That was all Zane had in mind. Of course it was. There was no reason to be so jittery because he was getting ready for bed. He was an honorable man. She believed that. Had to believe it. He wasn't going to pounce on her the minute the lights were out.

Lights! It would be pitch black in the room when they turned out the lights.

Becca hopped up and carried her new purchases

into the bathroom. She would leave the bathroom light on. That would help.

She stayed in the bathroom as long as she reasonably could, brushing her teeth, washing her face, combing her hair. Lining up her newly purchased items in straight rows, by size. Finally, when she could think of no more excuses to delay, she left the bathroom, leaving the light on.

Zane had turned off all the lamps except the one on her side of the bed. He was stretched out in the bed, hands behind his head, covers folded back to reveal his broad, bare, hair-covered chest. His eyes were closed. Becca's palms turned damp.

His shirt and jeans lay on top of his jacket and holster on the chair beside the door. Wondering if he'd left his briefs on had heat flushing her cheeks.

"Are you asleep?"

One of Zane's eyes opened a slit. "Almost."

"Oh. Uh, did you lock the door?" Instead of waiting for him to answer, she crossed the room and checked. The chain was on, the dead bolt secured. "Oh. Good. Do you think it's light out yet?" She lifted the edge of the blackout curtains and peered out. "It's still raining."

"Are you coming to bed?"

At the sound of his voice, she dropped the drapes and nearly jumped out of her skin. "What? Oh. Sure." Coming to bed. Such a small bed. "It's a nice room, don't you think? The paint looks fresh, and the carpet is brand new. I wonder if all the rooms have been redone."

With one eye, Zane watched her flitter around the room. She was as jumpy as a grasshopper on a hot griddle.

"One of my students last term moved to Crow Creek from Lindsay." Faster and faster her words ran together, but she couldn't seem to help it. "Did I tell you that?"

"No. I didn't know you were a teacher."

"Well, I am," she answered brightly. "High school math, geometry and algebra. Numbers are my thing, you know?"

"Glad to hear it. I'm sure you're a good one. Good night, Becca."

"Oh. Sure. You're tired. Good night." She ran a finger along the length of the dresser. Counted the hangers on the rod in the nook that passed for a closet. Six hangers.

"Are you going to get some sleep? We'll need to leave the minute the roads open."

Becca jumped. "Oh. Sure." She bit the inside of her jaw. "Did you check to see if there's a Gideon Bible in the room?" She hopped over to the nightstand on her side of the bed. "Here it is. It's like a law or something, you know? Every motel and hotel room has to have one. But you're trying to go to sleep, aren't you?"

Becca made the mistake of glancing at the bed. It looked even smaller than the last time she'd looked. If possible, her mouth turned drier, her palms more moist.

She forced herself to sit on the edge of the mattress. She could take off her shoes. She could do that much. And her socks. The socks could go. They were still a little damp anyway.

After taking them off, she jumped up and carried her socks to the bathroom, where she draped them over the shower rod. Then she made the mistake of looking into the mirror.

The woman staring back at her was plainly rattled.

Get a grip, Becca. Just go in there and crawl under the covers and go to sleep.

Something awful was going to happen, she just knew it. Becca and a man alone together in a motel room? The combination spelled disaster. It didn't matter that nothing intimate was going to happen. It didn't matter that all either of them wanted was a good night's sleep. She would jinx it, screw it up somehow. She just knew it.

He said her voice was sexy, but she knew he didn't really mean it. He wasn't going to jump her bones. *Even if you want him to,* came a sneaky voice from the back of her mind.

Oh, no. No, she most certainly did not want Zane Houston to jump her bones. Absolutely not. No way, José. She was not developing a case of the hots for a man she'd barely met.

So there.

As quietly as she could, she tiptoed back to the bed and stood there. "Zane? Are you awake?"

"No."

Oh. Stupid question. She took off her cardigan

and hung it in the closet nook. After a moment she crossed back to the bed and took a deep breath. After another moment she turned off the light, lifted the covers, and climbed into bed, fully clothed but for shoes and socks.

Zane felt the brush of denim against his calf. She'd left her clothes on. He couldn't blame her for that. A woman sharing a motel room and a bed with a man she knew nothing about couldn't be too careful. But she didn't need to worry about him. Never in his life had he pressured a reluctant female. Besides, now that he'd actually made it to bed, he was too damn tired to get out of line.

He was just about to fall asleep, when she shifted her weight. The carpet and paint may have been new, but the mattress was old and soft. It gave easily with each movement. He looked, and sure enough she was hugging the side to keep from rolling against him.

He let out a sigh. It was going to be a long night.

He shifted, trying to give her more room. His leg protested the move. He massaged it a moment, then gave up and blocked the pain from his mind.

Again he was almost asleep when the bed shook with her movements. About the fourth time it happened—not that he was counting—he gave up.

"Come here." He turned on his side and pulled her back against his chest. To keep her from flopping around, he left his arm around her. "Now be still and go to sleep."

Sleep? Becca thought frantically. He expected her to sleep snuggled up against him this way with her heart pounding ninety to nothing and her muscles quivering? His body put off heat like a blast furnace. His arm weighed her down. His knees pressed against the backs of hers. She would never be able to sleep this way.

But oddly enough, she did just that.

It was Zane who lay awake for more than an hour, wondering what the hell he'd done to himself. She was entirely too soft and comfortable snuggled up against him this way. They fit together like two spoons. It was disconcerting as hell.

The blast of a car horn outside their door at ten that morning startled them awake. Zane was stretched out on his back, and Becca was mortified to find herself sprawled atop his chest. They stared at each other for one heartbeat. Two.

Her heart was pounding. She should move away from him. Quickly. But there was a delicious heaviness in her breasts and loins that kept her pressed against him. She felt his heartbeat too, and it wasn't any calmer than hers.

Then she felt his body's other response to having a woman crawling all over him. Startled, she felt a flush steal up her face. "Oh."

Zane was shocked to feel a blush of his own. "Yeah. Oh."

"I didn't mean to crowd you," she said quickly, breathlessly. "I'm sorry."

To hell with it, Zane thought. It wasn't every day a man woke to find a woman on top of him. He curled his arms around her. "I'm not," he said, and he wasn't. There was a gray-eyed woman in his arms, and he was so damn tired of being alone.

Slowly he raised his head toward hers. "Good morning."

Becca shivered. His voice was raspy with sleep. His lips drew near. Panic threatened to choke off her breath.

Zane saw it in her eyes and stopped. "You're afraid."

"No," she said quickly. "Yes. I—" With a sharp cry she pulled away from him and sat on the edge of the bed, her back to him. "I'm sorry. I'm no good at this."

Zane eased a breath in and out slowly. "No good at what?"

"This." She waved a hand in the air, flopped it down on her lap. "Sex. I have bad luck with sex too."

"What do you mean, bad luck with sex?" He eased up and leaned back against the headboard.

"Just forget it, okay? For heaven's sake, I can't go to bed with a man I've known less than twenty-four hours."

"You already did go to bed with me. We're talking about something else now. Hey," he said when she flinched. "It's okay. You're right. It's too soon. I can wait until you're ready, darlin'."

Becca stiffened and turned slowly to face him. "Until I'm ready? You're sounding a little bit too sure of yourself for comfort, sugar."

Zane grinned. "I thought that'd get your attention. For the record, I was only after a good-morning kiss."

"That's what they all say," she muttered. "I might have been born in the dark, but it wasn't last night. Go take a cold shower."

"Good idea. I think I'll do just that." He flipped the covers aside and stood up. He felt her gaze on him like a hot, bold touch. His body reacted predictably.

Becca's eyes widened. She was staring and she knew it, but the sight of Zane Houston in nothing but Jockey shorts was something to behold. Words flew through her brain. Chest, arms, legs. Muscles. Strong. Gorgeous. Breathtaking. She barely noticed the scars on his right thigh, what with all the other . . . sights to see.

She'd been right, she thought as her face heated. He did need a cold shower.

"You might want to take one yourself," he told her.

Embarrassed at being caught staring, Becca jerked her gaze to his face. "Take one what?"

"A cold shower." He wasn't looking at her face. He was looking at the front of her T-shirt, where it draped and outlined her nipples, erect and aroused.

"We could take one together," he said, walking around the bed and toward the bathroom, "but I think that would defeat the purpose."

As he closed the bathroom door, Becca buried her face in her hands. Oh, Lord, oh, Lord. What was she supposed to do with all these feelings running loose inside her?

After her turn in the shower, Becca felt better. Steadier. More able to face Zane. Things would have been even better if she'd been able to put on clean clothes.

"Is it still raining?" she asked.

Zane snorted. "Is the Pope Catholic?"

"Funny. Did you call Harper?"

"Not yet. I'll do it while we're out getting breakfast. I assume you're hungry."

"I'm starved. But what's wrong with calling him from here?"

"His office probably has caller ID. I'd just as soon not let everyone there know exactly where we are."

"So what are you going to do? How are you going to call him? A pay phone will still show us in Lindsay, won't it? Since there's only one motel in town, they'll still know right where we are."

"I'm going to use a cell phone. The number won't show up on a caller ID box."

"And where," she asked, tugging on her sneakers, "are you going to get a cellular phone?"

Zane grinned. "I'm going to borrow one."

Which was exactly what he did, from an unlocked car parked on a quiet side street three blocks from the motel.

"You're entirely too good at stealing things," Becca mumbled as he slid into the car and flipped open the cellular phone and pressed the power button to turn it on. "I'm beginning to think you were something other than an OSBI agent."

"Relax. I'm not stealing anything."

"Only valuable airtime. This poor person's going to get billed for this."

"I'll leave money. Keep an eye out for anyone looking this way." Zane punched in the number for the Crow County Sheriff's Department. "Sheriff Montgomery, please."

While waiting for Harper to come on the line, Zane pulled a ten-dollar bill from his wallet and laid it on the car seat.

"Montgomery."

"It's me. Are we clear?"

"The line is secure. I'm checking on the other."

"Your men?"

"Yeah," Harper said heavily. "I hope you're wrong about that."

"I'd love to be. You have a better theory?"

"No. Tell me about the car at the motel."

"It was a dark gray four-door sedan, late model. I didn't get a look at him. The windows were tinted. But I saw the gun. It was a pistol that time, not a rifle."

"Did you get a tag number?"

"No. Never saw the back of the car. Makes me wish we lived in a state that required plates on the front."

"Yeah, that would be handy," Harp said. "Did you lose him?"

"I'm assuming so."

"What's that mean?"

"It means I haven't seen him."

"I won't ask where you are."

"Thanks. I need to stash Becca someplace safe. I don't want him or anyone else to be able to find her when I turn the tables on the son of a bitch."

"You're going after him."

"Hell yes, I'm going after him. Did you think I wouldn't?"

Listening while keeping her eyes peeled for anyone paying any attention to the fact that this was not their car, Becca bit her tongue. Whatever warmth that had survived her cold shower shriveled into an icy chill at the thought of Zane going after the man who was trying to kill him.

"Yeah, well, dig a little deeper. The connection has to be there somewhere. If you're sure it wasn't the desk clerk at the motel, and nothing was said over your radios, then the tipoff had to have come from one of your men."

Another shiver raced down Becca's spine. She knew the deputies Zane spoke of. Geoff Terrill she'd known all her life. She'd grown up with him, even dated him once in high school. Mike LaMott and Jim Graham had been deputies with the Sheriff's Department since Becca was a girl. She knew these men.

Yet, if Zane was right, one of them sent a killer after her and Zane last night.

They walked to a café down the street from the motel for breakfast, and by early afternoon the rain finally stopped. By the time the six o'clock newscast aired on television, the report was not good. Upstream, runoff was still pouring into the Washita, sending it farther out of its banks. Rivers and streams all over the state were out of their banks. Crops were underwater, livestock washed away, people drowned.

The Washita was expected to crest at sixteen feet above flood stage around midnight before finally starting to recede if there was no more rain. A very big if, according to the meteorologist.

Zane muttered a curse and turned away from the television to pace to the window and back. He was going stir crazy cooped up in the motel room. It didn't help that he was cooped up with a woman who couldn't stop talking. A woman he was starting to really like. A woman who had slept so trustingly in his arms.

With another curse he dropped the edge of the curtain and went back to the chair.

"How does pizza sound?" Becca asked.

"Fine." Anything. As long as it got them out of this room.

"You don't like sitting still," Becca commented.

"Not particularly."

"What do you do with your time since you're not with the OSBI any longer?"

"Do?"

"Yes, you know, *do*. You just admitted you don't like to sit still. How do you usually keep busy?"

If he told her, she would be disgusted. For a man who usually didn't worry about what people thought of him, he was suddenly reluctant to have her turn away. Which was exactly what she would do if he told her that during a great portion of the past year, to keep busy—and to forget—he drank. When he hadn't been drinking, he'd been looking for his next drink.

The mere reminder disgusted him. He could only imagine how someone as sweet and wholesome as Becca Cameron would react.

"Zane?"

"Not much," he finally answered. "A little of this, a little of that. You ready for that pizza?"

Becca studied him a moment, then said, "Yes. I'm ready."

She'd been too nosy again, asking him what he did with his time. She could tell he wished she hadn't asked. She could tell that he hadn't answered with the truth.

It hurt her, his evasion, and that was ridiculous. He didn't owe her explanations about himself or his life. His life and how he spent it were none of her business.

When was she ever going to learn to keep her mouth shut?

Riley swore and wiped the sweat from where it beaded above his upper lip. He knew it had been a gamble, but he'd been positive that his target had made it to Lindsay before the road was closed. But if the Mustang was there, it had become invisible.

How the hell could a bright orange Mustang just disappear? It should have been easy to find. It would have led him directly to the target.

Yet there was only one motel in town, and the closest thing to an orange Mustang that its parking lot could boast of was a yellow Pinto with orange rust.

His cell phone chirped. He ignored it, as he'd been doing all day. It was The Man. No one else had the number. No way in hell was Riley going to answer the phone and try to explain why he hadn't finished the job yet. No way in hell was he going to admit that he'd deliberately gotten himself flooded into this two-bit town on a hunch, only to have his prey elude him.

In frustration, he beat his fist against the steering wheel. If he didn't find his target and take it out, The Man would send someone after *him*.

"Come on, come on," he muttered, studying every car he passed. "Where are you? Show yourself to ol' Riley, huh? I promise it won't hurt but for just a minute."

He was ready, if only he could find the damn Mustang. His rifle was hidden in the trunk, but beneath the cover of his jacket he caressed his pistol, his fingers itching to pull the trigger.

What Riley didn't know was that if he had turned left instead of right at the last intersection, he wouldn't have needed his pistol or his rifle to finish the job. He could have run his quarry down with his car.

Zane checked on the Mustang, then he and Becca walked to the Pizza Hut for supper. She noticed he wasn't limping, but for once she refrained from saying anything. She even managed to keep quiet through the meal.

It was dark when they left the Pizza Hut, and unseasonably cool. Becca was glad she'd worn her cardigan. She tugged it around her and crossed her arms over her chest for warmth as they walked back to the motel. "Do you think we'll be able to leave tomorrow?" she asked.

Shortening his strides to match hers, Zane shrugged. "If the water recedes."

"Where will we go?"

"I still want to get to Oklahoma City. I have friends there. You'll be safe with them."

Becca wished his comment didn't make her feel like so much unwanted baggage.

"Not that I don't enjoy your company." He grinned slightly.

"Oh, yeah, sure."

Zane looked surprised. "You think I don't?"

"I don't see how you could, after all the trouble I've caused."

"Once and for all, nothing that's happened has been your fault. You got that?"

"No, I don't got that." She would have said more, but as they neared the door to their room, Zane held up his hand for quiet.

He stood next to the door and took a deep breath. Since leaving the motel an hour ago, something had been nagging at him, and he'd only just realized what it was. That sense that something wasn't quite right, that he should watch his step.

The last time he'd had that feeling was the night of the hit on Al and him, more than a year ago.

Now that sense of danger nearing put him on edge, sharpened his senses, pumped adrenaline through his blood. Was the trouble waiting for them inside the room, or was he overreacting, imagining things? He didn't know. And there was only one way to find out.

Becca moved to stand next to him, waiting for him to open the door. Zane motioned her back. "Stay there," he whispered.

"What's wrong?"

He shook his head. "Maybe nothing. Just stay there and let me check it out."

Becca felt the blood drain from her head. Something was wrong. Something was terribly wrong. She could see it on his face, in his eyes. In the way his lips thinned, hardened.

When he motioned her to stand back past the window to their room, she did so on trembling legs. When he reached for the gun in the holster beneath his arm, she nearly cried out.

She wanted to stop him, to keep him from opening that door and discovering whatever terror might be waiting inside. It didn't take a genius to realize that he thought perhaps the man who was after them might have found them, might be hiding in their room, waiting for them to walk in unaware.

With the key in one hand and gun in the other, Zane opened the door and stepped inside.

SIX

The room was empty. The television was still on—Zane had heard it from outside. The same lights they'd left burning were on. As near as Zane could tell, no one had been in during their absence. He would have called himself a fool for entering the room gun-first, but he'd always believed in the old adage of better safe than sorry.

After checking the bathroom, he was giving the room a final glance, his back to the door, when something hit his shoulder. He nearly dove for cover.

"Don't ever do that again!"

It was Becca shrieking at him. It was her fist that had hit his shoulder. As he whirled toward her, it came down on his chest. "Hey! What the—"

"You scared the *life* out of me. Don't you *ever* do that again." Both fists were flying now, pummeling him.

Zane tucked his Glock back in the holster, dropped the room key, and caught her hands against his chest before she could beat him black and blue. For such a little thing, she sure packed a wallop.

He got a look at her face, and swore. She was mad, all right, but she was scared too. Pale-faced, wide-eyed terrified. "I'm sorry," he told her. "Everything's okay. Everything's okay."

Beneath his hands, her fists tightened, tried to jerk free. When they couldn't, they finally relaxed. Her fingers spread across his chest, almost, he thought with a hard thump of his heart, almost like a caress.

"It's not okay." She stared up at him, trembling, eyes wide and stormy, lower lip quivering. "You thought he was in here, didn't you?"

"It wasn't likely. I was just being careful."

"Just being an idiot, you mean."

"I was wrong. He wasn't here." And the fact that he wasn't made Zane wonder what that prickly feeling along the nape of his neck as they'd crossed the street had been about. "He wasn't here," he repeated.

With a hard shove against his chest Becca freed herself from his hold. "He could have been." Whirling, she slammed the door, then turned back to him. "He could have been hiding in here, waiting for you to open the door. You'd have been dead before you even saw him."

"What should I have done, just stood out on the sidewalk all night? Let you walk in first? What?"

"I don't know!" she shouted, waving her arms in the air. "At least if I'd walked in first, he might not have shot me. And even if he had, that would have been more fair, since all of this is my fault anyway."

"Stop talking like an idiot." Zane grasped her arms to hold them still. "I thought I had the corner on guilt and self-blame, but, woman, you beat me to hell and back. Once and for all, none of what's happened is your fault."

"It is," she insisted, gripping his forearms. "I jinx everything. If I'd been minding my own business instead of looking through a telescope I wasn't supposed to even touch, I never would have come banging on your door. If I hadn't come banging on your door, that man out there would never have gotten a clear shot at you."

"If you hadn't come banging on my door, I'd have sat in the kitchen all night and maybe opened that damn bottle after all. I'd have gotten blind, stinking drunk—again—and he could have come right up to the window and blown my brains away. I'd never have known what hit me." He gave her a little shake for emphasis. "By coming to my door, you very likely saved my life, Becca."

Becca let go of his arms and covered her mouth with both hands. Her vision blurred. The picture he painted made her want to cry out in protest. She'd known Zane Houston barely twenty-four hours, yet she couldn't imagine a world without him. Could he be right? Could she accidentally have *helped*—for once—rather than harmed?

Then there were the words he'd left out, like why he'd been sitting at his table with his gun and a bottle. And his remark about getting drunk—again. There was more going on here than she realized. "Zane . . ."

"Hush," he said softly. "Just this once, Becca, hush."

And then he did the most astounding thing. He kissed her. Sort of. Almost. His head dipped down, his breath fanned her cheek. His lips brushed hers. Softly, gently. Just enough to send sparks shooting to her toes.

"Damn." Zane paused, stunned. He'd barely touched his mouth to hers, and he felt like he'd been poleaxed. Fireworks were going off inside his chest, his head. They clogged his lungs and clouded his thinking. All he could think to do was kiss her again.

So he did. For real this time.

This, Becca thought wildly as his mouth finally covered hers, was what she'd been fearing without even realizing it. Without understanding that she'd been wanting him to kiss her since the first time he'd reached out to reassure her last night in the car.

This was the reason her heart had been pounding against her ribs at odd moments for no apparent reason other than that she'd been looking at him, or had touched him, or been touched by him. This, plus flying bullets, she thought with a touch of hysteria.

But bullets couldn't hold her attention now. Not while Zane Houston was tasting her lips as if he were ready to devour them, and her. Everything in her focused on her mouth joined to his. Just kissing him stirred feelings inside her she'd never felt before. Heat. Longing. A sharp tingling down deep in her middle. A delicious heaviness in her breasts, like that morning when she'd awakened in his arms. Only stronger. She didn't know whether to run and hide from what was happening inside her, or throw herself at Zane and beg for more.

The matter settled itself when he slipped his arms around her and pulled her flush against his chest. Oh, the solidness of him, the rightness of being pressed against him. "Zane," she whispered against his lips.

"Yeah," he breathed, moving back just enough to stare at her. Things were happening that he hadn't anticipated and didn't understand. He'd known he wanted her. He'd assumed it would be great. But how could his mind go blank and his knees turn to rubber from just kissing a woman? What had possessed him to kiss her in the first place when he knew he shouldn't? His heart was pounding and his blood was pumping hot and fast. What was making him want to kiss her in the second place, and the third?

No delicate little pixie should be able to do this to him. "Becca . . ." He saw the uncertainty in her eyes along with the same need that he felt in his chest, his loins. "Rebecca," he whispered.

When his mouth reached for hers again, Becca met him halfway. No man had ever called her Rebecca. No man had ever made her name sound like a prayer. No man had ever looked at her the way Zane was looking at her, with awe, as though she was . . . special in some way. Special to him. As if he could see all of her, inside and out, and liked—very much—what he saw. His look melted something inside her that she hadn't realized had been frozen.

But trepidation wouldn't be so easily chased away. "I'm not . . ." Becca tried looking everywhere but at him.

With a thumb to her chin, he turned her head back. "Not what?"

Feeling all those delicious feelings fade, she wanted to weep. "I told you—I'm not any luckier at this than I am at anything else."

Zane heard the nerves in her voice and reined himself in. With a deep breath he slowly shook his head. "We're really going to have to do something about that attitude of yours." He placed a kiss on the turned-up tip of her nose. "What if I told you I could prove you wrong?"

Becca's breath caught. Possibilities blossomed. From somewhere came the nerve to ask, "Could you?"

Zane's smile came slowly. His eyes darkened. "Oh, darlin', just give me half a chance."

His cocky answer and his cocky grin took her breath away. Freed her. Sent bubbles of exhilaration shooting through her blood. With a laugh that was half nerves, half excitement, she wrapped her arms around his neck. "Well, then, sugar, what are you waiting for?"

Zane squeezed her tight, then sobered. "For you to tell me you're sure."

Oh, Lord, she could fall in love with this man if she wasn't careful. "I'm sure. For once in my life I'm feeling lucky. Very, very lucky."

His smile this time was soft. Devastating. "So am I."

She loved what his mouth did to hers. Feeling wild and brave and sexy for the first time in her life, she used her tongue to tease his and reveled in the groan that vibrated from his chest to hers.

Her hands turned greedy, rushing over him, touching him, feeling his strength in the hard muscles she found. His hands were as greedy, sliding over her, touching, cupping, and where he touched, she burned. And wanted more.

She smelled rain in his hair, motel soap on his skin. And something darker, deeper, the compelling scent that was his alone.

Becca understood sex. She'd had it before, once. But her head had never swam with it, her spirit had never soared. This was different. More. Stunning. When his hands slid up under her T-shirt to bare skin, she shivered. Nerves were gone. Excitement and instinct took over. She ran her hands up under his T-shirt and let her hungry hands feast on him.

Zane shuddered in reaction. She was getting to him, going to his head faster than aged whiskey. Her skin was soft as silk and he couldn't get enough of touching her, of having her touch him. He cupped a breast, small and firm, in his hand.

Becca shivered. A low moan of sheer pleasure worked its way up her throat. When he broke the kiss to peel off her shirt, she couldn't find a single reason to complain, except that she missed his mouth on hers. Until he put his mouth on her breast. Her knees buckled. She would have slid down his chest and ended on the floor if he hadn't been holding her.

But he was holding her, kept on holding her as he took her down to the bed. Zane had never made love with a woman whose hair was shorter than his. As he levered his weight on one forearm to keep from crushing her, he realized he liked it. Liked it very much. It was soft and cool to the touch and suited her delicate face perfectly. And it turned him on. His whole body tightened.

Becca nearly closed her eyes against the feel of his hands in her hair. She kept it short because there was nothing else to be done with it. It wouldn't hold a style or curl of any kind, not even a perm. She'd always hated it. But seeing Zane's eyes darken while he looked at it, touched it, made her feel beautiful in a way she never had before.

"It's as soft and fine as baby's hair," he said in wonder.

Becca returned the favor and threaded her fingers through his thick, dark mane. "Yours isn't," she murmured. "It's thick and full of life."

Zane closed his eyes and arched into her touch. Now that he knew the moment was at hand, so to speak, his sense of urgency was tempered by the need to take his time and experience all of her, savor every moment. It felt so damn good to be touched, really touched, the way she touched him.

"Zane?"

Her velvet, breathy voice drew his eyes open. The yearning on her face, the need in her eyes, stirred his blood.

"Kiss me," she whispered.

"With pleasure." He took her lips gently, savoring the taste and texture, building the intensity slowly. Anticipation stretched, tightened his nerves. Her hands slipped from his hair, down his back, up beneath his shirt. He shuddered. "I like the way you touch me."

His words sent her senses soaring. With Zane she felt beautiful, desirable, powerful.

He trailed hot, slow kisses down her neck, around her breasts, across their slopes. His mouth neared one nipple, then eased away toward the other, only to stop just short again. Over and over he tormented her, teased her, until she was arching and moaning, ready to beg. When he finally settled his mouth over a nipple, the pleasure was so intense that she cried out with it.

The sound shot through Zane like wildfire. He'd thought to take her slowly, easing them both up the slope gradually until they slid down the far side together. But her response, the way she dug her fingers into his back, was shredding his control. Her nipple against his tongue grew harder, like a small pearl. It drew his tongue again and again.

Becca went mad with it. When he suckled, he tugged on wires of sensation that reached clear to her core and induced a hot, heavy throbbing between her legs. She hadn't known, had never imagined so great a pleasure. When he moved to her other breast, it was more of the same. She was almost used to the sound of the tiny whimpers issuing from her throat.

When she thought her mind and body would shatter, he left her breast and trailed hot open-mouthed kisses to her navel, then to the waist of her jeans. It took him less than five seconds to remove the rest of her clothes, another five for his.

Hot skin against hot skin. Crisp chest hair against ultrasensitive nipples. Mouth against mouth, belly against belly. Between them a river raged out of control. Zane's weight settled between her legs, and she raised her hips eagerly to meet him.

Zane watched her face, her eyes, as he filled her. He shouldn't have, for the intensity of her pleasure was visible and nearly drove him over the edge. She was tight enough that he had to go slow for fear of hurting her, but she took all of him, to the hilt, and he'd never in his life felt anything to equal the sensation of joining his flesh with hers.

Becca gasped for breath, barely able to fathom the fullness of accommodating him, the thickness of her own blood in her veins, the trembling in her heart. If she had thought that making love with him would not change something deep and fundamental inside her, she had been wrong. This was more than pleasure. More than sex. At that moment, as she looked into his face and held his gaze, they were no longer two people thrown together by circumstances. They were one. A single entity.

And then she couldn't think at all as pleasure, and Zane Houston, took her flying. Again and again he filled her, withdrew, and filled her. She wrapped her legs around his hips and met him thrust for thrust, reaching with him for something she didn't quite understand.

Harder, faster, Zane felt the primal rhythm take control. She was with him. God, she was with him every step of the way. For a moment she shot ahead of him and he watched the climax in her eyes. But it was too intense to merely watch, and he followed her straight off the edge of the world. And off, and off, the shuddering force of it holding them in its grip, holding them, holding them, until finally her arms slipped bonelessly from his shoulders and he collapsed atop her, dazed by the strength of what had just happened.

Zane's first thought, sometime later, was that nothing like this had ever happened to him before. Nothing like Becca Cameron. Nothing like the shattering force of the climax she'd wrung from him. Somewhere between the back of his mind and the edge of his heart came the thought that his entire life had been directed to lead him to this moment, this joining. When his mind was clearer he would have to examine the conviction that he would never be the same. Making love with Becca had changed something inside him, altered something that he hadn't understood was off kilter.

Strength and breath returned enough to allow him to shift his weight to his forearms so he wouldn't crush her to death.

For a fleeting instant of panic, Becca feared he was leaving her, taking his warmth and strength and glorious body away. But by raising up onto his arms, he shifted his weight to his hips, settling himself firmly in the cradle of her thighs. Someone moaned. She thought maybe it was both of them.

"Are you all right?" His voice was even huskier now than that morning when it had been full of sleep.

An aftershock ran through her. She lifted her eyelids and found Zane staring down at her with an intensity that shook her because it matched what was going on inside her. "I'm not sure," she managed to say in answer to his question. "Are you?"

No, Zane thought. He wasn't all right. And yet he was more all right than he'd ever been in his life. "It's too soon to tell," he answered.

Those deep gray eyes of hers darkened. "It's only fair to tell you," she said, "that nothing even close to this has ever happened to me before."

Zane went rock still. "You weren't a virgin. I was too rough. Tell me you weren't a virgin. Did I hurt you?"

Becca's heart swelled to near bursting. The feeling came out on her face as a smile. "No, no, no, and no. I wasn't a virgin." Her smile faded, her eyes questioned. "But this . . . you . . . I never felt . . . the things you made me feel."

Zane swallowed, stunned. "You never had an orgasm?"

A blush stole up her cheeks, but smiling slightly, she held his gaze. "Was that what that was? I thought surely it was an earthquake, or that maybe we were back on that bridge and it finally gave way."

A shudder ripped through Zane, reaction to her words that made him both humble and chest-beating proud at the same time.

In response, Zane's body tightened, surged to life. The part of him still buried in her heat hardened, expanded. He sucked in a sharp breath between his teeth.

Becca's eyes widened. "Again?"

Blood pumped through his veins hot and heavy and fast. "I don't seem to have a choice."

Her arms came around him and her eyes glowed. "Thank goodness."

Sometime during the night Zane forced himself from Becca's warmth and turned off the lights and the television. When he returned to her arms, it felt as if he'd been away for months.

It shook him, the need for her that would not abate, but he went with it, let it hold him in its relentless grip because he couldn't seem to do anything about it. Whatever this spell was, he didn't want to break it. He couldn't get enough of her.

They slept like the dead, and woke to love again. And again. The light around the edge of the curtains changed from nighttime neon to daytime sunshine, and they made love again. They showered together and did things that Becca was sure that old porcelain had never seen before.

Few words were spoken throughout the night and morning. Few were needed. What was happening between them was too stunning, too intense for words.

Becca could not tell Zane what was in her heart. How could she explain to a man she'd known less than two days that she was forever changed because of him? He was at once tender and fierce, a combination that thrilled her, kept her off balance. Made her fall totally, completely, irrevocably in love with him.

Oh, Becca, you fool. What place was there for an unlucky klutz like her in the life of a strong, tough-minded ex-cop?

None. Surely none. She would not let herself hope for anything more than these few hours with him. But for these few hours, Zane Houston belonged to her. And she belonged to him.

For the first time in two weeks the sun was shining. The air, however, was still unseasonably cool. Becca was quiet as they walked down the street to the café for breakfast. Too quiet, Zane thought. From the minute she'd banged on his front door she had talked nonstop, until they made love. Now she hugged her cardigan around her and said nothing. Worried, he took her hand and drew her to a stop beside the street.

She looked up at him, those gray eyes full of a disconcerting combination of female satisfaction, mystery, and pain. The pain cut him like a knife. His hand tightened around hers. "Is something wrong?"

"No." Her smile was poignant. "No, Zane. Nothing is wrong." *Nothing*, she thought sadly, *except that I'm in love with you.*

At the stunned look that crossed Zane's face, terror shot through her. Had she spoken aloud what was in her heart? Dear God, she hoped not. A man like Zane, who probably knew dozens of women more worldly and sophisticated than herself, would not want to hear those words from her. They would make him uncomfortable. Maybe make him pity her, ruin what was left of their time together.

"Are you sure?" he asked, his thumb caressing her knuckles.

"That nothing's wrong?" She intentionally brightened her smile. "I'm positive."

A deep line appeared between his brows. "You don't lie worth a damn, Rebecca Ruth."

It was time, Becca decided, to lighten the mood. She feigned a scowl. "Nobody calls me Rebecca Ruth and lives, buster."

"I called you Rebecca last night and you didn't seem to mind."

Becca's breath caught. "That," she said, her voice going unintentionally husky at the memory, "was different."

Zane studied her, tried to read her. Whatever had been wrong was gone now. All he saw in her eyes was heat. His blood surged in response. "Damn." He drew her close. "Don't look at me like that."

"Like what?"

"Like you're remembering what it's like when I'm buried deep inside you."

That fast, with only those few words and the heat of his gaze scorching her, Becca felt her breasts tighten, her loins throb. "Oh, Lord have mercy."

"He already did that," Zane said solemnly. "He brought me you."

Stunned, Becca stared at him, breathless, needy, eyes filling with tears. "Zane . . ."

"Come here." He pulled her flush against his chest and, disregarding the traffic, both pedestrian and vehicular, he, who was not prone to public displays of affection or emotion, kissed her. He kissed her hard and thoroughly, tasting her fully, pressing her hips against the erection he couldn't control.

Loud heckling from a passing car full of teenagers broke them apart.

An hour later they were walking back from breakfast holding hands like two young, carefree lovers. Zane supposed that's what they were just then. He hadn't felt young and carefree in a hundred years, but with Becca, anything seemed possible.

But the weather had cleared and the river had crested. The flood waters were receding. He didn't want to think about returning to the real world and the threat that dogged them.

Studying Becca's smiling profile as they walked, he didn't notice the gray sedan that pulled up at the stop sign at the end of the block. But old instincts died hard. The hair along the back of his neck stood on end.

Startled by the feeling, so alien and unwelcome when all he wanted to do was drag Becca into his arms and feast on her mouth, Zane looked up in time to see the muzzle of a gun poke out of the half-open car window.

Becca felt the sudden tension in Zane's hand. From that point, everything seemed to happen in slow motion, as if in a movie. Zane shouted. With the hand that held hers—his left hand—he jerked her nearly off her feet to shelter her body with his. With his other hand he pulled his gun from the holster beneath his arm.

A shot sounded. Then another, so close upon the first that they sounded almost as one. Tires squealed. Somewhere nearby a woman screamed.

Becca bit back a scream of her own as Zane lifted her against his side and ran for cover between two buildings. All she could think was that he was protecting her, and risking himself. He was going to be shot.

They made it between the buildings, where Zane pressed her against the brick wall of one and covered her, his back to her, his gun drawn and aimed toward the street, waiting. Waiting.

"Go," he told her tightly. "Start toward the alley."

"Not without you," she protested.

"I'm right behind you. Don't argue. Go!"

Because to argue might put him in even more danger, Becca went. She nearly wept with relief when she realized that he was, indeed, coming with her.

Zane went, keeping himself between Becca and

the street with every step. He wasn't about to let her more than six inches away from him. Even that was too far, for a new twist had just developed. The man in the dark gray sedan had not been shooting at Zane, and it made the blood turn to ice in his veins. The man had taken direct aim at Becca.

SEVEN

Zane pushed Becca ahead of him until they reached the alley behind the buildings. "Wait." He drew her to a halt and, after glancing over his shoulder to make sure no one was behind them, pressed her against the brick wall beside them. Covering her with one arm, he leaned to the corner of the building and checked out the alley.

It was clear except for an old Chevy S-10 pickup. It would have to do. The driver's window was down, so he knew it was unlocked. He dragged Becca from the alley and toward the beat-up truck. "Get in and keep down."

Zane climbed in behind her and settled behind the steering wheel. "Key," he muttered. "Where's the damn key?" He checked above the sun visor, then beneath the floor mat. No key.

He looked at the ignition switch and swore. The pickup wasn't old enough to have the switch mounted in the dash so that he could reach under the dash, pull out the wires, and hot-wire the truck. This ignition switch was mounted on the side of the steering column, and it would take either tools he didn't have, or Arnold Schwarzenegger dressed as the Terminator, to get the switch off to gain access to the inside, where he could then start the truck and unlock the steering wheel.

"Son of a bitch."

"Keep looking," Becca said breathlessly. She reached for the ashtray. "Here!"

Zane grabbed the key and started the engine. With the gun still in his right hand, he put the pickup in gear and hit the gas. "I never would have found it," he said half to himself.

"Why not?"

Zane shook his head. "I used to smoke. Ashtrays are full of ashes. You don't put anything in them but butts and the occasional gum wrapper, if you don't mind starting a fire." He shook his head again. "I never would have looked there. Stay down," he told her. "All the way down. Sit on the floor."

Becca did as he ordered, and stared up at him, more frightened than she'd ever been in her life. But not totally for herself. "What about you?"

"I don't know how to break this to you, darlin'," he said grimly, checking the street for traffic, "but he wasn't shooting at me."

"What do you mean?" she squeaked. "If he catches sight of you behind the wheel, he'll shoot you."

"Maybe," he answered grimly, turning away from the main street toward a residential neighborhood. There was a red O.U. Sooners ball cap on the seat. Zane put it on and tugged the bill down low. "But I wasn't the one he was aiming at out on the street just now. His bullet plowed right smack into the utility pole that was directly behind you." He spared her a grim glance. "He was aiming at you, Becca."

Shock held her silent as Zane turned on first one street, then another, losing them in the warrenlike streets of the neighborhood and leaving their pursuer behind.

"Do you see him?" Becca asked, her throat dry.

"No. We've lost him. But stay down," he added tersely.

Becca's mind was in a whirl. She'd thought they were safe in Lindsay, but somehow the man had found them. There was terror in her, and confusion. Zane was convinced that the man had fired at her rather than at him. That made no sense. Who would want to kill her? She wasn't anybody.

If that weren't frightening enough, the man she'd spent the most incredible night of her life with had vanished. Zane Houston, the most tender and ferocious of lovers, was gone. Replaced by that hard-edged man she'd met at his door. The man who'd thrown her to the floor and demanded to know who sent her. He had that look about him again, the look of a stranger. A cop. A man suspicious of everyone and everything around him. Including her.

She felt as if someone had just carved open her chest and ripped her heart to shreds.

Zane felt much the same way. Confused. Bleeding inside. And angry. The rage threatened to choke him, and he didn't know where to focus it. On the shooter, certainly. The bastard had tried to kill Becca.

In his mind he pictured the other attempts, envisioned the angle and trajectory of the shots, and realized the man had been after Becca each time. It made Zane want to kill someone.

But the question that wouldn't be put aside for long was who was Becca Cameron? Who was she, what did she know, what had she done to warrant a hit? What deadly game was she mixed up in?

He would have his answers, he thought grimly. But not until he was sure they were safe from pursuit.

The neighborhood thinned out. Houses grew farther and farther apart past the edge of town. Ahead, an overgrown, rutted driveway led to a ramshackle, abandoned barn at the edge of a flooded wheat field. Zane slowed, turned onto the drive.

"Wait here." He threw the truck into park and climbed out. The big drive-through door was latched but not locked. It swung open with a loud creak of protest on rusty hinges. There were holes in the roof and pigeons in the loft. Boards missing from the back wall. Old hay and straw. Manure dried with age. It would do.

He drove the pickup through the door and sealed them inside.

Becca crawled up onto the seat and looked around. "Where are we?"

"An abandoned barn near the river."

"The river?" A sudden memory of that raging beast called the Washita made her stomach clench.

"Relax," he said tersely. "We're high and dry and out of sight. You wanna tell me why someone would go to the trouble to take out a contract on you?"

Becca had been expecting the question but not the anger behind it. For a moment she merely gaped at him. "You really do think he's after me, don't you?"

"I don't think it. I know it. What I want to know is why?"

"You think I know?" she cried. "You're the ex-cop with all the enemies. For crying out loud, I'm just a schoolteacher."

"Piss anybody off lately?"

"Enough to want to kill me? Not that I know of. Of course," she added sarcastically, "if this is about the football jock I flunked last fall, the whole town could have pooled their money to hire a killer. Other than that, I haven't a clue."

Zane forced a deep breath. She was telling the truth. If she was lying, those expressive eyes of hers would have given her away. He felt like a heel.

"Come here," he said quietly, holding out a hand to her.

She saw the change in him at once. The anger was gone. He believed that she didn't know what was going on. With a glad cry she launched herself at him.

Zane held her tight, felt her tremble. "I'm sorry," he whispered. "I'm an asshole."

"Yes," she managed to get out. "Sometimes you are." *But I love you anyway*, she thought, struggling to control the tears that threatened. "Do you really think he's after me?"

Zane cupped her cheek in his palm and met her gaze. "If I thought it would keep you safe, I'd lie and tell you no. But I can't, Becca. I saw his aim. It was deliberate, and it was at you. The bullet plowed into that post directly behind your head."

Her face turned ashen, her eyes nearly black.

Zane cursed himself.

Curled up against his chest, she shuddered. "What do we do now?"

"We sit tight right here until the roads open. Then we get you the hell out of here to someplace safe."

"You fired back at him, didn't you? Maybe you hit him. Maybe it's over."

"No." He couldn't let her hang on to a false hope like that. "I took out his side window, but I didn't hit him. He drove off."

There was another thing she hadn't yet thought

of, and he wouldn't bring it up. But a moment later he saw the horror of it dawn in her eyes.

"The deputies," she whispered rawly. "Oh, my God. If you're right and one of them is involved—Zane . . ."

She left the rest unsaid. That one of those men, whom she'd known all her life, had sent a killer after her. Not after the stranger she was with, but specifically after her.

"Don't think about it," he ordered harshly.

"Don't think about it?" she cried. "I've known them since I was a baby. All of them except Harper. You don't suppose—"

"No." But the thought crossed his mind. His friend and former fellow agent may have grown up in the area, but Harper had been back in Crow Creek for only a couple of years. But no. It was easier for Zane to believe someone Becca had known all her life had betrayed her than think that Harper Montgomery had turned bad. Yet for her, that would be the lesser of two evils. "Don't think about it," he repeated.

"I can't help it." Her lower lip quivered.

With a groan, Zane pulled her closer and kissed her. He wanted to pull her inside himself, protect her, keep her safe. God in heaven, he'd almost lost her today out on that street. It had been too close. Too damn close.

Something savage and primitive surged through his blood. She didn't resist when he pushed her down on the seat. He undid her jeans, pushed them down over her hips. Shoving his own jeans down to his thighs, he spread her legs and pushed into her.

Becca cried out, but not in pain. The minute he'd pushed her down on the seat she'd been ready for him, eager for his invasion. No soft kisses this time, no caresses. She didn't need them, didn't want them. Her wants and needs just then were too raw. He was giving her exactly what she craved.

But it wasn't just sex. Not for Zane. It was hot and primitive, mating stripped down to near savagery. It was possession, blatant and potent, a man claiming his woman, reaffirming that she was here, she was alive. And she was his. He drove against her, into her, again and again, until the surge that hit him was so powerful, he cried out with it.

What he cried was her name. The sound of it swept Becca along with him over the edge of awareness.

As the evening light began to fade beyond the cracks and holes in the walls of the old barn, Zane watched Becca's sleeping face. He'd have liked to join her and give his mind a rest, but he couldn't.

First, the chances of the bad guy finding them tucked away in this old barn were next to nothing, but Zane would not leave Becca's life to even that slim a chance. He would stay awake and keep watch. If he watched her, where she slept with her head in his lap, more than he watched the road through the crack in the door, well, hell, he was only human.

The weather had warmed. Every stitch of her clothes lay in a pile in the floorboard.

Second, he thought wryly, he couldn't join her in sleep because there wasn't room on the seat for him unless he slept on top of her. And hell, he'd been on top of her most of the day. Except for when she'd been on top of him.

A shiver of remembered heat trickled down his spine. If he lay down with her on that vinyl seat again, there would be no sleep for either of them.

No more, he warned himself. She wouldn't admit it, but she was sore from making love about a dozen times since last night.

Good God, he hadn't been that rambunctious as a randy teenager.

As the light faded, the air cooled. "Becca." He smoothed his hand over her silky hip. "Becca, wake up."

With her face against his jean-clad thigh, she smiled. "Why?"

"Because you're going to get cold soon. You should probably put some clothes on."

"Spoilsport." But she felt the chill in the air and knew he was right. It was time she got dressed.

The reluctance with which she silently acknowledged the need struck her as humorous, and she laughed.

"What are you laughing at? It's my own sport I'm spoiling, not just yours."

She sat up, and he reluctantly let her slide from his touch. "I was just thinking."

"About what?"

"That I've never lain around naked all day with a man before."

Zane grinned. "Yeah?"

"Yeah."

"So what do you think? Think you might like to do it again sometime?"

She arched a brow. "Depends on the man."

"Tease."

Putting on her clothes, Becca laughed harder than Zane thought necessary for the occasion. "What's so funny?"

She pulled her wrinkled T-shirt over her head, then reached for her cardigan. "Me. This"—she motioned toward him, them, the pickup and barn—"is so unlike me. I've never been this way before," she added, sobering. "I've never felt free to reach out and touch a man the way I do with you."

"Darlin', you can reach out and touch me anywhere you want, anytime."

Becca grinned and slipped on her cardigan while scooting away from him. "Don't give me that husky voice of yours. Not when I've just put my clothes on."

Zane chuckled. He was damn tempted to pull those clothes right back off her, but he stifled the urge. One more round and neither one of them would be able to walk for a week.

"This isn't exactly how I usually behave either," he confessed.

"I'm glad to hear I'm not the only one going a little crazy here."

A cool draft floated through the open window beside Zane. He reached to roll up the window and found out that it was broken and wouldn't budge. With a shrug, he gave up. "I guess we'll just have to sit real close together to keep warm."

Becca slid across the seat and tucked herself against his side. "What a hardship."

Between the loose change in his front pocket and whatever she had in the pocket of her sweater, Zane had to shift her a little to ease the gouging. "I hate to bring it up, but we have to talk about what's happening. The danger you're in."

She tensed against him.

Zane wrapped his arm around her shoulders and rubbed her arm through her sweater. "Think, Becca. Who would have a reason to come after you?"

She tried to pull away from him, but he held her close.

"I don't know," she cried. "I've thought and thought. Zane, there's no one. I'm not important enough to anyone for something like this. I teach school, and in the summer I tutor, or help out at the library. I don't do anything controversial. There's nothing. Nothing."

"Okay," he said, rubbing her arm and pulling her closer. "Okay. Have you made anyone angry lately?"

"Not that I know of."

She shifted against him, and whatever it was in her pocket jabbed at him again. "What is that?"

"Oh, sorry." She felt around in her pocket and came out with a roll of exposed, undeveloped film. "I forgot I had this."

"What's on it?"

She shrugged and dropped the roll into her purse. "Just another one of my screwups."

"I thought you were going to work on that attitude."

Becca ran her hands through her hair. "Yeah, well, this one was minor. I can at least hide it."

"Hide what?" Maybe talking about whatever she'd done would take her mind off the fact that someone was trying to kill her.

"A photo I messed up. I was trying to help my uncle with his book. It didn't exactly work out."

"Jim's writing a book?"

"Sort of." She told him about the book Uncle Jim was putting together about birds of Crow County. "He didn't have a cardinal yet, so I thought I'd help him out."

"You didn't get the cardinal?"

"Oh, I got the cardinal, all right. A beautiful shot of him in flight. Unfortunately, when the film is developed I'm sure he'll look more like the hood ornament on a Firebird than anything else. The key subject in that shot was a white-plumed gold-necked passenger pigeon."

"A what?"

Becca laughed and explained about the car that had come along just as she'd snapped her shot.

Everything inside Zane went still. "This passenger pigeon. He was in the car?"

"Yeah. What? You have a funny look on your face."

One by one Zane's muscles tightened. "What did he look like, this passenger?"

"What difference does it make? I'd never seen—"

"What did he look like, Becca?"

Becca frowned. "He had white hair. Snow white. Dark tan skin, a big nose. That's all I remember."

"You said something about gold-necked."

"Necklaces. He had at least a half dozen gold chains around his neck. What's wrong? Zane . . . do you know who he is?"

Zane felt a fine trembling start in his hands and work its way up to his neck. "Where did you see him? Where did you take the picture?"

"They turned down your road on their way to the Bar B. I was standing on the porch."

"When?" he demanded.

"Around noon, the day I met you. Zane, what—"

"You said *they*. Who else?"

Becca had no idea what was going on, but Zane's eyes had turned fierce, like a predator's. Hard, keen. Ice cold.

"Who else?" he demanded.

"He was with Mark Hammond, foreman over at the Bar B in Smith County."

"In a Firebird?"

"That's right. Are you going to tell me—"

"Was anyone else in the car with them?"

"Not that I could see. Zane—"

"Did either of them see you?"

Becca shrugged. "Not that I remember. Not while I was looking, anyway. As far as I could tell, they didn't even glance my way."

"Who else knows you took that picture?"

"No one."

"Are you sure?" His hand tightened on her arm.

"Zane, the film's not even developed. Even I haven't seen the photo. What in blazes is going on? Who is this man?"

"Unless I miss my guess," Zane said darkly, "you've just described the man who hired the hit on my partner and me last year." Zane swore viciously and hit the steering wheel with his fist. "I *knew* that bastard was in the area. I *knew* it. Tell me again. Everything."

Becca folded her arms across her chest. "Not until you tell me what you're talking about."

Zane's breath was coming fast. He put his head back against the edge of the seat and ordered himself to calm down. Until the Washita receded, he couldn't go anywhere. He couldn't get to Bowen.

"A year ago last winter," he said, "my partner and I were part of a special task force appointed by the state attorney general to work with the ATF and investigate the sudden appearance of assault rifles among gangs across the state."

"Assault rifles? They're illegal, right?"

"Illegal as hell. Fully automatic AK-47s. Pull the trigger once and spray bullets until you run out. Street value, two grand apiece. Coming in straight out of China."

"China? I thought AK-47s were Russian."

"They are. Were. They're being manufactured in China these days. A boatload slipped through customs and offloaded an estimated four million dollars' worth of them. Next thing you know, fourteen-year-old gang members in the heartland of America are mowing each other down with them. We had a suspect, several suspects, but we were after the head of the Oklahoma connection. We knew who he was but didn't have enough evidence to hold him. But we were getting close. Closer than we thought."

As full dark fell inside the barn, Becca shivered. "How close?"

"Close enough for him to hire a hit on us."

"On you and your partner? Is that . . . when you were shot?"

"That was it. February twenty-second. The night I got my partner killed."

Becca's indrawn breath echoed in the cab of the pickup.

"I told you you didn't have the corner on guilt," Zane added.

So this was it, Becca thought. This was the torment she'd seen in his eyes that first night. Dear Lord, was it only two nights ago? This was the reason he sat alone at his kitchen table with a bottle in one hand and a gun in the other. He blamed himself for his partner's death.

Becca placed a hand on his chest and felt the slow, hard beat of his heart. "What happened?"

Zane closed his eyes and saw it all again behind his lids. "I was too slow. He came out of nowhere. Al and I met the ATF half of our task force for dinner, to talk about our next move. Make plans. We were headed across the parking lot toward our cars. Bullets started flying."

Becca wrapped her arms around his chest and held him tightly. "And you were shot."

"Took one in the leg," he said. "The shooter drew down on me again while I went for my gun. Just as he opened fire, Al jumped in front of me."

"Oh, Zane."

"I must have blacked out for a minute or two." His voice was an emotionless monotone. "The next thing I knew, the shooter was gone. Al . . . I held his hand while he died."

Becca buried her face against Zane's shoulder to hide the hot tears she couldn't help.

"I was too slow. I should have—"

"Don't," she cried. "It wasn't your fault. Do you hear me? It wasn't your fault. You know it wasn't."

Zane waited until his breathing leveled before speaking again. "In my head I know it. It's my gut that's not convinced. I had on my vest, Al didn't. I could have taken those shots. Goddammit, he had a wife and two kids. Nobody would have missed me."

"No!" Becca raised her head and tried to see his face through the darkness. "Don't say that!"

He rolled his head toward her. "It sounds maudlin, I know. But it's the truth."

"I suppose that makes me nobody, then. I'd probably be dead by now if you're right and someone *is* after me. What happened to the man who shot you?"

"They got him. It's his trial I'm supposed to testify at next month."

"He's not the man you were after?"

"Just a hired gun. Like this fellow in the gray sedan." Zane leaned up and flipped on the radio. "Let's see what the water's doing."

Garth Brooks was crooning a ballad.

"This man you were after," Becca said. "You think he's the man in my picture?"

"I'm almost certain of it. I'll know as soon as we get the film developed."

Becca sighed. "I meant to do that right after . . . Oh, my God."

"What?"

"I just remembered. There is someone who knows about the photo."

"Who?"

"Geoff Terrill."

"The deputy?"

"I told him about it when I went to town that

afternoon. I meant to have the film developed then, but I'd forgotten it."

"What did you do?"

"I went home."

"And the next time you stuck your nose out of the house—"

"Was when I ran to your door."

"All right," Zane said. "We've got that nailed down."

"Nailed down?" she cried. "A man I've known all my life, a man I went to school with, a man I *dated*, is trying to help get me killed, and you say *all right*?"

"I'm sorry." Zane pulled his mind out of the past and away from the current details to focus on Becca. "I'm sorry. Come here. Don't think about it. Maybe we're wrong. Maybe it wasn't Terrill."

"It was," she said in a small voice. "It had to have been. He's the only one who knew about the picture. And he made the reservations for us at the motel. It had to have been him."

He held her and rocked her, wishing he could protect her from the pain of betrayal. All he could do was say again, "Don't think about it."

They sat in silence but for the radio, and held each other as the night turned cold. At nine-thirty the newscaster advised that State Highway 76 north out of Lindsay—the only road out of the town that did not cross the Washita—was estimated to be re-opened within the hour.

"That's it," Zane said. "We're outta here."

❖———❖

Riley sat in his parked car and shivered. The night had cooled, but still the sweat rolled off him.

He had lost them. By the time he'd circled the block they were nowhere in sight. After hours of searching every street in town, he was no closer to finding them. He cursed viciously.

At least this time he'd gotten a clear look at the man with his target. He had no choice. He had to call The Man.

This news, at least, might keep The Man from killing him outright for failing to take out the target. The Man would want to do this job himself.

"It's Riley," he said into the phone when The Man came on the line. "No, I haven't got her yet. I'm holding off for now because I think you're going to want to finish this job personally."

"And why," came that smooth, soft voice, "would I want to do that?"

"Because I finally got a look at the man with her."

"I do not care who is with her."

"You will when I tell you it's Zane Houston."

EIGHT

They had two choices about how they left town. One, drive the stolen pickup and hope the police were too busy reopening the highway to pay attention to the vehicles lined up to leave town; or, two, retrieve the Mustang and hope the bad guy didn't see them.

It was a crap shoot.

"At least with the police we'll only end up in jail," Zane pointed out as they left the barn behind and worked their way back through the neighborhood streets toward the center of town.

"Yes," Becca agreed. "Where we'd be sitting ducks, and if it's all the same to you, I'd just as soon not end up doing five to ten for grand theft auto. I vote for the Mustang."

Since that was what Zane preferred too, he didn't argue with her. "The Mustang it is."

They drove to where they'd left the car, and parked the pickup in its place behind the old shed.

"I want you to get in the back and lie down," Zane told her.

"Zane, we don't have time for that now."

A startled bark of laughter escaped him before he could stop it. "God, I love you." He kissed her hard and fast, then opened the passenger door on the Mustang and flipped the front seat forward. "I mean," he said, laughter still ripe in his voice, "I want you to stay hidden in the back until we're out of town."

With a blush staining her cheeks, Becca cleared her throat. "Oh."

Their luck held. They made it out of town without spotting the gray sedan. That they had decided on the Mustang turned out to be the best choice after all, as only one lane of the highway was open, and police were there directing traffic, letting a few cars leave town, then halting northbound vehicles to let those kept out of town by the flood return.

For nearly a mile, one narrow strip of pavement down the middle of the highway was all that was above water. Everything else was covered.

But once past the flooded area that had been closed for two days, the road was clear and dry. Traffic thinned, and Zane drove with a heavy foot.

Becca ignored the discomfort of being scrunched up into the small, dark backseat. He hadn't meant it, was all she could think. He'd said he loved her, but he hadn't meant it. He'd been joking, that was all.

That she wanted it to be otherwise should have shocked her. She'd known him only two days. Falling in love in two days wasn't possible. It was crazy, irresponsible, and foolish.

So why did her heart ache with the thought of never seeing him again when this was over?

But Zane had other things on his mind than Becca Cameron. She remembered her first sight of him, sitting at his kitchen table caressing that deadly gun with one hand and a bottle of forgetfulness in the other. How could he blame himself for his partner's death?

But she knew how. Classic survivor's guilt. Even if he didn't believe he caused Al's death, she understood that he could still feel guilty for being the one to survive. She understood it only too well.

"Becca, are you awake?" he called softly over his shoulder toward the backseat.

"No one could sleep in a space this small."

"You can crawl up here now, if you want."

The speed with which she squeezed herself between the bucket seats and into the passenger seat was her answer.

Zane had the sudden urge to pull over to the side of the road and drag her onto his lap. She'd been away from him—all the way in the back-seat—for more than thirty minutes. It was ridiculous. It was asinine. It was scary as hell. But there it was, staring him in the face. He'd missed her.

In the glow from the dash lights and the head-lights of an occasional oncoming car on the two-lane blacktop, tension and fatigue lined her face. And something else he didn't like the looks of. There was guilt there, self-blame. He knew the look because it was the same one he saw in the mirror every time he looked at himself. That sort of sick-to-your-stomach look. The look that made a person turn away from his own reflection in pain and dis-gust. He hated the sight of it on her face much more than he did on his own. He stroked her silky-soft cheek with his knuckles. "Why don't you try to get some sleep?"

Becca shook her head, took his hand in both of hers, and held it on her lap. "I'm not sleepy."

"Something on your mind?"

"You."

Zane hesitated. "Is that good?"

She kept her gaze trained on the road before them. "You could have been killed because of me."

Bingo. There it was. "I wasn't."

"But you could have been, more than once. Es-pecially this afternoon, when you deliberately put yourself between me and a bullet."

Zane relaxed his hold on her hand and gave her a negligent shrug. "I was a cop for too long. Some-times the old training just kicks in." If with Becca it was more instinct than training, that would be his secret for now. Until he figured out what it meant.

"Are you saying you didn't think about the fact that you were shielding me from a bullet with your own body? That you could have been shot in my place?"

"There wasn't time to think. I did what I've been trained to do."

"Protect and serve, huh?"

"Something like that. Do you think I could just stand there and let a man shoot you?"

She smiled softly. "No, I don't think you could. I don't think you could stand by and watch anyone be hurt without trying to help, trying to protect them. Was . . . was your partner the same way?"

"Al?" he asked, surprised. "Yeah, sure. We had the same training."

"And the same protective instincts?"

Zane shrugged. "I guess." It seemed odd to talk about Al and not feel that familiar pain grind through him. Oh, it hurt, hurt plenty, but this time it didn't take his breath away. Maybe that was a sign that he was learning to live with the guilt. Finally. "What are you getting at?"

She stroked her fingers across the back of his hand. Finally she said, "You know how you told me you feel like his death is your fault?"

Zane didn't answer. He didn't see the point.

"Then you should have some small idea of how I would have felt if you'd been killed because you'd put yourself between me and a bullet, the way Al did for you."

Score one for Rebecca Ruth. He knew exactly

how she would have felt, and he couldn't stand the thought of her going through what he himself had been through during the past year.

But this was different. There'd been no need for Al to jump in front of Zane the way he'd done. Zane had known the risks of his profession and had accepted them years before. But Becca . . . Becca was innocent. She couldn't begin to protect herself from the type of man who was after her. "If you're asking me to stand aside and let somebody shoot you next time, forget it."

Staring straight ahead rather than looking at him, Becca laughed grimly. "I'm too big a coward to ask for that. But if you have the right to put yourself between me and a bullet, because that's what you're trained to do and that's what your instincts tell you, don't you think Al had that same right?"

"Now you're talking nonsense," he said tightly.

"Am I? It's okay for you to sacrifice yourself for someone you barely know, but it's not okay for him to try to shield someone he probably cared a great deal for? If he was anything like you, I don't think he'd thank you for the thought."

"It's not the same thing. Not the same thing at all. I didn't need protecting. He should have been protecting himself."

"Is that what you would have done? If the gunman had been about to kill Al, would you have left him to it and protected yourself?"

Zane ground his teeth in frustration. She was

twisting everything around, trying to . . . to what? Give him a way to live with what had happened? A reason to let go of his guilt?

"What right," she said quietly, "do you have to feel guilty because your partner did what came naturally?"

Zane took one breath. Two. "You don't know what you're talking about."

"If you have a right to your guilt, you have to allow me the right to mine," she said.

And maybe, just maybe, Zane thought, they were both right. And both wrong.

Zane waited until he reached the busy streets of Oklahoma City before stopping to use a pay phone. The first chance he got when this was over, he vowed to replace the cell phone he'd gotten rid of last year.

He scrapped his plan to stash Becca someplace safe. That had been born of the belief that she'd been an innocent bystander and he could get her out of the line of fire. Now that he believed she was the target, he wasn't letting her out of his sight.

It was midnight when he pulled into the alley behind a small shopping strip and turned off his headlights. "I'm going back to the pay phone out on the corner to make a call. Wait here. I won't be long."

Her eyes were huge in her face. "Be careful."

Zane squeezed her hand in reassurance. "I will."

He hated to leave her. She looked so lost and alone. But he had to talk to Trace.

OSBI agent Trace Youngblood had been Harper Montgomery's partner for years, until Harper retired a couple of years back. Zane had been out of the picture for more than a year, so he didn't know who Trace partnered with these days, but it wouldn't matter.

Zane could have called Newman or Helms, the agents who had replaced Al and him on the task force, but he didn't have their numbers. In addition, they didn't know him the way Trace did. For all Newman and Helms knew, Zane was still neck deep in the nearest bottle of booze. Trace would trust him, would believe him.

Calling Trace was a predictable move on Zane's part, from the viewpoint of anyone who knew him well from the old days. The four men, Zane, Al, Trace, and Harper, used to hang together a lot. But just then it was more important for Zane to get help from someone he trusted with his life, someone with whom he could trust Becca's life, if it came down to it, than go it on his own.

Trace answered on the second ring. "Youngblood."

"It's Houston."

There was a rustling sound, like that of a man throwing off bedcovers and sitting up. "Where are you?"

"You don't sound surprised to hear from me."

"Did you think I would be? Harp called me this

morning when he heard the report of shots being fired in Lindsay. He figured that was you, and that you would head this way the minute you could."

"Predictable," Zane muttered.

"Are you all right?"

Something in Trace's tone told Zane the question was not a casual one, and had nothing to do with gunshots in Lindsay. "I'm sober, if that's what you mean."

Silence. Then an audible exhale. "Sorry. I had to ask."

"I don't blame you. I wouldn't want to stick my neck out for a drunken bum either." And a drunken bum was exactly what Zane had been until he'd realized that if he kept at it, he could jeopardize the trial and Al's killer might walk.

"Am I going to be sticking my neck out?" Trace asked, his casual tone saying that he accepted Zane's word at being sober.

"I hope not, but I could use a little help here."

"What can I do?"

"I need to get a roll of film developed."

"Tonight?"

"Tonight."

"Must be pretty interesting film."

"Try a snapshot of Roger Bowen driving down the road in front of my house two days ago."

No explanations were needed. Trace knew that Zane had rented the house in Crow County because the weapons drop was suspected of being in the area. He knew, understood, that Zane had felt useless in solving the case after the shooting and that hanging around to catch a glimpse of Bowen was the only thing Zane had been able to do. Trace let out a low whistle.

"Yeah. My words exactly."

"Where are you now?"

"In Oklahoma City."

"Anyone on your tail?"

Zane eyed the traffic whizzing by on South Western. "No." Not, Zane thought, unless someone had gone to a hell of a lot of trouble setting up a relay of different vehicles to take over the tail every few miles. If Bowen was behind the attempts on Becca's life—which Zane was convinced of—that was possible. And here he stood at a well-lit intersection in plain view.

A relay surveillance took time and coordination to set up, and it ran well only when the route was known in advance so teams could be set in place. If Bowen was guilty of even half the things Zane thought he was, the man could handle the coordination with no problem. And Zane's route wouldn't take a genius to figure out. But the back of his neck wasn't prickling. He felt safe enough for now. "No tail that I've been able to spot."

"If you haven't spotted one, it's either not there or it's invisible. Meet me at the office—"

"Unh-unh. I've got a passenger. The office is too obvious a place for me to go. I don't want anyone finding her."

"That would be your landlord's niece, Becca Cameron."

"Right."

"Okay. Denny's at Sixty-third and May. One hour. It's the closest place to the office that's open this time of night, and they've got a back room that can't be seen from the street."

"Will do. Oh, and, Trace?"

"Yeah?"

"Drive something you won't mind swapping for my Mustang. I'm too easy to spot."

Trace chuckled. "Hot damn. I've been trying to get that car away from you for years. Don't worry. I'll swap you for something nobody will look twice at."

Zane groaned. "Not your wife's van."

Trace's chuckle held the ring of evil. "See you in an hour."

Becca waited in the car, as Zane had asked, but she didn't wait well or easily. She didn't like the idea of Zane standing out on the corner, in plain view of the traffic, talking on the phone. She didn't like the idea of sitting here where it was safe while he put himself in possible danger for her yet again.

She didn't like much about anything, she realized. She felt . . . off balance. Disoriented by everything that was happening. A stranger was trying to kill her. A friend was apparently helping. Bullets had flown, and might yet fly again before this was over. Her entire life had been turned upside down. And in the midst of it all, she'd met a man the likes of which she'd never met before. Strong. Courageous. Honorable. Tender, loving, loyal.

Staring out the back window to watch for Zane's return, she wrapped her arms around herself and shivered. Lord help her, she'd fallen in love.

Becca didn't hear whatever Zane said to the hostess at Denny's, but it got results. The woman seated them alone in the back dining room with no fuss, no questions.

As soon as the hostess left them, Zane flipped open his menu. "I don't know about you, but I'm starved."

"Shouldn't we wait for your friend?" Becca asked.

"Trace? Nah. We'll be doing him a favor if we're finished eating when he gets here. Since he got married a few years ago he's had to start watching his waistline. He claims his wife's goal in life is to make him fat with her cooking."

Becca cocked her head. There was a relaxed tone in his voice when he spoke of Agent Youngblood that she'd never heard from him before. "You like him, don't you?"

Zane looked up from his menu, his brow raised in question. "Trace? Sure. Why?"

She shrugged. "It shows in your voice."

They ordered and were just finishing their meal

when Agent Youngblood arrived. He was a big man, part Indian, with straight black hair just reaching his collar. And the most startlingly blue eyes Becca had ever seen. He had that same air of watchfulness about him as Zane, and exuded that same sense of confidence and competency.

"Pleasure to meet you," he told Becca when Zane introduced them. "I understand you've attracted the attention of one of our, shall we say, less honorable citizens."

"So it seems," she answered, not surprised that he knew her circumstances. Zane would have told him.

"So," Trace said to Zane, "tell me what we've got."

Zane filled him in on everything that had happened and about the photograph Becca had taken.

Trace tapped his pen against the small notepad where he'd been taking notes. "I agree this deputy, Terrill, is probably involved, since he's the only one who knew about the photograph. I'll get Harper started on him. This man driving the Firebird—" He checked his notes. "Mark Hammond. You know him?" he asked Becca.

"He's the foreman over at the Bar B Ranch just across the line in Smith County."

"And that's the direction they were heading?"

"Yes. There's not much else out there in that direction. I can't imagine they were heading anywhere else."

"Do you know who owns the Bar B?" Zane asked.

Becca's eyes widened.

"What?" Zane asked.

"I don't know if it means anything, but the Baileys, Chuck and Cynthia, they own the ranch. But they're not home. They went with Uncle Jim and Aunt Sue on the cruise."

Zane's gaze went blank. Becca could practically hear the wheels turning. "Your aunt and uncle take two of these trips a year, right?"

"How did you—Jim told you?"

"Yeah. One every January, and one in June, right?"

Becca nodded.

"Do the Baileys go with them?"

"Sure. Sue and Cynthia Bailey are sisters. The two couples have vacationed together for years."

"That's it," Trace said eagerly. "That matches the dates of the shipments we know about. Hammond must be acting as middleman every time his boss leaves town."

Becca shuddered. The thought of deadly automatic weapons being shipped through a ranch right next to her aunt and uncle's, through Sue's sister's home, on their way to street gangs, made ice form in the pit of her stomach.

Zane saw her shiver and automatically wrapped his arm around her shoulders for comfort and warmth.

Trace raised an eyebrow at the move.

Zane raised an eyebrow right back at him, but said nothing.

"What happens now?" Becca asked.

"Now we turn your film over to Trace," Zane said, "and he gets it developed. We get a positive ID on Bowen, tie him to the area."

"And bring in the task force," Trace finished. "We'll get that bastard yet. Nice piece of work the two of you have done."

"Pure dumb luck," Becca muttered.

"Yeah." Zane looked down at her and squeezed her shoulder. "But it wasn't all bad luck, was it?"

The teasing glint in his eye drew a smile from her. "No. Not all bad luck."

Trace Youngblood took the Mustang to deliver the film to a photographer friend with his own darkroom who wouldn't mind—too much—being dragged out of bed at two in the morning. From there he would go by the bureau and check the computer for the latest information on the case and notify the OSBI agents Newman and Helms, who had replaced Zane and Al on the task force.

"Your new chariot, ma'am." Zane waved his arm toward a dented, rusted Dodge van, its maroon paint chipped and peeling.

Becca studied it a moment, then gave him a look. "I take it the OSBI doesn't pay their agents much?"

Zane laughed. "This belongs to Lillian, Trace's

wife. He's been after her for years to junk the thing and get a new car, but she says she keeps it for sentimental reasons. There's no figuring that woman."

Becca smiled thoughtfully. "You sound like you like her too."

"Everybody likes Lillian. It's impossible not to."

So, Becca thought as he held the door open and she climbed into the passenger seat of the van. Zane Houston wasn't quite the loner she'd assumed. He had friends. People he liked and respected. From what she'd seen, they—at least Trace Youngblood, and, she recalled, Harper Montgomery—liked and respected him too.

The rush of what felt ridiculously like jealousy made her feel small. But with the exception of the thirty minutes they had spent in Harper's office in Crow Creek, Becca had had Zane entirely to herself from the minute she'd met him. Until now. Now the outside world was intruding. Now she would have to share him with people who knew more about him than she did. Eventually, soon, she acknowledged painfully, she would lose him.

Things were happening. They weren't isolated by a flood, weren't running from a killer. They had help. The situation would soon be resolved, and everyone could go back to their lives. There would be no reason for Zane to see her again. Unless he wanted to, she thought hopefully. Desperately. *Please let him want to.*

But things like that didn't happen to Becca, and

she knew it. Her luck at sex may have changed with Zane, but the man himself was temporary in her life. She had to remember that.

The rest of her luck was running about par for the course. Who else but Bad Luck Becca could take a photograph of a bird and end up with a hit man trying to kill her?

Zane drove to a motel on Thirty-ninth and checked them in while she waited in the van. Soon he came out and drove them to the other end of the motel and parked in front of their room. As she climbed out of the van, Becca noticed a child's safety seat behind the driver's seat.

A baby seat. It made Becca yearn for a child of her own. A child, she admitted, that she could already be carrying, thanks to their carelessness the night before and that afternoon.

"They might need that," she told Zane.

"Yeah, you're right. I'll tell Trace. He can get it when I meet him later. If he forgets it, Lillian will never let him hear the end of it."

Becca smiled, as she knew was expected, but as she walked with Zane to the door of their room, she realized with sudden clarity that she would welcome a child of Zane's.

Becca knew she wasn't the type of woman men chased after. She'd never had dates line up at her door. She knew every man in Crow Creek, had known them all her life. To them she was just Becca, the sister of one of their friends, the teacher of one of their children, the woman around whom accidents and bad luck happened. She was a friend. To some, a very good friend. But nothing more.

But Zane . . . Zane saw her differently. Made her feel different. He made her feel desirable. He sought her opinions and valued them. He saw past her youthful looks and acknowledged that she had a brain.

For those things alone, Becca could love him. But her feelings went beyond the way he treated her to the type of man he was.

Yes, she would welcome a child of his. She pressed a hand to her abdomen and hoped there already was a child, because she knew her time with Zane was running out. The very things she loved about him, his strength of purpose, his ability to put aside his own feelings and look after the needs of a stranger, his willingness to risk himself for someone else . . . those things made him the type of man who would probably never think of settling down with a woman and raising a family. At least, not a woman like her.

Chilled at the thought of losing him, she stepped aside while he unlocked the door, then entered the room.

Another average motel room, although newer than their last one. In the far corner sat a vanity, and a closet area stood just outside the bathroom. A television was bolted to the dresser. A small table and two chairs were placed beside the door. And dominating it all, two double beds with a nightstand

and a pair of lamps mounted on the wall between them.

Two beds. One for each of them.

Becca felt as though she'd already lost him. He might not have requested separate rooms—he felt obligated to protect her, after all—but he must have requested the separate beds.

"Excuse me." With her face averted, she rushed into the bathroom and closed the door before she could embarrass herself by crying in front of him.

She wasn't going to cry. Tears were foolish and a waste of time. Maybe he hadn't asked for two beds. Maybe that was all they had.

Or maybe, she thought with a pain in the region of her heart, maybe what little good luck she'd known in the past two days had just run out.

Speculation was useless. She wasn't going to assume anything. She was going to march out there and ask him point-blank if he was tired of making love with her and preferred to sleep alone.

She was going to ask him. Right after she did something about the way she looked, she thought with horror as she glanced in the mirror. Good Lord, she looked, as Uncle Jim would say, like she'd been dragged through a knothole backward.

Her clothes were wrinkled, as well they should be. Last night while she and Zane had made love in the motel, her jeans and T-shirt had lain in a crumpled pile on the carpet. For most of today they'd lain in a crumpled pile on the floorboard of their "borrowed" pickup. There was no help for her clothes.

But she could comb her hair and wash her face, which she did, and felt somewhat better for it.

Zane was standing between the beds, using the remote control to flip through the channels on the television, wondering what was taking Becca so long.

It had been, in his opinion, a moment of madness that had made him request two beds. A moment of nobility that was fast slipping past his grasp. He should offer to let her sleep alone. Their entire situation had been crazy from the minute she'd pounded on his front door. Everything had happened too fast, as though time had been compressed.

He'd never taken her on a date, never brought her flowers or any of the other things women liked. But he'd made love with her more times, and more intensely, than with any other woman. He felt closer to her than he'd ever felt to another person, except maybe Al, and in a completely different way.

She thought she knew him, but she didn't. She didn't know that he'd sunk to such depths of self-pity, self-blame, grief, that he'd stayed drunk for months rather than face reality. She wouldn't want a man like that if she knew. She deserved better. Sweet, funny Becca with her gallant honor, her willingness to try to keep a stranger from harming himself, when Zane still wasn't sure if that man was worth saving.

But damn, she'd gotten to him. He didn't know how he was going to survive without her when this was over. Didn't know if he could stand to let it be over, whatever this thing was between the two of them.

When she stepped out of the bathroom he stopped flipping through the TV channels and looked up at her. With the push of one button the television turned off. He tossed the remote onto the bed nearest the door. Be damned, he wasn't ready to start putting, or even allowing, distance between them.

"What is it?" she asked, setting her purse down next to the television.

Zane studied her face, the lines of fatigue, the wariness in her eyes. The words came hard, as he knew they would, but he forced himself to say them. "I asked for two beds on purpose."

Something flickered in her eyes, but he wasn't sure what it was. "You—" She paused and licked her lips. "You did?"

Zane's stomach tied itself in a knot. It had been hours since he'd tasted those lips. He was getting tired of waiting. But the decision had to be hers. "I thought you might like to have a choice whether or not to sleep alone."

Becca felt her knees tremble. He was offering her a graceful way to end what they'd shared. All she had to do was say so and she could sleep alone. Perhaps in a bed of her own she could get her equilibrium back. Perhaps she could shore up her reserves and try to forget the incredible night and day they'd spent making love.

The thought of spending the night away from him—even if the distance was only a few feet—nearly panicked her. She would be a fool to take a separate bed, unless that was what he preferred she do. Their time together was dwindling rapidly enough without her rushing it.

"Why," she asked, steeling herself for possible rejection, "would you think I would want to do that?"

Zane swallowed. "Considering how we met, everything that's happened since, you might be having second thoughts."

"It sounds to me like you are."

Holding her gaze, Zane shook his head. "I'm only wondering why you'd waste your time on a loser like me."

"It's my time, and I don't think it's wasted. You're not a loser, Zane Houston, and don't you ever let me hear you say that again."

NINE

Her response sent Zane's heart pounding in relief and blood surging to his loins. In two long strides he had her in his arms. "It's just as well," he said, leaning down to kiss her, his voice rough. "I don't think I would have let you sleep alone anyway."

Becca felt her knees give way in sheer, utter relief. He wasn't tired of her yet. No man who kissed a woman the way he was kissing her was interested in sleeping alone. "You're the one," she managed to say as he trailed his mouth down her neck, "who got us a room with two beds. I thought . . ."

"When we get tired of one," he growled against her neck, "we can move to the other."

He stepped backward and took her with him, kissing her, nibbling on her, until he felt the bed against the backs of his legs. Their clothes, Becca noticed briefly, ended up in a pile again. By the time they made it to the bed, the tightness in her breasts and heavy heat in her loins were more pronounced than ever before. The strength of her need for him, sudden and sharp, bordered on the frightening.

Stretched out with her on the bed, Zane looked into her eyes and paused with his hand halfway to her breast. "What's wrong?"

"Nothing," she quickly assured him.

Still, he hesitated. He didn't believe her. "For a minute there," he said softly, "you looked . . . scared."

In a moment of total honesty, Becca took his hand in hers and pressed it against her naked breast. Her eyes closed for a moment, the better to hold in the exquisite sensation. "It's just that it would be so easy to become addicted to you. It's a little scary."

"Believe me," he said, replacing his hand with his mouth, flicking his tongue across her beaded nipple and reveling in her gasp of pleasure, "I know exactly what you mean."

And he did. Two days. He'd know her only two days, intimately only one. When he'd offered her a separate bed he'd done so because he thought he had to, out of fairness to her. If she'd taken him up on it, he doubted he'd have let her sleep alone. He would have told her it wasn't safe. That she needed protection. Close protection. Anything, as long as they were together.

Addicted? That was as good a term as any, he supposed. All he knew was that after a solid night and full day of making love with her, he hadn't begun to slake his hunger for this particular woman. If anything, it grew stronger each hour. And she was right. It was scary. Scary as hell.

But not scary enough for him to begin to deny either of them the pleasure they could give each other. He wouldn't even try. Couldn't. Not when those soulful gray eyes of hers were shining like silver. Not when her breast swelled to fit his hand and her color heightened and her lips parted.

With a groan of surrender he took what she offered and gave back everything he had, everything he was. Flesh met flesh and turned slick with the sweat of passion. There was a pounding against his chest, and he couldn't tell if it was his heart or hers, or both. When her hand slid down his chest, his stomach, and grasped him, he groaned again. Her touch was like velvet fire.

Urgency built like a raging wildfire. He rolled until she was beneath him, cradling him in her arms and between her silken thighs. One slow slide, and he was home. She took him deep, and he took her hard and fast. Sooner than he would have liked, yet not nearly soon enough, their mingled cries of completion filled the room.

Trace couldn't contact them because Zane hadn't been sure where he and Becca would spend the night. They'd made arrangements for Zane to contact Trace at four that morning. That should give Trace enough time to have the film developed, get to the office computer, and alert at least the OSBI members of the task force assigned to track down the illegal weapons.

Zane hated waking Becca just to tell her he was going out to the pay phone in the lobby to call Trace. But he didn't want her waking up alone and wondering where he'd gone. As gently as he could, he shook her awake and told her where he was going.

She mumbled something he couldn't understand. He had to ask her to repeat it.

"Cold," she said, curling up in a tight ball beneath the covers. "I'll get cold without you."

Funny how such a simple statement could make a man weak in the knees. "Here." He grabbed for the pile of clothes on the floor at the foot of the bed and came up with her T-shirt. "Put this on, and I'll be back as fast as I can."

She was still half asleep. He had to hold her steady while she pulled on her shirt or she would have fallen over. Once she had the shirt on, he tucked her back beneath the covers, made sure the T-shirt was tugged down to her thighs for warmth, then kissed her temple. "Go back to sleep." He softened the order with another kiss. Then another. "I'll be gone only a few minutes."

Damn, what was happening to him? Closing the door and leaving the room without her felt as if he were tearing off a strip of his own skin. Deep. He was getting in way too deep. He just wasn't sure he was willing to do anything about it.

He dialed the number for Trace's cell phone. Trace answered on the first ring.

"What have you got?" Zane asked.

"Not much we can use in court, but a few little things. It's definitely Bowen in the photograph, but there's nothing in the shot worth hiring a hit on the photographer for, so for now we have to assume your theory is right, that he just doesn't want anyone to be able to place him in the area at this time. That has to mean another shipment's coming through."

Zane's only reply was a grunt of acknowledgment.

"I woke up Newman. He's on his way into the office. Meanwhile I've been playing around on the computer. It's spitting out some information right now. I want to run it by you. Where can we meet?"

Zane glanced out the window of the lobby. "There's an all-night coffee shop next to the motel. We're over on Thirty-ninth, just west of Portland. How long before you get here?"

"The printer just finished. I'll be there in fifteen minutes max. I won't be driving your car. Just in case."

"Good. Right now Becca's safe. I don't want to give anyone any way to find her."

"That's what I thought you'd say. Newman just walked in."

"Bring him along," Zane said. "If he hears all

this firsthand tonight, he can get things rolling faster."

"We'll do. See you in fifteen."

Instead of going back to the room and waking Becca up again to tell her he was meeting Trace and Newman, Zane let her sleep and went directly to the coffee shop. He met the two men out front in the parking lot.

"Newman." Zane greeted the agent with a handshake.

Before coming to the Bureau a couple of years before Zane left, Frank Newman had done more than a few undercover stints. He'd run into Roger Bowen and Buddy King before. He'd been the perfect man to take over Zane's spot on the task force.

"Houston," Newman said, shaking his hand. "Good to see you."

What he didn't say, but if the look in his eyes meant anything, was *Good to see you sober, with your head on straight.* Zane couldn't blame him for that.

"Where's Helms?" Zane asked him.

Newman gave an exaggerated shudder. "He's on his honeymoon. The idiot went and got married."

Trace slapped Newman on the back. "You'll survive. You can hold out for the rest of us."

"Speaking of wives and families," Zane said to Trace, "there's a baby seat in the back of the van

you might want to pick up before Lillian finds out
you forgot it."

"Thanks. You're right. She'd skin me."

"You poor slob," Newman said with a hangdog
look for Trace.

"Yeah," Zane commiserated. "He has to go
home to the same beautiful woman night after
night. Has to put up with rugrats who look just like
him and call him Daddy. Hell of a life."

And in silence Zane thought, *Where do I sign up?*

He dismissed the idea. He wasn't husband or
father material, not by any stretch of the imagination.

Still, to see a child of his with clear silver
eyes . . .

Heat flashed through his veins, fast and unexpected. There could already be a child. How many
times had he made love with Becca with no protection?

"Come on, you clowns. Let's get to work."
Trace turned and entered the coffee shop. They
took a table in the back corner, where, out of habit,
each put his back to a wall and faced the room and
the door.

"We've got a connection," Trace said when the
hostess left them. Excitement lit his eyes. "Bowen
to Buddy King."

"No way, man," Newman protested. "We've
been working that angle for months and haven't
been able to connect those two."

"It's weak," Trace admitted, "and it's sure not evidence, but it's there."

Zane tensed, eager. "What is it?"

"Mark Hammond, the one driving Bowen around in the Firebird, is none other than Buddy King's cousin on his mama's side."

Zane's grin came slow and wide. "Well, well, well. And here Becca thought she brought everyone around her bad luck. King's cousin, huh?"

"What Firebird?" Newman asked. "What's in the envelope?" He nodded to the manila envelope Trace had brought with him.

In as few words as possible, Zane explained. Then he turned to Trace. "Cousins?" He grinned again. "How about that."

"First cousins. Their mothers are sisters."

Zane let the satisfaction roll through him, then settled down. "Okay, now, what have we got that we can use?"

Trace frowned. "Not much."

"No kidding," Newman said. "You can't arrest a guy for who his relatives are. Although that would come in handy now and then."

Trace tossed the manila envelope to Zane. "These are the photographs Becca shot two days ago. With them we can put Bowen in the area on a specific date, in the company of Buddy King's cousin, Mark Hammond, and we can check out the Bar B. It's not much, but it's more than we had."

Zane thumbed through the photographs and

pulled out the one of Bowen. "Has anyone else seen these?"

"Only me and the guy who developed the film. And now Newman. There's a blowup of that one," Trace offered.

While Zane picked it up, he asked, "Did you call Harper and alert him about the good deputy Geoff Terrill?"

"I did. He'll handle it."

"Who's Terrill?" Newman asked. "What's he got to do with all this?"

"He's a Crow County deputy. He's the only other person who knew Becca took this shot, so he has to be the one who passed the information to Bowen."

Newman whistled between his teeth. "One of Harper's deputies is dirty?"

"He said he'd handle it," Trace said tersely.

Zane read Trace like an open book. He'd taken offense at Newman's comment. That a deputy was dirty didn't imply that the sheriff was, but the look in Newman's eyes hinted that at the least, Harper Montgomery had slipped up somehow. Trace wouldn't stand for any criticism of his former partner.

But Zane had to give Newman the benefit of the doubt. He'd come to work for the OSBI mere weeks before Harper had retired, so he didn't know him the way longtime agents knew him.

Newman shrugged. "If you say he'll handle it, then it's as good as handled."

"That's right," Trace said.

But Zane's mind had already left Geoff Terrill and Harper Montgomery behind. The blowup of Roger Bowen now held his attention fully. And then some.

"What is it?" Trace asked.

Frowning hard, Zane studied the blowup. "I don't know. There's something about this—" Then he swore, hard and fast. His gut clenched, and a wave of pain and outrage swamped him.

"What?" Newman demanded. "You found something?"

"Oh, yeah, I found something." Zane swore again. "Another connection between Bowen and King." He tossed the blowup across the table to land between Trace and Newman. "Take a look at that necklace on Bowen."

Trace snorted. "Which one? Son of a bitch could start his own jewelry store. He must be wearing damn near a dozen."

"The one with something hanging from it. The only one that's not just a chain."

"Okay. So?"

Zane closed his eyes and told his heart to quit racing, his stomach to quit rolling. "It's—it was—Al's."

As one, Trace and Newman jerked their gazes up to Zane's. "You're sure?" they demanded.

Grinding his back teeth together, Zane nodded. "Positive. Mary Jo is a jewelry designer. She made that for him for their anniversary or something.

Custom made. One of a kind. Those little stones are her and their kids' birthstones."

"Damn." Trace rubbed a hand over his face. "I remember how proud he was of that necklace. One of Mary Jo's original designs. He'd shown that necklace to everyone in sight, like a new parent with the first photo of the baby."

"I remember," Newman said.

Zane took a deep breath, let it out slowly. "He was wearing it the night of the hit."

As though speaking of it aloud threw open the door to his memory, pictures flooded Zane's mind. Like watching the news. Film at eleven. Zane and Al, arriving in separate cars to meet with the other half of their task force, the two agents from ATF.

The four of them had sat in a private back room at the restaurant on Twenty-third and laid out their plans. They were going to crack down on Bowen, keep him under twenty-four-hour surveillance, watch every step he took, every move he made. They were sure he was the man responsible for the illegal AK-47s ending up in the hands of street gangs across the state. And they were going to stop him—cold.

Over dinner they'd laid out their plans, made a few adjustments as ideas were kicked back and forth. They were ready. Zane and Al's part would start the next morning with a visit to Roger Bowen. They wouldn't get anything out of him, they knew. But the task force's first priority was to stop the spread of those automatics. If that meant making their second objective, catching the man responsible, that much harder, they would live with it. As long as the flow of illegal weapons was halted.

If Bowen knew they were after him, he'd have to slow down, maybe put his operation on hold. That should keep any more guns from coming into the state, at least for a while. Bowen wouldn't like that. The last shipment carried an estimated street value of four million dollars.

After their little visit the next day, Zane and Al were to start digging deeper into Bowen's in-state activities to tie him to the shipments that had already reached Oklahoma and been sold on the street. The ATF agents, Zucker and Hewitt, would work back to the shipment's arrival in the U.S., tracing its route, looking for any connection to Bowen, or anyone else, for that matter.

The four men left the restaurant together that night. Their meeting hadn't been secret, just private, so there was no need to act as though they hadn't met.

They had scattered through the parking lot, each headed for his own car. Zane and Al had parked near each other at the south end of the lot, near the street. It was dark. The lights in that part of the lot were out.

The shooter had been waiting for them.

"You're sure about the necklace?" Trace asked, jerking Zane into the present.

"You said you remembered it."

"Yeah, but I couldn't positively swear that this is it." He tapped the photograph.

"I can. Mary Jo could," Zane said. He remembered the way the lights in the restaurant had bounced off the twisted gold nugget with its birthstone gems as Al had shown it off to Zucker and Hewitt, the waitress, the busboy—anyone who would look.

Zane shook his head to shut off the memories. "Mary Jo came to see me in the hospital." That, too, was something he would like to forget. Mary Jo Simpson coming to comfort *him*, the man her husband died protecting. "The necklace hadn't been in Al's personal belongings. She asked me about it. We all assumed it had just gotten lost in the parking lot and somebody found it later and picked it up. There's no question. That was the necklace Al was wearing that night. The only way Bowen could have gotten it is directly from the killer. You know King's rep. He likes his little trophies, but he's not into flesh."

"Okay." Newman tapped his finger against the blowup. "But even if you're right that that is Al's necklace, you know Bowen will just say he picked it up at some flea market."

Trace raised a brow in mock horror. "Roger Bowen is much too fastidious to ever admit having been near a flea market. And if he bought it anywhere else, he should have gotten a receipt."

"Which he saw no need to keep." Newman

raised both hands as if in surrender. "I'm just playing devil's advocate here."

"Fine," Zane muttered. "But this is a damn sight more than the task force has had in the past. Are you going to run with it or not?"

"Oh, I'll run with it, all right." Newman slid the stack of photos back into the manila envelope. "First thing in the morning. How can I reach you?"

Zane nodded toward the motel across the parking lot. "Room 115. But I don't even want Zucker and Hewitt knowing that. The whole damn task force has been snakebitten from the beginning. One blind alley after another, then the hit. The same thing that happened to Al and me could happen to you guys. I don't want Becca caught in the cross fire. You watch your back. I want to see you nail this bastard."

"We'll get him. You can count on it."

More asleep than awake, Becca heard the key in the lock and smiled. She wouldn't be cold much longer. Damn motel air conditioner anyway, she thought grumpily as she pulled the covers up to her eyes. It roared like a jet engine and kept the room as cold as the inside of a walk-in freezer. But the minute it cycled off, the room became unbearably stuffy. Feast or famine. Cold or stuffy.

She'd take the cold. Zane would soon warm her. Meanwhile she curled up on her side, her face toward the door, and waited.

She must have drifted off. She never heard the door open or close. The next thing she was aware of was a large, sweaty hand clamping itself over her mouth.

She came abruptly, terrifyingly, awake. Behind the hand she screamed. She tried to jerk away and felt something cold and round and metal press against her right temple.

"Don't move," a hoarse voice warned, "unless you want your boyfriend to walk in and find your brains scattered all over the wall."

Becca froze in sheer terror, except for the violent trembling that started in the pit of her stomach and worked its way outward. *Zane!*

The two lamps mounted on the wall between the beds came on, momentarily blinding her. When her vision cleared, she saw not the man with his hand over her mouth, but the other, the one standing between the beds, who had turned on the lights. The man with the snow-white hair and gold chains. The man she had unwittingly captured on film. The man who wanted her dead.

Her throat closed on a ball of terror.

"Are you going to scream if I take my hand away?" the man holding her asked. She could see the dark shape of the gun he held to her head, could feel his fingers bruising her cheek and jaw, but, lying on her side the way she was, she couldn't see his face. Behind the hand, another involuntary scream sounded.

"Stop that." The hand tightened across her face. "Do it again and I'll knock you cold, bitch."

"Is she the one?" the white-haired man asked calmly.

"She's the one, all right."

The first man *tsk*ed. "Such a little thing to cause so much trouble. If you promise not to scream," he told Becca smoothly, "I'll tell him to take his hand off your mouth."

It was all Becca could do to nod her head in agreement. She had to get the man's hand off her mouth. She had to have some way to warn Zane before he walked in.

Slowly the hand slipped away from her mouth, but the gun remained at her temple. She couldn't stop shaking.

"Riley, I believe you're scaring the young lady."

"Who are you," Becca managed to get out. "What do you want? I don't have more than twenty dollars in my purse, but you're welcome to it."

"Twenty dollars?" the man with the white hair said in outrage. "That's terrible. If I didn't have more pressing matters to tend to, I'd offer you a loan. Imagine having only twenty dollars. Can you imagine such a thing, Riley?"

"No, sir."

"Take the gun away from her head, Riley." The man's voice was so cool and smooth, sophisticated. Slick. It sent chills down Becca's arms. "After all, we don't want her so terrified that she can't answer our questions."

The instant the gun moved from her head, Becca scrambled up and crouched against the headboard, clutching her pillow and bedcovers for whatever protection she could find. "Wha—" Her mouth was so dry, her voice cracked. "What do you want?" But she was very much afraid that she knew the answer.

"We'll start," the man with the white hair said, "with a certain photograph, and, naturally, it's accompanying negative."

So, Becca thought with another shiver. Zane had been right. It was her they were after. The entire scenario seemed unreal to her. She got her first look at the man who'd held the gun to her head, and he looked like somebody's favorite uncle. Brown hair and eyes, a cleft in his chin, a paunch sagging against his belt. A nervous uncle, she decided. Sweat sheened his face, and she'd felt it on his hand.

She shuddered at the reminder.

The other man looked like a modern-day version of a snake oil salesman. Maybe a used car salesman. From Florida, with that dark tan of his. Still, nothing too terribly sinister about him.

Both men looked like someone she might pass on the street. They spoke in reasonable tones, no shouting.

Yet they had come to kill her. Of that Becca had no doubt. Her, and possibly Zane, if he showed up.

"The photograph and negative?" he asked again, arching a brow.

"I don't know what you're talking about."

White teeth, almost as white as his hair, flashed behind his smile. "Now, why did I know you were going to say that? Search her purse, Riley."

They would find nothing in her purse. At least, nothing of interest to them. When they didn't find what they were looking for, would they kill her?

"Nothing in here," Riley said.

"Where are they?" The man's voice took on an edge. "You took a photograph of me the other day, and I want it."

"H-how did you know?" But she knew how he knew. She'd told only one person—Geoff. That someone she'd known her whole life could send a killer after her . . . she still couldn't accept it. She had no choice but to believe it, but she couldn't accept it.

"I have my ways. Where is the photograph, Miss Cameron."

"Y-you know my name."

"I know a great deal about you. Now, where is the photograph, and the negative?"

Becca licked her lips. She had to stall them, think of a way to get past them, warn Zane before he walked in unaware. "If you know anything about me, you should know, then, that my luck's not the greatest."

"Luck, Miss Cameron? Yes, I would say it was your bad luck to take that photograph. Who put you up to it, Houston?"

"Put me up to it?"

"He did, didn't he?"

"I didn't even know him until later that night," she protested. "I'd never met him before. The picture was an accident. I . . . there was this bird . . . a cardinal. I was taking a picture of a cardinal, when it flew in front of the car." Lord, she was rattling on like an airhead. But at least he was listening rather than shooting.

"My, that *was* bad luck, was it not?" the white-haired man said. "However, I'm still waiting, Miss Cameron." He pulled a gun from the pocket of his jacket. "And I grow impatient."

"You know I didn't get the film developed," Becca said in a rush. "I didn't have time."

"Not even during your two days in Lindsay?" the second man asked.

Becca whipped her head toward him and glared. "It was you! You're the one who shot at us. You scared the life out of me."

The man smiled and made a slight bow. "At your service."

The words "you're not a very good shot" came to mind, but she swallowed them. Under the circumstances, it seemed slightly more than foolish to speak them. That they whispered through her mind at all told Becca she was on the verge of hysteria.

She turned back to the first man. "I lost it."

"Lost . . . what?"

"The film. I lost it. In addition to having bad luck, I'm also a klutz."

His white hair seemed to glow in the lamplight as he rounded the bed and took her by the arm.

Becca winced at his tight hold. "You're hurting me."

"I assure you, Miss Cameron, I'll do more than hurt you if you don't give me the film."

"I don't have it!"

"Riley, get over by the door and keep watch. My favorite former OSBI agent should be returning any minute."

"He's not coming back," she said in a rush.

"Nice try."

"No, really." Becca rose to her knees, as if to better make her point. "He figured I was safe now that we're in the city."

"Zane Houston has a responsibility streak in him a mile wide. He would never leave you here alone for more than a few minutes, to talk with his friend, Agent Youngblood."

Becca felt the blood drain from her face. How could he know? Had Trace Youngblood told him? Was Zane wrong about his friend? *Zane! Stay away, Zane!*

"The film. Now," the man barked.

"I don't have it! I told you, I lost it."

The man's eyes narrowed to angry slits. "And where," he said slowly, "did you lose it?"

To say that Becca thought fast would be inaccurate. Thought had little to do with the activity in her mind as she tried to think of what to say. It was more like mice scrambling through a maze. "It was his fault." She pointed at the man over by the door. Riley. "When he shot at us in Lindsay—I know I had it just before that. I was going to take it to get it developed. But when we ran for cover it must have fallen out of my pocket. It's his fault," she repeated, pointing at Riley again, purposely letting her voice rise in pitch, as though she were nearing hysteria, which wasn't far from the truth. "Really, Mr.—what *is* your name anyway?"

The man with white hair blinked. "You don't know my name?"

"How could I? We've never met."

"Surely Zane Houston would have told you."

"You know Zane?"

"We've met."

"Well, why didn't you tell me?" Shaking on the inside like a bowl of gelatin, Becca prepared to give the performance of her life. Enter one airhead. "If you're a friend of Zane's . . . my name's Becca." Ignoring his gun, she held her hand out to him. With a grin that she hoped was impish, she added, "Most of my friends call me Bad Luck Becca. Please, here, have a seat. How long have you known Zane?"

The man with the white hair—what *was* his name?—gave the other man a look that seemed to ask if she'd lost her mind. Becca was wondering the same thing, but she couldn't think of any other way to get the men to lower their guard.

"I'm sorry Zane's not here, but the truth is, we had a little falling out." She managed what she hoped was a credible pout. "He called me an airhead."

The man called Riley made a strangled sound and covered his mouth with his hand.

"Can you believe the nerve? Me! An airhead!"

"How . . . undiplomatic of him," the white-haired man said, his lips pursing.

Becca sniffed. "He made me mad. I told him to get out. So he won't be coming back. And if he did, I wouldn't let him in," she added emphatically.

"What do you want to do?" Riley asked his boss.

Bowen, Becca remembered. That was his name. Roger Bowen. He looked at her for a moment, making her feel like a bug under a microscope.

"I think," he said slowly, his voice dripping ice, "we'll wait. I believe our young schoolteacher here is trying to pull the wool over our eyes, Riley. Now, where," he said to her tightly, "is the film?"

TEN

Zane said good-bye to Trace and Newman and crossed the parking lot, heading for the motel and Becca. A gust of warm south wind played with a discarded plastic cup, sending it bouncing across the pavement. Once the weather had cleared earlier that day, it had stayed clear. Above him stars started winking out. It would be daylight soon, and it would be hot. He'd been gone longer than he'd planned.

It startled him to acknowledge yet again that he didn't like being away from Becca. Somehow, within a scant two days the woman had wormed her way into his mind and he didn't even want to try to get her out.

Okay. If he was honest, his mind wasn't the only place she'd taken up residence. He'd never been in love before, but this had to be it. This constantly thinking of a woman, being willing to do anything to keep her safe, wanting her every waking minute, dreaming of her when he slept.

Dreaming. Of her, of the two of them together. Becca had no idea of the gift she had given him when she'd slept in his arms and kept the nightmares at bay. The last two nights were the first time in more than a year that Al's face had not haunted him.

As he strolled toward the door of their room, he shook his head in wonder at how she had changed him so quickly, so completely. She'd made him smile again, made him laugh. And it felt good.

He supposed he would always feel guilty about Al, for surviving when Al hadn't, but Becca had made him admit to himself that he wasn't to blame for his partner's death. Buddy King and Roger Bowen were to blame. And Al's own instincts. If positions had been reversed, Zane wouldn't have thought twice about throwing himself in front of his partner to save him. And he'd have been damn mad if anyone tried to tell him that wasn't his right. Becca had seen that. Had made Zane see it.

The light in their room was on. She was awake and waiting for him. Zane smiled, put his key in the lock, and opened the door.

Something kept the door from opening all the way, and for half a second, which felt like a lifetime in hell, it didn't occur to him what it might be. He couldn't, in that instant, think past the sight of Roger Bowen holding Becca before him with his gun to her ear.

Becca's wide, terrified eyes darted to the side, to the wall behind the door. Suddenly the reason the door wouldn't swing all the way open became clear. There must be another man.

It never occurred to Zane to step back through the door before the other man could get the drop on him. Never occurred to him to turn and run for help. He couldn't leave Becca. No way.

Everything seemed to happen in slow motion, as it had out on the street in Lindsay. Becca met his gaze, but instead of terror in her eyes now, there was purpose. That look she'd had right before she'd spilled her coffee on Harper's desk to avoid answering his question.

She was going to do something. Zane wanted to shout at her. *Don't move!* But it wouldn't matter. If they didn't do something, Bowen would kill her. That much was plain on the man's face.

"I think I'm going to faint," Becca cried shrilly. Her eyes rolled back in her head. Her body went limp and started sliding from Bowen's grasp.

Bowen shouted and tried to hold on to her.

Zane reached beneath his jacket for his gun, and at the same time slammed his shoulder against the door.

The man behind the door cried out, and his gun arced through the air and fell to the floor. As the door bounced back, Zane stepped aside, then, when the door swung shut, moved in and placed his hand over the bastard's face. With a shout of rage he rammed the man's head into the wall.

The man slid to the floor, unconscious.

Bowen shouted again, and from the corner of his eye Zane saw the man haul a struggling Becca back into the crook of his arm and put the gun to her head. Zane turned and aimed. "Don't do it, Bowen."

"You seem to have left me no choice." The voice was still smooth and modulated, every hair was still in place, the clothes straight and immaculate. But sweat beaded Bowen's face.

"There's no need to kill her. Let her go."

"People are so predictable," Bowen said, disappointment coloring his voice. "Can you think of nothing new to say?"

"The film has already been developed," Zane said, keeping his gun aimed at Bowen's chest. "Prints are already with the OSBI. Becca's already given her statement. Killing her now won't save you. It'll only get you in deeper. Tell me how you found us and maybe I can help you."

"Surely you don't take me for a fool."

"I don't know," Zane drawled. "Any man who would walk around wearing a necklace taken off a murdered OSBI agent can't be too bright."

A muscle in Bowen's cheek spasmed. His eyes widened, then narrowed.

"Oh, that's funny. You didn't know, did you?" Zane taunted. "Don't tell me you forgot about Buddy King's little habit of collecting trophies. This time he gave it to you."

"I bought this necklace from a reputable jeweler."

"Which necklace is that, Bowen? Did I say which necklace I was talking about? Let her go now. You don't need her anymore. Spilling the name of your informant will do you a hell of a lot more good than killing an innocent woman."

"Especially," came Trace's voice from behind Zane, "when you're outnumbered."

Roger Bowen had not accumulated several million dollars in offshore accounts because he was stupid. He released Becca and threw down his gun.

"Nice timing," Zane told Trace over his shoulder as he crossed toward Becca.

"I came back for the baby's car seat."

"Here." He shoved Bowen in Trace's direction. "Take care of this baby too."

Becca was never entirely sure what happened after that. Somehow Bowen was gone and Zane was there and she was in his arms, where she not so quietly went to pieces.

Zane wasn't in much better shape. He didn't start shaking until he got his arms around her, but then he had to lean against the wall to remain upright.

They had no privacy. Within minutes the Oklahoma City police, OSBI agents, and two agents from the ATF arrived. During the confusion, arrests, and questioning, Zane and Becca became separated.

Becca repeated her story over and over, first for

a police officer, then an OSBI agent, then another
agent, until she was no longer certain what she was
saying. By six o'clock that evening, Harper Montgomery was walking her to the door of her parents'
house and she had no clear memory of how they'd
gotten there.

She turned suddenly and gripped Harper's arm.
"Zane?"

"He's still in the city." Harper patted her hand.
"He'll be in touch as soon as they're through with
him."

Outwardly, life had returned to normal, Becca
mused as she stared out her front window. She was
back in her own home, and her family had stopped
hovering. Mostly. Although she was certain that if
she backed her car out of her driveway, no fewer
than three neighbors would report in immediately
to her mother, as no doubt instructed.

But Becca didn't mind. Two weeks earlier, she'd
almost lost more than a person should have to lose.
She'd always loved her family, but now she had a
new appreciation for them, as well as for the blessing of another day to be alive.

She'd be going to her parents' for supper tonight. Afterward she'd promised to change the oil
in her mother's station wagon. Becca doubted the
oil needed changing. Her mother was just trying to
cheer her up by giving her something fun to do.

Roger Bowen was in jail with his lips sealed

tight. His bevy of high-powered attorneys hadn't yet been able to get him out on bail, and probably never would, if the media were to be believed.

Geoff Terrill would be arraigned the following week for his part in the attempt on Becca's life. Before being arrested, he had ransacked her aunt and uncle's house looking for the roll of film Becca had shot. She'd been able to straighten it up a bit before they'd returned from their cruise.

The Crow County Sheriff's Department was looking for a new deputy.

The OSBI was looking for a new agent to replace Frank Newman. Newman was the one responsible for Roger Bowen finding Becca that night at the motel. He'd overheard Trace talking to Zane on the phone, and before following Trace to the meeting, he'd passed along Becca's location to Roger Bowen. According to the news media, Newman had been secretly feeding Bowen information since his days undercover with the DEA. It had been Newman who'd helped arrange the hit on Zane and his partner, so that Newman could get himself appointed to the task force, thus having access to even more information of direct benefit to his old friend Roger.

Aunt Sue's sister, Cynthia Bailey, and her husband, Chuck, were looking for a new foreman, since Mark Hammond was in jail on a half dozen or more illegal-weapons charges. Mark's wife was so broken up about it that she'd been seen out with three different men in as many nights. But a certain rodeo queen down in Ardmore was genuinely devastated and had been to visit Mark in jail twice.

Becca had been kept up-to-date on everything that was happening. Everything, that is, except for the whereabouts of one Zane Houston. She had not heard from him, not a word.

"Let's face it, Becca," she murmured to herself. "He's moving on with his life. It's time you did the same thing."

She'd been right about her mother's station wagon. The oil hadn't needed changing, but she changed it anyway because it seemed to make her parents happy. By the time she left their house at dusk to walk the three blocks home, her face felt as if it were going to crack from forcing itself to smile when she didn't feel like smiling.

The streetlights were on by the time she turned the last corner and started up her street. Shadows deepened under shrubs and across porches. On her porch, a long shadow rose and stepped out into the light.

Becca's heart leapt into her throat. "Zane!"

He stuffed his hands in the front pockets of his jeans and hunched his shoulders. "It occurred to me," he said, "that I never told you I loved you."

Becca's heart fluttered in her throat. "No. No, you didn't."

"Well, I do."

"You . . . do?"

"Yeah."

"Oh. Oh . . . well."

"Oh, well?" His voice rose slightly. "Is that all? I don't suppose maybe you feel the same."

Becca tried to moisten her lips, but her mouth was too dry. "I . . . I suppose maybe I do."

Mouth pursed, Zane nodded and studied the sidewalk between his feet for a moment. Then he raised his head. "I got drunk."

"You . . . got drunk?"

"For months, after Al was killed. I turned into a lush. I don't plan on it ever happening again, but I thought you should know."

"Oh. Okay. Thank you for telling me. Why are you telling me?"

"I have a job now."

"You do? A job?"

"Yeah, it seems there was an opening in the county sheriff's office."

"Oh."

"Wanna get married?"

"Wha—" For a moment her voice failed her. "What?" she managed to say.

"I said, do you want to get married. Maybe have a couple of kids. You know—married."

"You . . . want us—you and me—to get married?"

"I do."

"So do I."

Zane let out the breath he'd been holding and pulled her into his arms. "Thank God." Then he kissed her. "I'm sorry I took so long. . . ." His voice trailed away as his mouth busied itself with hers.

Becca kissed him back, struggling to swallow her tears. "I was afraid I'd never see you again."

"I'm sorry." He planted hurried kisses across her face. "I got crazy. I got scared. I was afraid you didn't want me the way I wanted you. I mean, why should you?"

"Because I love you," she said around the lump in her throat.

"I was hoping you'd say that."

Her mother had the news of their impending wedding before they made it inside Becca's house to consummate the engagement.

THE EDITORS' CORNER

Have no fear, spring is here, bringing with it four April LOVESWEPTs to help ward off the last vestiges of winter. April also brings back four of your favorite authors weaving love stories filled with excitement and danger, honor and trust, romance and passion, just for you. Our courageous heroines and their gorgeous male counterparts must overcome many obstacles to get to that happy ending. Join them on their journeys to happily ever after!

A houseful of kids brings a family together in Marcia Evanick's first installment of her **WHITE LACE** & **PROMISES** trilogy, **DADDY MATERIAL,** LOVESWEPT #830. For weeks Adam Young has been on a desperate mission—to find the woman with whom he'd shared the most passionate night of his life. After watching Emily Pierce frolicking with her children, Adam realizes his most difficult task will be wooing a woman whose heart belongs to her kids. Emily doesn't want to play Cinderella to Adam's Prince Charming, but can she ignore his promises of forever? Marcia brings together a prince of a guy with a pretty young widow in a celebration of delicious fun and touching joy that will renew your faith in happily ever afters.

SILENT WARRIOR John McShane senses the desperation in Cali Ellis's plea for help in LOVE-SWEPT #831, by Donna Kauffman. Now, after he had flown to the Caribbean to rescue her, Cali refuses to leave without answers, and John finds that she still has the power to ignite his desire. John had been Cali's anchor when grief shattered her heart, but could a hero rugged enough to haunt a woman's dreams convince this defiant beauty that he'd fight to keep her forever? In a sexy tale of breathless pursuit and irresistible danger, Donna Kauffman throws this fierce warrior and his ladylove into the fires of restless passion and ultimate possession.

Suzanne Brockmann steams up the pages, as Kayla Grey and Cal Bartlett fight an undeniable attraction that is so right, yet so **FORBIDDEN**, LOVE-SWEPT #832. Sure, Kayla was saved from a drenching storm by a man who'd given her shelter, but did that merit the reckless urge to kiss the handsome cowboy? Cal can't believe he nearly made love with the woman who'd betrayed his brother's memory, but shame wars with desire when Kayla insists that Liam might still be alive. Can a man who's tasted paradise sacrifice the woman he loves? Suzanne answers that question in this sensual tale of honor, trust, and the forbidden fruits of love.

RaeAnne Thayne lets the sparks fly when Andrea

McPhee and Will Tanner fall **IN TOO DEEP,** LOVESWEPT #833. Andrea can't resist teasing Sheriff Tanner about his roadside manner after he stops her for speeding on a Wyoming back road. The sassy rebel gets under Will's skin, seeping through the barriers he's erected to protect his heart from the sorrows of the past. Driven by vengeance and a desire he cannot define, Will softens when Andrea confesses her own demons of grief and loss. Together they each must learn to let go of the past and to seek sanctuary in the love of a lifetime. RaeAnne Thayne writes with wrenching emotion and tender humor in a story of healing hearts and second chances.

Happy reading!

With warmest wishes,

Shauna Summers

Joy Abella

Shauna Summers

Editor

Joy Abella

Administrative Editor

P.S. Look for these Bantam women's fiction titles coming in March. In **A THIN DARK LINE,** the boundaries between the law and justice and love and murder are crossed in the newest hardcover from the *New York Times* bestselling author of GUILTY AS

SIN, Tami Hoag. Hailed by *Rave Reviews* as "a genre superstar," Elizabeth Thornton returns with **THE BRIDE'S BODYGUARD,** a novel about a mysterious stranger and a young woman who believes she's eluded a neglectful guardian's clutches. In **PLACES BY THE SEA,** highly acclaimed author Jean Stone explores the choices that a woman who has everything she could ever ask for must face—until she learns that true love is what she really wants. And immediately following this page, preview the Bantam women's fiction titles on sale *now*!

For current information on Bantam's women's fiction, visit our new web site, *Isn't It Romantic*, at the following address: **http://www.bdd.com/romance**

Don't miss these extraordinary books
by your favorite Bantam authors

On sale in February:

*LONG AFTER
MIDNIGHT*
by *Iris Johansen*

*THE SCOTSMAN
WORE SPURS*
by *Patricia Potter*

LONG AFTER MIDNIGHT
BY IRIS JOHANSEN

An explosive new hardcover novel of suspense
by bestselling author
Iris Johansen

*Research scientist Kate Denby is on the verge of a major
medical breakthrough that could save countless lives. But
there's someone who doesn't want her to finish her work.
Someone not interested in holding out hope—but in buying
and selling death.*

She didn't look like a warrior, sitting there on the
boy's bed, Ishmaru thought in disappointment. She
looked soft and womanly, without spirit or worth.

He peered through the narrow slit afforded by the
venetian blinds covering the window of the boy's
room.

Look at me. Let me see your spirit.

She didn't look at him. Didn't she know he was
there, or was she scorning his threat to her?

Yes, that must be it. His power was so great tonight, he felt as if the stars themselves must feel it.
Coup always brought added strength and exultation
in its wake. The little girl had felt his power even
before his hands had closed around her throat. The
woman must be taunting him by pretending she was
not aware he was watching her.

His hands tightened on the glass cutter in his
hand. He could cut through the glass and show her he
could not be ignored.

No, that was what she wanted. Even though he was quick, he would be at a disadvantage. She sought to lure him to his destruction as a clever warrior should do.

But he could be clever too. He would wait for the moment and then strike boldly in full view of these sheep with whom she surrounded herself.

And before she died, she would admit how great was his power.

Joshua remained awake for almost an hour, and even after his eyes finally closed, he slept fitfully.

It was just as well they were going away for a while, Kate thought. Joshua wasn't a high-strung child, but what he'd gone through was enough to unsettle anyone.

Phyliss's door was closed, Kate noted when she reached the hall. She should probably get to bed too. Not that she'd be able to sleep. She hadn't lied to Joshua: she was nervous and uneasy . . . and bitterly resentful. This was her home, it was supposed to be a haven. She didn't like to think of it as a fortress.

But, like it or not, it was a fortress at the moment and she'd better make sure the soldiers were on the battlements. She checked the lock on the front door before she moved quickly toward the living room. She would see the black-and-white from the picture window.

Phyliss, as usual, had drawn the drapes over the window before she went to bed. The cave instinct, Kate thought as she reached for the cord. Close out the outside world and make your own. She and Phyliss were in complete agree—

He was standing outside the window, so close they were separated only by a quarter of an inch of glass.

Oh God. High concave cheekbones, long black straight hair drawn back in a queue, beaded necklace. It was him . . . Todd Campbell . . . Ishmaru . . .

And he was smiling at her.

His lips moved and he was so near she could hear the words through the glass. "You weren't supposed to see me before I got in, Kate." He held her gaze as he showed her the glass cutter in his hand. "But it's all right. I'm almost finished and I like it better this way."

She couldn't move. She stared at him, mesmerized.

"You might as well let me in. You can't stop me."

She jerked the drape shut, closing him out.

Barricading herself inside with only a fragment of glass, a scrap of material . . .

She heard the sound of blade on glass.

She backed away from the window, stumbled on the hassock, almost fell, righted herself.

Oh God. Where was that policeman? The porch light was out, but surely he could see Ishmaru.

Maybe the policeman wasn't there.

Didn't Michael tell you about bribery in the ranks.

The drape was moving.

He'd cut the window.

"Phyliss!" She ran down the hall. "Wake up." She threw open Joshua's door, flew across the room, and jerked him out of bed.

"Mom?"

"Shh, be very quiet. Just do what I tell you, okay?"

"What's wrong?" Phyliss was standing in the doorway. "Is Joshua sick?"

"I want you to leave here." She pushed Joshua toward her. "There's someone outside." She hoped he was still outside. Christ, he could be in the living room by now. "I want you to take Joshua out the back door and over to the Brocklemans."

Phyliss instantly took Joshua's hand and moved toward the kitchen door. "What about you?"

She heard a sound in the living room. "*Go.* I'll be right behind you."

Phyliss and Joshua flew out the back door.

"Are you waiting for me, Kate?"

He sounded so close, too close. Phyliss and Joshua could not have reached the fence yet. No time to run. Stop him.

She saw him, a shadow in the doorway leading to the hall.

Where was the gun?

In her handbag on the living room table. She couldn't get past him. She backed toward the stove. Phyliss usually left a frying pan out to cook breakfast in the morning. . . .

"I told you I was coming in. No one can stop me tonight. I had a sign."

She didn't see a weapon but the darkness was lit only by moonlight streaming through the window.

"Give up, Kate."

Her hand closed on the handle of the frying pan. "Leave me *alone*." She leaped forward and struck out at his head with all her strength.

He moved too fast but she connected with a glancing blow.

He was falling. . . .

She streaked past him down the hall. Get to the purse, the gun.

She heard him behind her.

She snatched up the handbag, lunged for the door, and threw the bolt.

Get to the policeman in the black-and-white.

She fumbled with the catch on her purse as she streaked down the driveway toward the black-and-white. Her hand closed on the gun and she threw the purse aside.

"He's not there, Kate," Ishmaru said behind her. "It's just the two of us."

No one was in the driver's seat of the police car.

She whirled and raised the gun.

Too late.

He was on her, knocking the gun from her grip, sending it flying. How had he moved so quickly?

She was on the ground, struggling wildly.

She couldn't breathe. His thumbs were digging into her throat.

"Mom." Joshua's agonized scream pierced the night.

What was Joshua doing here? He was supposed to be— "Go away, Josh—" Ishmaru's hands tightened, cut off speech. She was dying. She had to move. The gun. She had dropped it. On the ground . . .

She reached out blindly. The metal of the gun hilt was cool and wet from the grass.

She wasn't going to make it. Everything was going black.

She tried to knee him in the groin.

"Stop fighting," he whispered. "I've gone to a great deal of trouble to give you a warrior's death."

Crazy bastard. The hell she'd stop fighting.

She raised the gun and pressed the trigger.

*"Charming humor, page-turning intrigue,
and characters so real they step out of the page.
A winner."*
—Iris Johansen, *New York Times* bestselling author
of *THE UGLY DUCKLING*

THE SCOTSMAN
WORE SPURS

BY PATRICIA POTTER

*Andrew Cameron, a penniless Scottish earl, comes to
America seeking a simple life. But he soon finds himself
rescuing a wealthy rancher and hiring on as a cattle
drover. A scrawny, scruffy young boy joins the drive, but
Drew quickly discovers that behind the facade is beautiful
Gabrielle Parker, out to find her father's killer.*

Drew ignored the hooting from the two cowboys riding with him as he gingerly—very gingerly—picked
himself up from the ground.

The fall was ignominious. He couldn't ever remember falling from a horse before. Horsemanship
was one of the few accomplishments he claimed—that
and gaming.

Kirby had warned him that cutting horses were
unlike any other animal, their movements quick and
sometimes unexpected when they saw a cow wandering off. The pinto Drew was riding had done just
that, moving sharply when he'd just relaxed after a
very long day in the saddle.

"Uncle Kirby said you could ride," Damien

Kingsley said nastily. "What other tall tales did you hand him?"

Drew forced a wry smile to his face. He had been the butt of unending razing since he'd first gone on the Kingsley payroll a week earlier. His Scottish accent and unfamiliarity with cattle hadn't helped the image of tenderfoot.

"What do they have for horses in Scotland?" another man scoffed.

Damien, sitting a small roan, snickered. "You ain't going to be any use at all."

Drew tested his limbs. They seemed whole, if sore. He eyed the pinto with more than a little asperity, and the bloody beast bared its teeth as if laughing. Damn, but every bone in his body ached. He had raced horses, had ridden them long distances, but sitting in a saddle eighteen hours a day for a week strained even his experienced muscles. The thought of three months of this shriveled his soul.

Learn cow. That's what Kirby called learning the cattle business. In some strange ungrammatical way, the expression fit. But Drew was beginning to think he'd just as soon jump off the edge of the earth. He'd had no experience with cattle in Scotland, and his enthusiasm for being a cattle baron now had dimmed to the faint flicker of a dying candle.

Yet he'd never been a quitter, and he didn't much like the idea of starting now, nor did he want to see the triumph spreading across Damien's and his brother's faces. Even less did he want to disappoint Kirby.

He started for the pinto.

"Well, lookit that, will ya!" The exclamation came from a drover called Shorty, and all looked out in the direction the man pointed. Drew's own gaze followed the pointing arm.

Drew saw the most moth-eaten, woebegone, and decrepit beast he'd ever had the misfortune to see. Perched precariously on its bony back sat a small figure whose hat was as decrepit as the horse he rode.

"Mebbe Scotty could ride that," one of the men said, laughing uproariously at his own joke and using the name the other drovers had given Drew.

Drew would have loved to cram that laughter down his throat, along with his hat, but that would just make trouble for Kirby. He wondered how long he could curb a temper that had never been known for its temperance.

Then he watched, with the others, the slow approach of the rider.

The boy was enveloped by a coat much too big for him, and only a portion of his face was visible. Under the dirty slouch hat, a pair of dark blue eyes seemed to study him before they lowered and moved on to the other riders before going blank.

"I'm looking for the foreman," he mumbled in a voice that seemed to be changing.

"What for?" one of the men said, using his elbow to nudge a companion. "Want to sell that fine horse of yours? The fellow near the pinto may be interested."

Guffaws broke out again, and the boy's eyes went back to Drew, resting there for a moment. "Lookin' for a job," he said, ignoring the jibe. "Heard they might be hirin' here."

"Pint-size cowboys?" Damien said. "You heard wrong. We're full hired. More than full hired," he added, tossing a disagreeable look at Drew.

"Read about the drive in the newspaper," the boy

said. "It said they be needing help. I want to see the foreman."

Drew admired the boy's persistence, especially in light of the snickers that had just been transferred from himself to the lad. But the drive *was* full hired. A number of much more promising looking cowboys had been turned down. He himself wouldn't have had a chance of hiring on, even at the miserly wage of fifty dollars and keep, had he not been Kirby's friend. It seemed every cowboy in the West wanted to ride with Kirby Kingsley on what was being called a historic drive.

"I'll take you," Drew said. "Follow me."

He took the reins of his horse and limped toward the corral where Kirby was making a final selection of horses to take. There would be ten horses per man, one hundred and eighty mounts in all, not including the sixteen mules designated for the two wagons that would accompany them.

"Mr. Kingsley?" He had stopped calling Kingsley by his first name when he went into his employ, especially around the other men. He had no wish to further aggravate their resentment toward the Scottish tenderfoot.

Kirby turned around, noticed his limp and gave him a grimace that passed for a smile. "Told you about those cutting horses."

"So you did," Drew said wryly. "I won't make the mistake of underestimating them again."

"Good. Nothing broken, I take it."

"Only my pride."

Kirby's lips twitched slightly, then his gaze went over to the boy. "That a horse, boy?"

The boy flushed, and the chin raised defiantly.

"He has heart. Just 'cause no one ever took care of him . . ."

Kirby's smile disappeared. "You have a point. What's your name?"

"Gabe. Gabe Lewis."

"And what's your business?"

"I heard you was hiring."

"Men," Kirby said. "Not boys."

"I'm old enough."

"What? Fourteen? Fifteen?"

"Sixteen," the boy said angrily, "and I've been making my own way these past three years."

"You ever been on a drive?"

The boy hesitated, and Drew could almost see the wheels turning inside his head. He wanted to lie. He would have lied if he hadn't thought he might be caught in it. "No, but I'm a real fast learner."

"We don't need any more hands," Kirby said, turning away. The easy dismissal brought a deeper flush to the boy's face.

"Mr. Kingsley?"

Kingsley swung back around, irritation deepening the lines in his face. He waited for the boy to continue.

The boy's voice became a plea. "I'll do anything, Mr. Kingsley. Maybe I'm not so big, but I'm a real hard worker."

Kirby shook his head.

"I need the job real bad," the boy said in one last desperate plea.

"By the looks of that horse, I'd agree," Drew said helpfully. Strangely enough, he sensed his help wasn't welcome. The boy's gaze cut to his only for a briefest second, but there was no missing the scowl in them.

Kirby looked thoughtful for a moment. "Pepper,

our cook, was complaining yesterday about his rheumatism. Maybe we could use someone to help him out. You up to being a louse, boy?"

"A louse?" The boy's eyes widened, and Drew noticed again how very blue they were.

"A cook's helper," Kirby explained. "A swamper. Clean up dishes, hunt cow chips, grind coffee. You ever done any cooking?"

"Of course," the boy said airily. Drew sensed bravado, and another lie, but Kirby didn't seem to notice. From the moment the boy had mentioned he was desperate, the rancher had softened perceptibly. Drew saw it, noted it. And it surprised him. There was nothing soft about Kirby Kingsley.

He knew, despite the fact he had saved Kirby's life, that if he couldn't pull his own weight he would be gone. His job had been based on the fact that Kirby had seen him shoot—and ride—and believed the rest would come easily enough.

If painfully.

But this slip of a boy sat a horse like a beginner, and he obviously lied about his ability to cook. Those dark blue eyes darted around just enough to say so. And he didn't look strong enough to control a team of four mules. Drew's eyes went to the numerous—but odd—bits and pieces of clothing; it was too hot for so much clothing, which meant he was trying to conceal a thin frame or feared someone would take what little he had if he didn't keep them close to his person.

But if Kirby had noted all these things, and Drew was sure he had because little escaped the man, he made no mention of them.

"My cook has to agree," Kirby was telling the

boy. "If he does, I'll pay you twenty dollars and found."

The boy nodded.

"You can't cut it, you're gone," Kirby added.

The boy nodded again.

"You don't have much to say, do you?" Kirby asked.

"Didn't know that was important." It was an impertinent reply, one Drew might have made himself, and he took another look at the boy's face.

There was no stubble, but the lad's skin was darkened by the sun and none too clean. But then the cook was none too fastidious himself, although Kirby proclaimed his food the best among cattle-drive cooks. That distinction appeared dubious at best—at least to Drew. Texas beef, he'd discovered, was tough and stringy, and the Kirbys' Mexican cook at home spiced it with hot peppers. He wondered if Pepper did the same, and he briefly longed for a piece of fresh salmon or good Scottish lamb.

He quickly discarded the thought. He doubted he would ever return to Scotland, where few of his memories were happy ones. If he had to suffer tough, tasteless beef to banish them, he would consider it more than a good trade.

"Drew?"

Kirby's sharp question broke his rambling throughts and he turned his attention to the man next to him.

"Get the kid some food. I'll talk to Pepper."

"I need to take care of my horse," the boy said. "Give him some oats if you got any."

"I'm Drew Cameron," he said.

The boy looked at him suspiciously and without warmth. "You talk funny."

"I'm from Scotland," Drew explained. "The other hands call me Scotty."

The boy didn't look satisfied, but didn't ask any more questions, either. Instead, still hunched in the coat, he followed Drew into the barn and then into a stall. Drew found some oats and poured them into a feed bucket. The horse looked at him with soft, grateful eyes, and he understood the boy's attachment. Hell, he'd had a horse he'd loved. Too much. Bile filled his throat as he remembered.

"I can take care of him alone," the boy said rudely.

"You got a name for this horse?"

"Billy, if it's any of your business."

"Hell of a name for a horse."

"It ain't your horse."

"No," Drew conceded as he watched the boy take off the bit, then the saddle. He struggled with it, and not just because the saddle was heavy. There was no deftness that comes with practice. His gaze went to the boy's hands. Gloves covered them. New gloves.

And the clothes were fairly new though some effort had been extended to hide that fact. Dirt was too uniform for it to have been accumulated naturally, and the denim trousers were still stiff, not soft and pliant. Something else didn't ring true. The "ain't," perhaps. Drew had an ear for nuances of sounds.

The natural skill had been invaluable in gaming; he could always detect a false note: desperation, bluffing, fear. He thought he detected all three now.

Why? Unless the boy had something to hide other than a need for a job. Could he be a runaway, or something else? Something more ominous?

Drew hadn't forgotten the ambush nor the possibility that someone might try again. And he remembered the ambusher's words. *That little guy.* He very much doubted this slip of a boy could be involved, but he had seen danger and dynamite come in much smaller packages.

He immediately dismissed the idea as quickly as it flitted through his mind. Those last few months in Scotland had raised his caution. A man he'd never suspected—a trainer of horses—had proved to be a murderer and kidnapper. Many things, and people, had not been as they seemed.

"Where are you from?" he asked.

The boy's vivid blue gaze bore into his. "Places."

Drew grinned. It was an answer he'd given frequently. He merely nodded. The boy's business was his own until proved otherwise.

"The bunkhouse is the next building. Take any that doesn't look occupied," Drew said. He'd moved to the bunkhouse himself. There were several empty cots.

"When do we leave?"

Drew heard an anxious note in the boy's voice.

"In two days," Drew said.

"What do you do?" the boy asked unexpectedly, his eyes narrowing.

Drew shrugged. "Just a cowhand," he said, "and if I want to stay that way, I'd better get back to work." He turned, oddly discomfited by the hostility in the boy's vivid blue eyes.

What the bloody hell, anyway. The lad was none of his business.

On sale in March:

A THIN DARK LINE
by Tami Hoag

*THE BRIDE'S
BODYGUARD*
by Elizabeth Thornton

*PLACES BY
THE SEA*
by Jean Stone